# Volume Three
## by Choi Kyung-ah

# English Adaptation
## by Sarah Dyer

Los Angeles • Tokyo • London

# ALSO AVAILABLE FROM TOKYOPOP®

PLANETES
PRIEST
PRINCESS AI
PSYCHIC ACADEMY
RAGNAROK
RAVE MASTER
REALITY CHECK
REBIRTH
REBOUND
REMOTE
RISING STARS OF MANGA
SABER MARIONETTE J
SAILOR MOON
SAINT TAIL
SAIYUKI
SAMURAI DEEPER KYO
SAMURAI GIRL REAL BOUT HIGH SCHOOL
SCRYED
SEIKAI TRILOGY, THE
SGT. FROG
SHAOLIN SISTERS
SHIRAHIME-SYO: SNOW GODDESS TALES
SHUTTERBOX
SKULL MAN, THE
SMUGGLER
SNOW DROP
SORCERER HUNTERS
STONE
SUIKODEN III
SUKI
THREADS OF TIME
TOKYO BABYLON
TOKYO MEW MEW
TOKYO TRIBES
TRAMPS LIKE US
UNDER THE GLASS MOON
VAMPIRE GAME
VISION OF ESCAFLOWNE, THE
WARRIORS OF TAO
WILD ACT
WISH
WORLD OF HARTZ
X-DAY
ZODIAC P.I.

## MANGA NOVELS
CLAMP SCHOOL PARANORMAL INVESTIGATORS
KARMA CLUB
SAILOR MOON
SLAYERS

## ART BOOKS
ART OF CARDCAPTOR SAKURA
ART OF MAGIC KNIGHT RAYEARTH, THE
PEACH: MIWA UEDA ILLUSTRATIONS

## ANIME GUIDES
COWBOY BEBOP
GUNDAM TECHNICAL MANUALS
SAILOR MOON SCOUT GUIDES

## TOKYOPOP KIDS
STRAY SHEEP

## CINE-MANGA™
ALADDIN
ASTRO BOY
CARDCAPTORS
CONFESSIONS OF A TEENAGE DRAMA QUEEN
DUEL MASTERS
FAIRLY ODDPARENTS, THE
FAMILY GUY
FINDING NEMO
G.I. JOE SPY TROOPS
JACKIE CHAN ADVENTURES
JIMMY NEUTRON: BOY GENIUS, THE ADVENTURES OF
KIM POSSIBLE
LILO & STITCH
LIZZIE MCGUIRE
LIZZIE MCGUIRE MOVIE, THE
MALCOLM IN THE MIDDLE
POWER RANGERS: NINJA STORM
SHREK 2
SPONGEBOB SQUAREPANTS
SPY KIDS 2
SPY KIDS 3-D: GAME OVER
TEENAGE MUTANT NINJA TURTLES
THAT'S SO RAVEN
TRANSFORMERS: ARMADA
TRANSFORMERS: ENERGON

# For more information visit www.TOKYOPOP.com

03.03.04T

Translator - Jennifer Hahm
English Adaptation - Sarah Dyer
Copy Editor - Troy Lewter
Retouch and Lettering - Riho Sakai
Cover Layout - Anna Kernbaum
Graphic Designer - James Dashiell

Editor - Bryce P. Coleman
Digital Imaging Manager - Chris Buford
Pre-Press Manager - Antonio DePietro
Production Managers - Jennifer Miller, Mutsumi Miyazaki
Art Director - Matt Alford
Managing Editor - Jill Freshney
VP of Production - Ron Klamert
President & C.O.O. - John Parker
Publisher & C.E.O. - Stuart Levy

JAN 2 9 2016

E-mail: info@TOKYOPOP.com
Come visit us online at www.TOKYOPOP.com

 A **TOKYOPOP** Manga

TOKYOPOP Inc.
5900 Wilshire Blvd. Suite 2000
Los Angeles, CA 90036

*Snow Drop Vol. 3*

ISBN: 1-59182-686-1

First TOKYOPOP printing: May 2004

10 9 8 7 6 5 4 3 2 1
Printed in the USA

## Previously in

When So-Na returns to high school after a traumatic experience, it isn't quite the smooth transition she'd hoped it would be. For one thing, her best friend, Ha-Da, ticks her off more than he calms her down. For another, there's the gorgeous student-model, Hae-Gi, who is quickly becoming an unexpected romantic entanglement. And then there's Sun-Mi, spoiled rich-girl extraordinaire. Sun-Mi's used to getting whatever she wants, and unfortunately for So-Na, she's decided she wants Hae-Gi.

# C·O·N·T·E·N·T·S

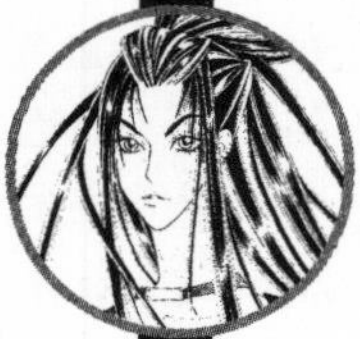

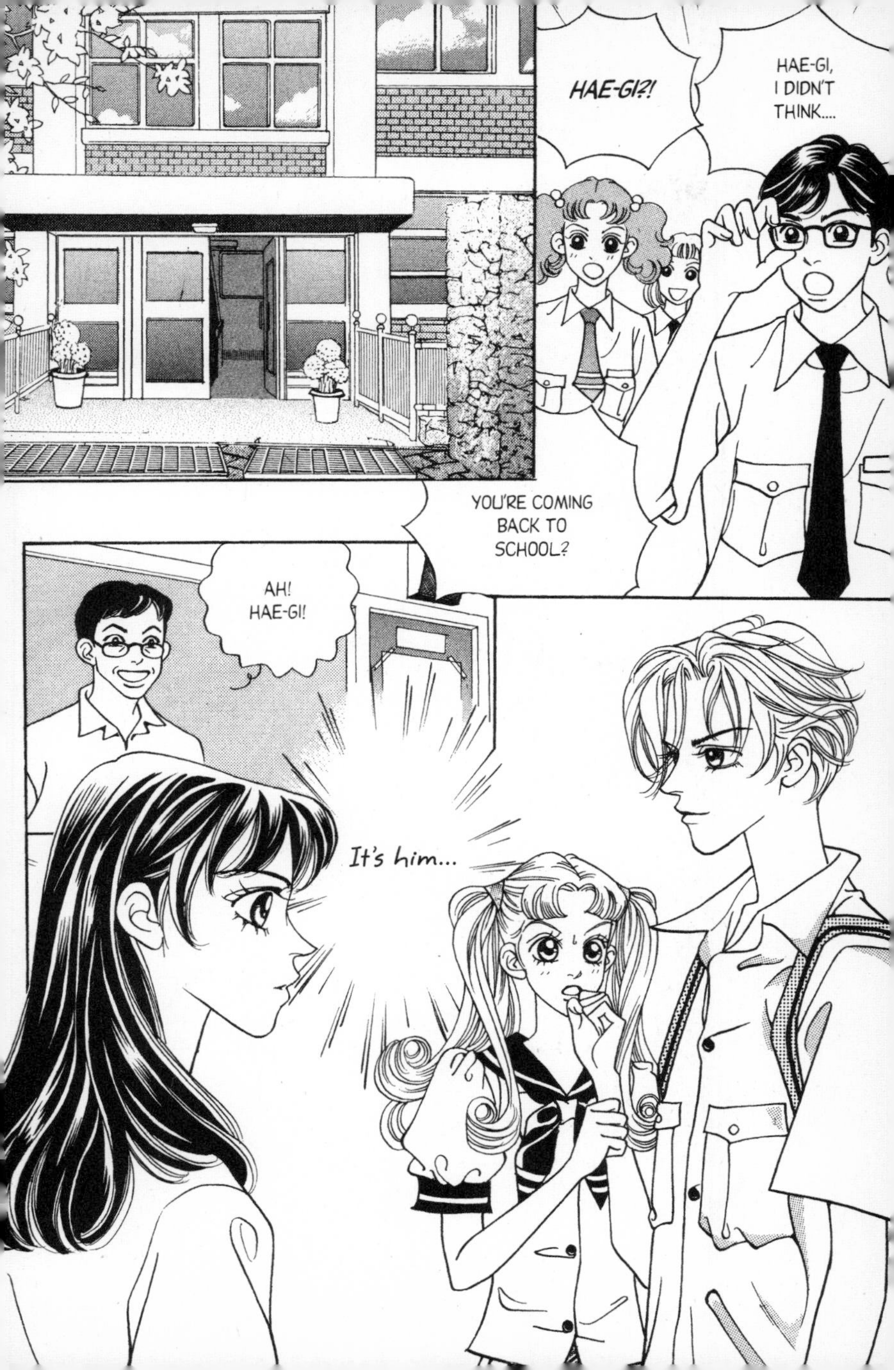
HAE-GI?!
HAE-GI, I DIDN'T THINK....
YOU'RE COMING BACK TO SCHOOL?
AH! HAE-GI!
It's him...

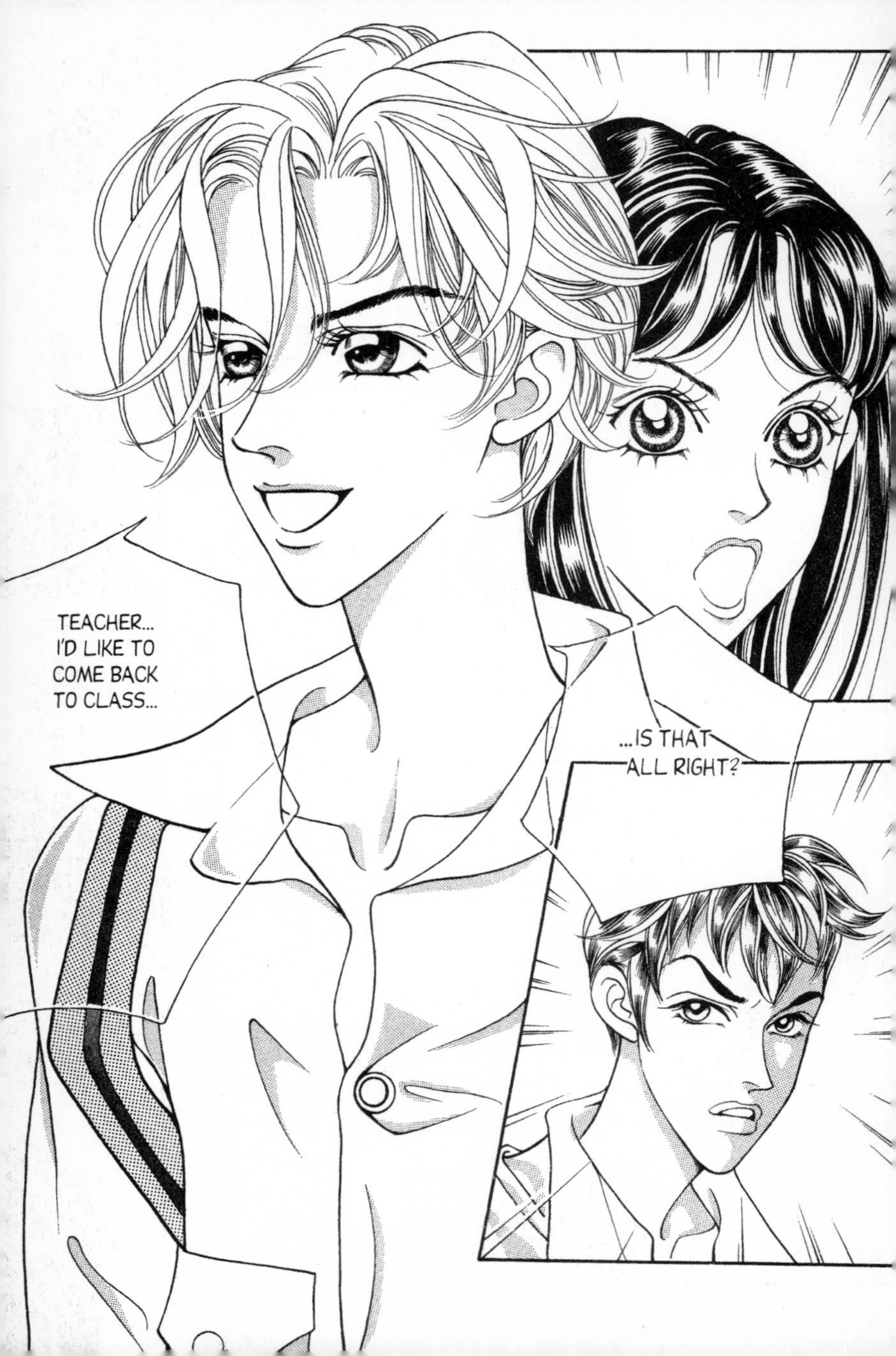
TEACHER... I'D LIKE TO COME BACK TO CLASS...
...IS THAT ALL RIGHT?

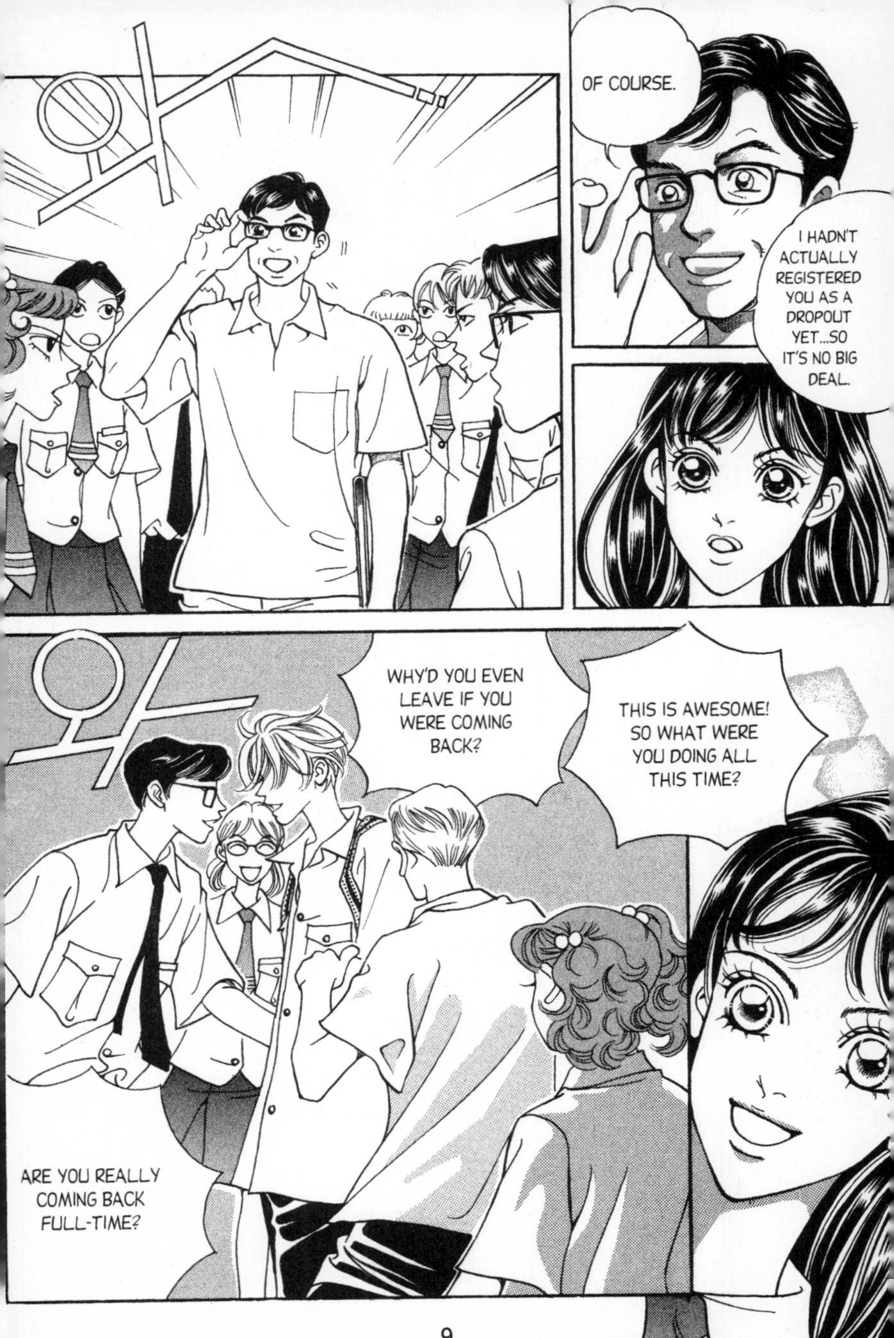
OF COURSE.
I HADN'T ACTUALLY REGISTERED YOU AS A DROPOUT YET...SO IT'S NO BIG DEAL.
WHY'D YOU EVEN LEAVE IF YOU WERE COMING BACK?
THIS IS AWESOME! SO WHAT WERE YOU DOING ALL THIS TIME?
ARE YOU REALLY COMING BACK FULL-TIME?

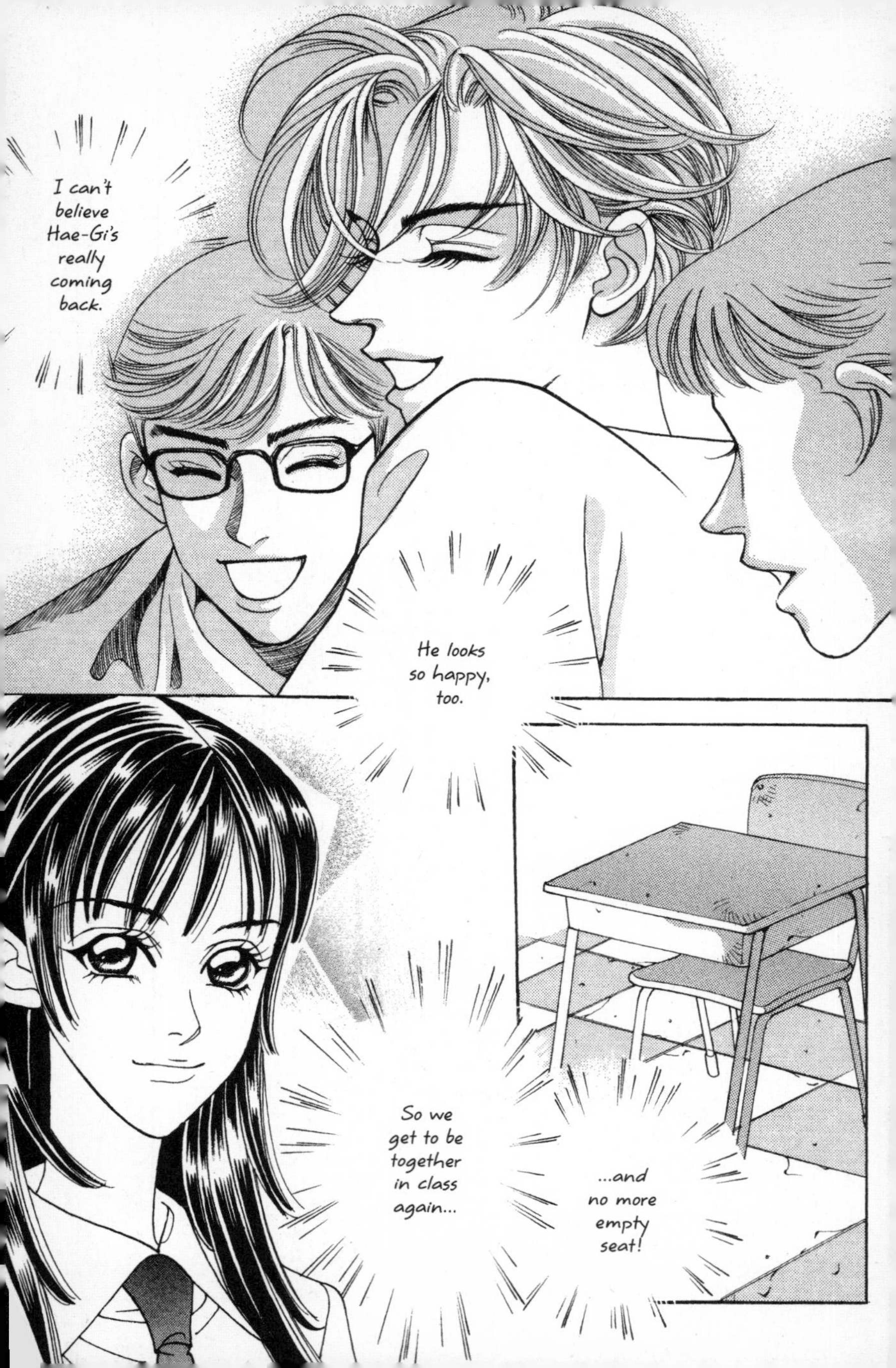
I can't believe Hae-Gi's really coming back.
He looks so happy, too.
So we get to be together in class again...
...and no more empty seat!

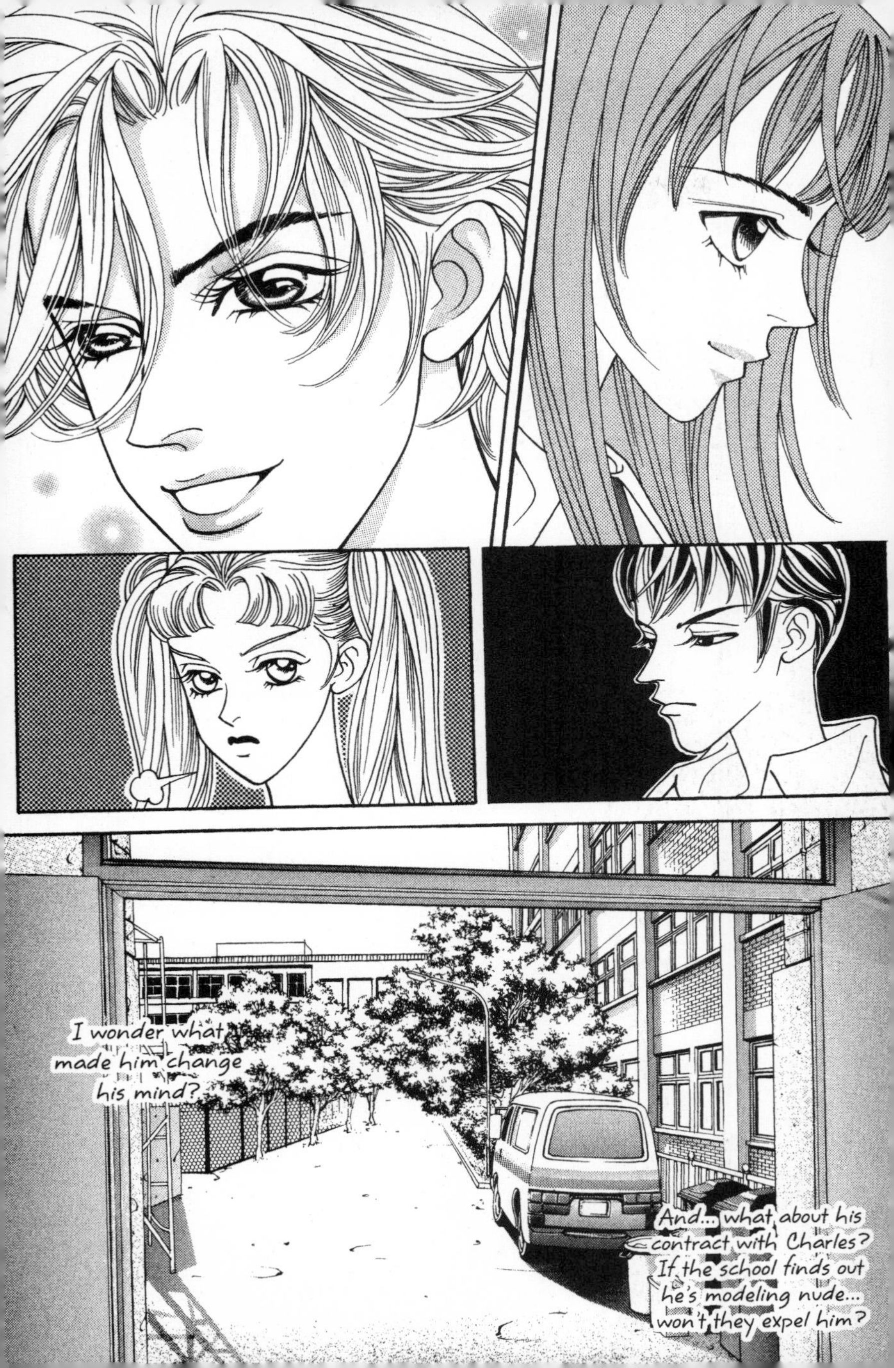
I wonder what made him change his mind?
And... what about his contract with Charles? If the school finds out he's modeling nude... won't they expel him?

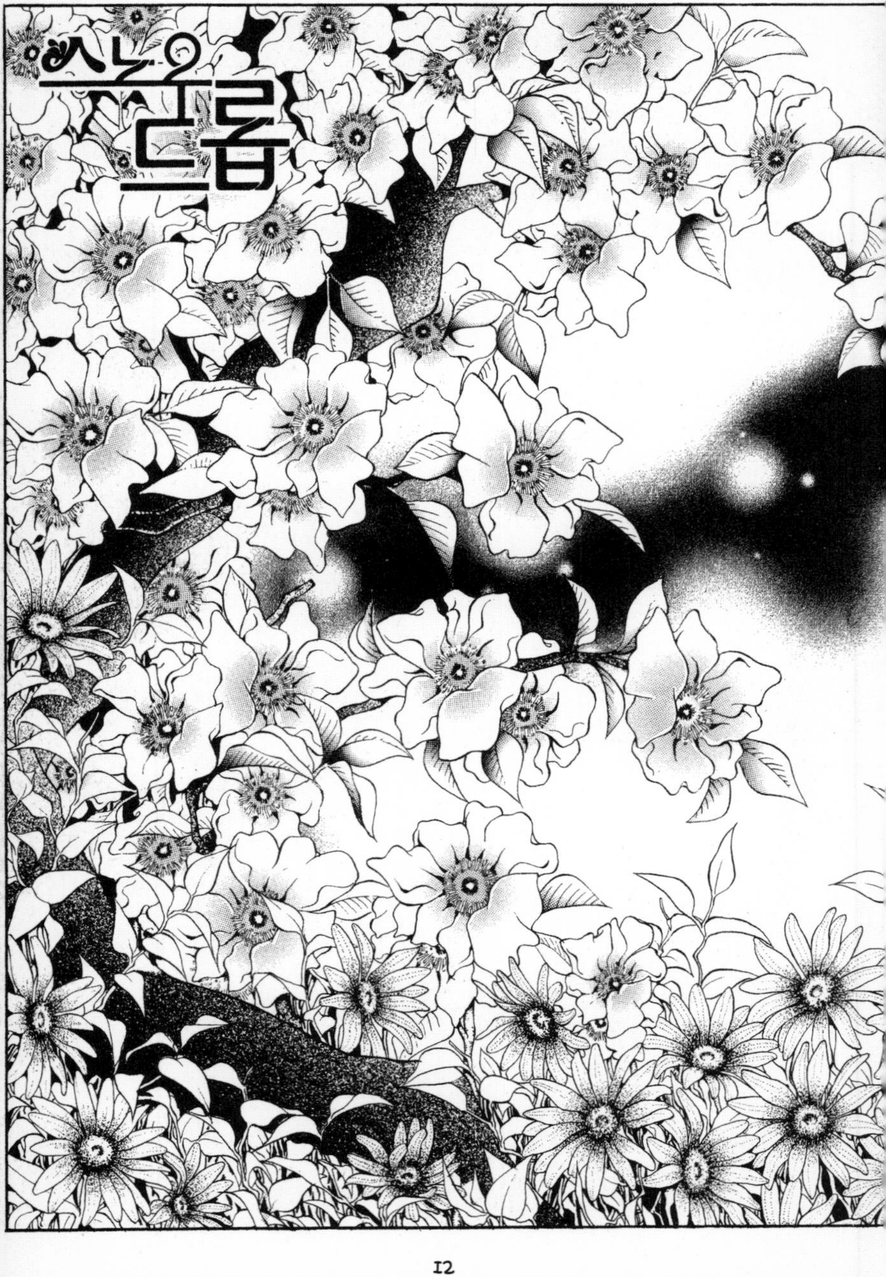

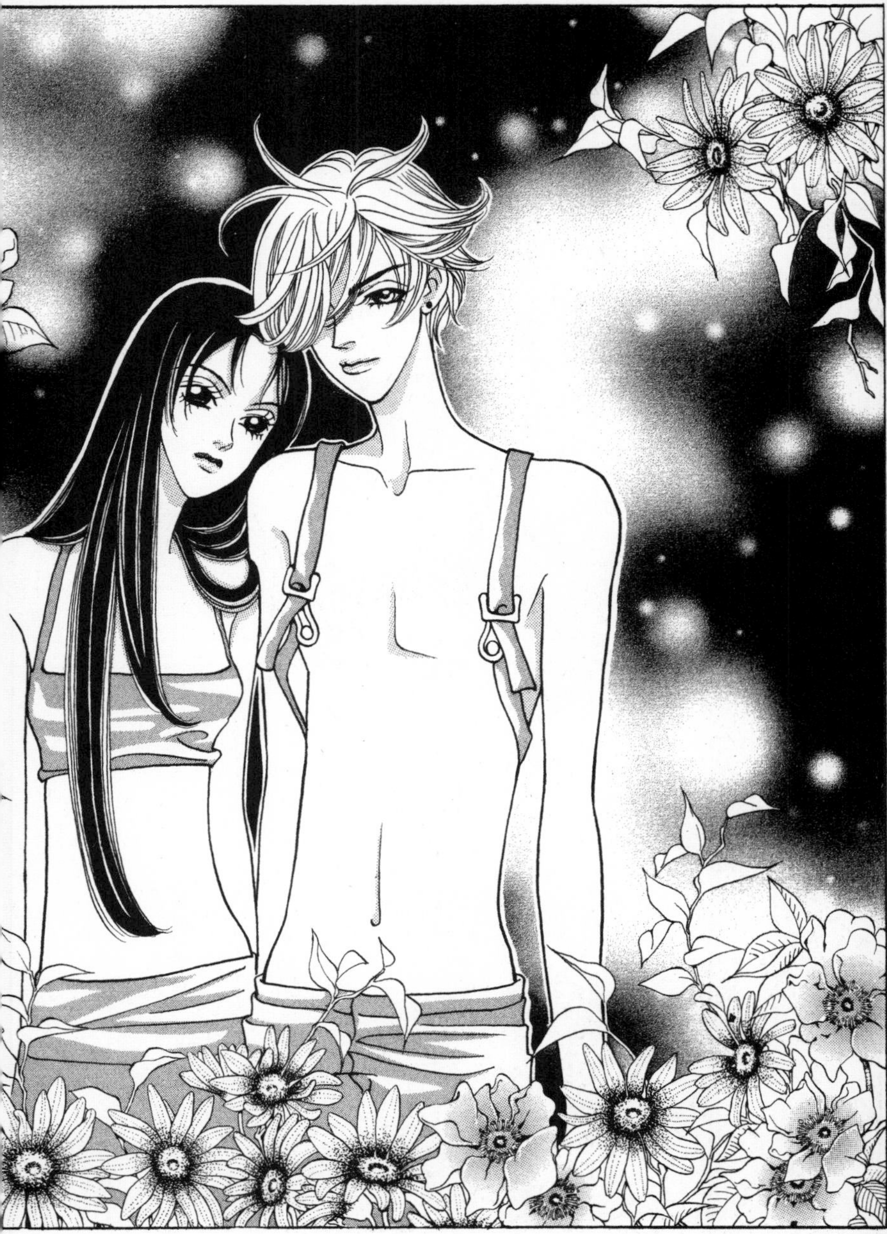

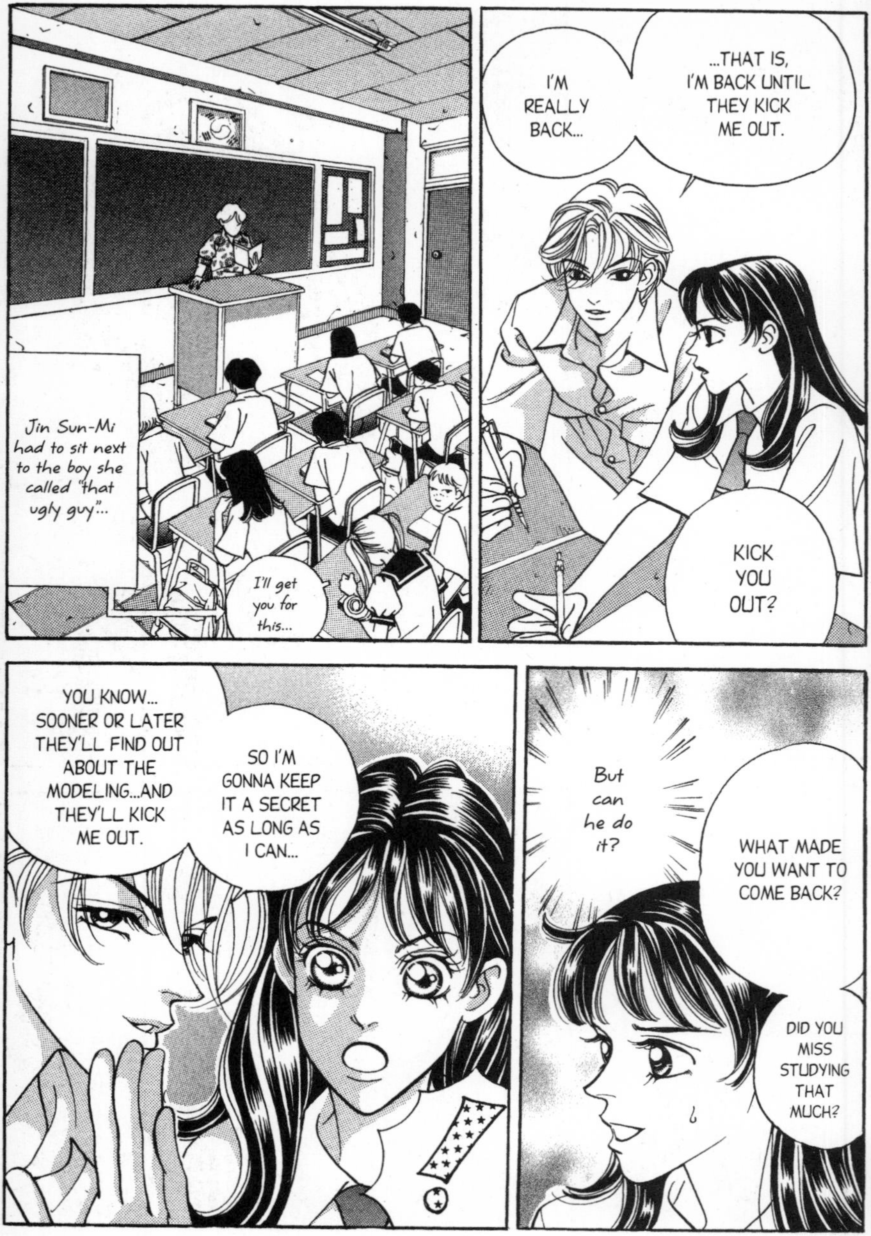
Jin Sun-Mi had to sit next to the boy she called "that ugly guy"...
I'll get you for this...
I'M REALLY BACK...
...THAT IS, I'M BACK UNTIL THEY KICK ME OUT.
KICK YOU OUT?
YOU KNOW... SOONER OR LATER THEY'LL FIND OUT ABOUT THE MODELING...AND THEY'LL KICK ME OUT.
SO I'M GONNA KEEP IT A SECRET AS LONG AS I CAN...
But can he do it?
WHAT MADE YOU WANT TO COME BACK?
DID YOU MISS STUDYING THAT MUCH?

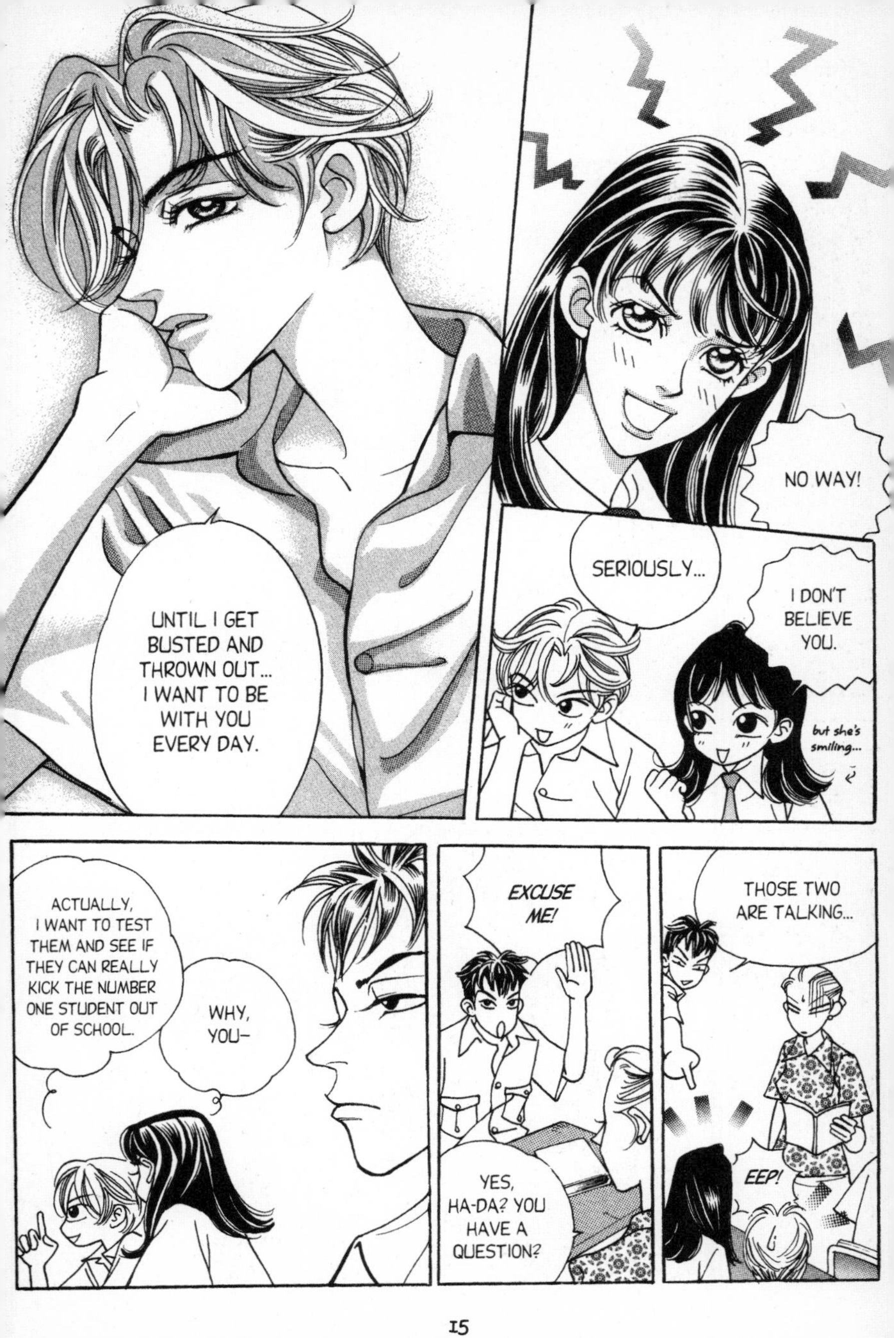
UNTIL I GET BUSTED AND THROWN OUT... I WANT TO BE WITH YOU EVERY DAY.
NO WAY!
SERIOUSLY...
I DON'T BELIEVE YOU.
but she's smiling...
ACTUALLY, I WANT TO TEST THEM AND SEE IF THEY CAN REALLY KICK THE NUMBER ONE STUDENT OUT OF SCHOOL.
WHY, YOU–
EXCUSE ME!
YES, HA-DA? YOU HAVE A QUESTION?
THOSE TWO ARE TALKING...
EEP!

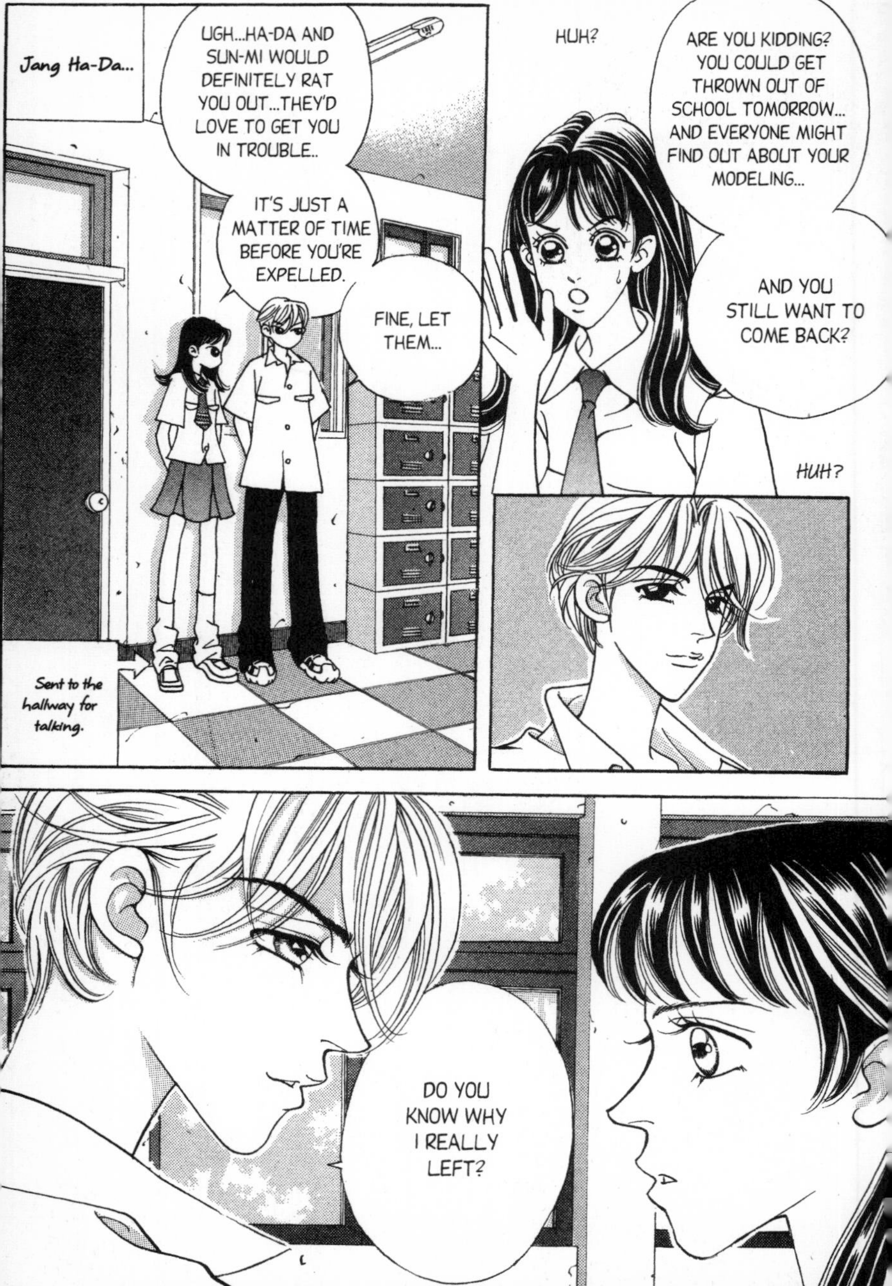
Jang Ha-Da...
UGH...HA-DA AND SUN-MI WOULD DEFINITELY RAT YOU OUT...THEY'D LOVE TO GET YOU IN TROUBLE..
IT'S JUST A MATTER OF TIME BEFORE YOU'RE EXPELLED.
FINE, LET THEM...
Sent to the hallway for talking.
HUH?
ARE YOU KIDDING? YOU COULD GET THROWN OUT OF SCHOOL TOMORROW... AND EVERYONE MIGHT FIND OUT ABOUT YOUR MODELING...
AND YOU STILL WANT TO COME BACK?
HUH?
DO YOU KNOW WHY I REALLY LEFT?

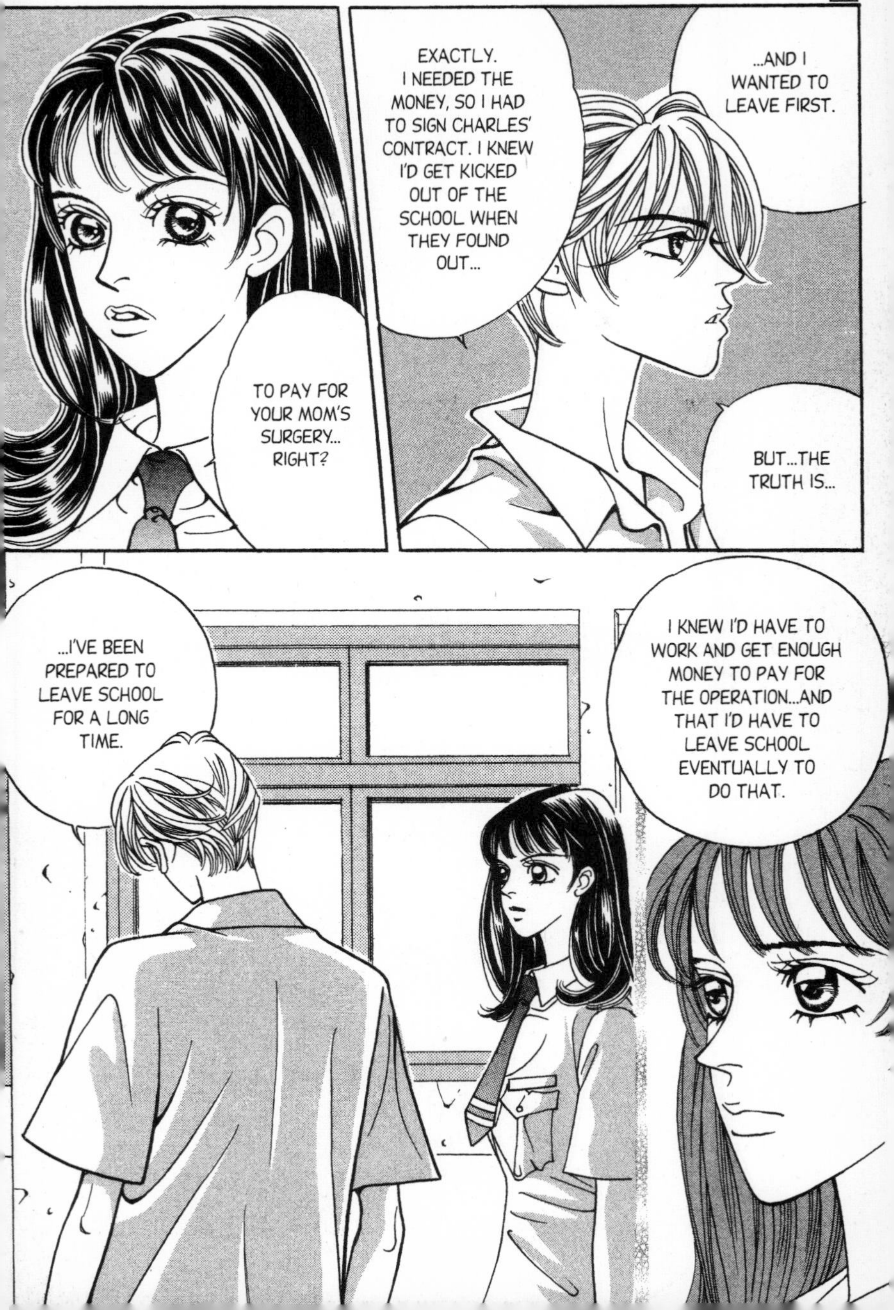
TO PAY FOR YOUR MOM'S SURGERY... RIGHT?
EXACTLY. I NEEDED THE MONEY, SO I HAD TO SIGN CHARLES' CONTRACT. I KNEW I'D GET KICKED OUT OF THE SCHOOL WHEN THEY FOUND OUT...
...AND I WANTED TO LEAVE FIRST.
BUT...THE TRUTH IS...
...I'VE BEEN PREPARED TO LEAVE SCHOOL FOR A LONG TIME.
I KNEW I'D HAVE TO WORK AND GET ENOUGH MONEY TO PAY FOR THE OPERATION...AND THAT I'D HAVE TO LEAVE SCHOOL EVENTUALLY TO DO THAT.

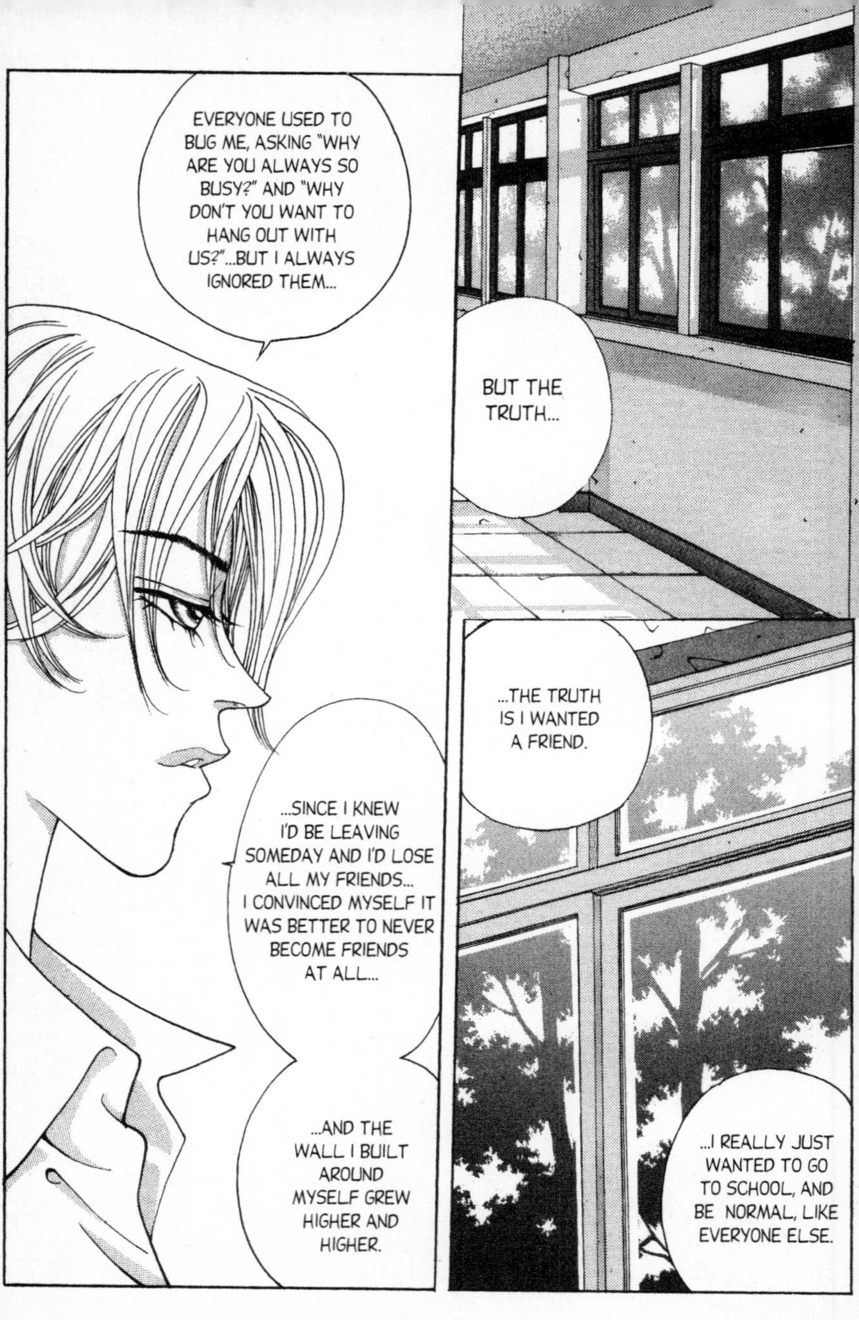
EVERYONE USED TO BUG ME, ASKING "WHY ARE YOU ALWAYS SO BUSY?" AND "WHY DON'T YOU WANT TO HANG OUT WITH US?"...BUT I ALWAYS IGNORED THEM...
...SINCE I KNEW I'D BE LEAVING SOMEDAY AND I'D LOSE ALL MY FRIENDS... I CONVINCED MYSELF IT WAS BETTER TO NEVER BECOME FRIENDS AT ALL...
...AND THE WALL I BUILT AROUND MYSELF GREW HIGHER AND HIGHER.
BUT THE TRUTH...
...THE TRUTH IS I WANTED A FRIEND.
...I REALLY JUST WANTED TO GO TO SCHOOL, AND BE NORMAL, LIKE EVERYONE ELSE.

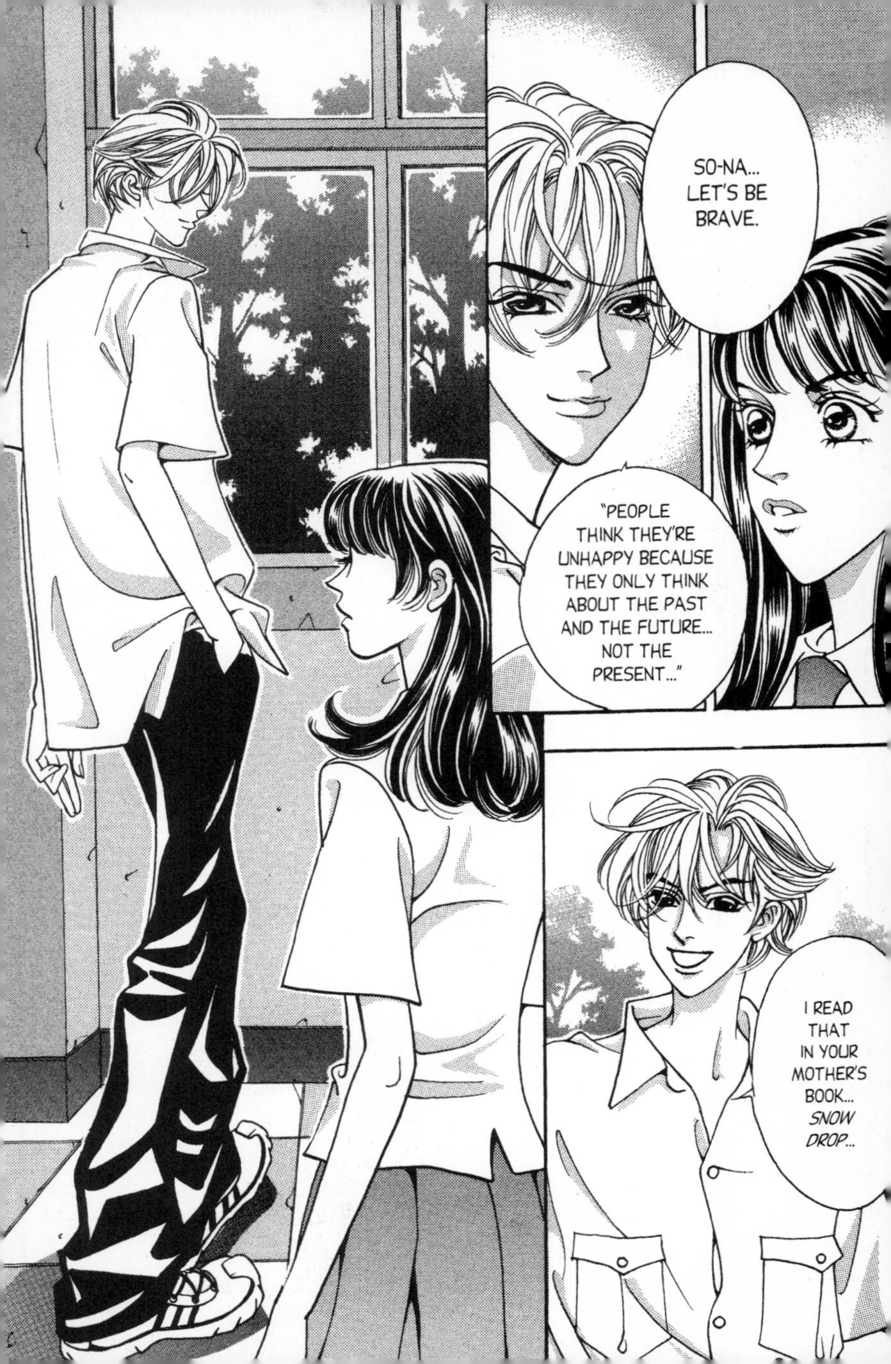
SO-NA... LET'S BE BRAVE.
"PEOPLE THINK THEY'RE UNHAPPY BECAUSE THEY ONLY THINK ABOUT THE PAST AND THE FUTURE... NOT THE PRESENT..."
I READ THAT IN YOUR MOTHER'S BOOK... *SNOW DROP*...

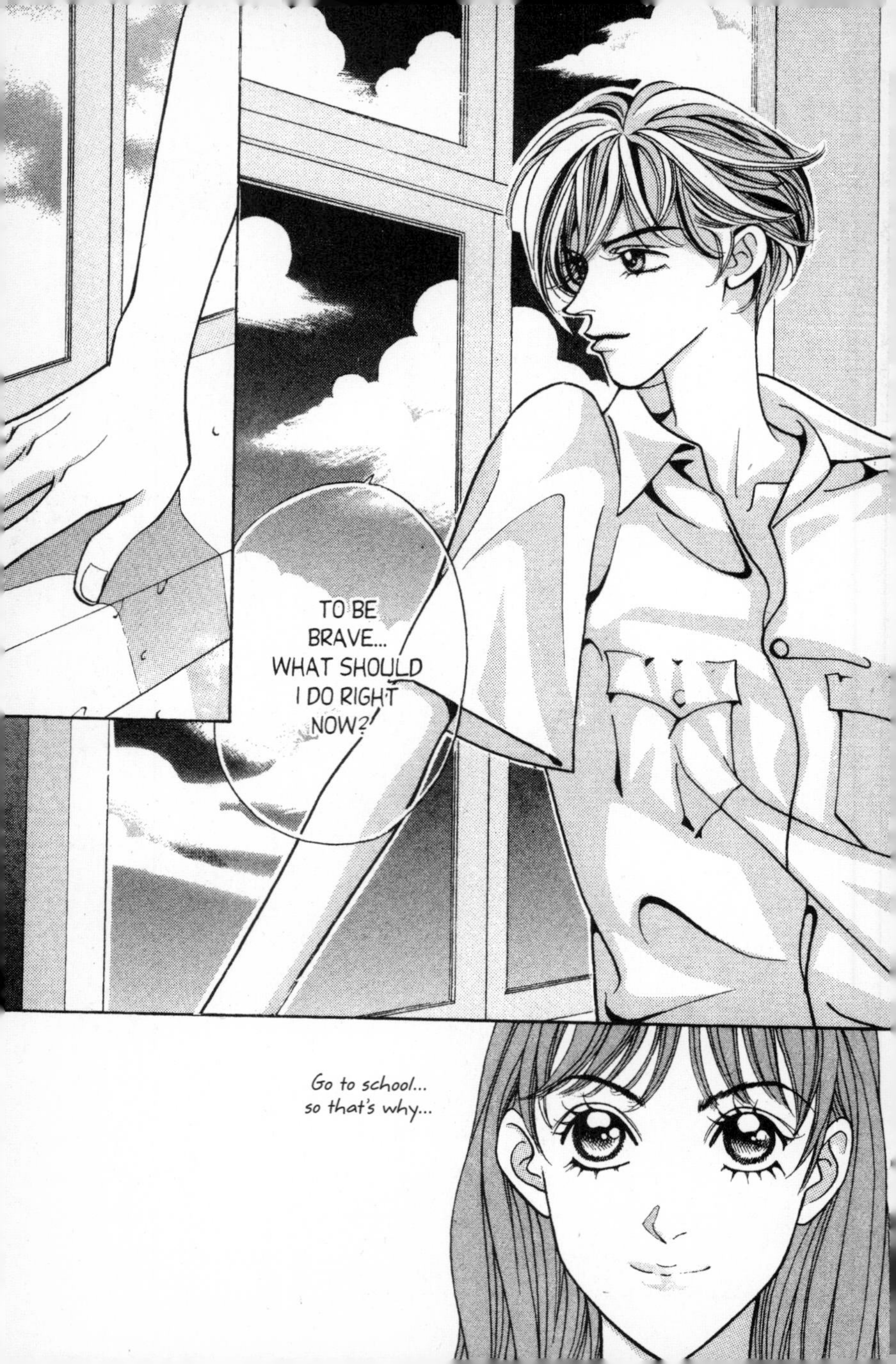
TO BE BRAVE... WHAT SHOULD I DO RIGHT NOW?
Go to school... so that's why...

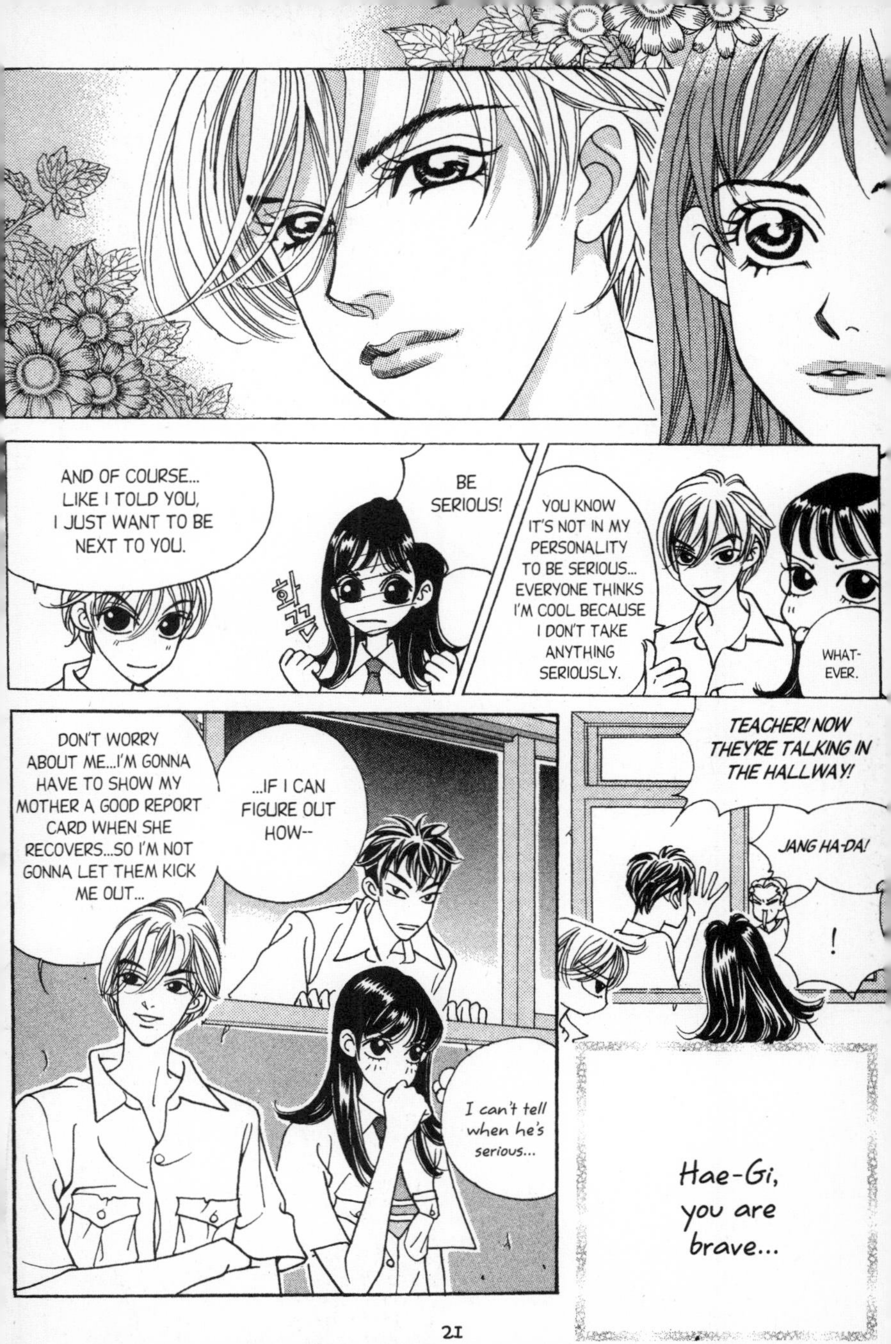
AND OF COURSE... LIKE I TOLD YOU, I JUST WANT TO BE NEXT TO YOU.
BE SERIOUS!
YOU KNOW IT'S NOT IN MY PERSONALITY TO BE SERIOUS... EVERYONE THINKS I'M COOL BECAUSE I DON'T TAKE ANYTHING SERIOUSLY.
WHAT-EVER.
DON'T WORRY ABOUT ME...I'M GONNA HAVE TO SHOW MY MOTHER A GOOD REPORT CARD WHEN SHE RECOVERS...SO I'M NOT GONNA LET THEM KICK ME OUT...
...IF I CAN FIGURE OUT HOW--
I can't tell when he's serious...
TEACHER! NOW THEY'RE TALKING IN THE HALLWAY!
JANG HA-DA!
!
Hae-Gi, you are brave...

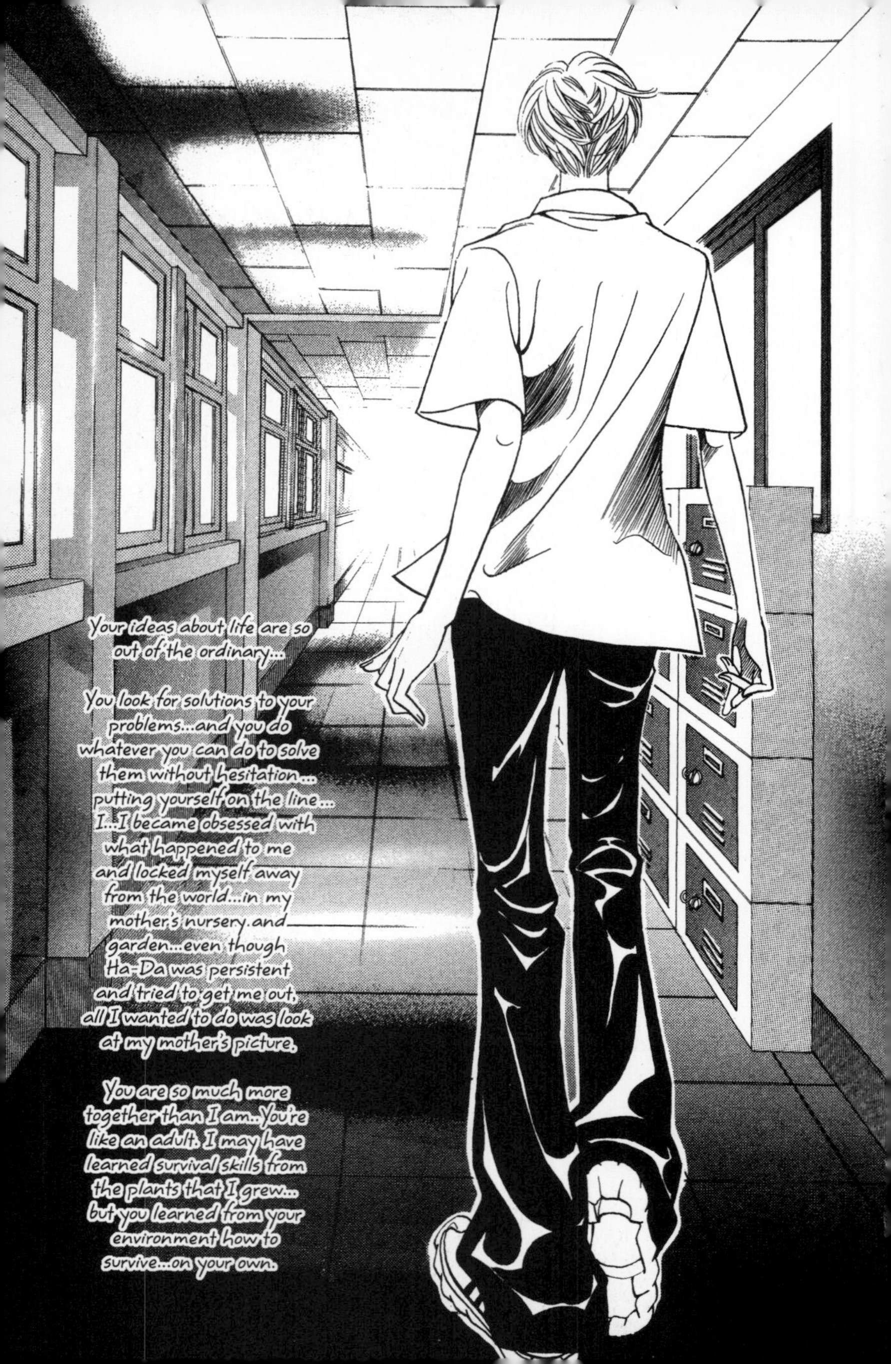
Your ideas about life are so out of the ordinary...
You look for solutions to your problems...and you do whatever you can do to solve them without hesitation... putting yourself on the line... I...I became obsessed with what happened to me and locked myself away from the world...in my mother's nursery and garden...even though Ha-Da was persistent and tried to get me out, all I wanted to do was look at my mother's picture.
You are so much more together than I am...You're like an adult. I may have learned survival skills from the plants that I grew... but you learned from your environment how to survive...on your own.

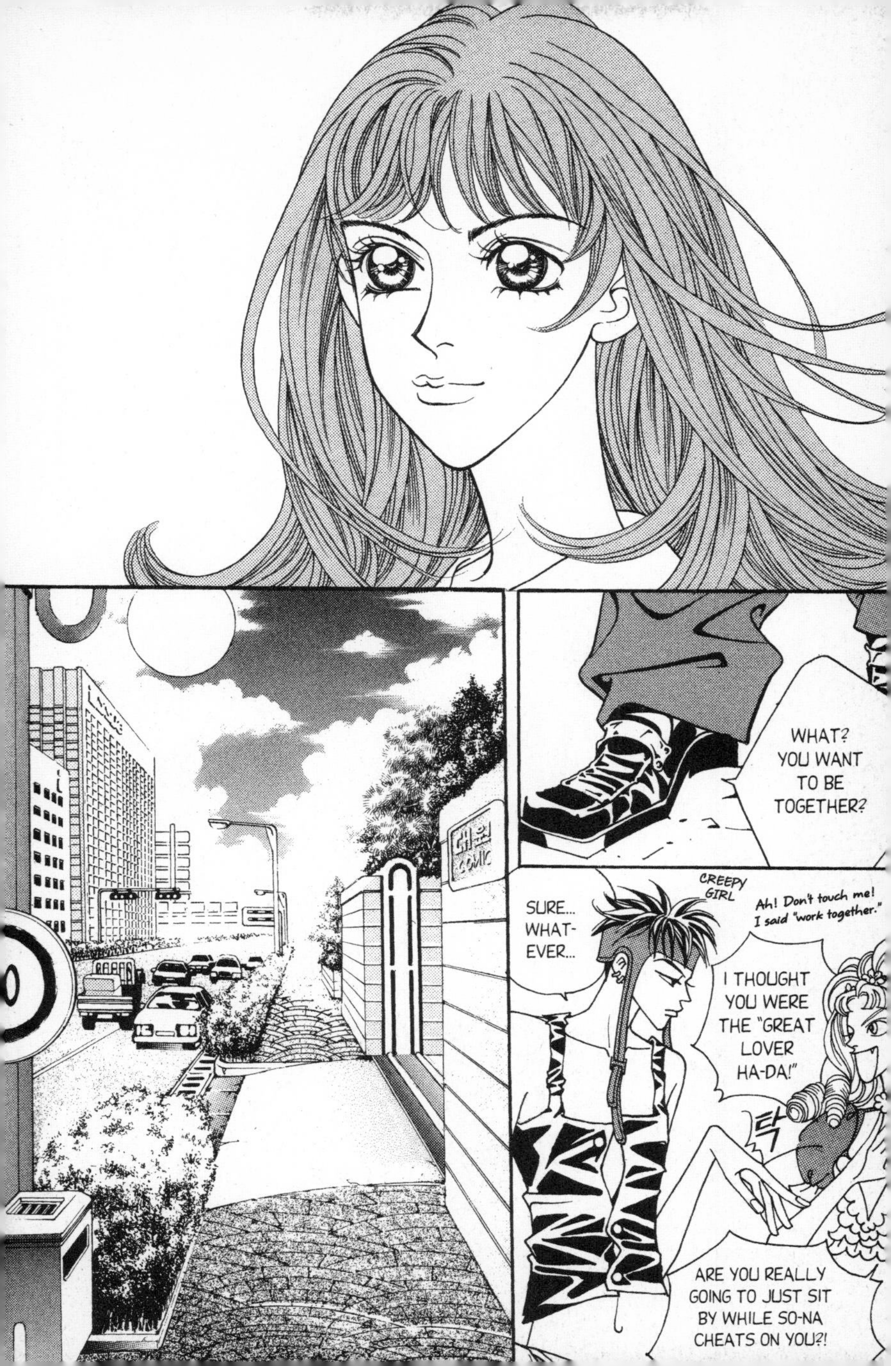
WHAT? YOU WANT TO BE TOGETHER?
SURE... WHAT-EVER...
CREEPY GIRL
Ah! Don't touch me! I said "work together."
I THOUGHT YOU WERE THE "GREAT LOVER HA-DA!"
탁
ARE YOU REALLY GOING TO JUST SIT BY WHILE SO-NA CHEATS ON YOU?!

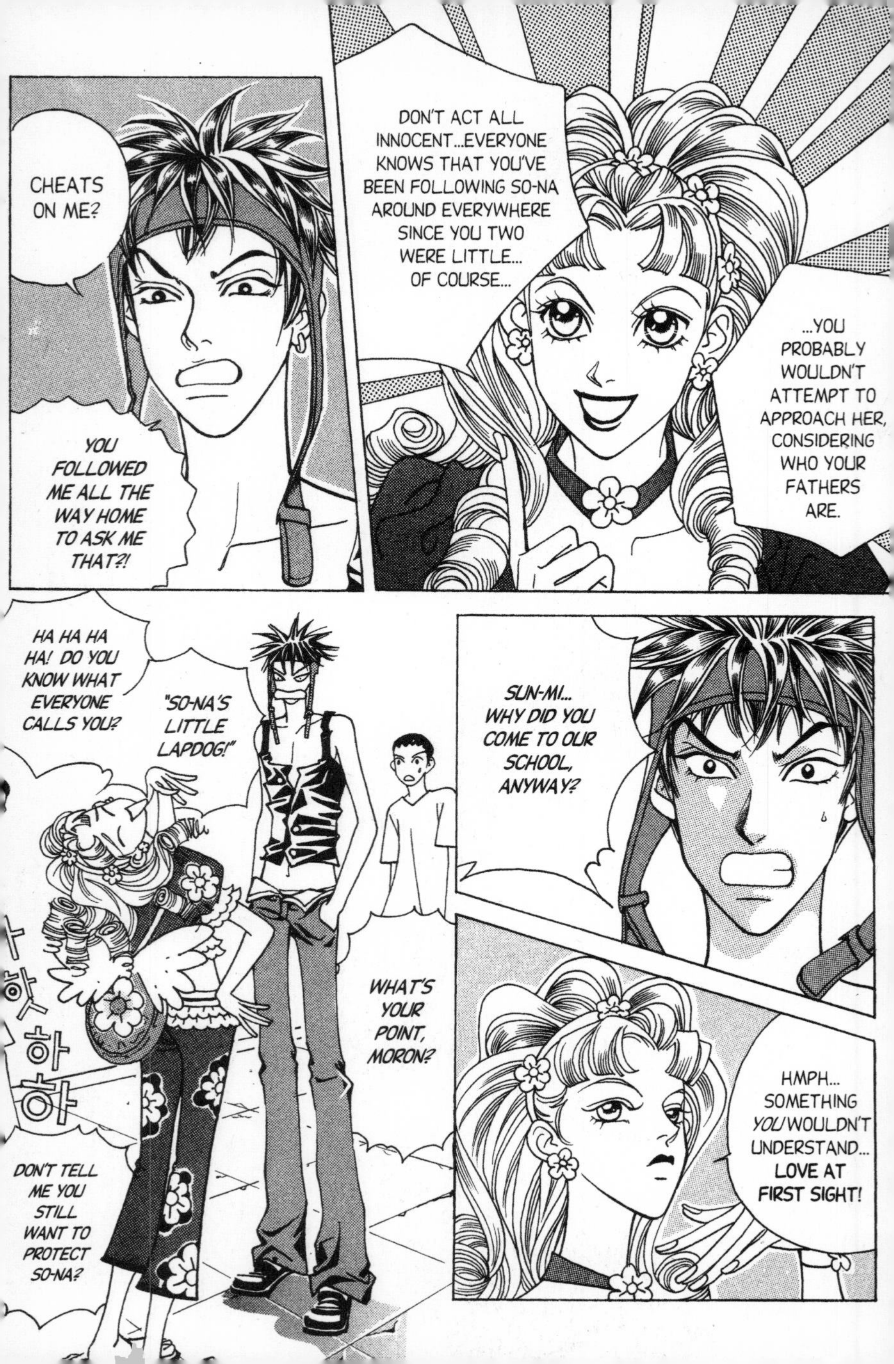
CHEATS ON ME?
YOU FOLLOWED ME ALL THE WAY HOME TO ASK ME THAT?!
DON'T ACT ALL INNOCENT...EVERYONE KNOWS THAT YOU'VE BEEN FOLLOWING SO-NA AROUND EVERYWHERE SINCE YOU TWO WERE LITTLE... OF COURSE...
...YOU PROBABLY WOULDN'T ATTEMPT TO APPROACH HER, CONSIDERING WHO YOUR FATHERS ARE.
HA HA HA HA! DO YOU KNOW WHAT EVERYONE CALLS YOU?
"SO-NA'S LITTLE LAPDOG!"
하하하
WHAT'S YOUR POINT, MORON?
DON'T TELL ME YOU STILL WANT TO PROTECT SO-NA?
SUN-MI... WHY DID YOU COME TO OUR SCHOOL, ANYWAY?
HMPH... SOMETHING *YOU* WOULDN'T UNDERSTAND... **LOVE AT FIRST SIGHT!**

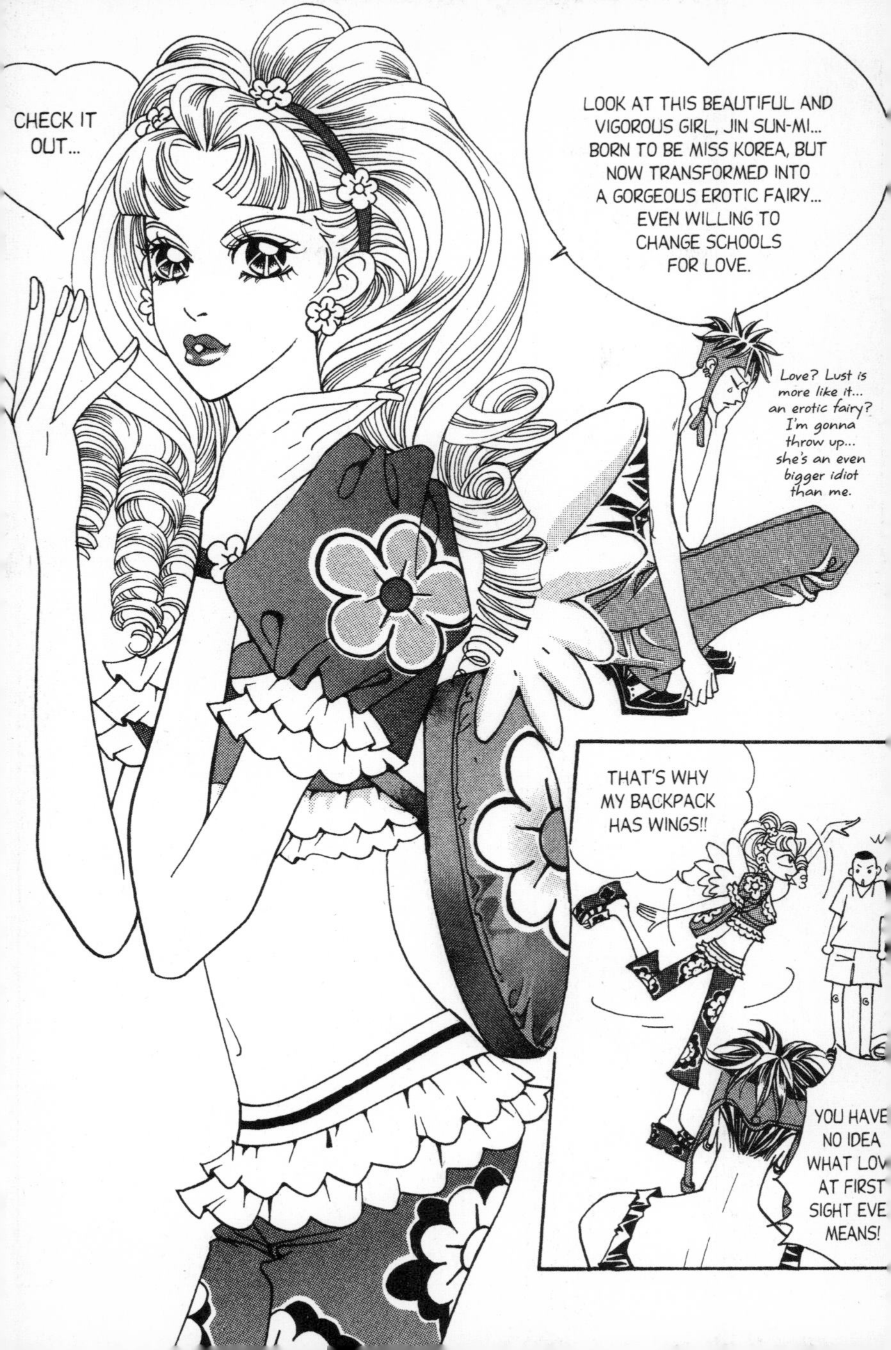
CHECK IT OUT...
LOOK AT THIS BEAUTIFUL AND VIGOROUS GIRL, JIN SUN-MI... BORN TO BE MISS KOREA, BUT NOW TRANSFORMED INTO A GORGEOUS EROTIC FAIRY... EVEN WILLING TO CHANGE SCHOOLS FOR LOVE.
Love? Lust is more like it... an erotic fairy? I'm gonna throw up... she's an even bigger idiot than me.
THAT'S WHY MY BACKPACK HAS WINGS!!
YOU HAVE NO IDEA WHAT LOV AT FIRST SIGHT EVE MEANS!

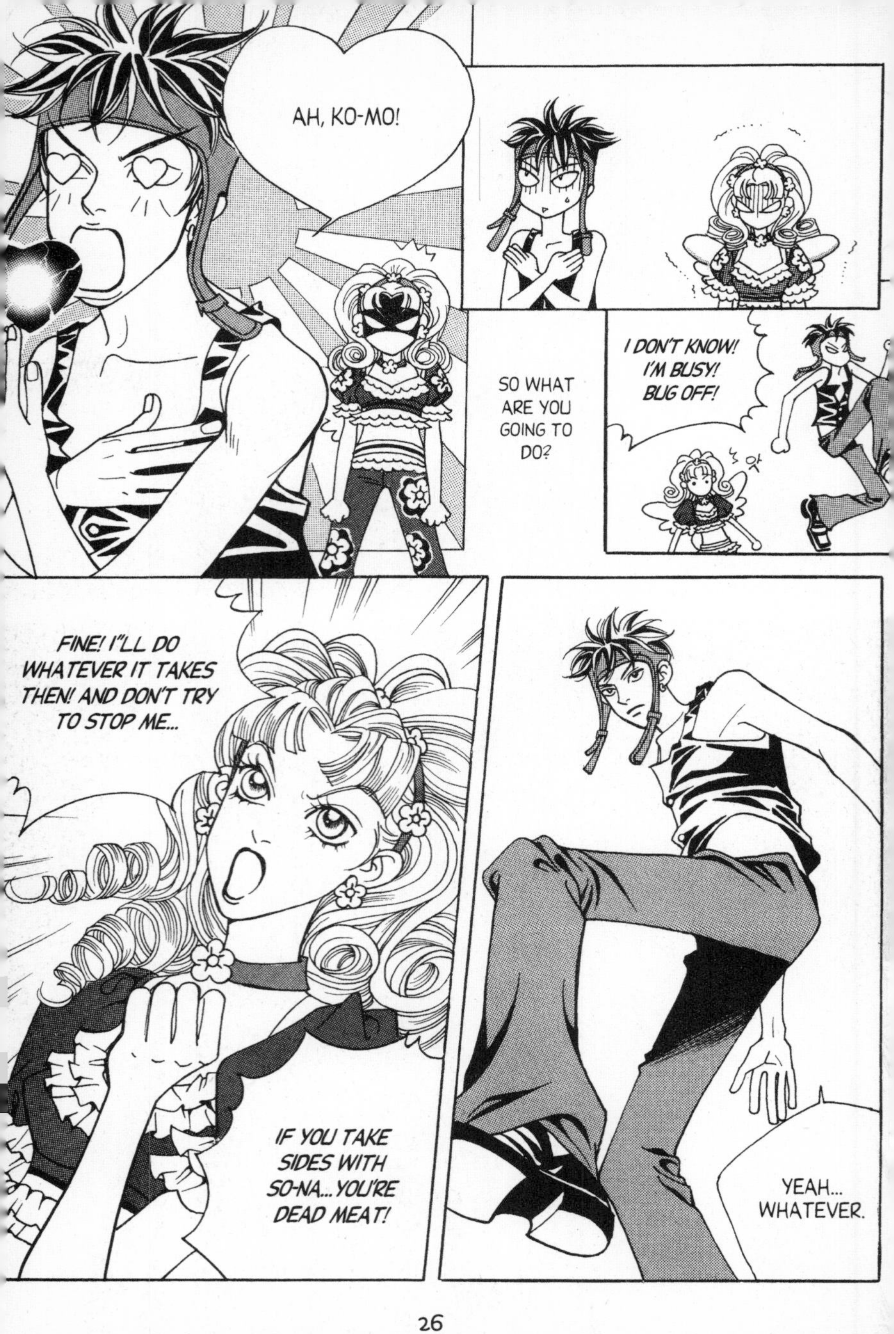
AH, KO-MO!
SO WHAT ARE YOU GOING TO DO?
I DON'T KNOW! I'M BUSY! BUG OFF!
FINE! I'LL DO WHATEVER IT TAKES THEN! AND DON'T TRY TO STOP ME...
IF YOU TAKE SIDES WITH SO-NA... YOU'RE DEAD MEAT!
YEAH... WHATEVER.

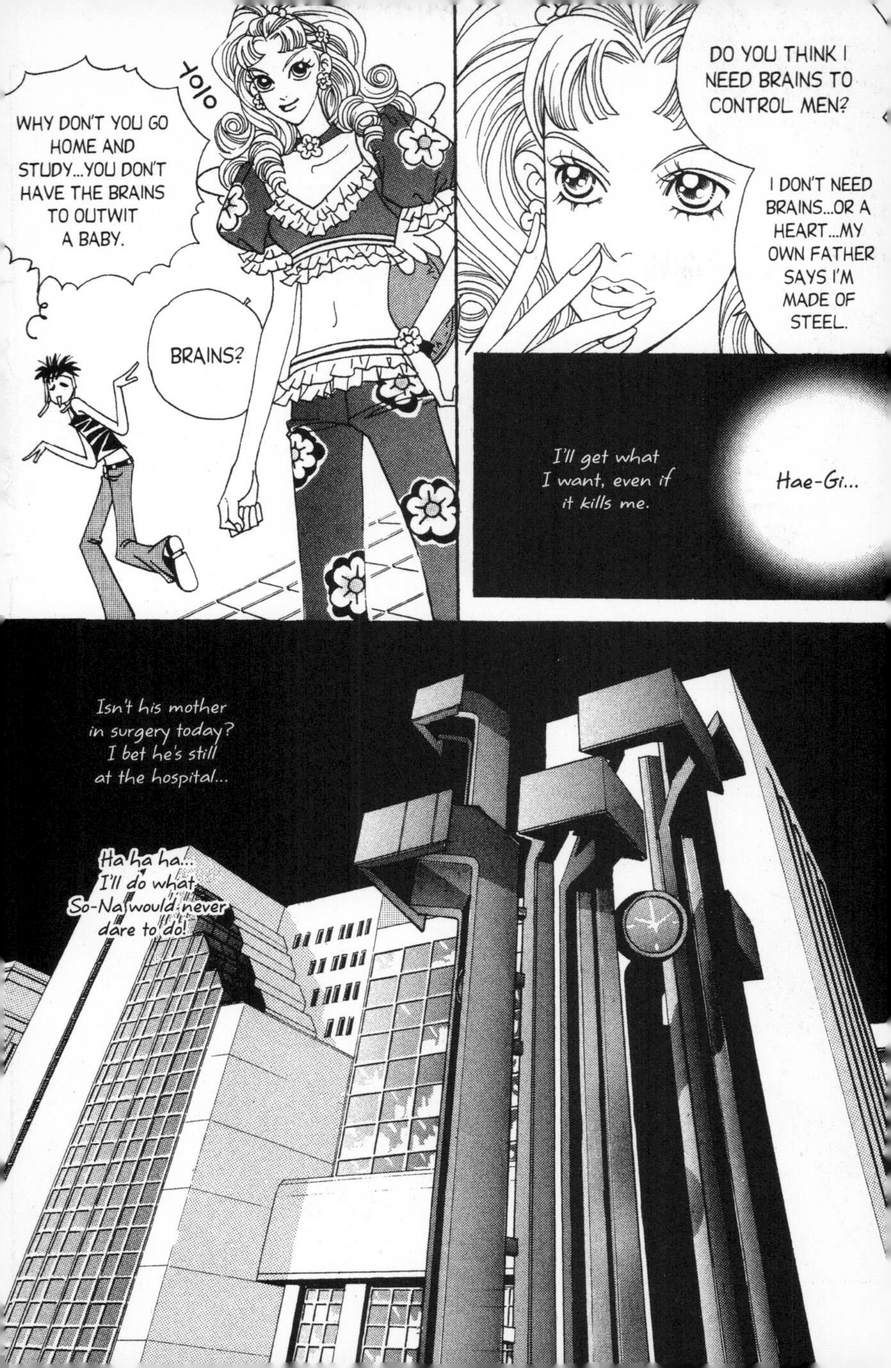
WHY DON'T YOU GO HOME AND STUDY...YOU DON'T HAVE THE BRAINS TO OUTWIT A BABY.
BRAINS?
DO YOU THINK I NEED BRAINS TO CONTROL MEN?
I DON'T NEED BRAINS...OR A HEART...MY OWN FATHER SAYS I'M MADE OF STEEL.
I'll get what I want, even if it kills me.
Hae-Gi...
Isn't his mother in surgery today? I bet he's still at the hospital...
Ha ha ha... I'll do what So-Na would never dare to do!

SURGERY IN PROGRESS

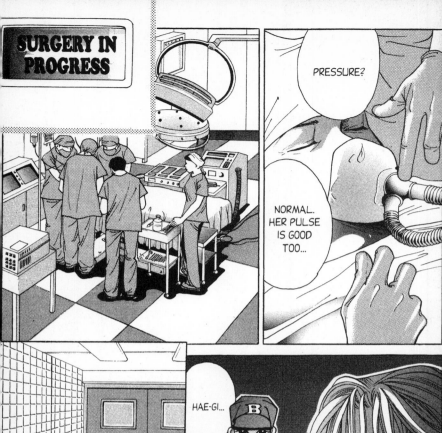

PRESSURE?

NORMAL. HER PULSE IS GOOD TOO...

HAE-GI...

ABOUT TIME YOU SHOWED UP.

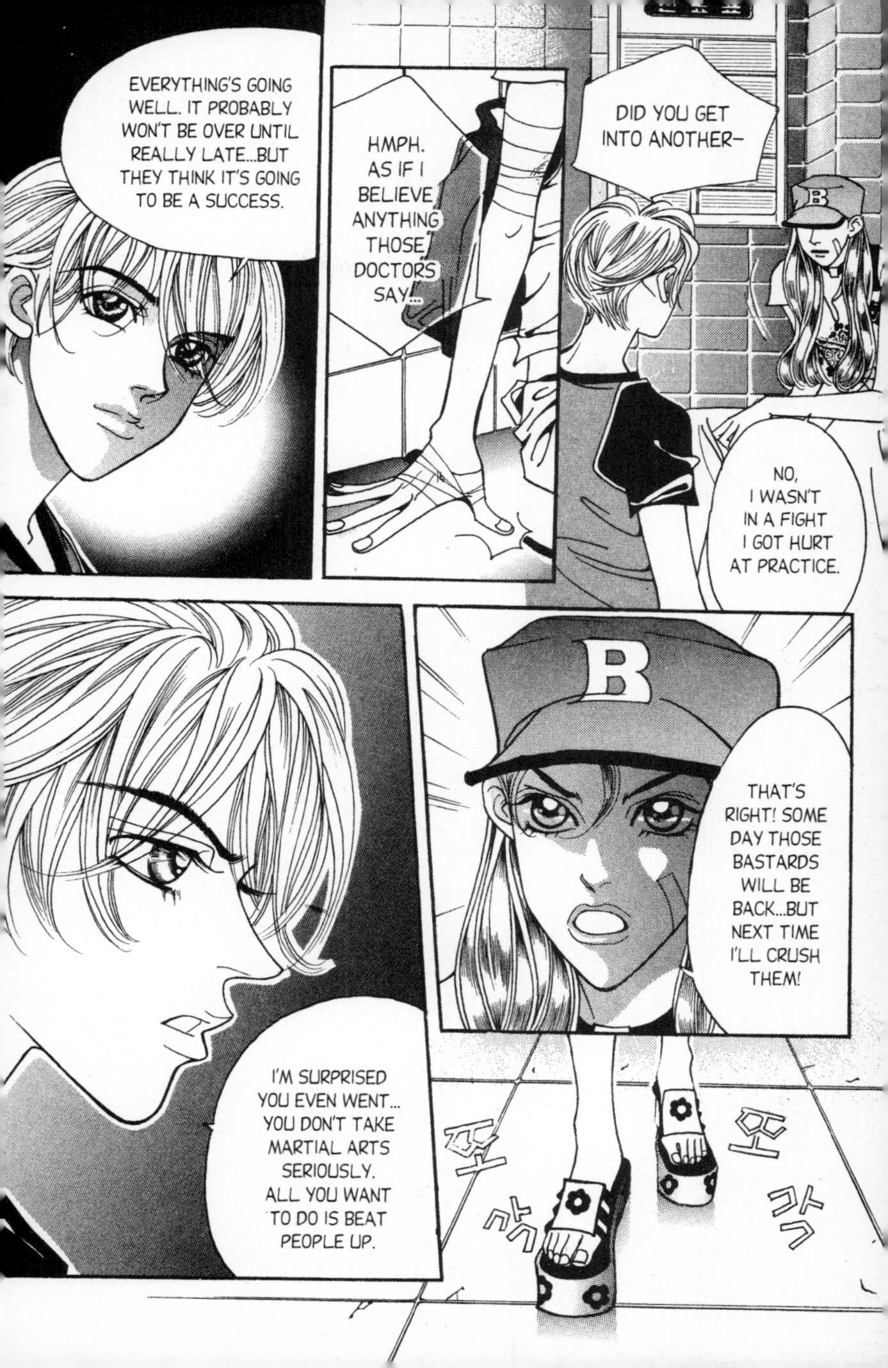
EVERYTHING'S GOING WELL. IT PROBABLY WON'T BE OVER UNTIL REALLY LATE...BUT THEY THINK IT'S GOING TO BE A SUCCESS.
HMPH. AS IF I BELIEVE ANYTHING THOSE DOCTORS SAY...
DID YOU GET INTO ANOTHER—
NO, I WASN'T IN A FIGHT I GOT HURT AT PRACTICE.
I'M SURPRISED YOU EVEN WENT... YOU DON'T TAKE MARTIAL ARTS SERIOUSLY. ALL YOU WANT TO DO IS BEAT PEOPLE UP.
THAT'S RIGHT! SOME DAY THOSE BASTARDS WILL BE BACK...BUT NEXT TIME I'LL CRUSH THEM!

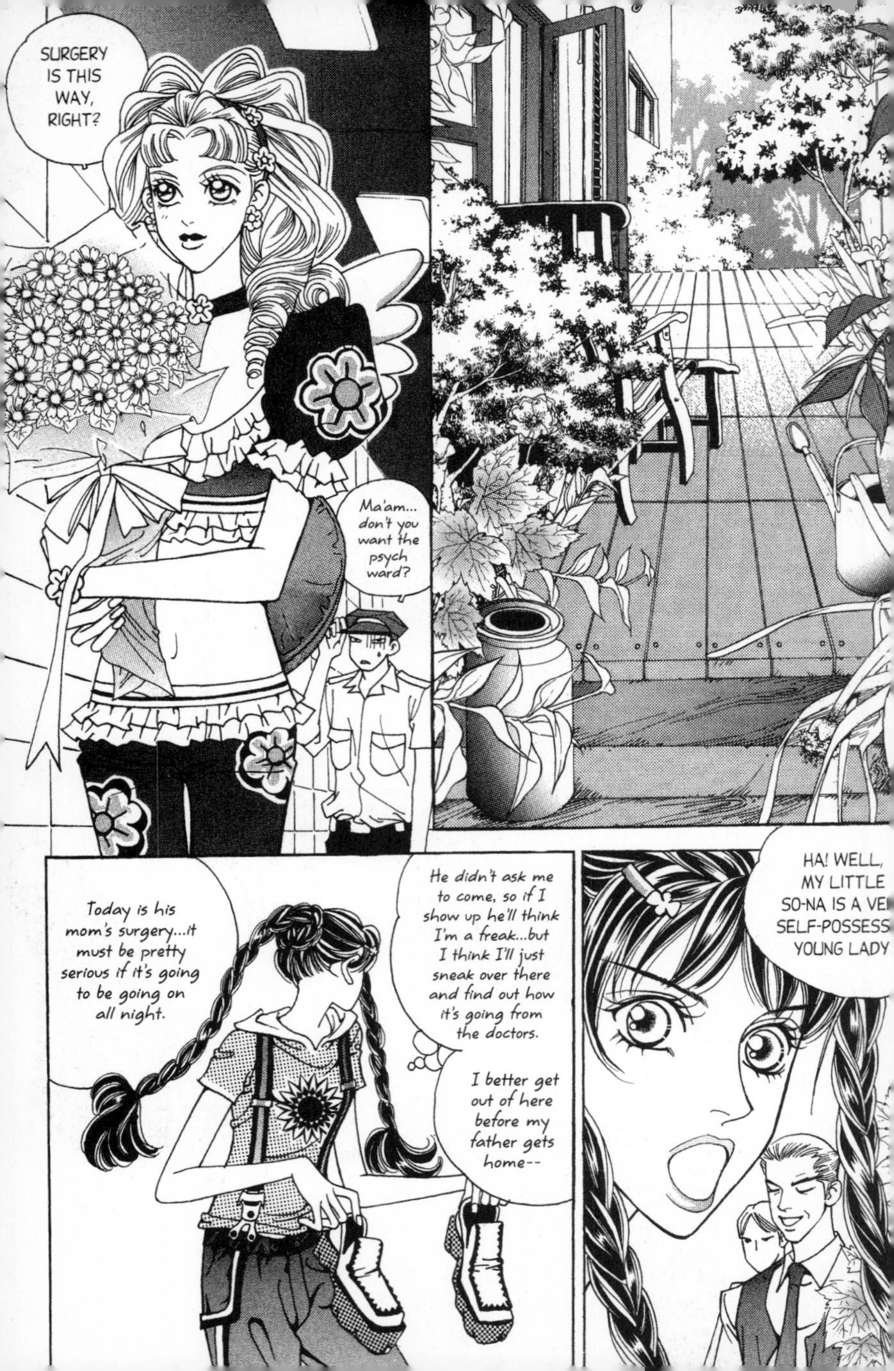
SURGERY IS THIS WAY, RIGHT?
Ma'am... don't you want the psych ward?
Today is his mom's surgery...it must be pretty serious if it's going to be going on all night.
He didn't ask me to come, so if I show up he'll think I'm a freak...but I think I'll just sneak over there and find out how it's going from the doctors.
I better get out of here before my father gets home--
HA! WELL, MY LITTLE SO-NA IS A VE
SELF-POSSESS
YOUNG LADY

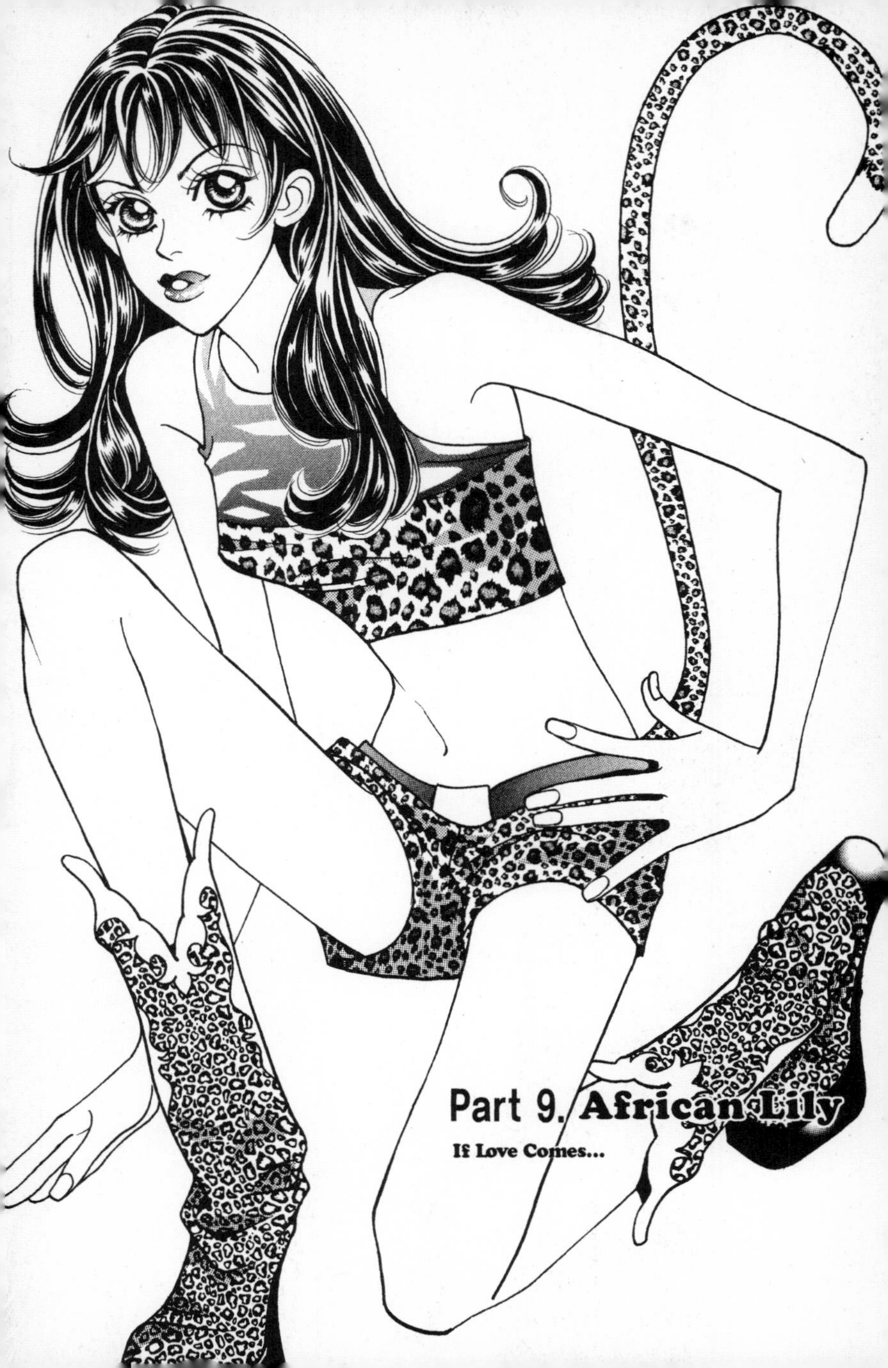

# Part 9. African Lily

**If Love Comes...**

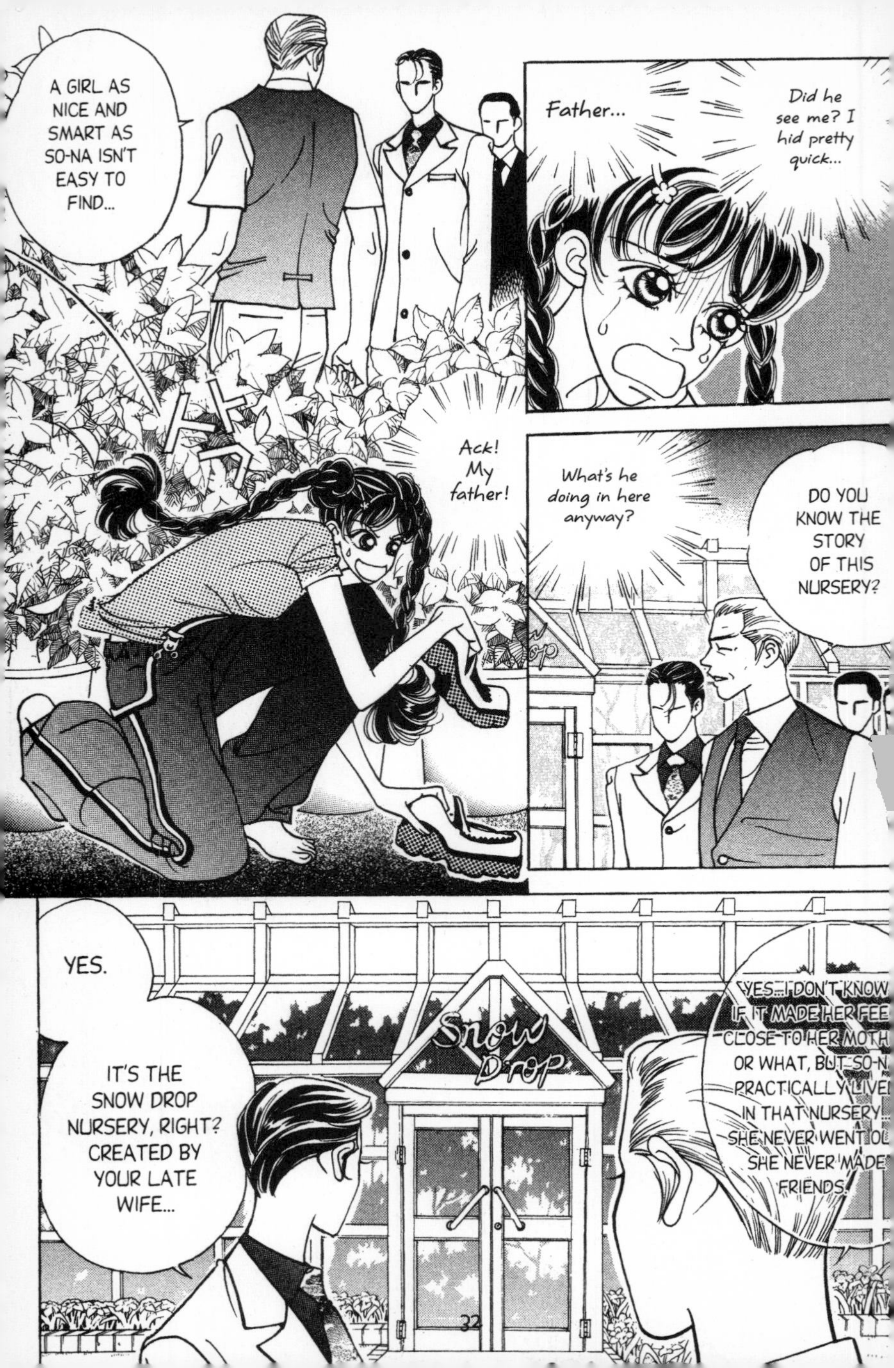
A GIRL AS NICE AND SMART AS SO-NA ISN'T EASY TO FIND...
Ack! My father!
Father...
Did he see me? I hid pretty quick...
What's he doing in here anyway?
DO YOU KNOW THE STORY OF THIS NURSERY?
YES.
IT'S THE SNOW DROP NURSERY, RIGHT? CREATED BY YOUR LATE WIFE...
Snow Drop
YES...I DON'T KNOW IF IT MADE HER FEE CLOSE TO HER MOTH OR WHAT, BUT SO-N PRACTICALLY LIVE IN THAT NURSERY... SHE NEVER WENT OU SHE NEVER MADE FRIENDS.

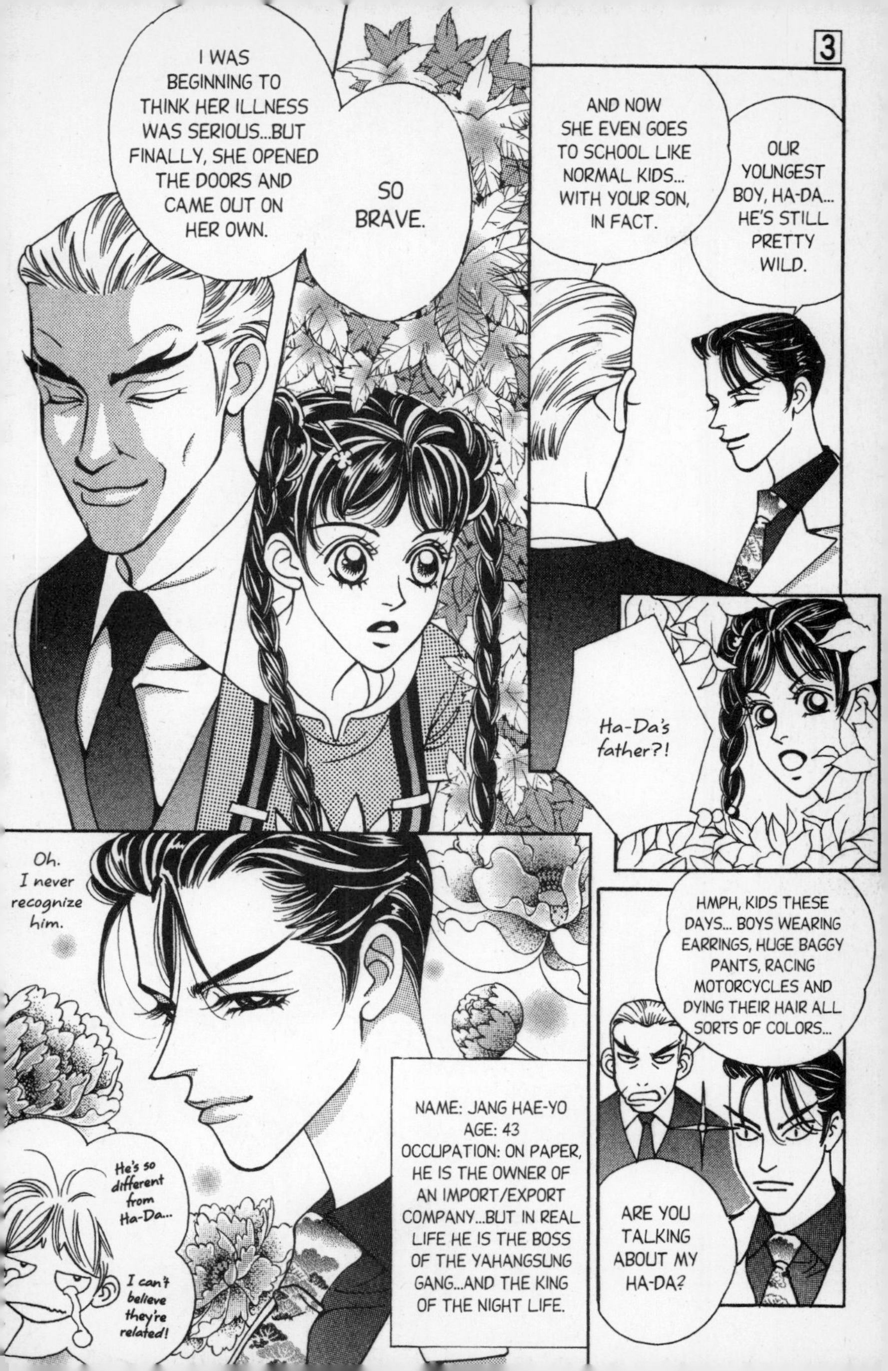
3
I WAS BEGINNING TO THINK HER ILLNESS WAS SERIOUS...BUT FINALLY, SHE OPENED THE DOORS AND CAME OUT ON HER OWN.
SO BRAVE.
AND NOW SHE EVEN GOES TO SCHOOL LIKE NORMAL KIDS... WITH YOUR SON, IN FACT.
OUR YOUNGEST BOY, HA-DA... HE'S STILL PRETTY WILD.
Ha-Da's father?!
Oh. I never recognize him.
He's so different from Ha-Da...
I can't believe they're related!
NAME: JANG HAE-YO AGE: 43 OCCUPATION: ON PAPER, HE IS THE OWNER OF AN IMPORT/EXPORT COMPANY...BUT IN REAL LIFE HE IS THE BOSS OF THE YAHANGSUNG GANG...AND THE KING OF THE NIGHT LIFE.
HMPH, KIDS THESE DAYS... BOYS WEARING EARRINGS, HUGE BAGGY PANTS, RACING MOTORCYCLES AND DYING THEIR HAIR ALL SORTS OF COLORS...
ARE YOU TALKING ABOUT MY HA-DA?

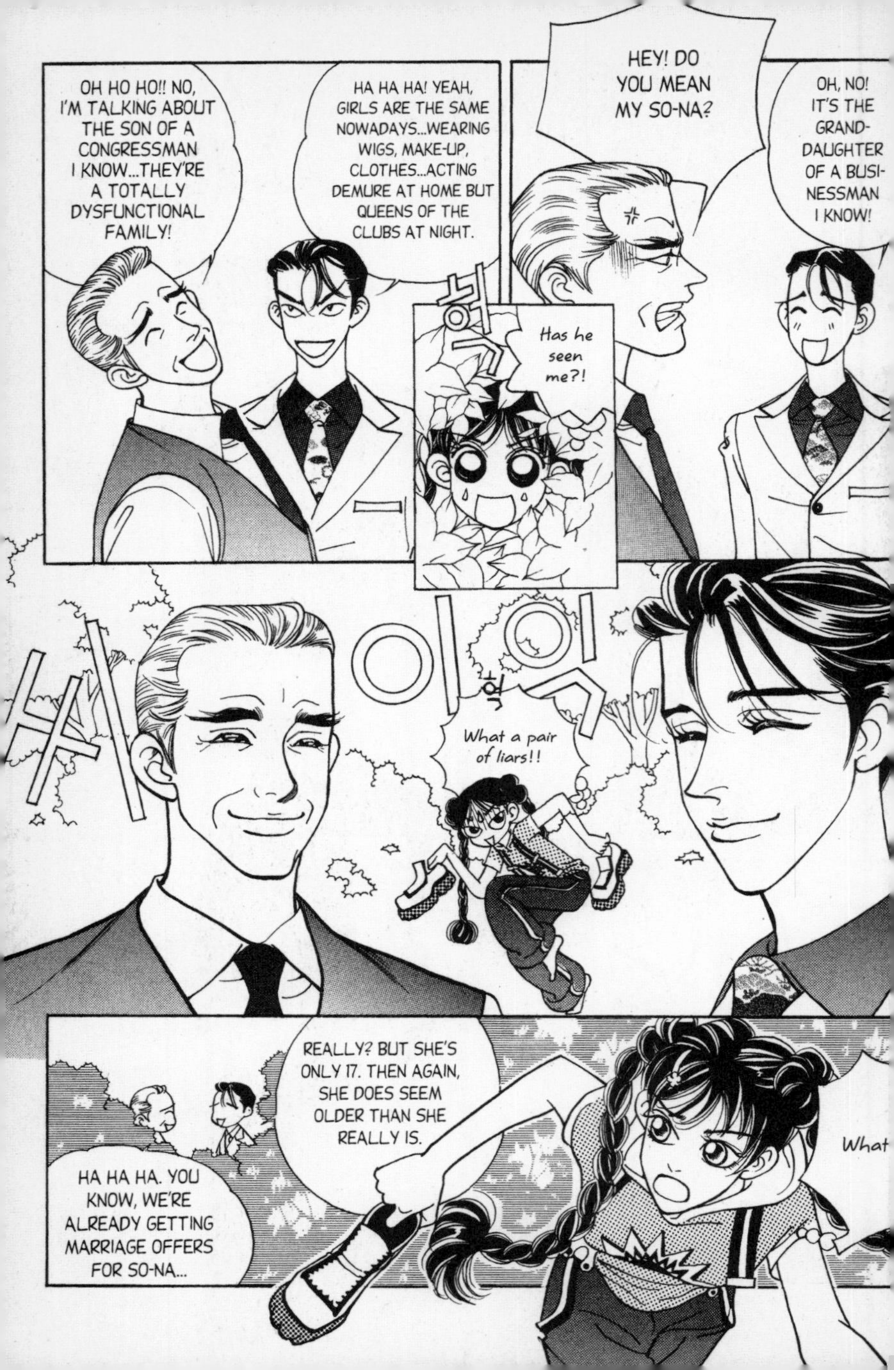
OH HO HO!! NO, I'M TALKING ABOUT THE SON OF A CONGRESSMAN I KNOW...THEY'RE A TOTALLY DYSFUNCTIONAL FAMILY!
HA HA HA! YEAH, GIRLS ARE THE SAME NOWADAYS...WEARING WIGS, MAKE-UP, CLOTHES...ACTING DEMURE AT HOME BUT QUEENS OF THE CLUBS AT NIGHT.
HEY! DO YOU MEAN MY SO-NA?
OH, NO! IT'S THE GRAND-DAUGHTER OF A BUSI-NESSMAN I KNOW!
Has he seen me?!
What a pair of liars!!
HA HA HA. YOU KNOW, WE'RE ALREADY GETTING MARRIAGE OFFERS FOR SO-NA...
REALLY? BUT SHE'S ONLY 17. THEN AGAIN, SHE DOES SEEM OLDER THAN SHE REALLY IS.
What

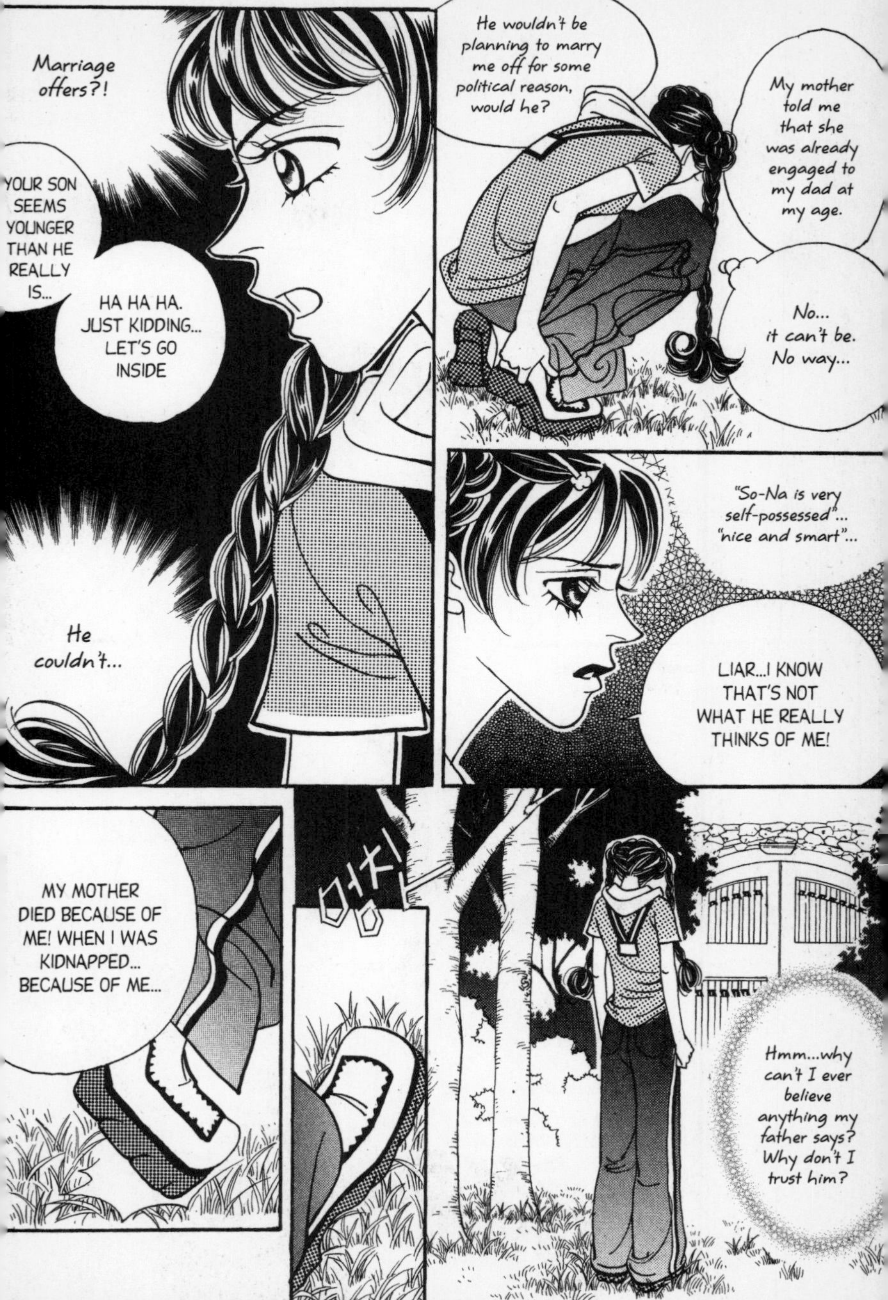
Marriage offers?!
YOUR SON SEEMS YOUNGER THAN HE REALLY IS...
HA HA HA. JUST KIDDING... LET'S GO INSIDE
He couldn't...
He wouldn't be planning to marry me off for some political reason, would he?
My mother told me that she was already engaged to my dad at my age.
No... it can't be. No way...
"So-Na is very self-possessed"... "nice and smart"...
LIAR...I KNOW THAT'S NOT WHAT HE REALLY THINKS OF ME!
MY MOTHER DIED BECAUSE OF ME! WHEN I WAS KIDNAPPED... BECAUSE OF ME...
Hmm...why can't I ever believe anything my father says? Why don't I trust him?

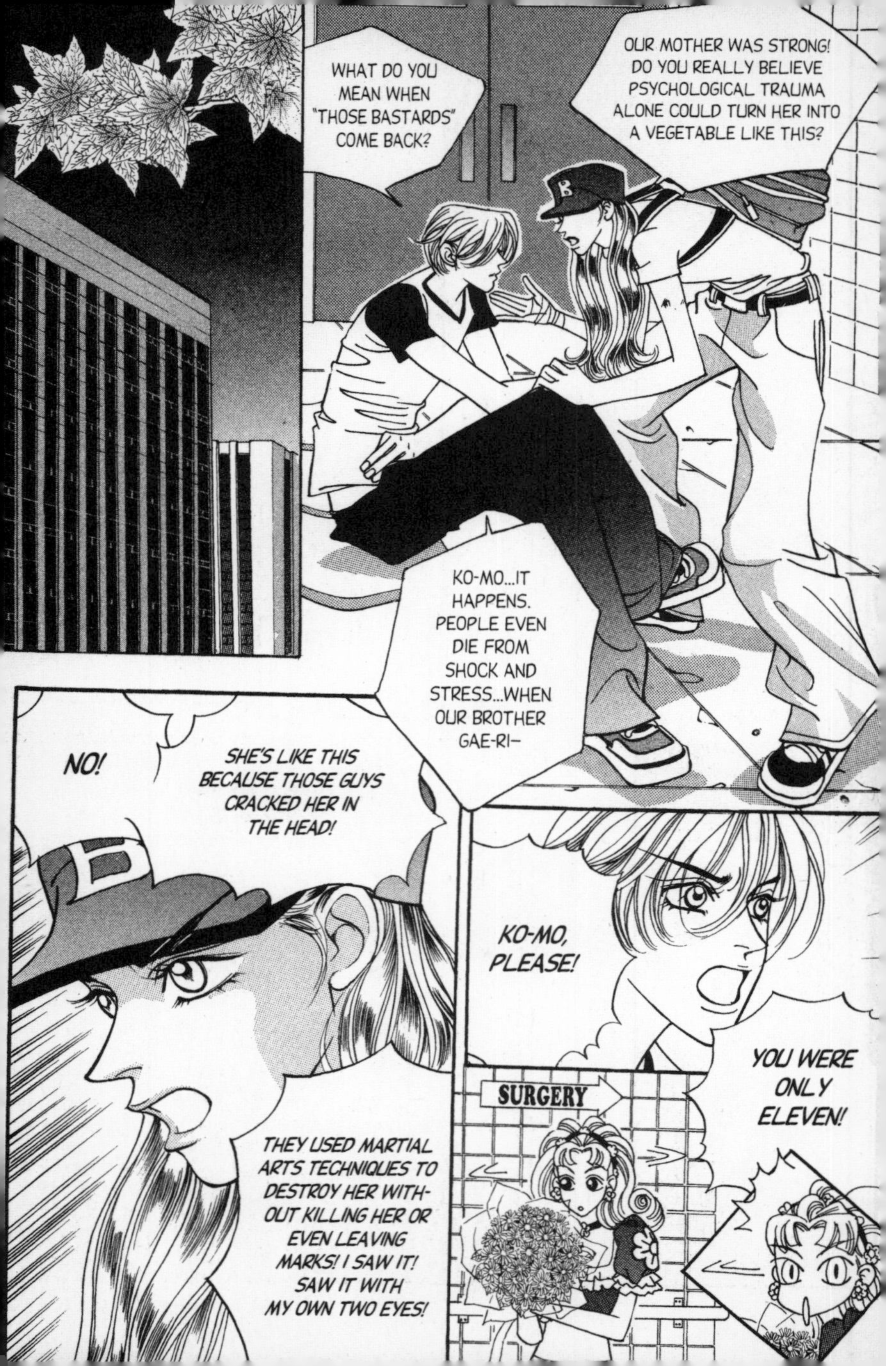

WHAT DO YOU MEAN WHEN "THOSE BASTARDS" COME BACK?
OUR MOTHER WAS STRONG! DO YOU REALLY BELIEVE PSYCHOLOGICAL TRAUMA ALONE COULD TURN HER INTO A VEGETABLE LIKE THIS?
KO-MO...IT HAPPENS. PEOPLE EVEN DIE FROM SHOCK AND STRESS...WHEN OUR BROTHER GAE-RI–
NO!
SHE'S LIKE THIS BECAUSE THOSE GUYS CRACKED HER IN THE HEAD!
THEY USED MARTIAL ARTS TECHNIQUES TO DESTROY HER WITH-OUT KILLING HER OR EVEN LEAVING MARKS! I SAW IT! SAW IT WITH MY OWN TWO EYES!
KO-MO, PLEASE!
YOU WERE ONLY ELEVEN!
SURGERY

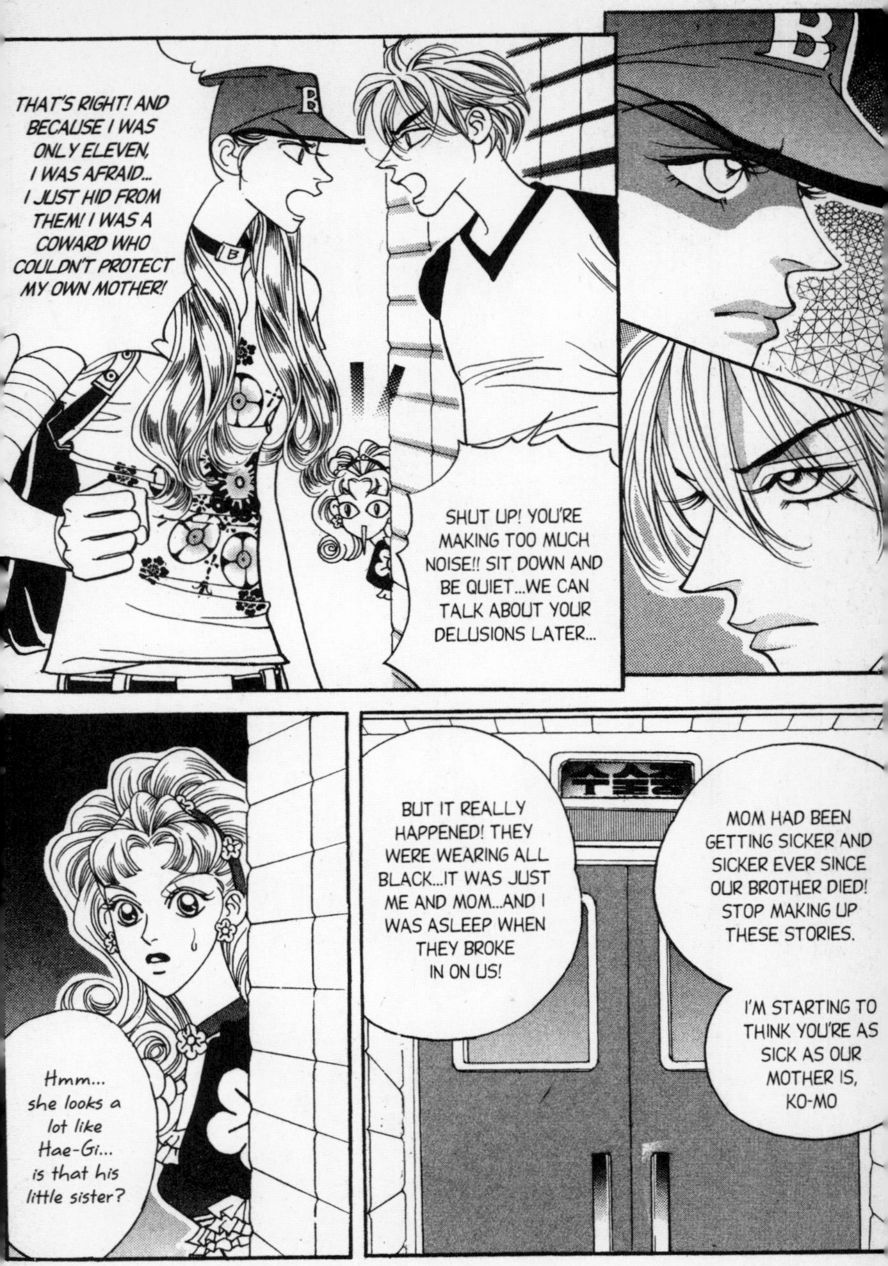
THAT'S RIGHT! AND BECAUSE I WAS ONLY ELEVEN, I WAS AFRAID... I JUST HID FROM THEM! I WAS A COWARD WHO COULDN'T PROTECT MY OWN MOTHER!
SHUT UP! YOU'RE MAKING TOO MUCH NOISE!! SIT DOWN AND BE QUIET...WE CAN TALK ABOUT YOUR DELUSIONS LATER...
Hmm... she looks a lot like Hae-Gi... is that his little sister?
수술중
BUT IT REALLY HAPPENED! THEY WERE WEARING ALL BLACK...IT WAS JUST ME AND MOM...AND I WAS ASLEEP WHEN THEY BROKE IN ON US!
MOM HAD BEEN GETTING SICKER AND SICKER EVER SINCE OUR BROTHER DIED! STOP MAKING UP THESE STORIES.
I'M STARTING TO THINK YOU'RE AS SICK AS OUR MOTHER IS, KO-MO

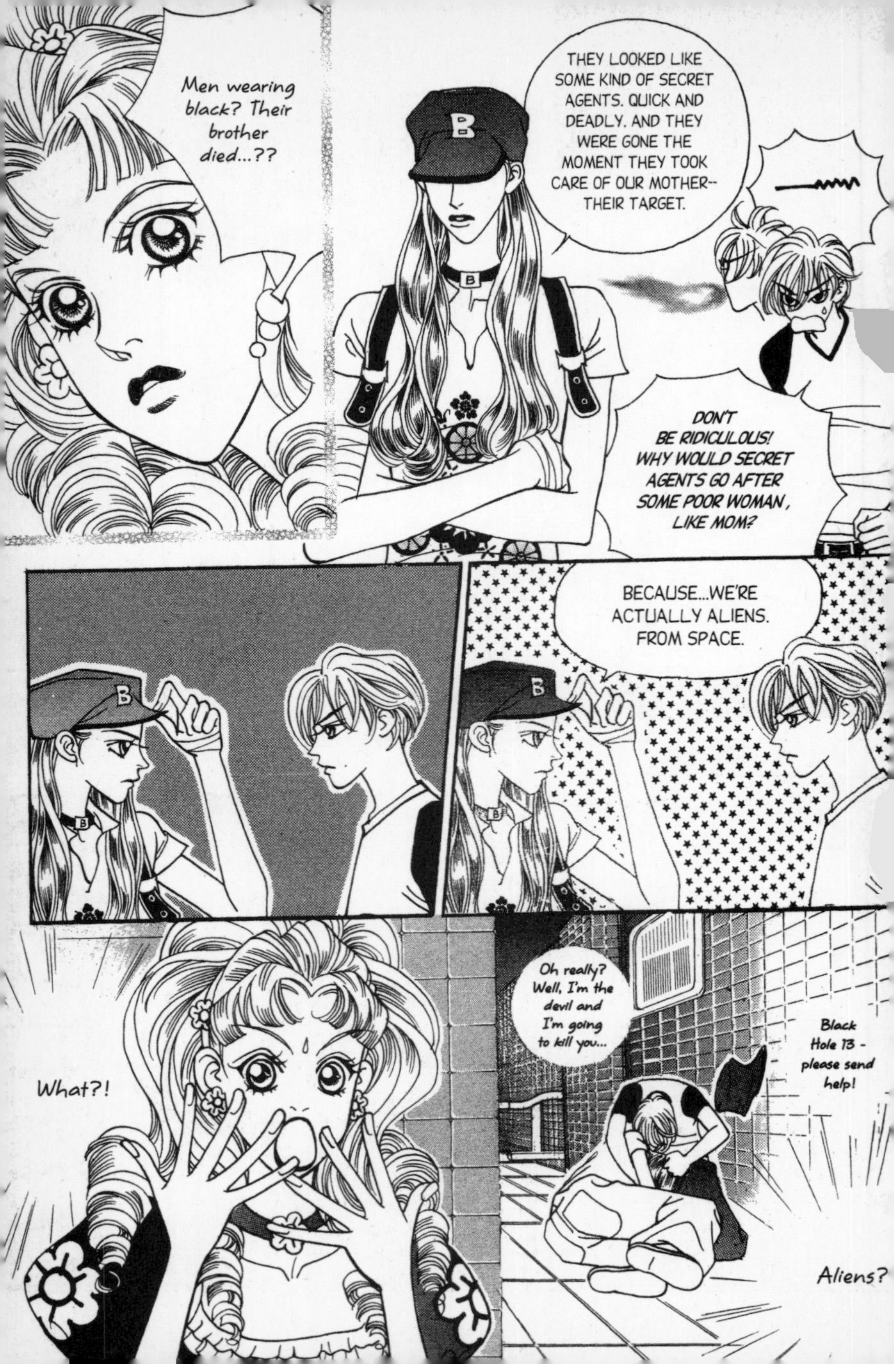
Men wearing black? Their brother died...??
THEY LOOKED LIKE SOME KIND OF SECRET AGENTS. QUICK AND DEADLY. AND THEY WERE GONE THE MOMENT THEY TOOK CARE OF OUR MOTHER-- THEIR TARGET.
DON'T BE RIDICULOUS! WHY WOULD SECRET AGENTS GO AFTER SOME POOR WOMAN, LIKE MOM?
BECAUSE...WE'RE ACTUALLY ALIENS. FROM SPACE.
What?!
Oh really? Well, I'm the devil and I'm going to kill you...
Black Hole 13 - please send help!
Aliens?

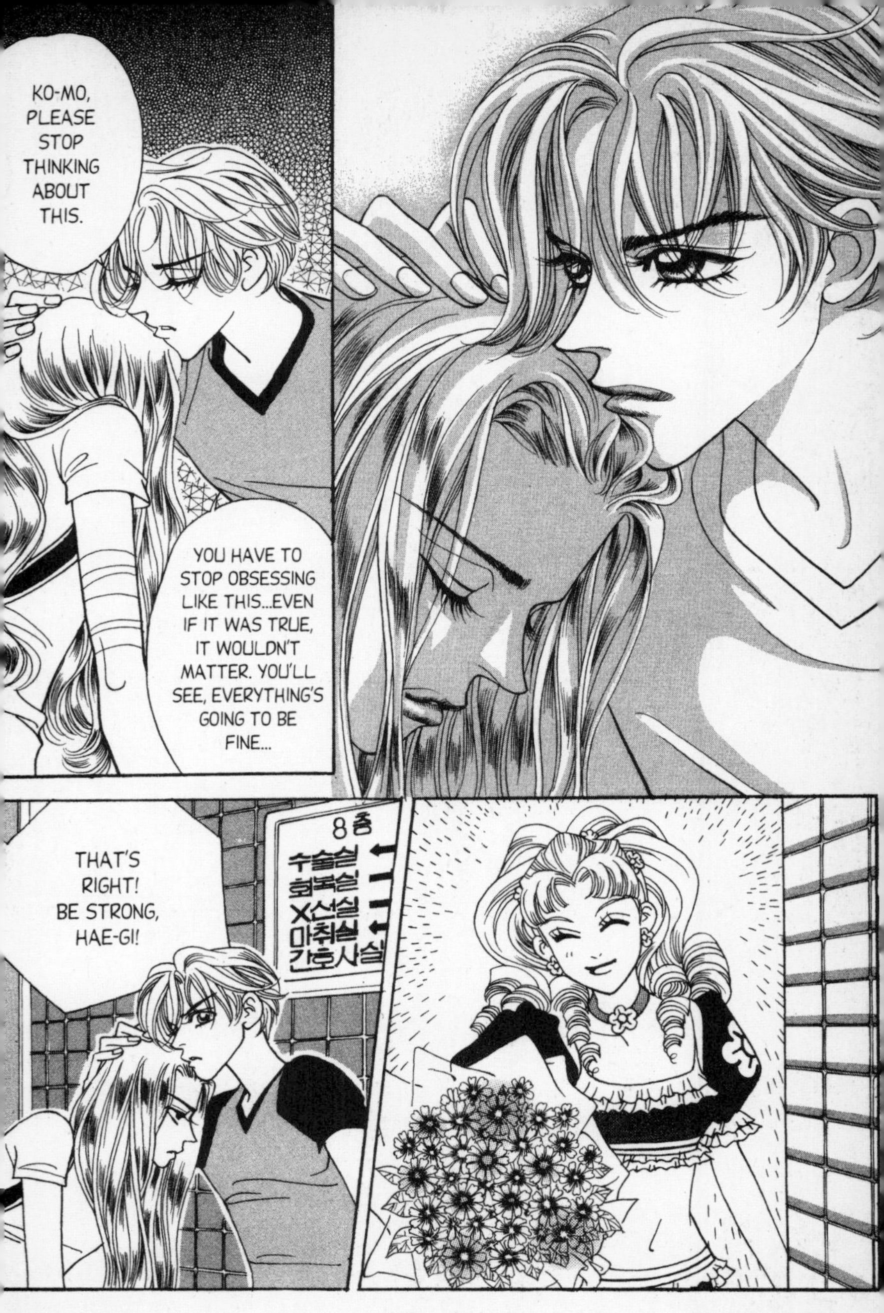
KO-MO, PLEASE STOP THINKING ABOUT THIS.
YOU HAVE TO STOP OBSESSING LIKE THIS...EVEN IF IT WAS TRUE, IT WOULDN'T MATTER. YOU'LL SEE, EVERYTHING'S GOING TO BE FINE...
THAT'S RIGHT! BE STRONG, HAE-GI!
8층
수술실
회복실
X선실
마취실
간호사실

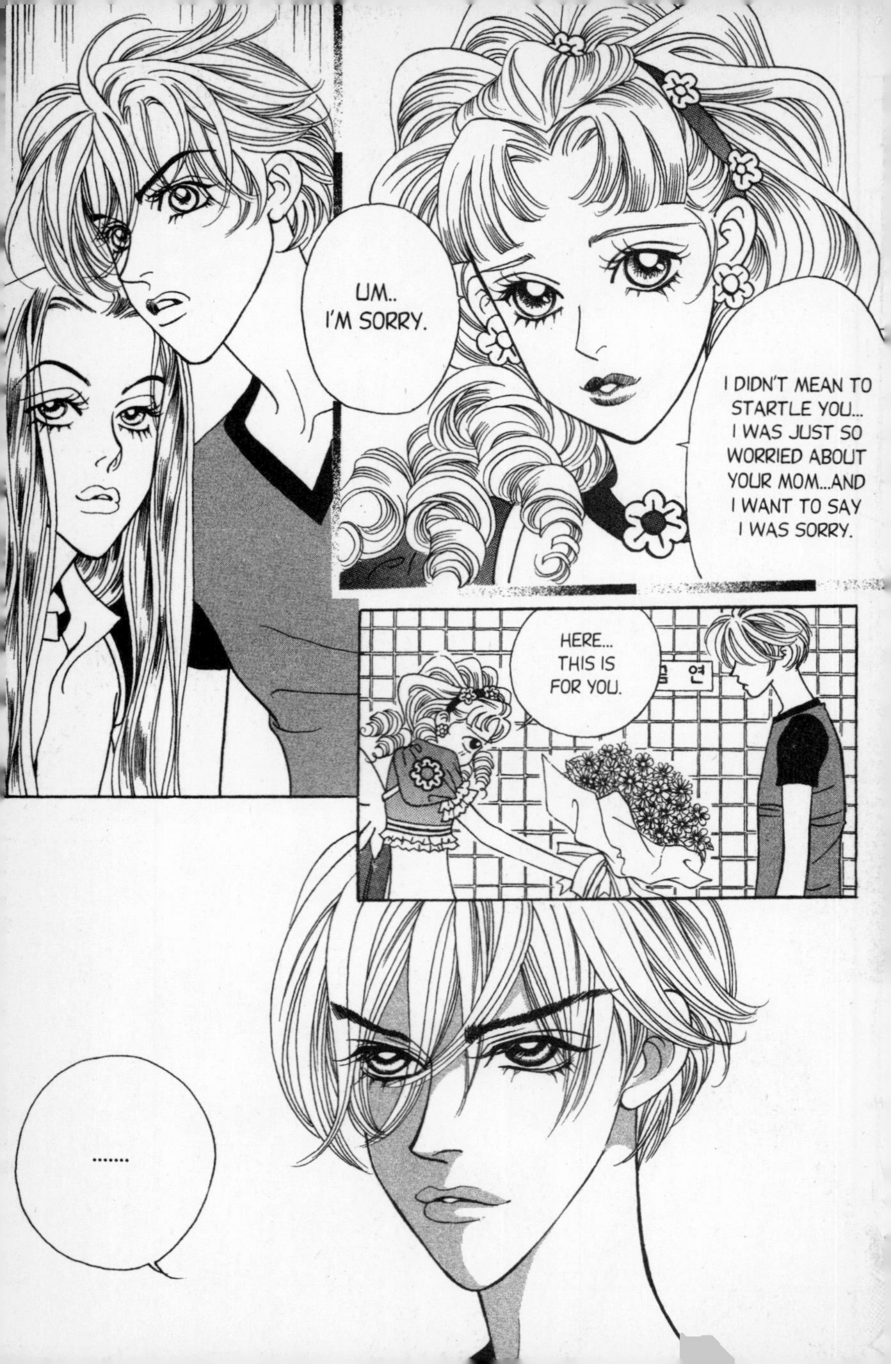
UM..
I'M SORRY.
I DIDN'T MEAN TO STARTLE YOU... I WAS JUST SO WORRIED ABOUT YOUR MOM...AND I WANT TO SAY I WAS SORRY.
HERE... THIS IS FOR YOU.
.......

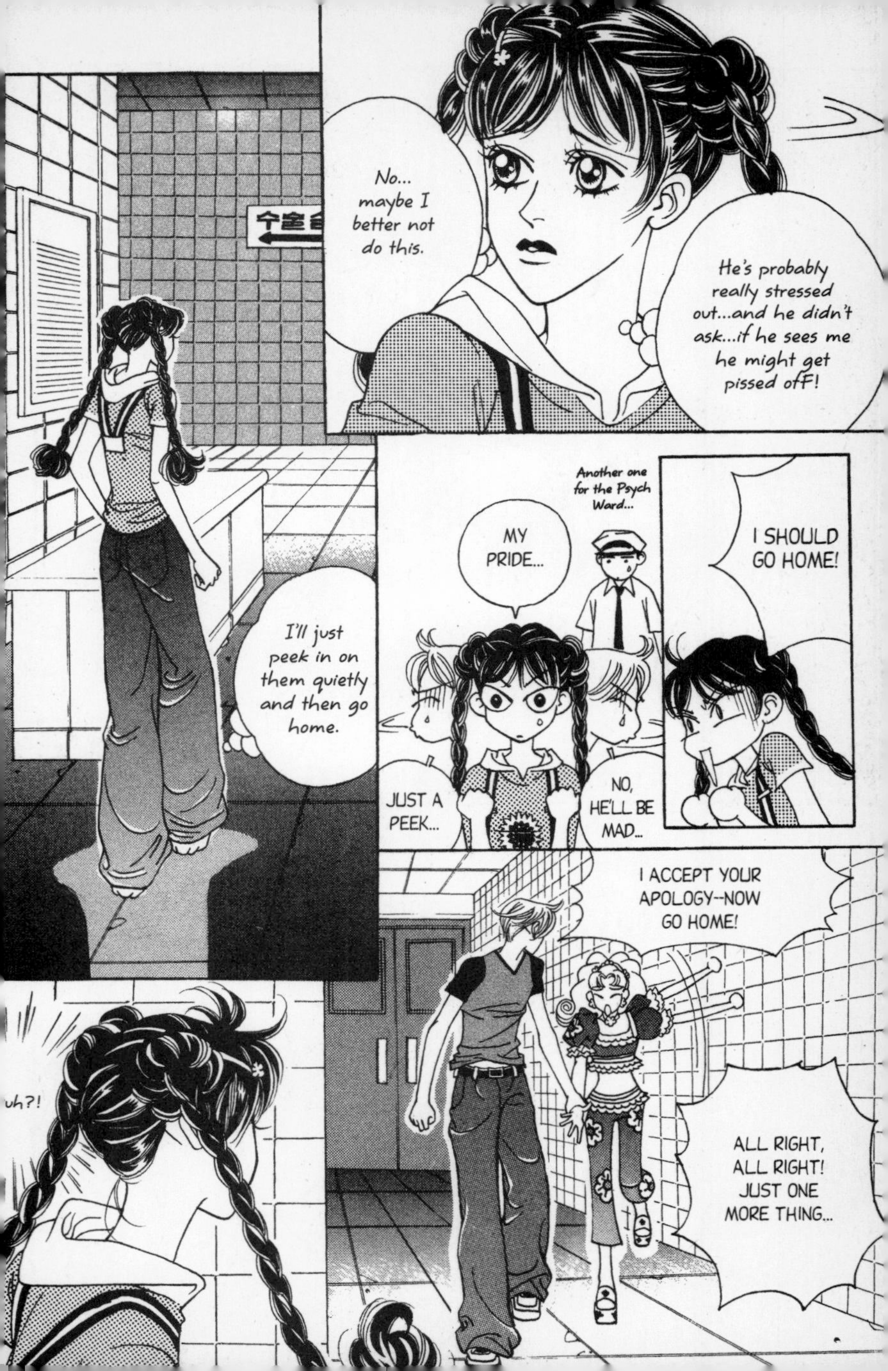
I'll just peek in on them quietly and then go home.
No... maybe I better not do this.
He's probably really stressed out...and he didn't ask...if he sees me he might get pissed off!
Another one for the Psych Ward...
MY PRIDE...
JUST A PEEK...
NO, HE'LL BE MAD...
I SHOULD GO HOME!
uh?!
I ACCEPT YOUR APOLOGY--NOW GO HOME!
ALL RIGHT, ALL RIGHT! JUST ONE MORE THING...

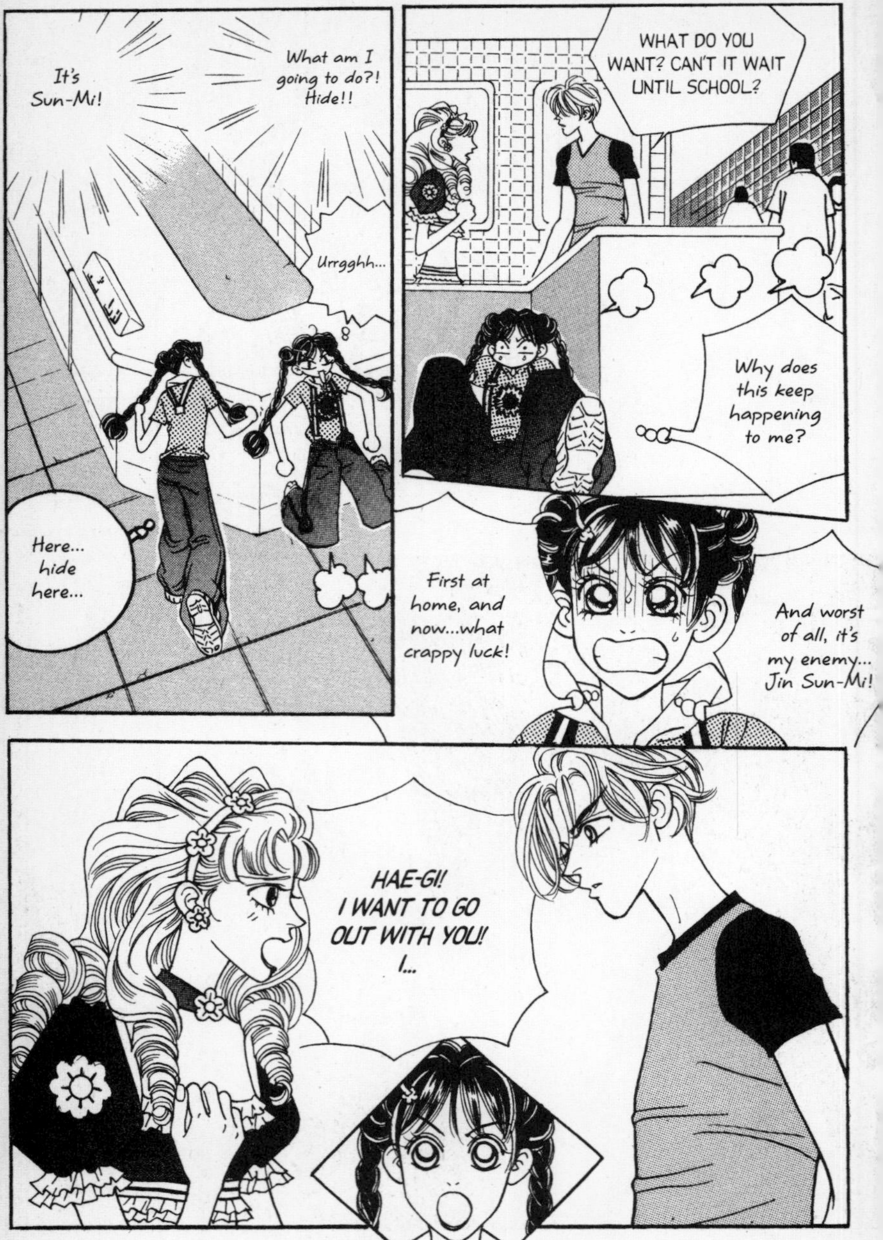

It's Sun-Mi!
What am I going to do?! Hide!!
Urrgghh...
Here... hide here...
WHAT DO YOU WANT? CAN'T IT WAIT UNTIL SCHOOL?
Why does this keep happening to me?
First at home, and now...what crappy luck!
And worst of all, it's my enemy... Jin Sun-Mi!
HAE-GI! I WANT TO GO OUT WITH YOU! I...

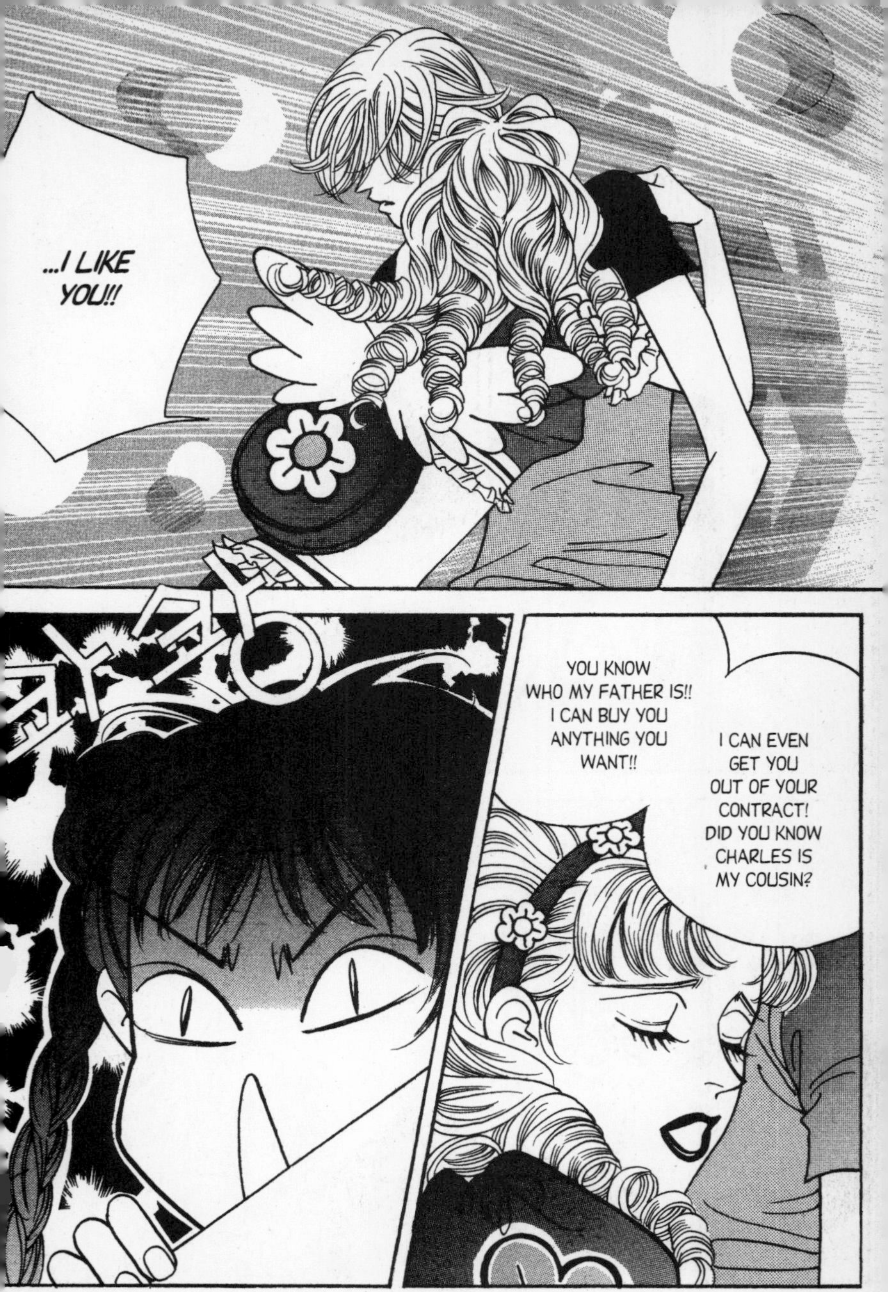
...I LIKE YOU!!
YOU KNOW WHO MY FATHER IS!! I CAN BUY YOU ANYTHING YOU WANT!!
I CAN EVEN GET YOU OUT OF YOUR CONTRACT! DID YOU KNOW CHARLES IS MY COUSIN?

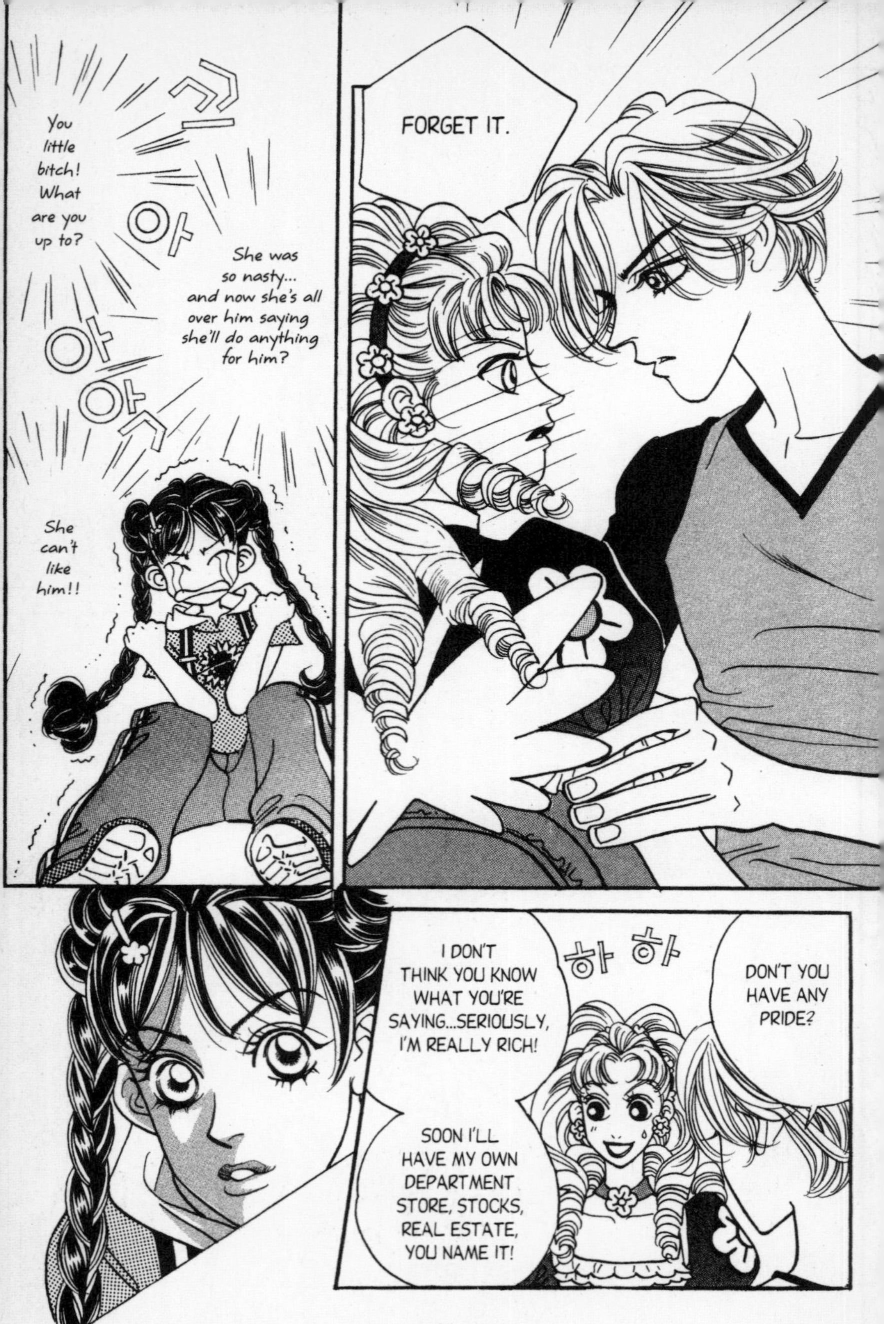
You little bitch! What are you up to?
She was so nasty... and now she's all over him saying she'll do anything for him?
She can't like him!!
FORGET IT.
I DON'T THINK YOU KNOW WHAT YOU'RE SAYING...SERIOUSLY, I'M REALLY RICH!
하 하
DON'T YOU HAVE ANY PRIDE?
SOON I'LL HAVE MY OWN DEPARTMENT STORE, STOCKS, REAL ESTATE, YOU NAME IT!

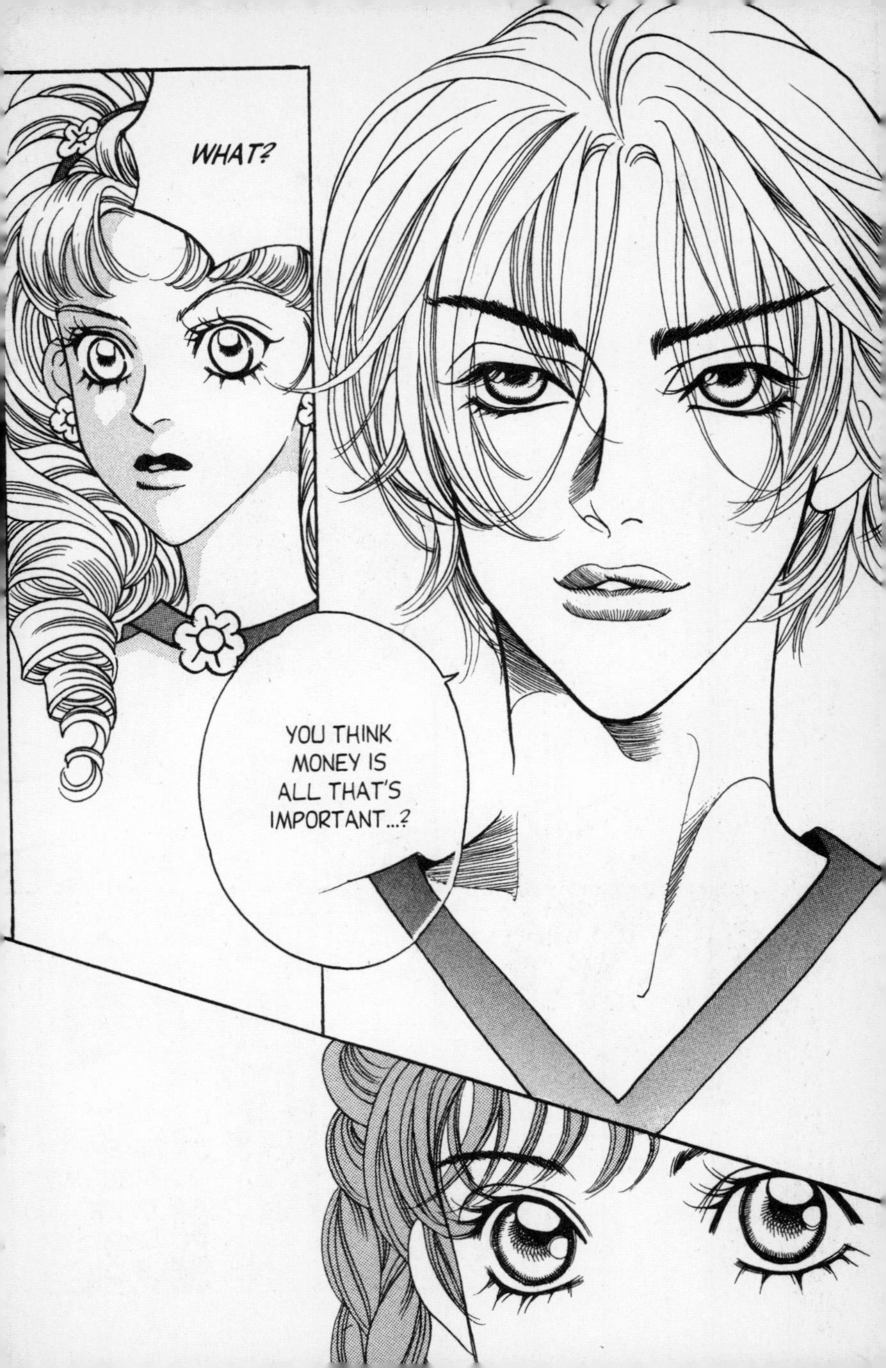
WHAT?
YOU THINK MONEY IS ALL THAT'S IMPORTANT...?

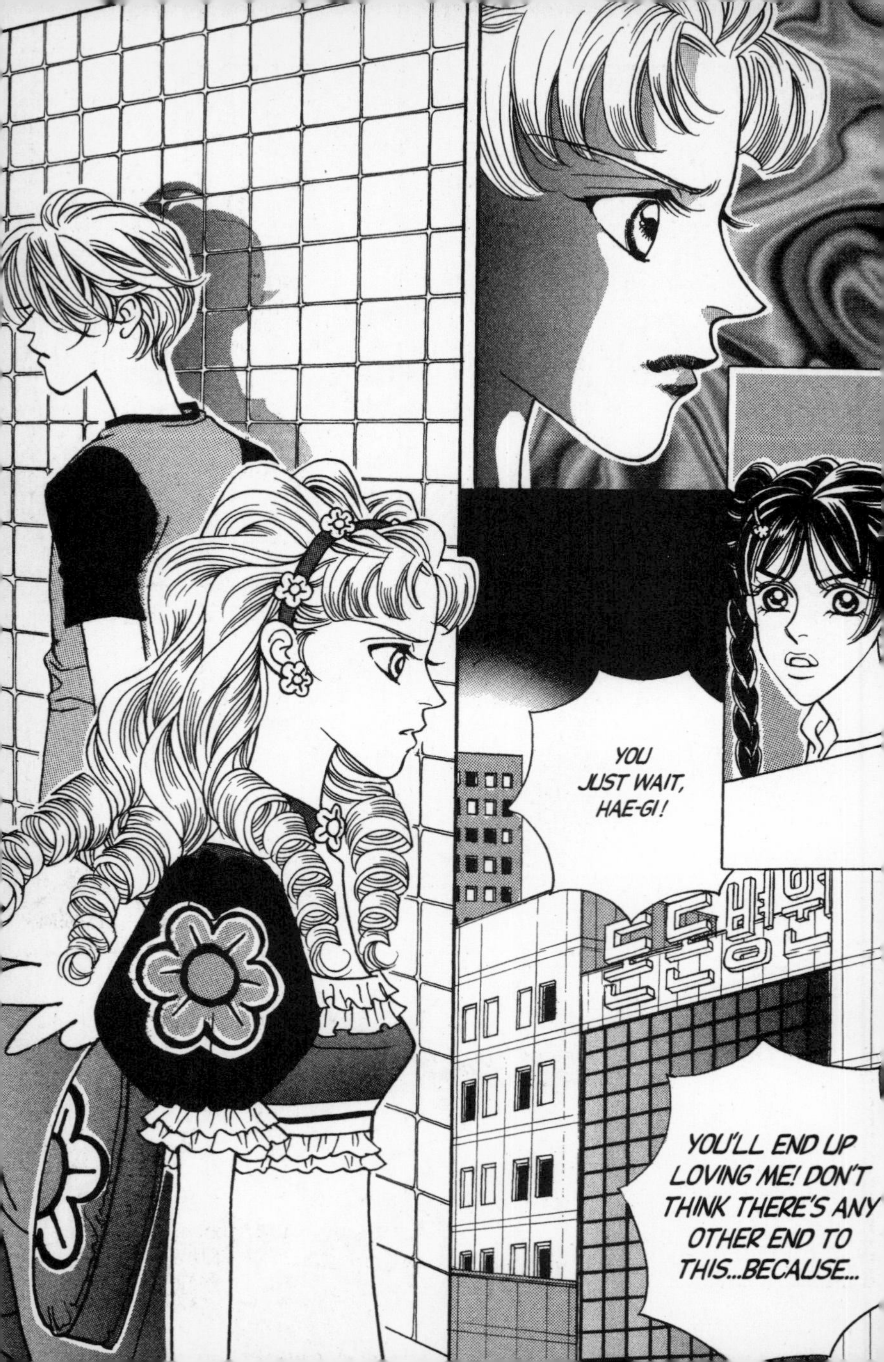
YOU JUST WAIT, HAE-GI!
YOU'LL END UP LOVING ME! DON'T THINK THERE'S ANY OTHER END TO THIS...BECAUSE...

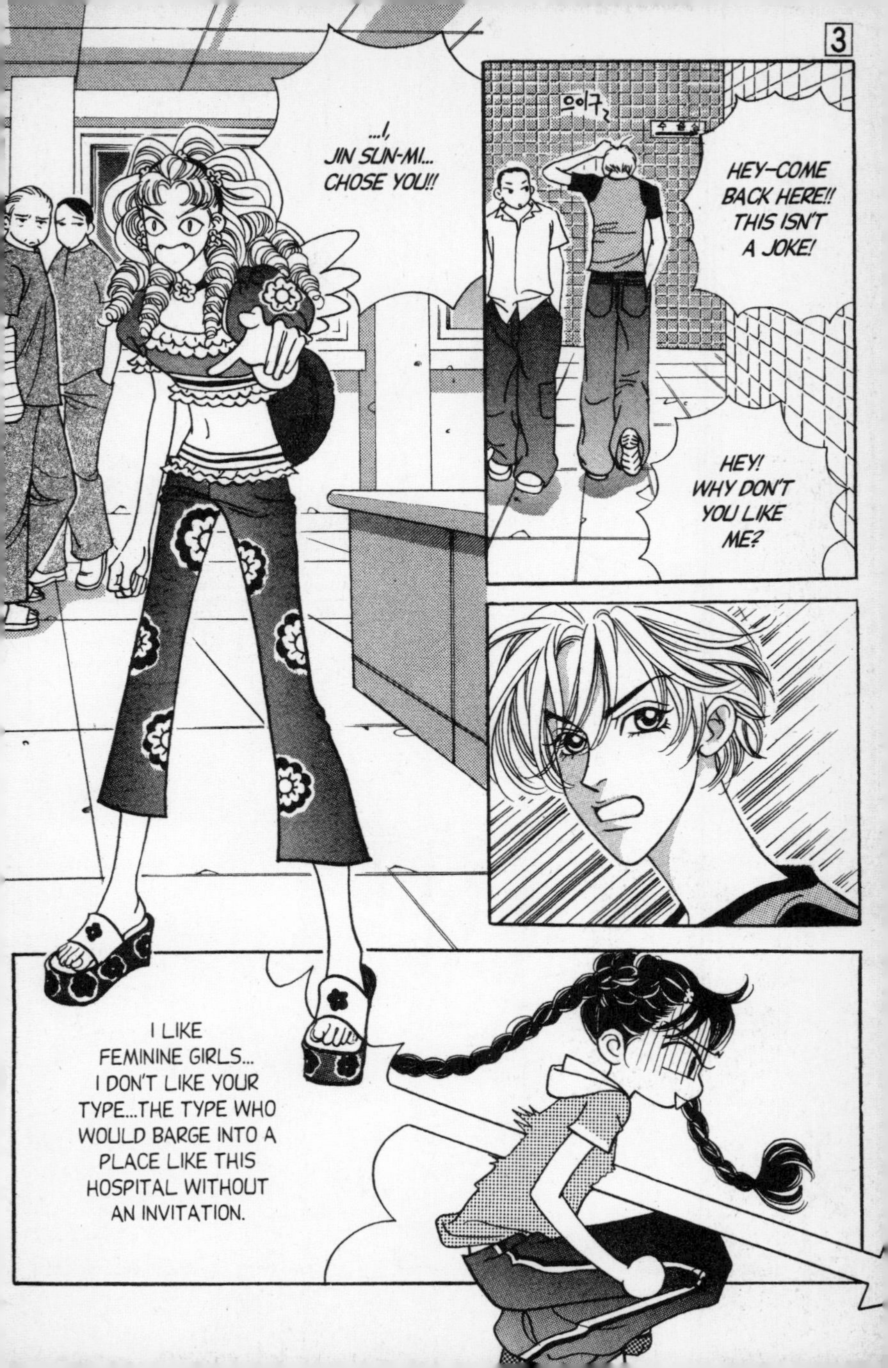
...I, JIN SUN-MI... CHOSE YOU!!
으이구
HEY—COME BACK HERE!! THIS ISN'T A JOKE!
HEY! WHY DON'T YOU LIKE ME?
I LIKE FEMININE GIRLS... I DON'T LIKE YOUR TYPE...THE TYPE WHO WOULD BARGE INTO A PLACE LIKE THIS HOSPITAL WITHOUT AN INVITATION.

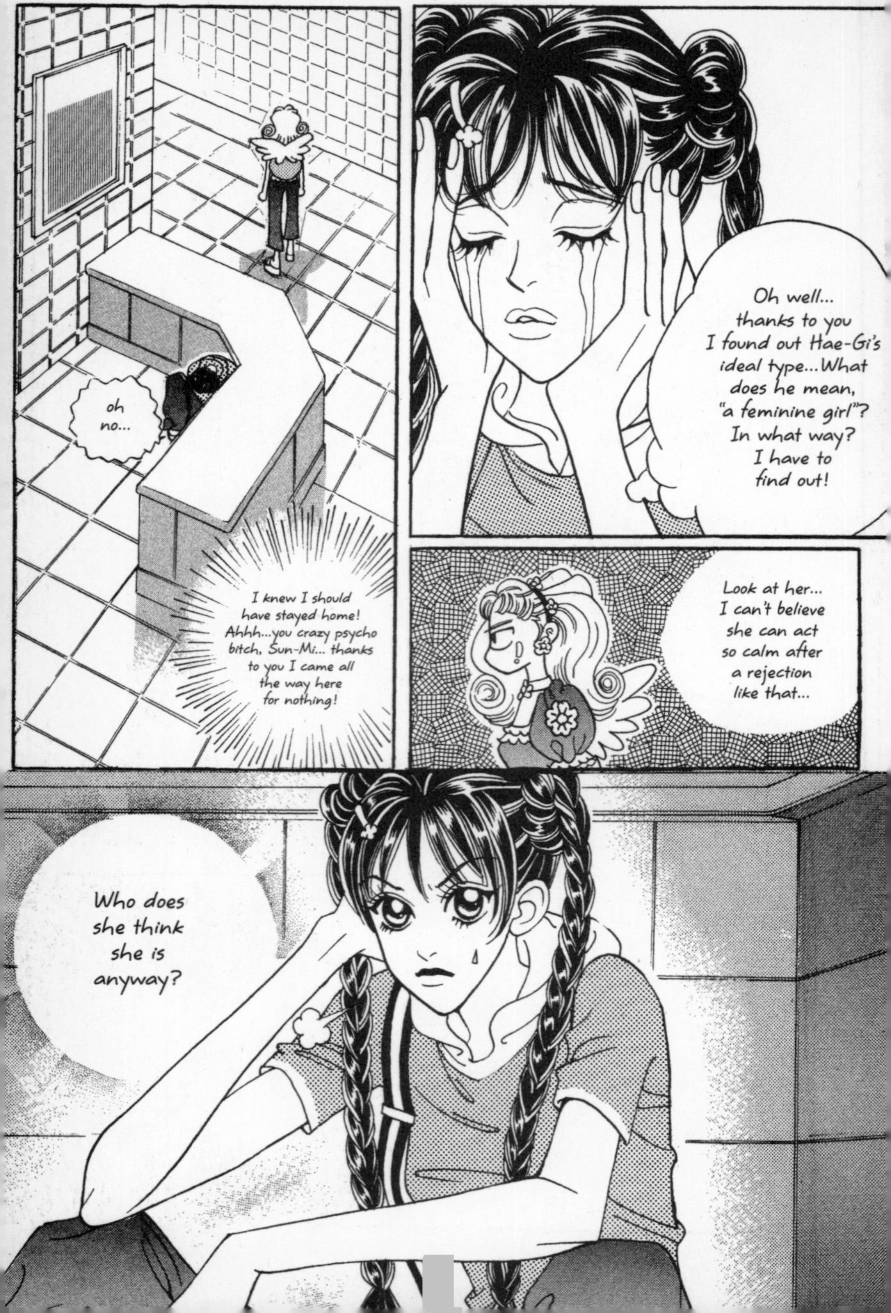
oh no...
I knew I should have stayed home! Ahhh...you crazy psycho bitch, Sun-Mi... thanks to you I came all the way here for nothing!
Oh well... thanks to you I found out Hae-Gi's ideal type...What does he mean, "a feminine girl"? In what way? I have to find out!
Look at her... I can't believe she can act so calm after a rejection like that...
Who does she think she is anyway?

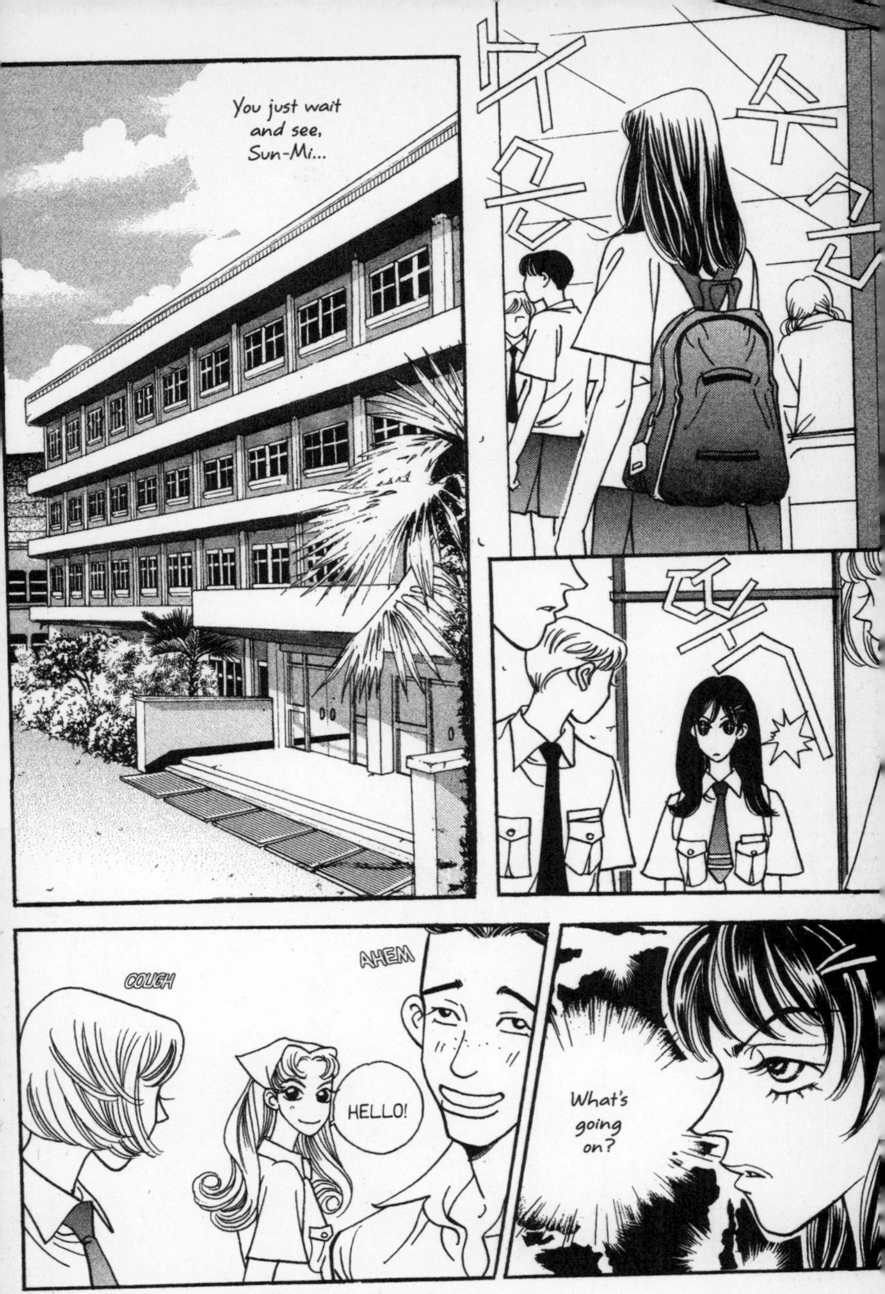
You just wait and see, Sun-Mi...
COUGH
AHEM
HELLO!
What's going on?

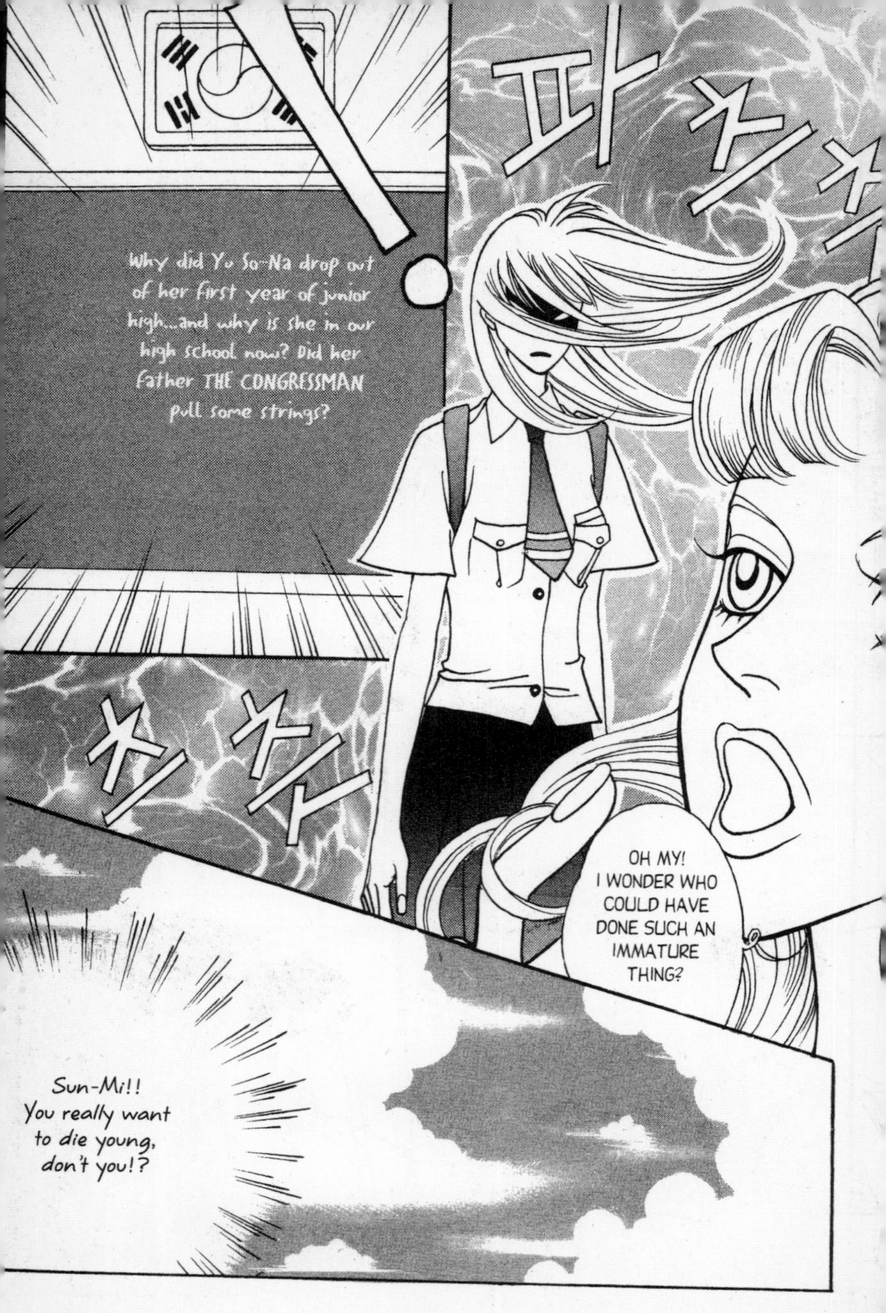
Why did Yu So-Na drop out of her first year of junior high...and why is she in our high school now? Did her father THE CONGRESSMAN pull some strings?
OH MY! I WONDER WHO COULD HAVE DONE SUCH AN IMMATURE THING?
Sun-Mi!! You really want to die young, don't you!?

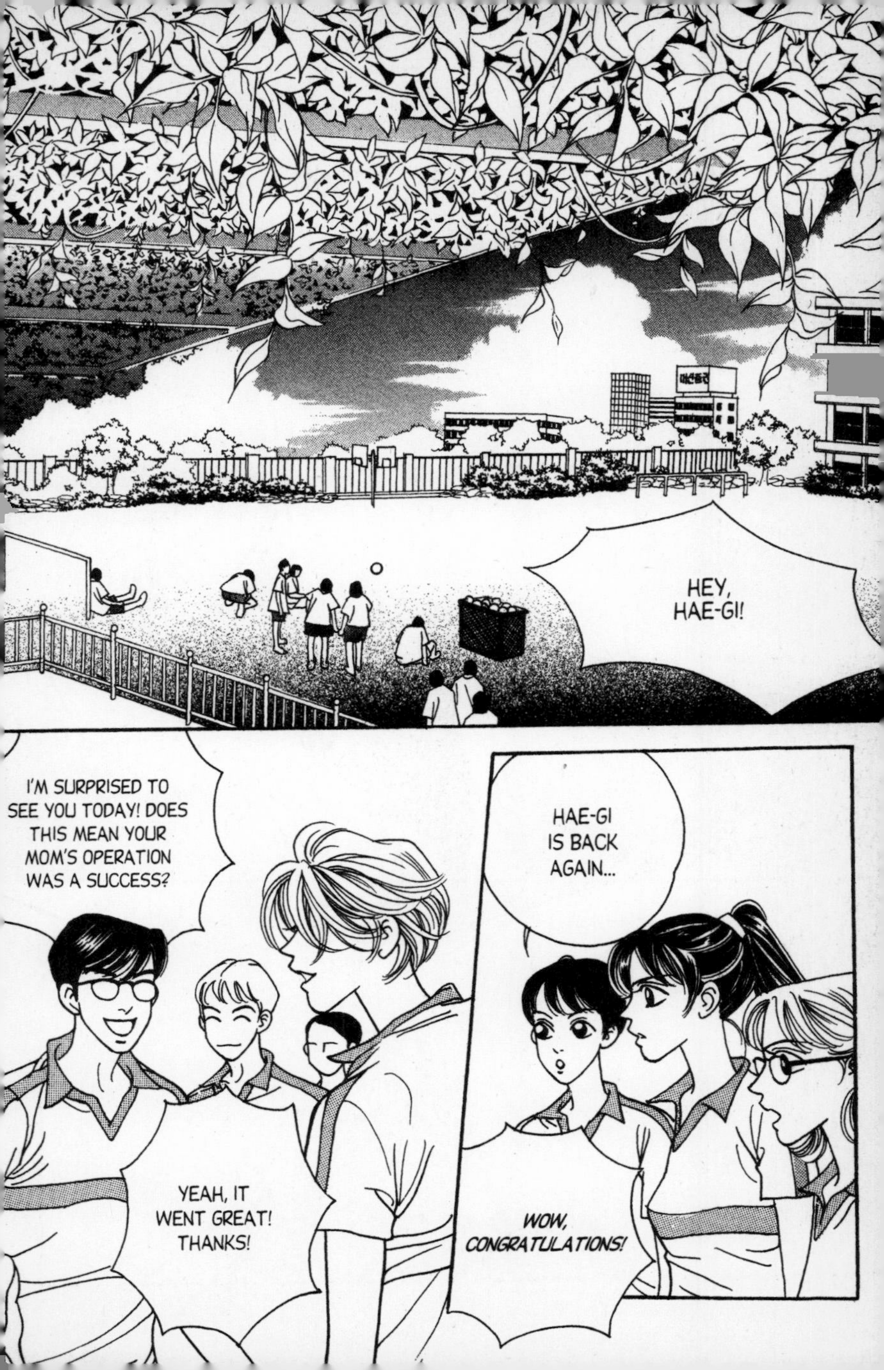
HEY, HAE-GI!
I'M SURPRISED TO SEE YOU TODAY! DOES THIS MEAN YOUR MOM'S OPERATION WAS A SUCCESS?
YEAH, IT WENT GREAT! THANKS!
HAE-GI IS BACK AGAIN...
WOW, CONGRATULATIONS!

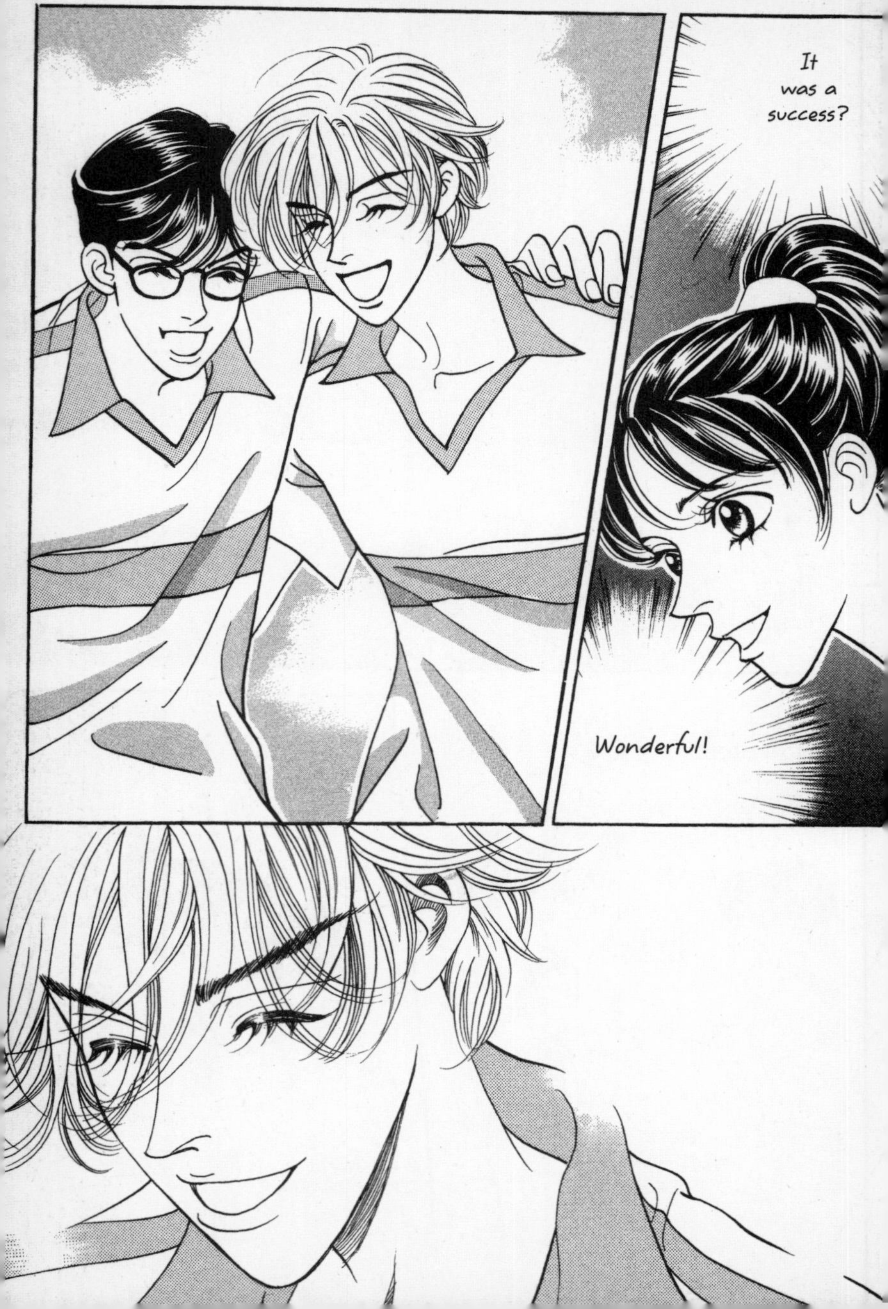
It was a success?
Wonderful!

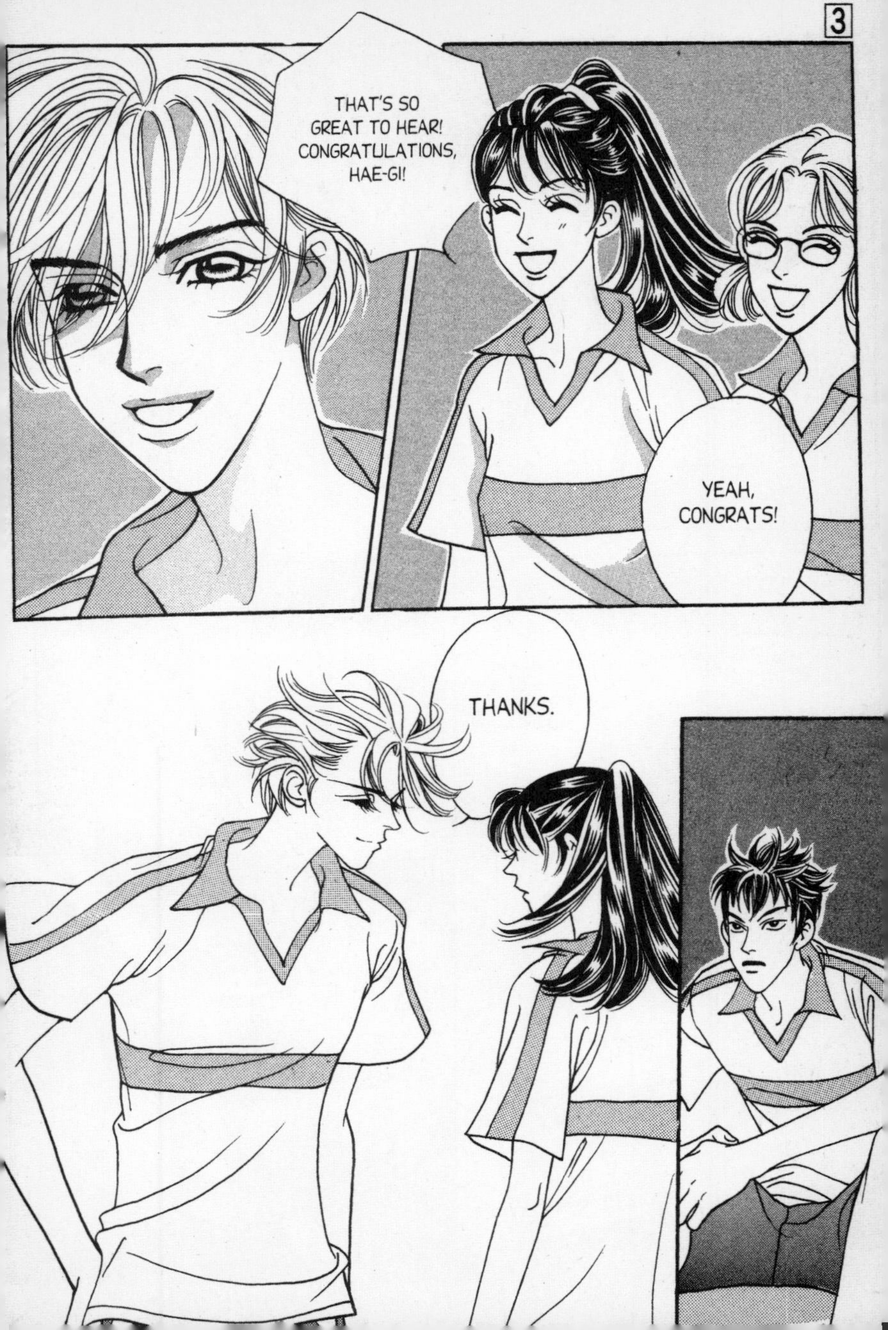
THAT'S SO GREAT TO HEAR! CONGRATULATIONS, HAE-GI!
YEAH, CONGRATS!
THANKS.

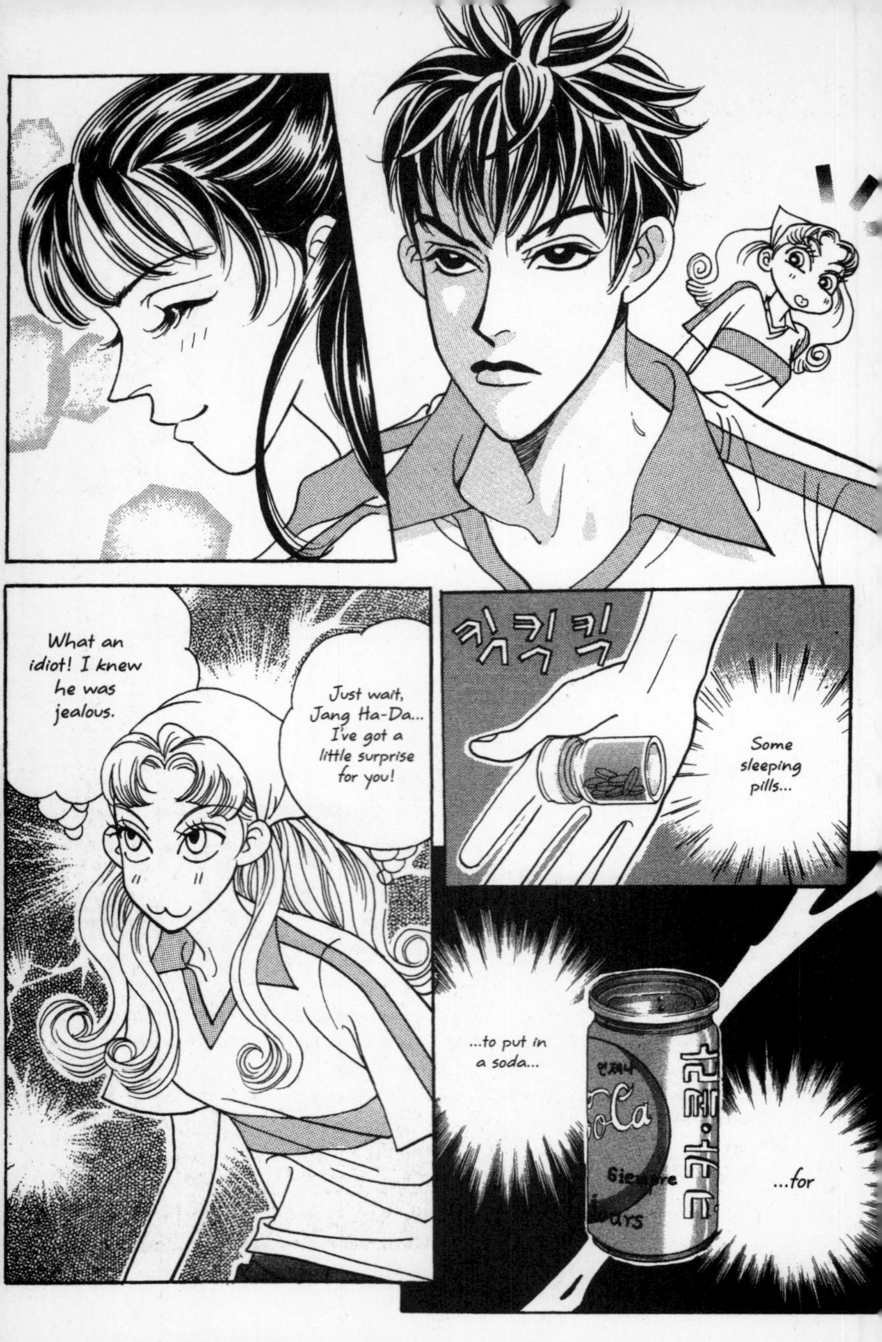
What an idiot! I knew he was jealous.
Just wait, Jang Ha-Da... I've got a little surprise for you!
킥킥킥
Some sleeping pills...
...to put in a soda...
...for

# 스노우 드롭

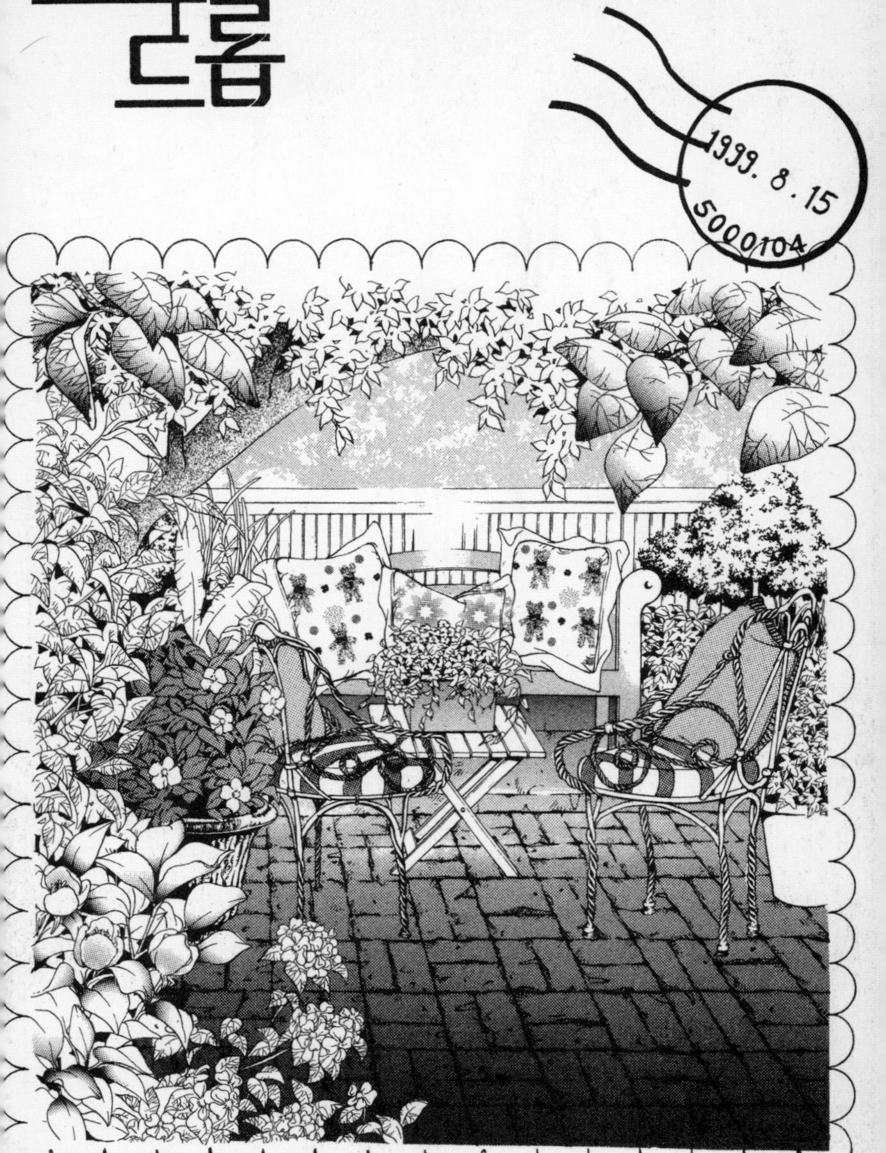
1999. 8. 15
5000104

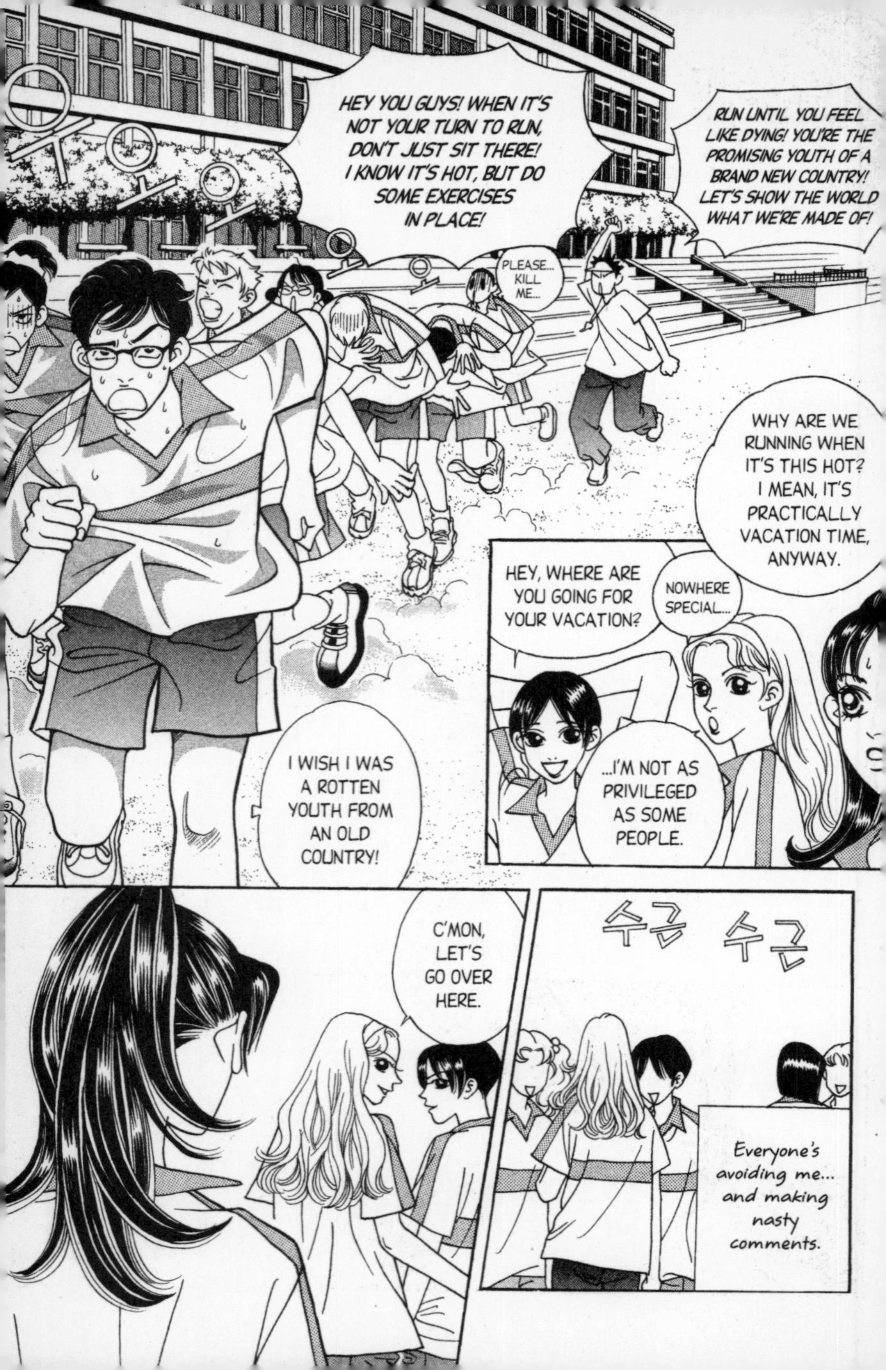
HEY YOU GUYS! WHEN IT'S NOT YOUR TURN TO RUN, DON'T JUST SIT THERE! I KNOW IT'S HOT, BUT DO SOME EXERCISES IN PLACE!
RUN UNTIL YOU FEEL LIKE DYING! YOU'RE THE PROMISING YOUTH OF A BRAND NEW COUNTRY! LET'S SHOW THE WORLD WHAT WE'RE MADE OF!
PLEASE... KILL ME...
WHY ARE WE RUNNING WHEN IT'S THIS HOT? I MEAN, IT'S PRACTICALLY VACATION TIME, ANYWAY.
I WISH I WAS A ROTTEN YOUTH FROM AN OLD COUNTRY!
HEY, WHERE ARE YOU GOING FOR YOUR VACATION?
NOWHERE SPECIAL...
...I'M NOT AS PRIVILEGED AS SOME PEOPLE.
C'MON, LET'S GO OVER HERE.
수군 수군
Everyone's avoiding me... and making nasty comments.

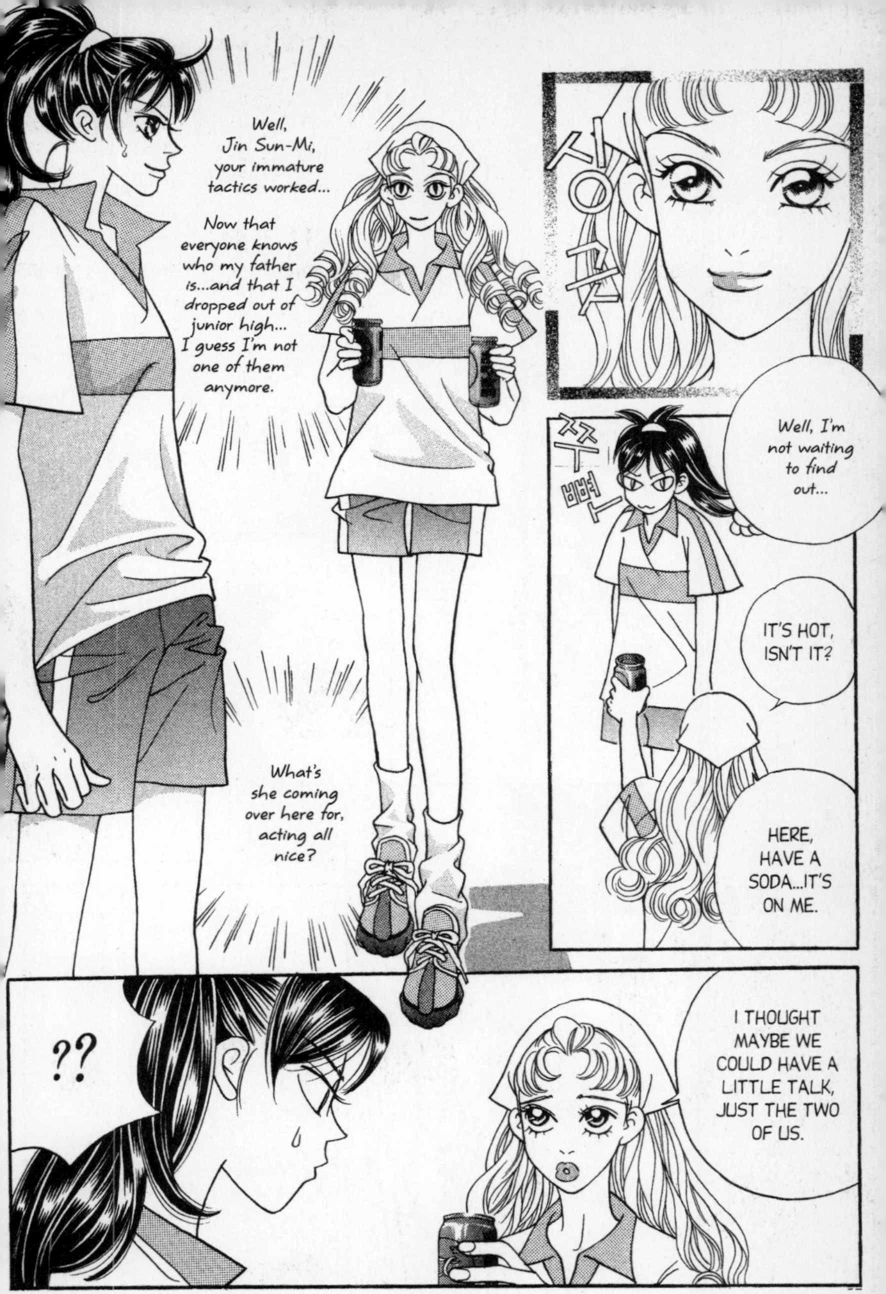
Well, Jin Sun-Mi, your immature tactics worked...
Now that everyone knows who my father is...and that I dropped out of junior high... I guess I'm not one of them anymore.
What's she coming over here for, acting all nice?
Well, I'm not waiting to find out...
IT'S HOT, ISN'T IT?
HERE, HAVE A SODA...IT'S ON ME.
??
I THOUGHT MAYBE WE COULD HAVE A LITTLE TALK, JUST THE TWO OF US.

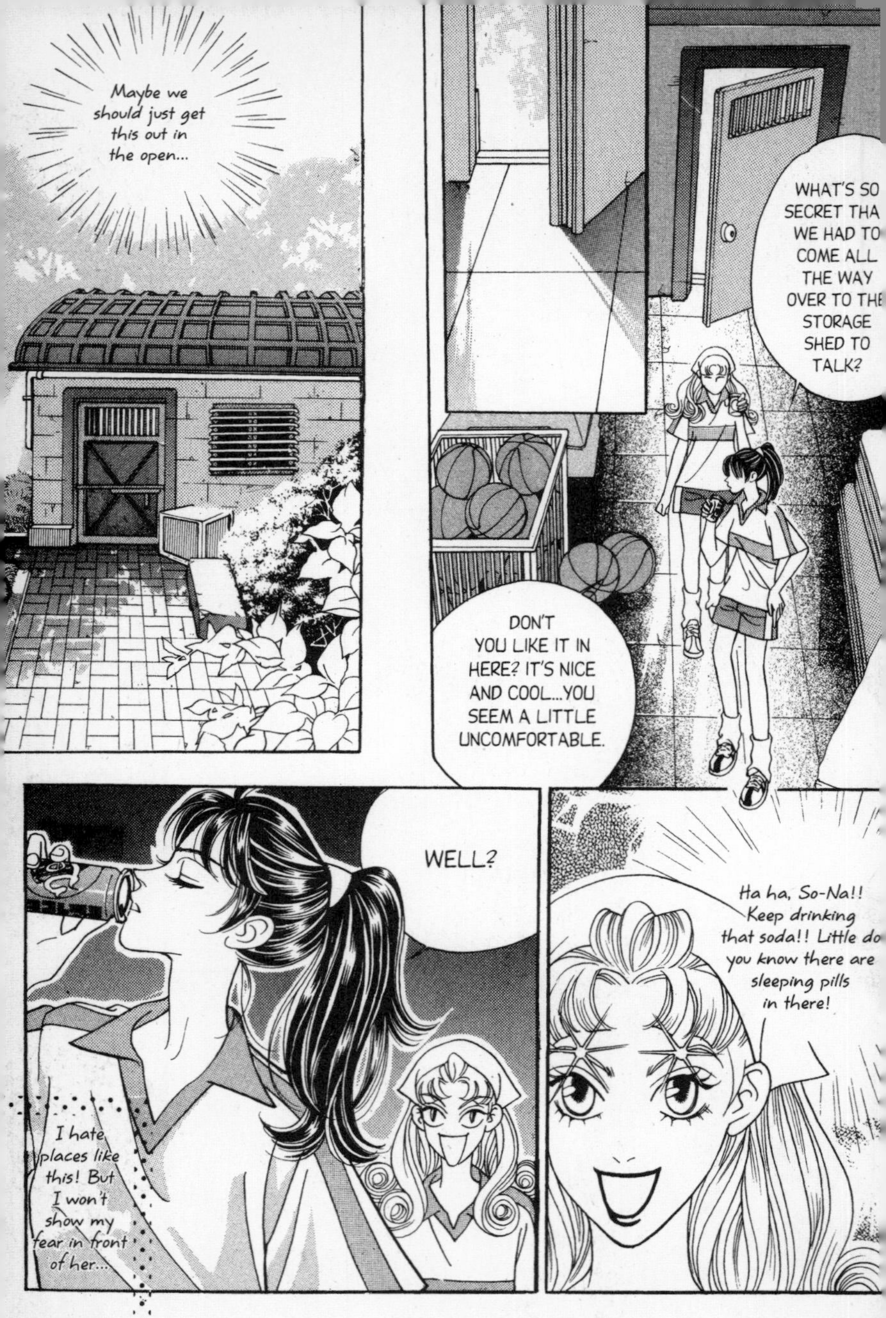
Maybe we should just get this out in the open...
WHAT'S SO SECRET THA WE HAD TO COME ALL THE WAY OVER TO THE STORAGE SHED TO TALK?
DON'T YOU LIKE IT IN HERE? IT'S NICE AND COOL...YOU SEEM A LITTLE UNCOMFORTABLE.
WELL?
I hate places like this! But I won't show my fear in front of her...
Ha ha, So-Na!! Keep drinking that soda!! Little do you know there are sleeping pills in there!

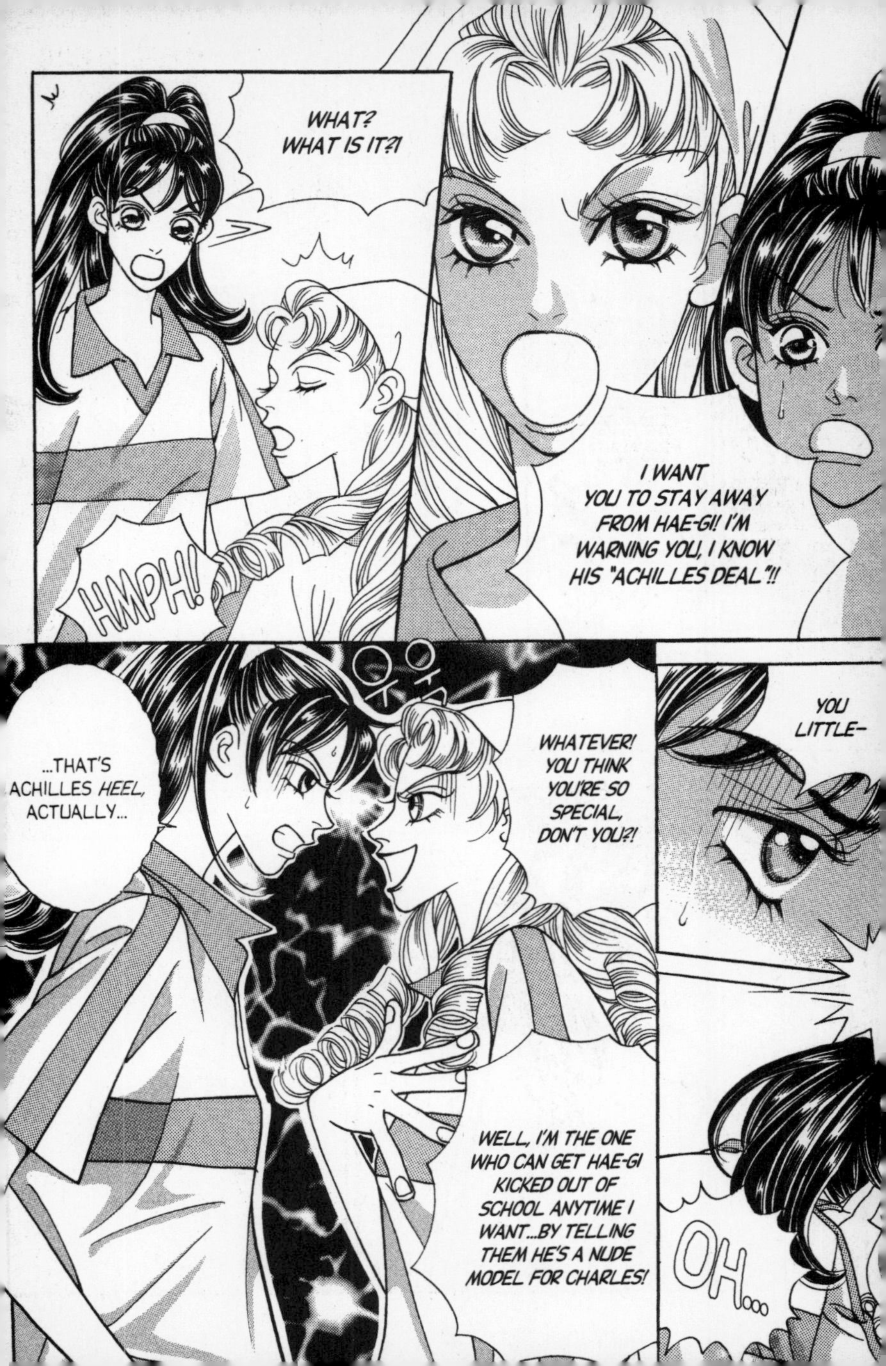
WHAT? WHAT IS IT?!
HMPH!
I WANT YOU TO STAY AWAY FROM HAE-GI! I'M WARNING YOU, I KNOW HIS "ACHILLES DEAL"!!
...THAT'S ACHILLES *HEEL*, ACTUALLY...
WHATEVER! YOU THINK YOU'RE SO SPECIAL, DON'T YOU?!
WELL, I'M THE ONE WHO CAN GET HAE-GI KICKED OUT OF SCHOOL ANYTIME I WANT...BY TELLING THEM HE'S A NUDE MODEL FOR CHARLES!
YOU LITTLE—
OH...

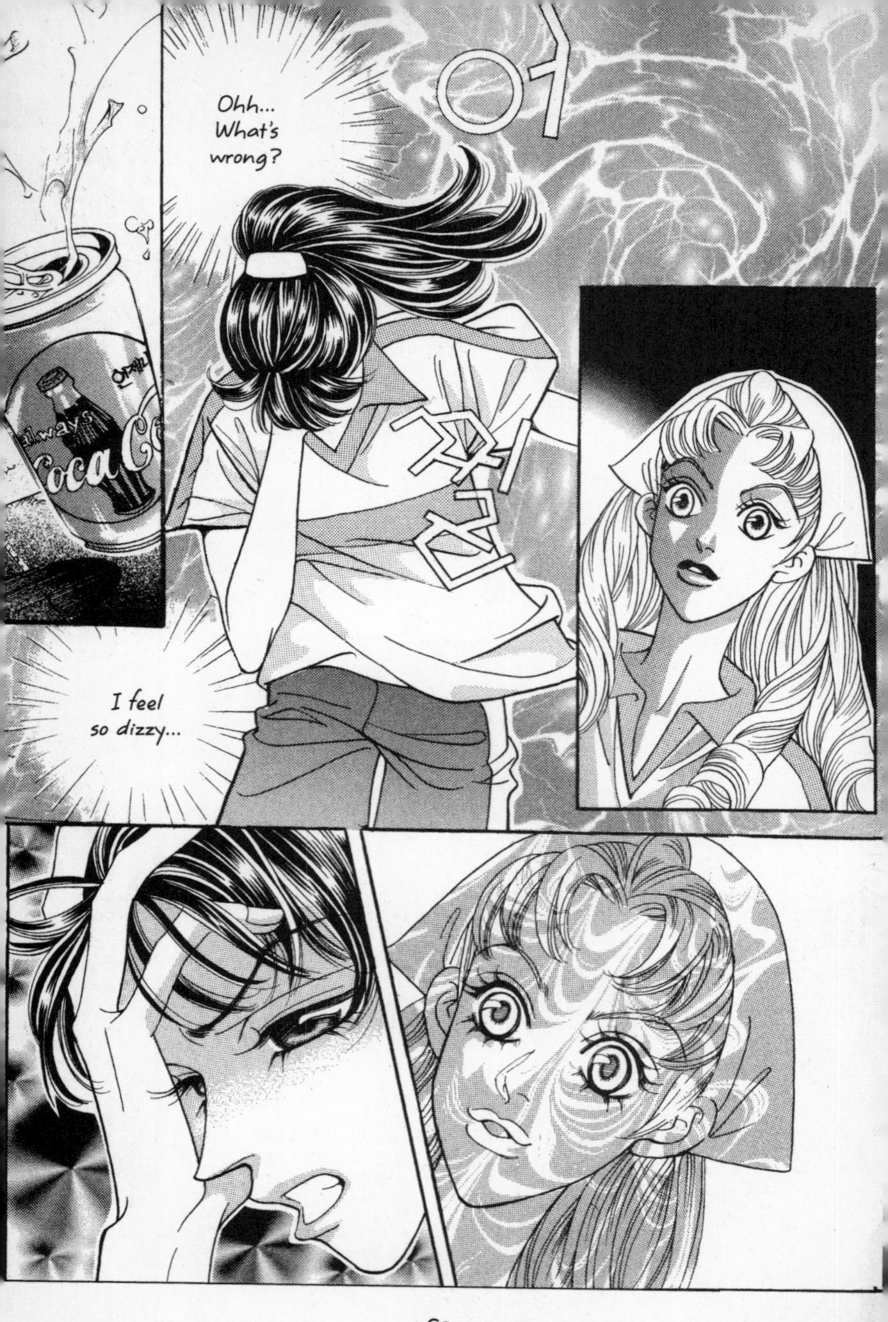
Ohh... What's wrong?
I feel so dizzy...

3

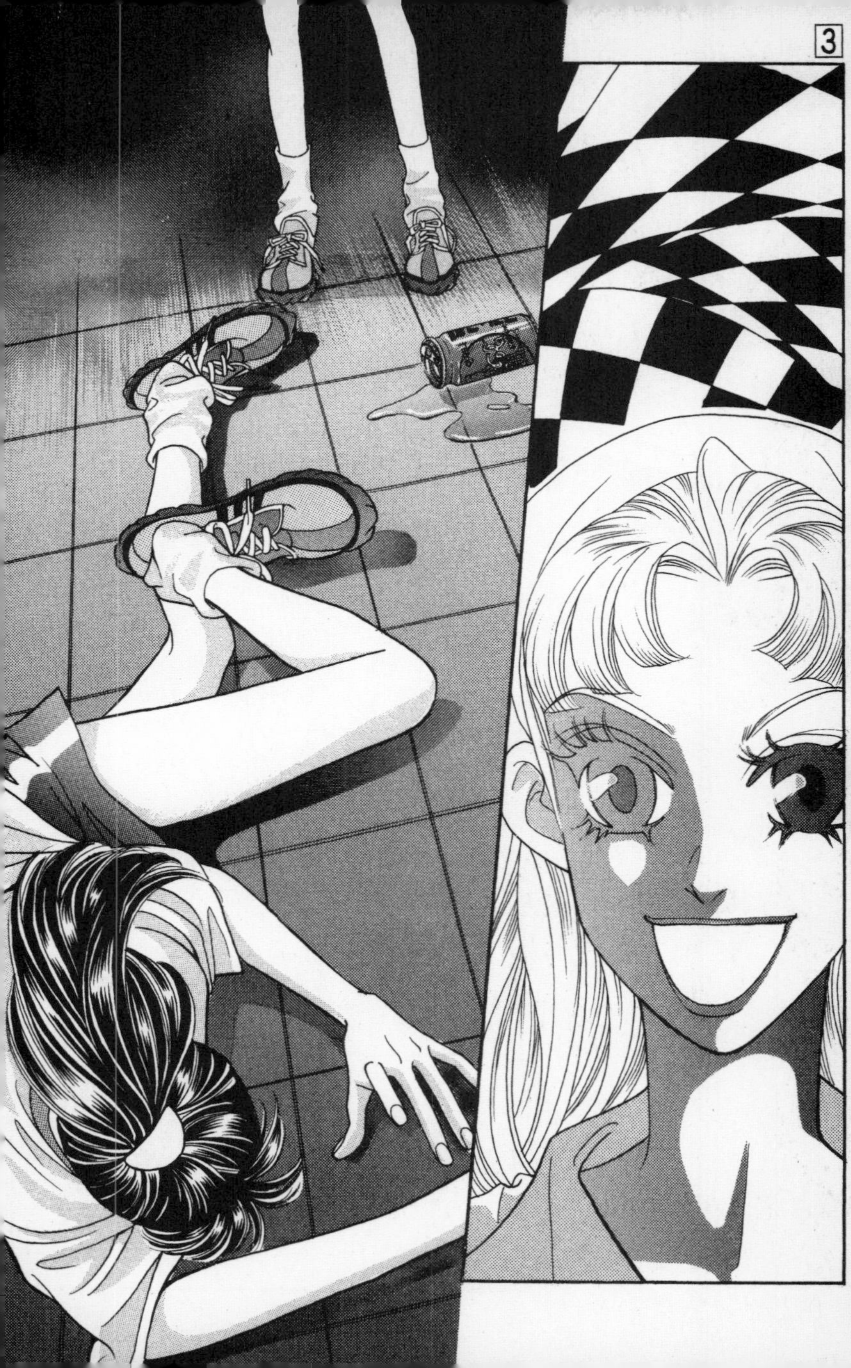

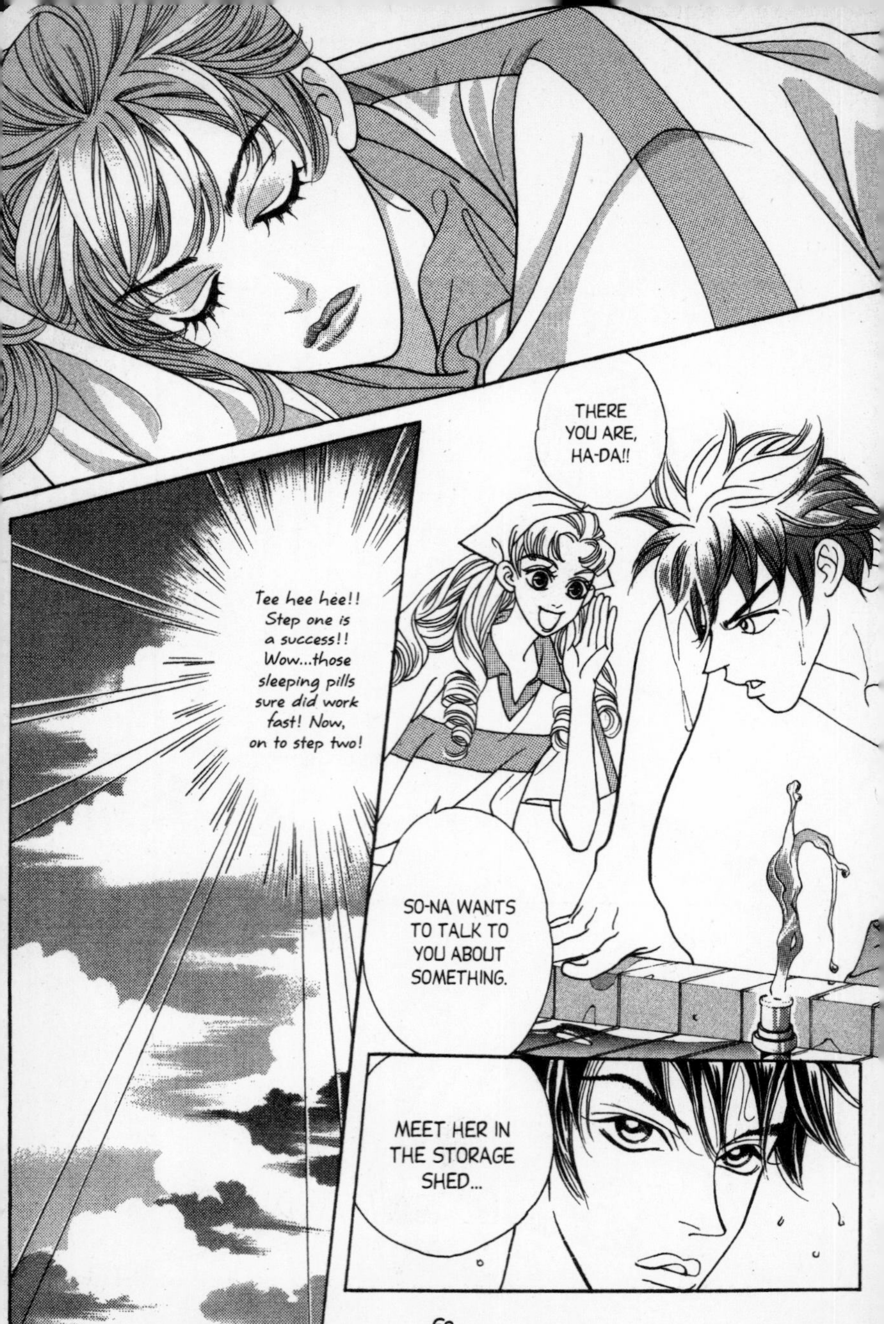
Tee hee hee!! Step one is a success!! Wow...those sleeping pills sure did work fast! Now, on to step two!
THERE YOU ARE, HA-DA!!
SO-NA WANTS TO TALK TO YOU ABOUT SOMETHING.
MEET HER IN THE STORAGE SHED...

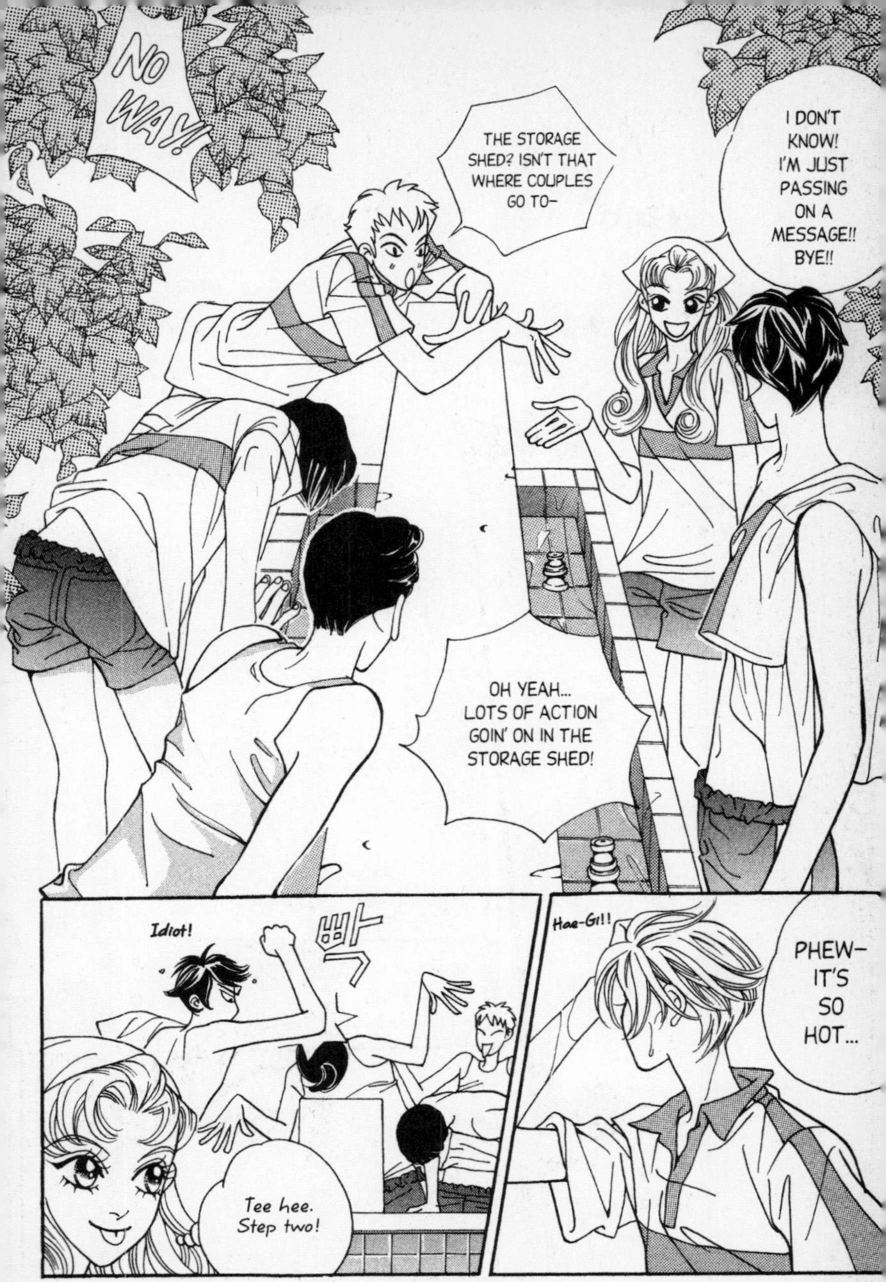
NO WAY!
THE STORAGE SHED? ISN'T THAT WHERE COUPLES GO TO–
I DON'T KNOW! I'M JUST PASSING ON A MESSAGE!! BYE!!
OH YEAH... LOTS OF ACTION GOIN' ON IN THE STORAGE SHED!
Idiot!
빡
Tee hee. Step two!
Hae-Gi!!
PHEW– IT'S SO HOT...

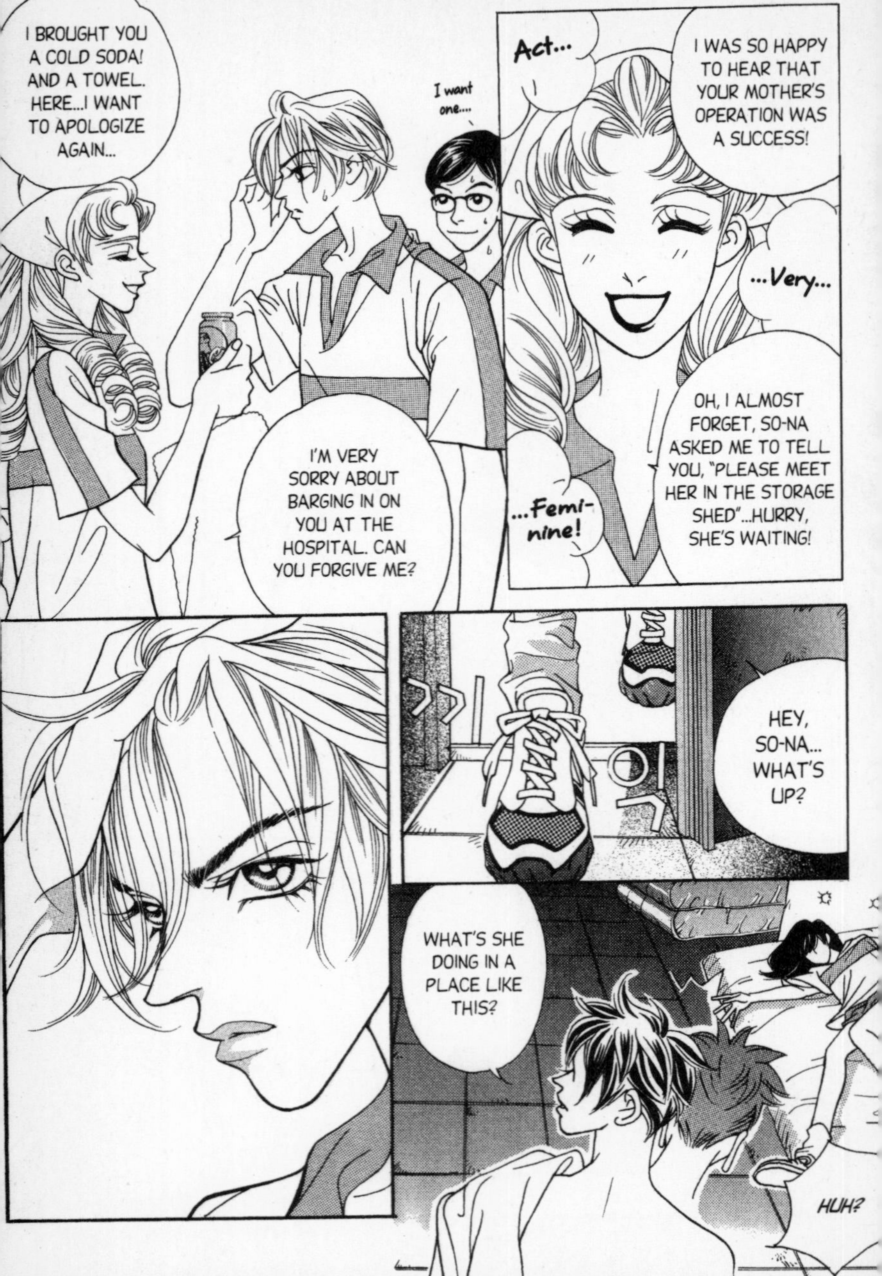
I BROUGHT YOU A COLD SODA! AND A TOWEL. HERE...I WANT TO APOLOGIZE AGAIN...
I'M VERY SORRY ABOUT BARGING IN ON YOU AT THE HOSPITAL. CAN YOU FORGIVE ME?
I want one....
I WAS SO HAPPY TO HEAR THAT YOUR MOTHER'S OPERATION WAS A SUCCESS!
Act...
...Very...
...Femi-nine!
OH, I ALMOST FORGET, SO-NA ASKED ME TO TELL YOU, "PLEASE MEET HER IN THE STORAGE SHED"...HURRY, SHE'S WAITING!
HEY, SO-NA... WHAT'S UP?
WHAT'S SHE DOING IN A PLACE LIKE THIS?
HUH?

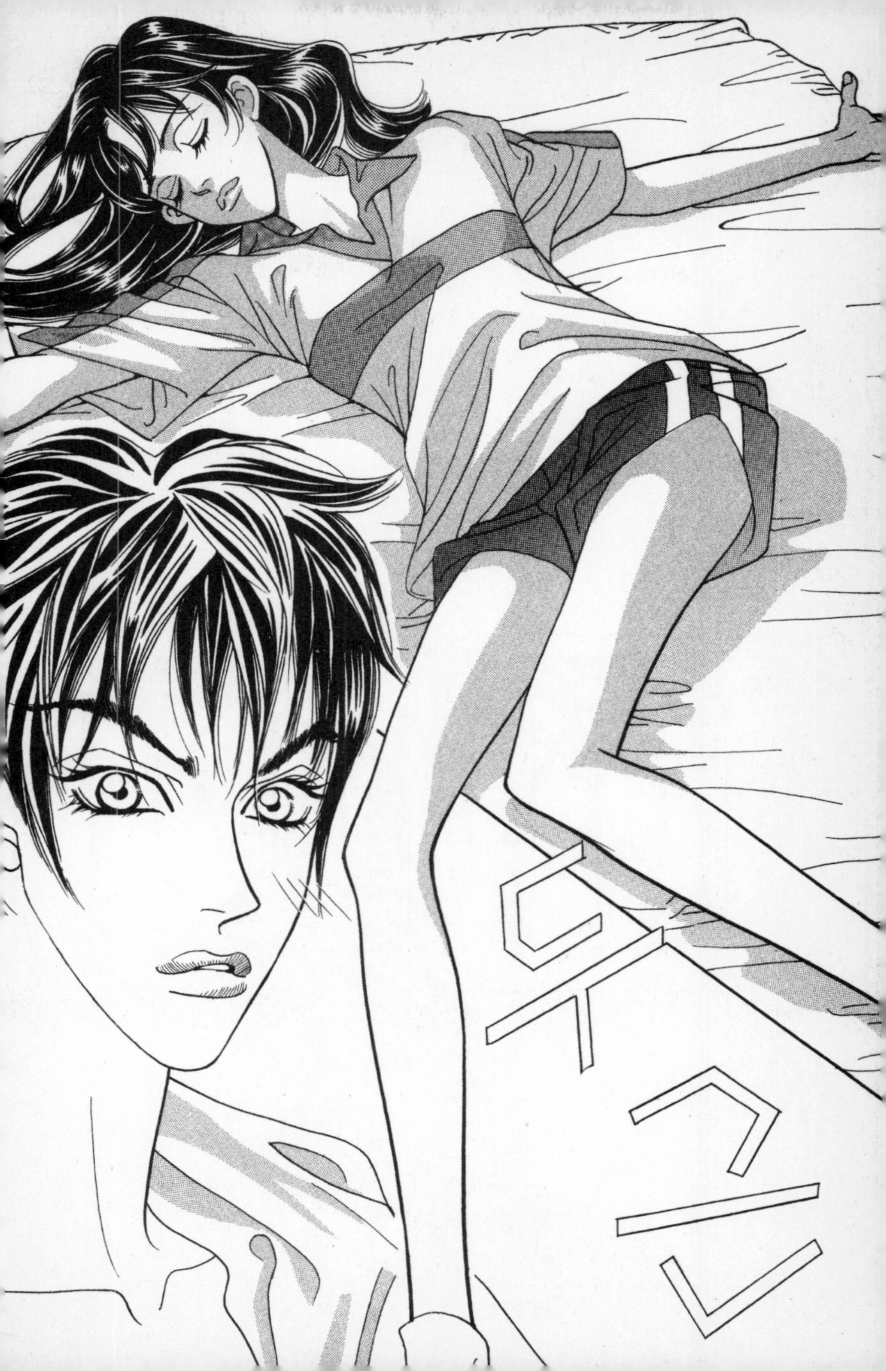

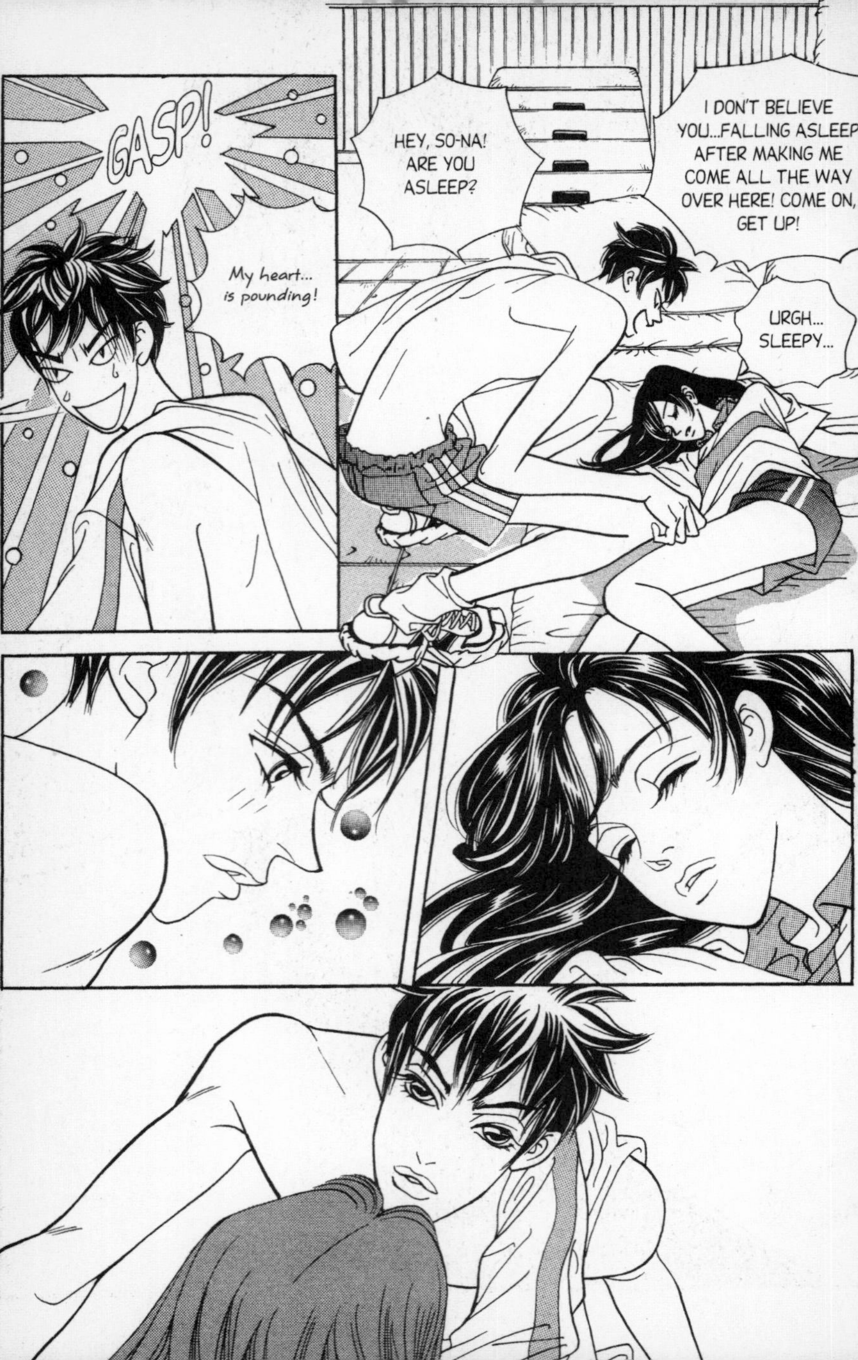
GASP!
My heart... is pounding!
HEY, SO-NA! ARE YOU ASLEEP?
I DON'T BELIEVE YOU...FALLING ASLEEP AFTER MAKING ME COME ALL THE WAY OVER HERE! COME ON, GET UP!
URGH... SLEEPY...

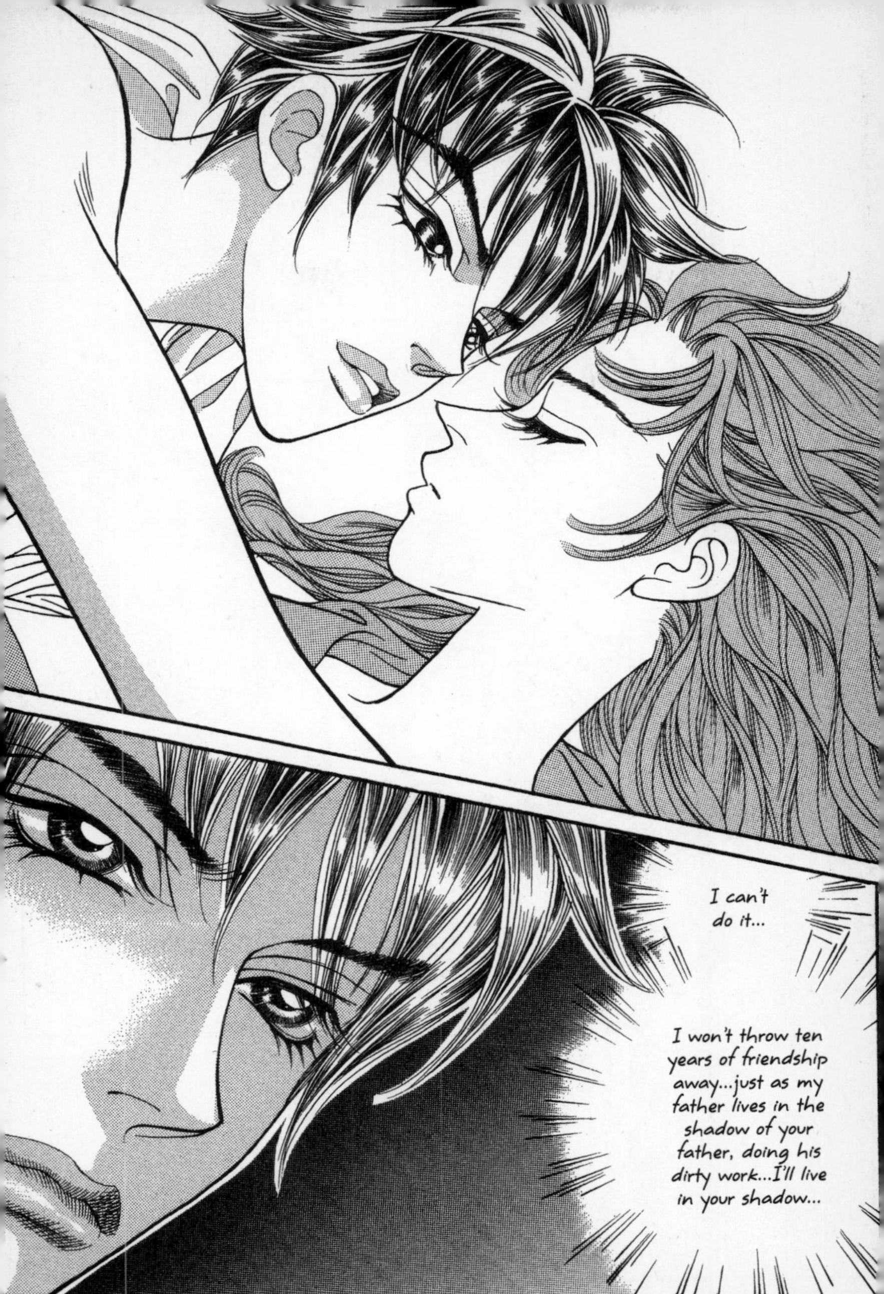
I can't do it...
I won't throw ten years of friendship away...just as my father lives in the shadow of your father, doing his dirty work...I'll live in your shadow...

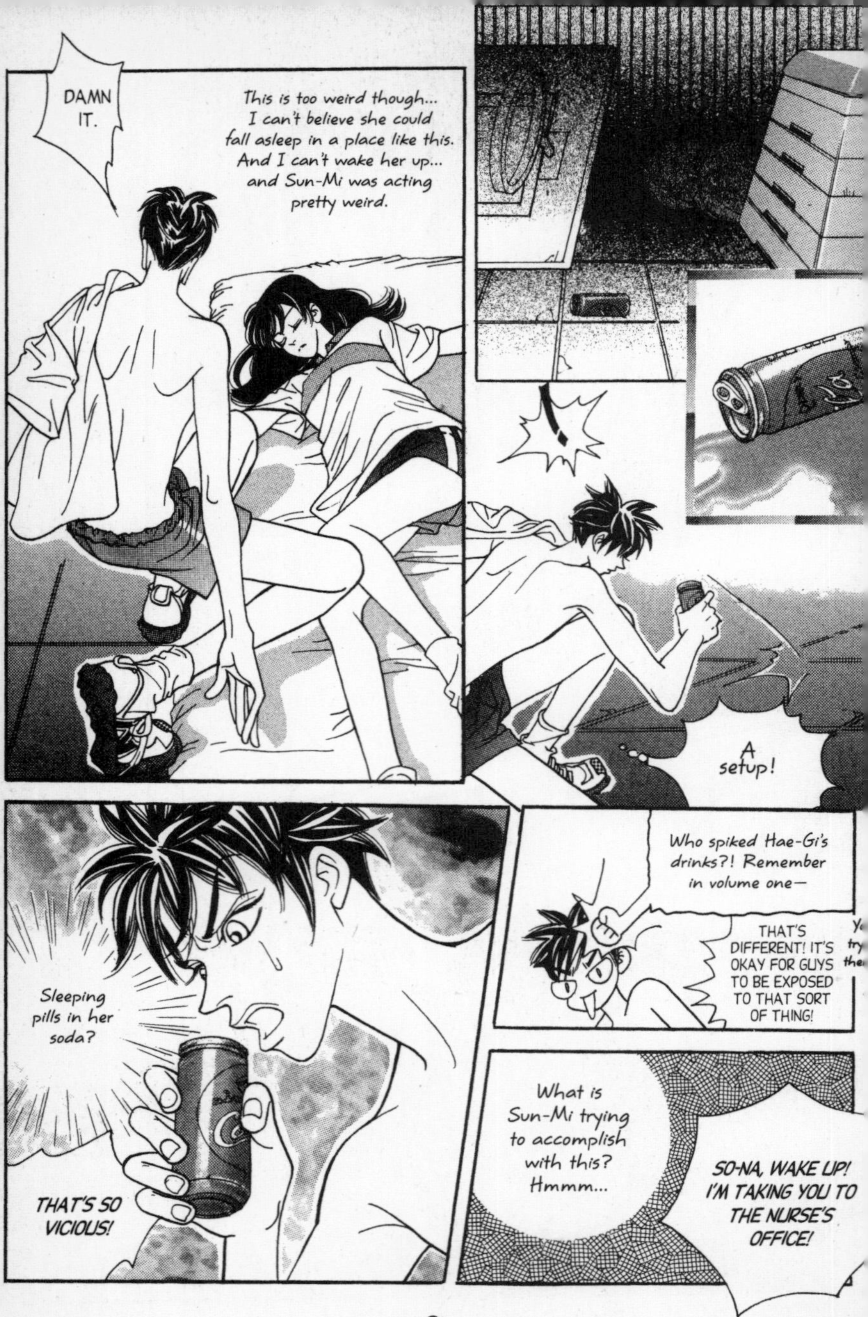
DAMN IT.
This is too weird though... I can't believe she could fall asleep in a place like this. And I can't wake her up... and Sun-Mi was acting pretty weird.
!
A setup!
Sleeping pills in her soda?
THAT'S SO VICIOUS!
Who spiked Hae-Gi's drinks?! Remember in volume one—
THAT'S DIFFERENT! IT'S OKAY FOR GUYS TO BE EXPOSED TO THAT SORT OF THING!
What is Sun-Mi trying to accomplish with this? Hmmm...
SO-NA, WAKE UP! I'M TAKING YOU TO THE NURSE'S OFFICE!

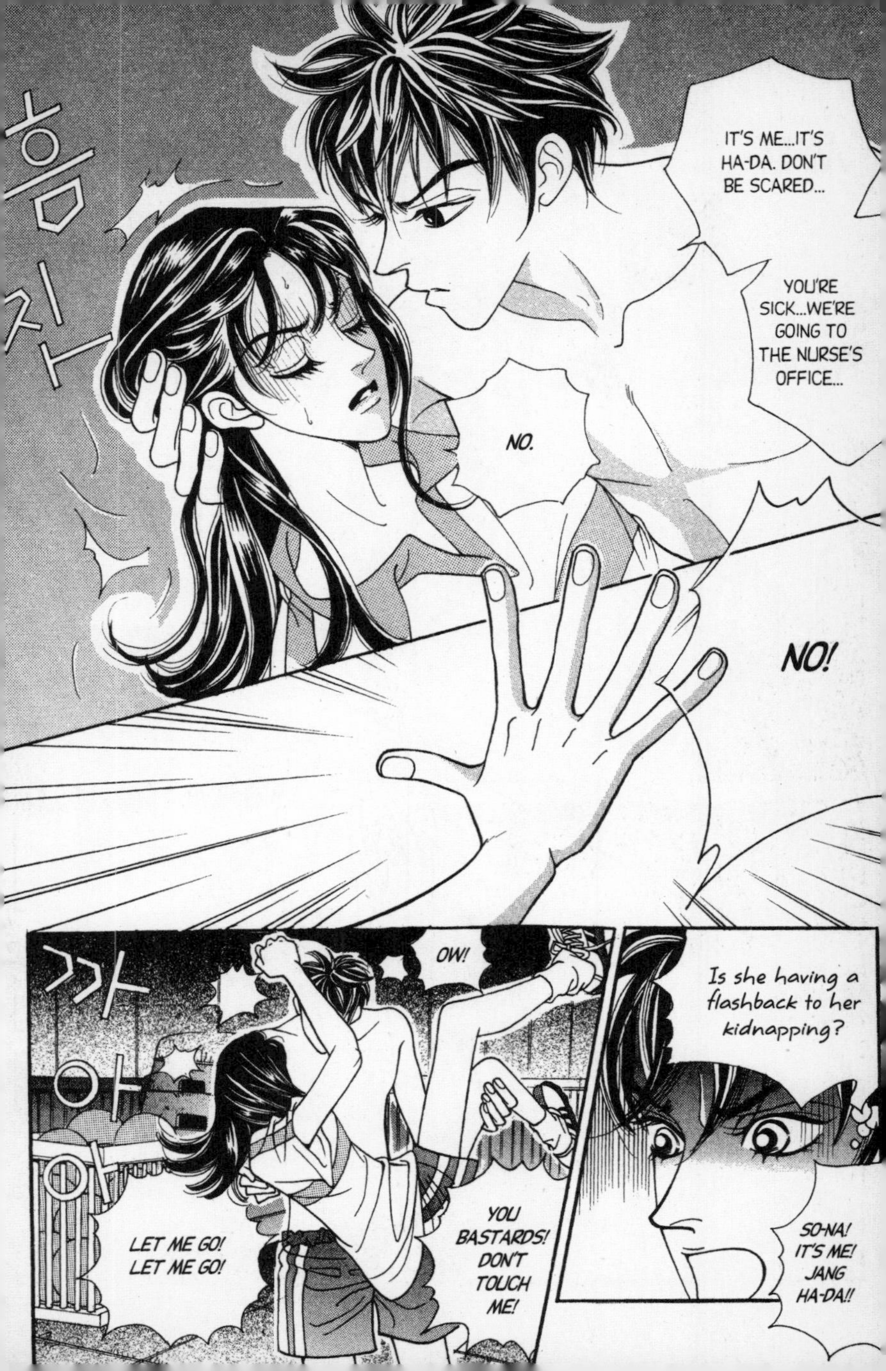
IT'S ME...IT'S HA-DA. DON'T BE SCARED...
YOU'RE SICK...WE'RE GOING TO THE NURSE'S OFFICE...
NO.
NO!
OW!
LET ME GO! LET ME GO!
YOU BASTARDS! DON'T TOUCH ME!
Is she having a flashback to her kidnapping?
SO-NA! IT'S ME! JANG HA-DA!!

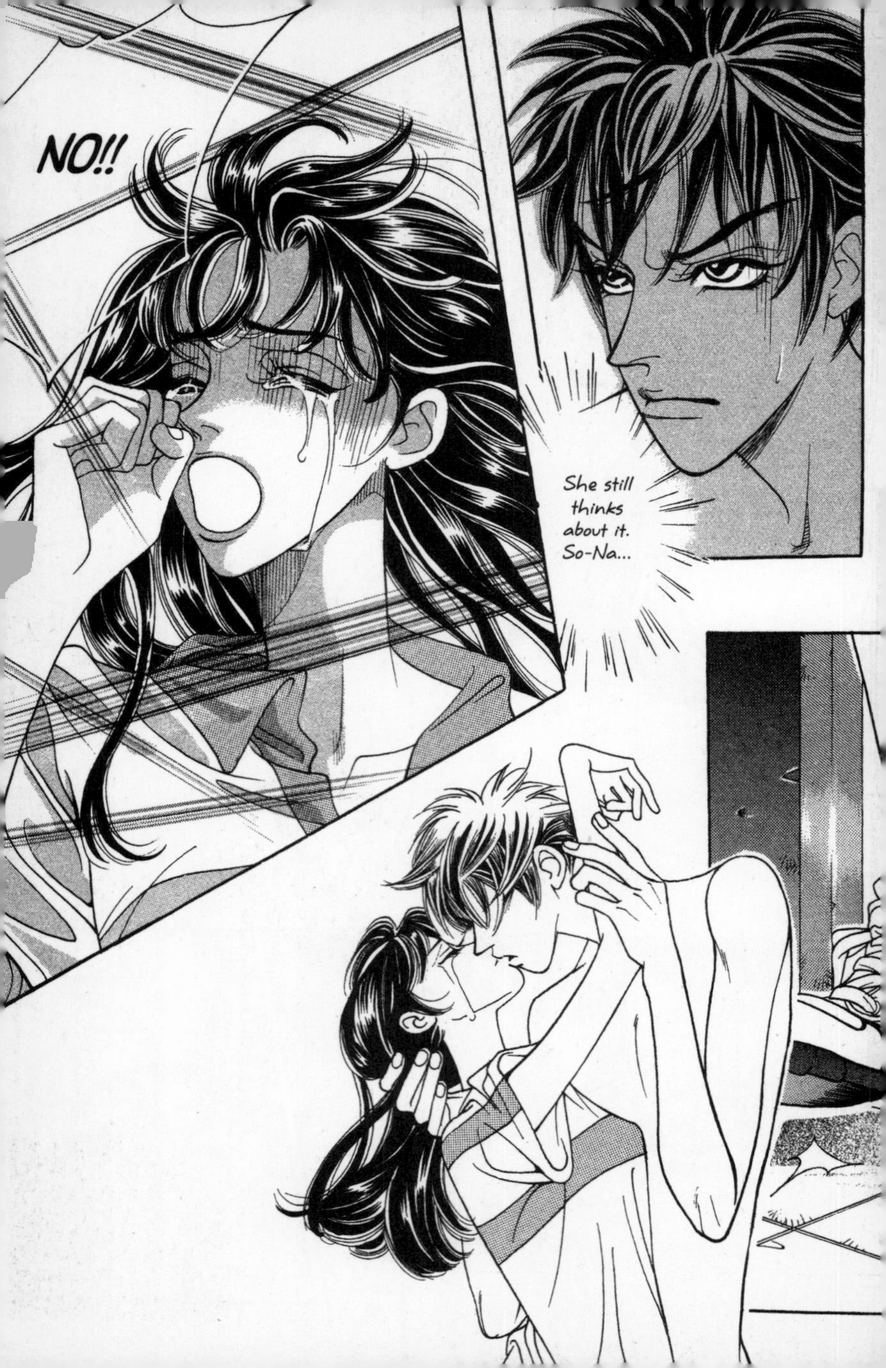
NO!!
She still thinks about it. So-Na...

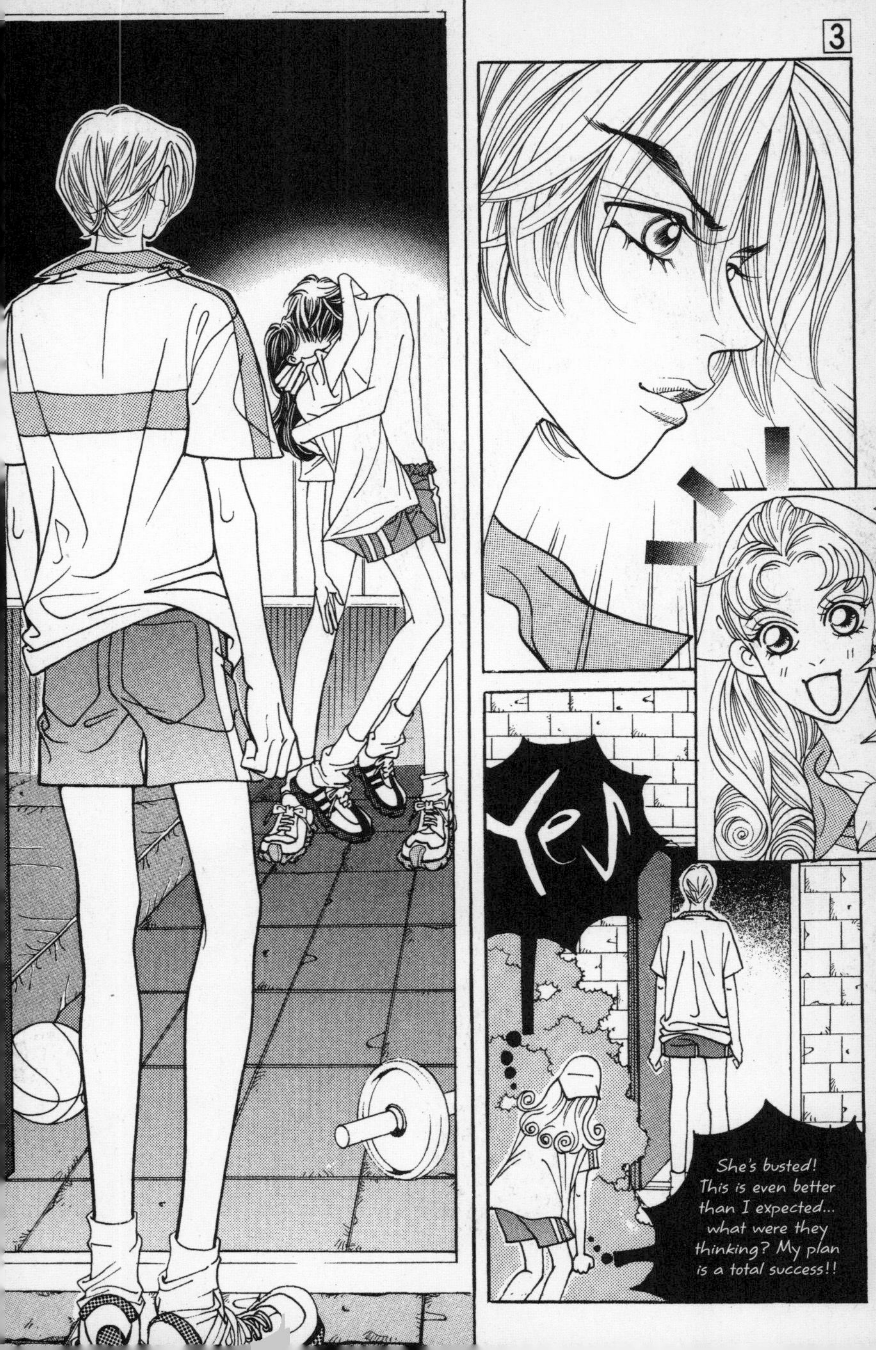
3
Yes
She's busted! This is even better than I expected... what were they thinking? My plan is a total success!!

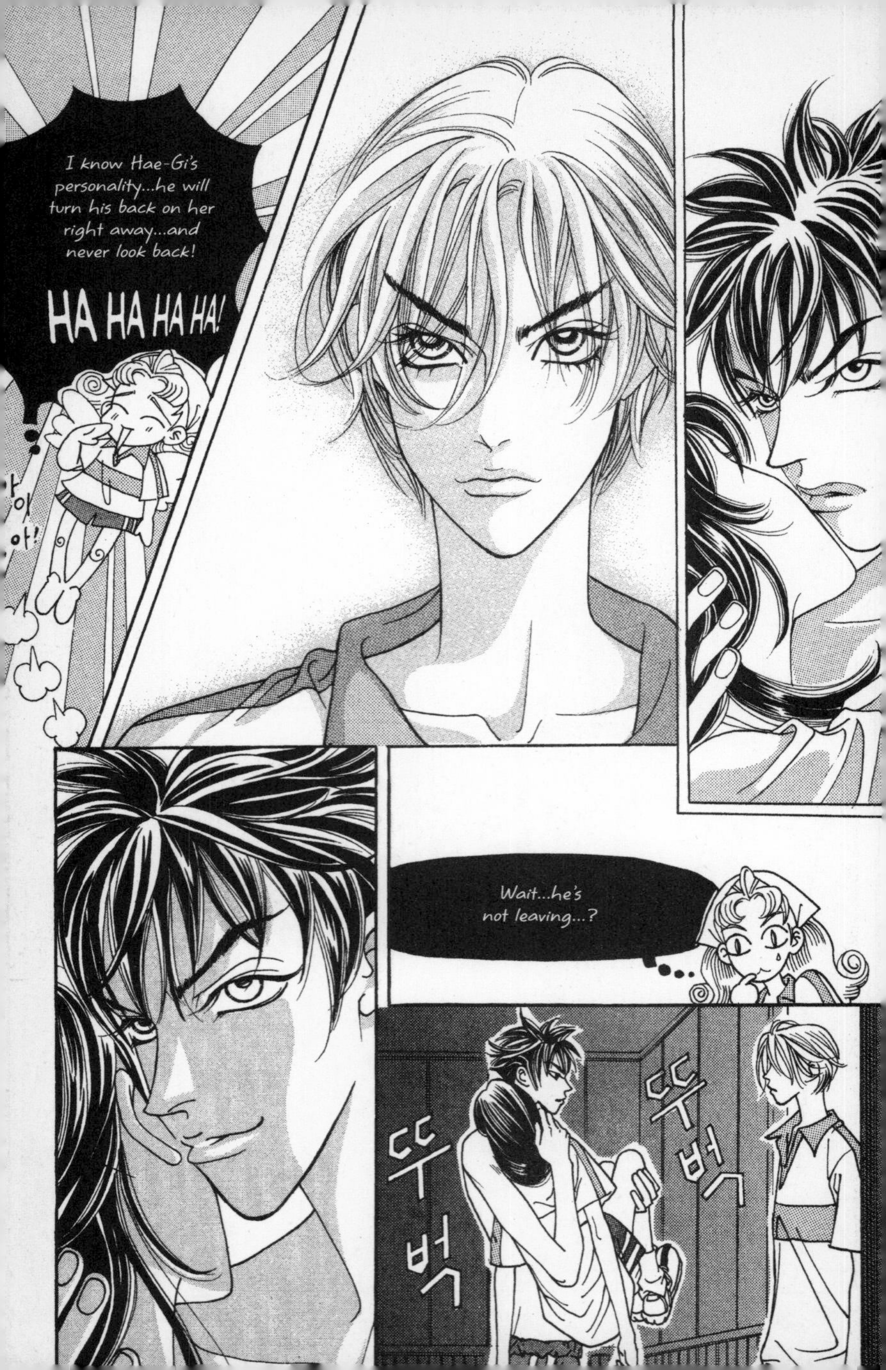
I know Hae-Gi's personality...he will turn his back on her right away...and never look back!
HA HA HA HA!
Wait...he's not leaving...?
뚜벅
뚜벅

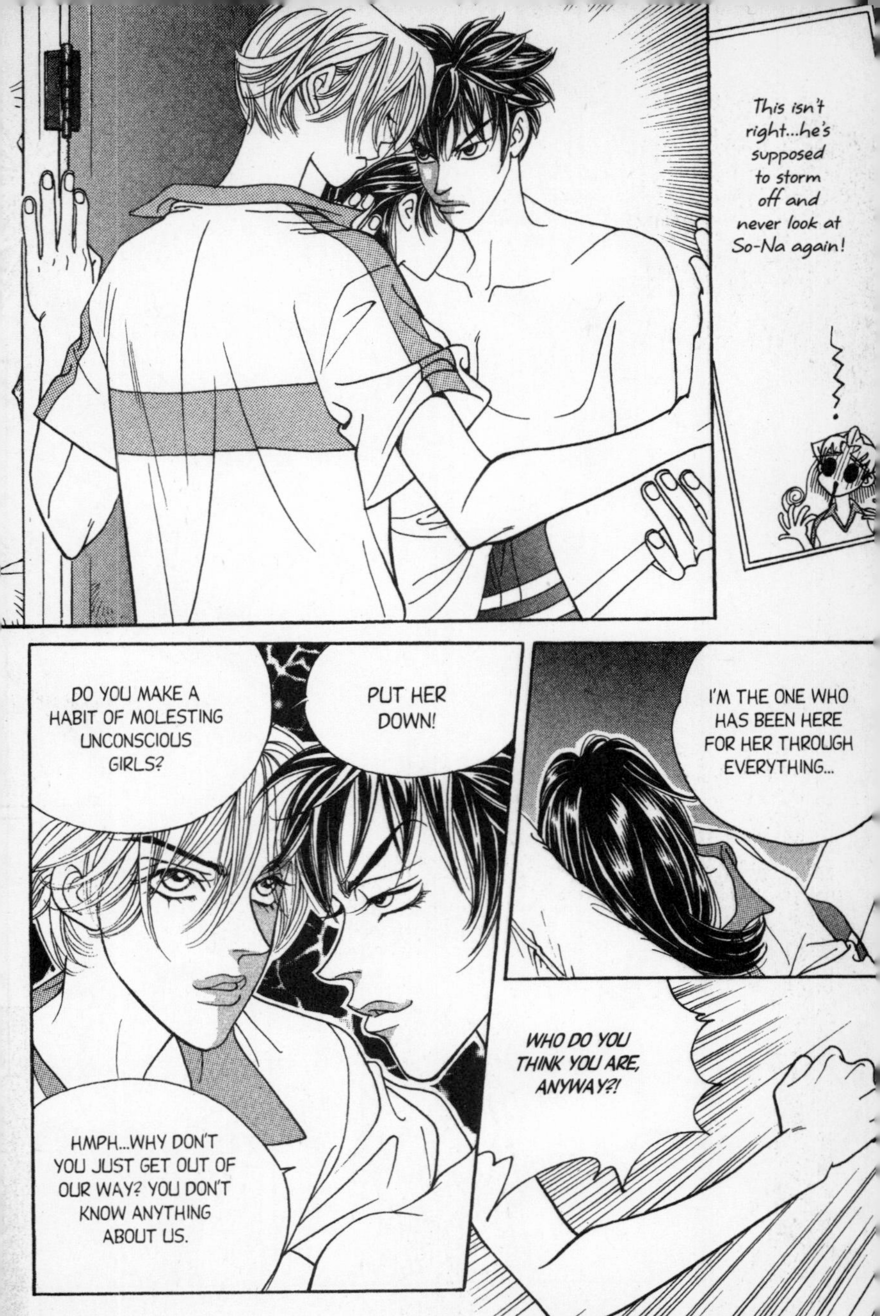
This isn't right...he's supposed to storm off and never look at So-Na again!
DO YOU MAKE A HABIT OF MOLESTING UNCONSCIOUS GIRLS?
PUT HER DOWN!
HMPH...WHY DON'T YOU JUST GET OUT OF OUR WAY? YOU DON'T KNOW ANYTHING ABOUT US.
I'M THE ONE WHO HAS BEEN HERE FOR HER THROUGH EVERYTHING...
WHO DO YOU THINK YOU ARE, ANYWAY?!

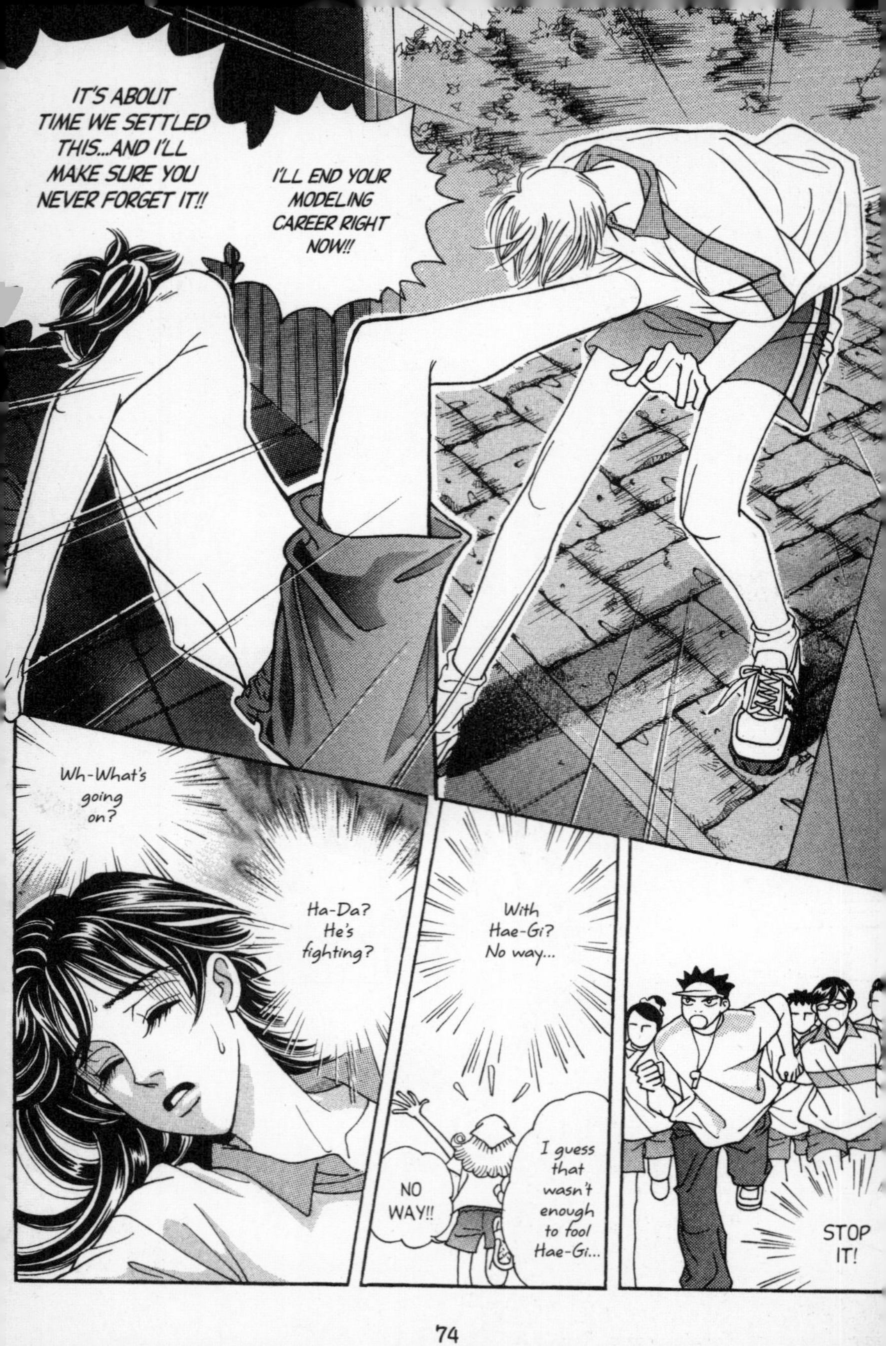
IT'S ABOUT TIME WE SETTLED THIS...AND I'LL MAKE SURE YOU NEVER FORGET IT!!
I'LL END YOUR MODELING CAREER RIGHT NOW!!
Wh-What's going on?
Ha-Da? He's fighting?
With Hae-Gi? No way...
NO WAY!!
I guess that wasn't enough to fool Hae-Gi...
STOP IT!

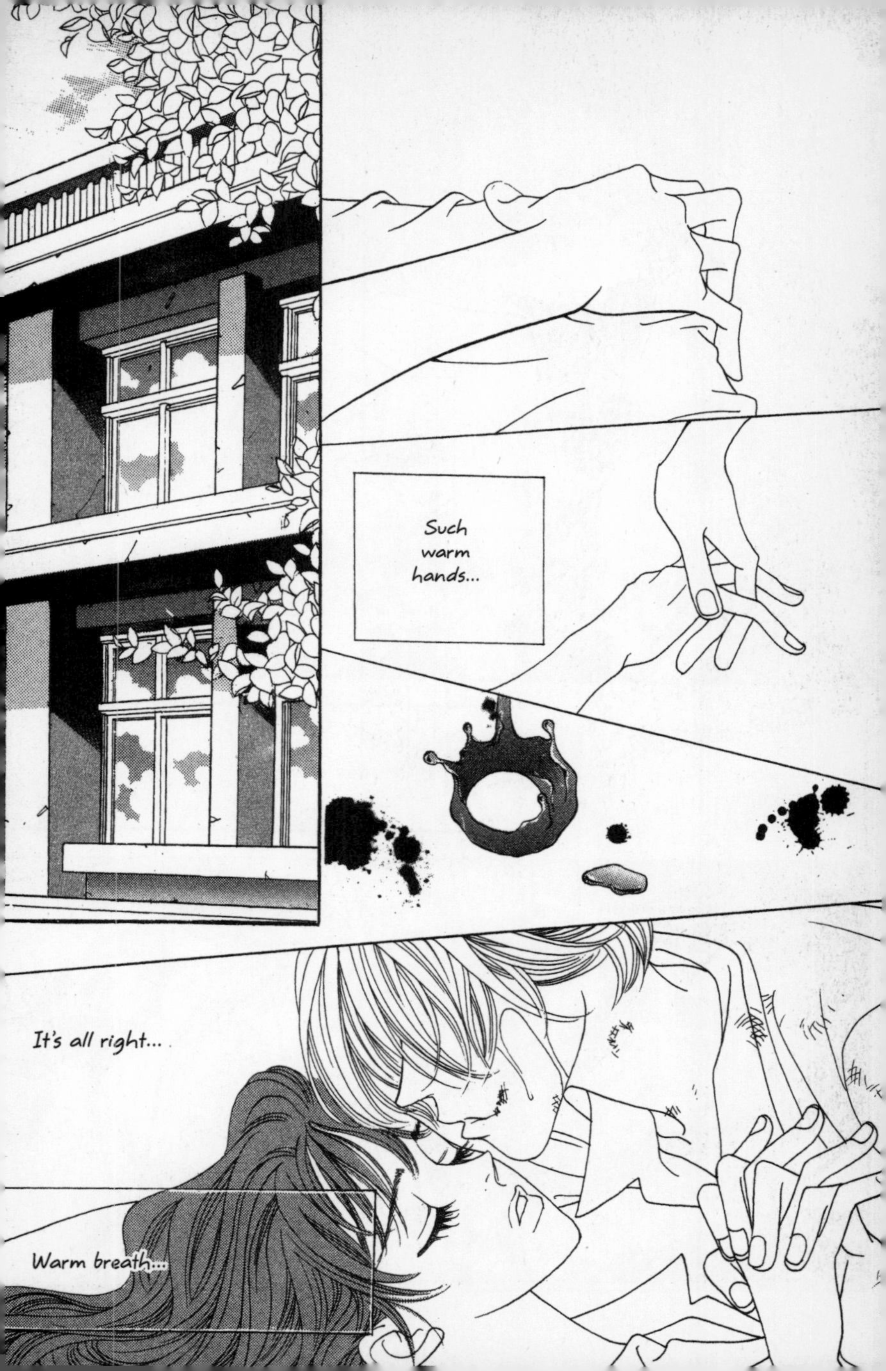
Such warm hands...
It's all right...
Warm breath...

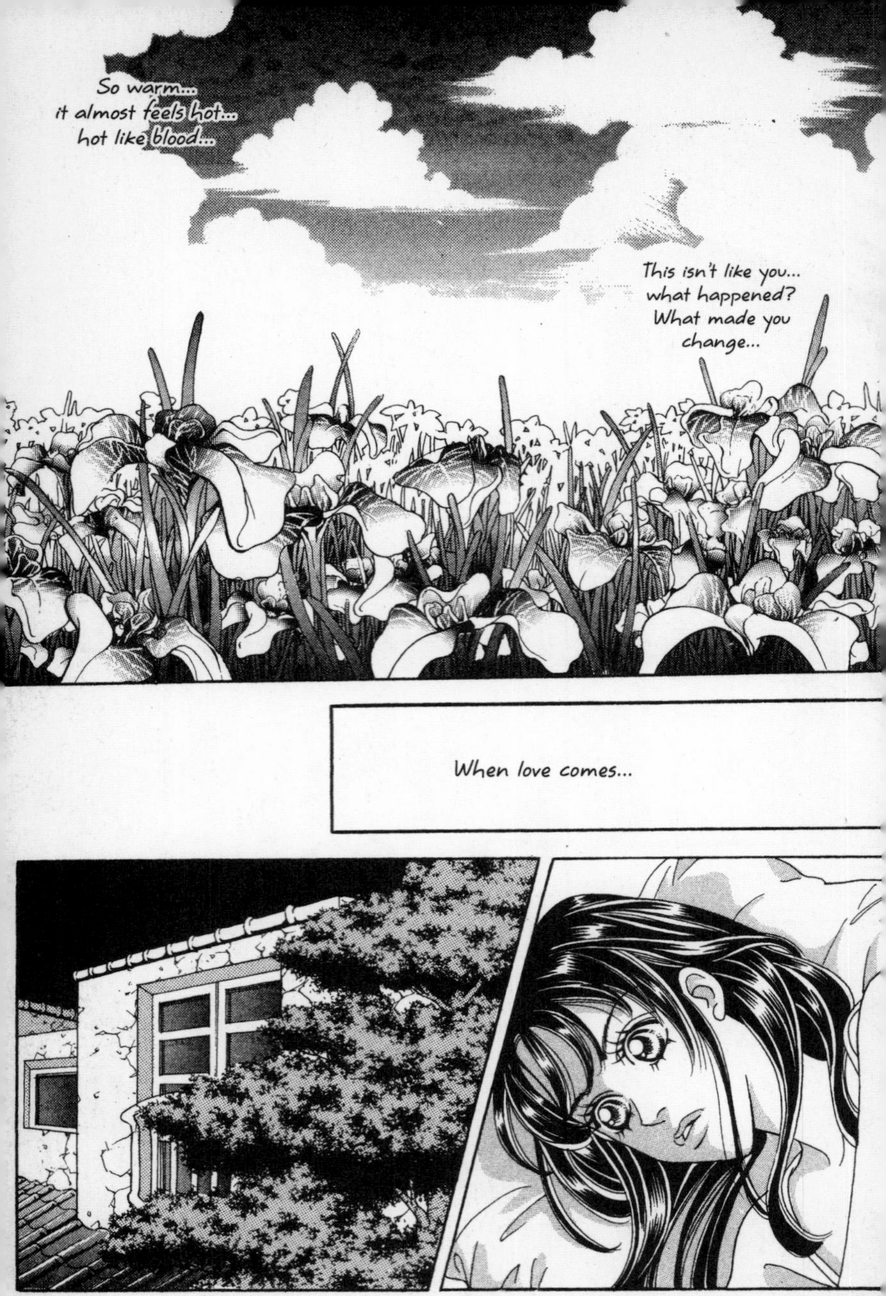
So warm... it almost feels hot... hot like blood...
This isn't like you... what happened? What made you change...
When love comes...

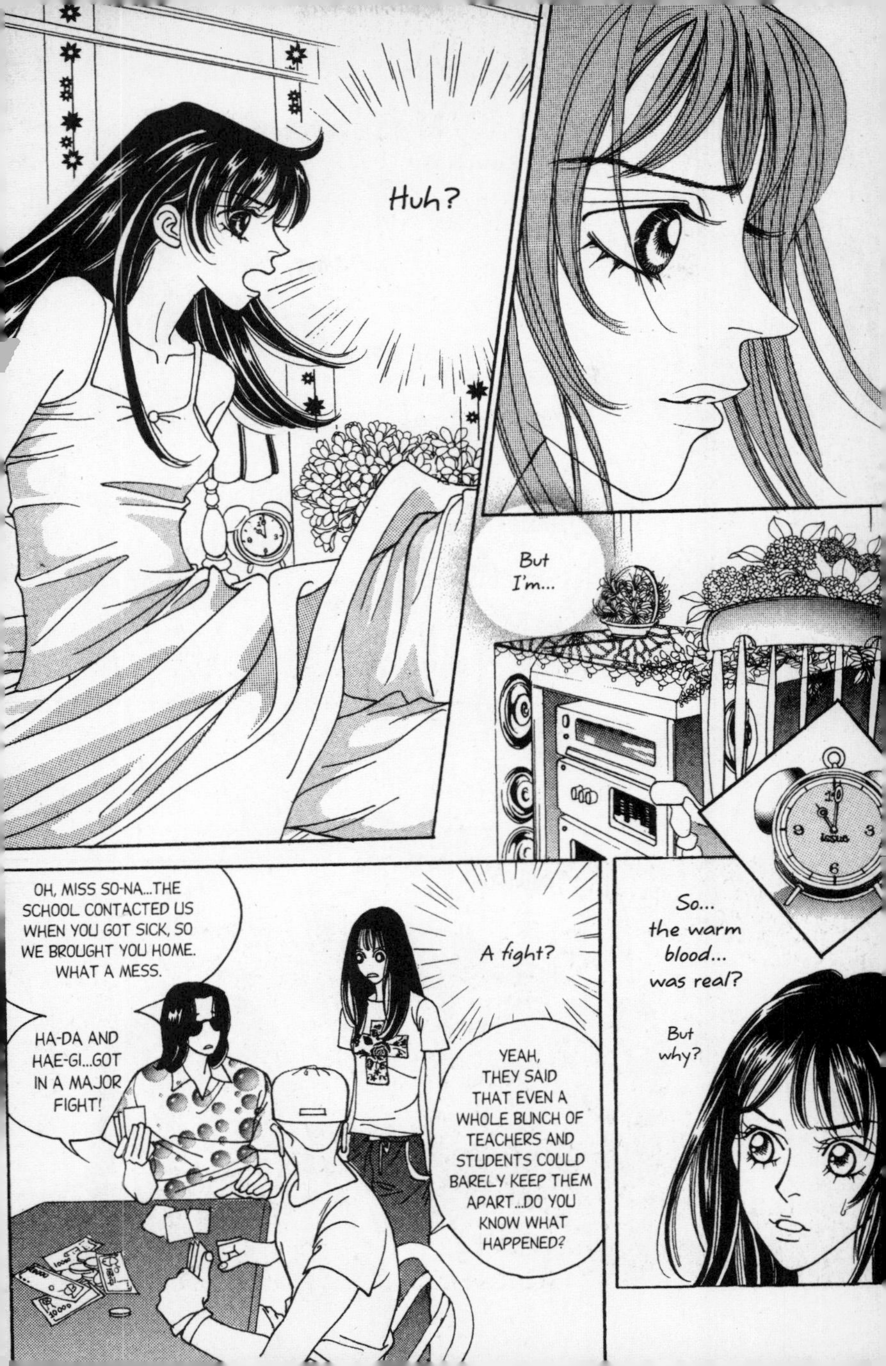
Huh?
But I'm...
OH, MISS SO-NA...THE SCHOOL CONTACTED US WHEN YOU GOT SICK, SO WE BROUGHT YOU HOME. WHAT A MESS.
HA-DA AND HAE-GI...GOT IN A MAJOR FIGHT!
A fight?
YEAH, THEY SAID THAT EVEN A WHOLE BUNCH OF TEACHERS AND STUDENTS COULD BARELY KEEP THEM APART...DO YOU KNOW WHAT HAPPENED?
So... the warm blood... was real?
But why?

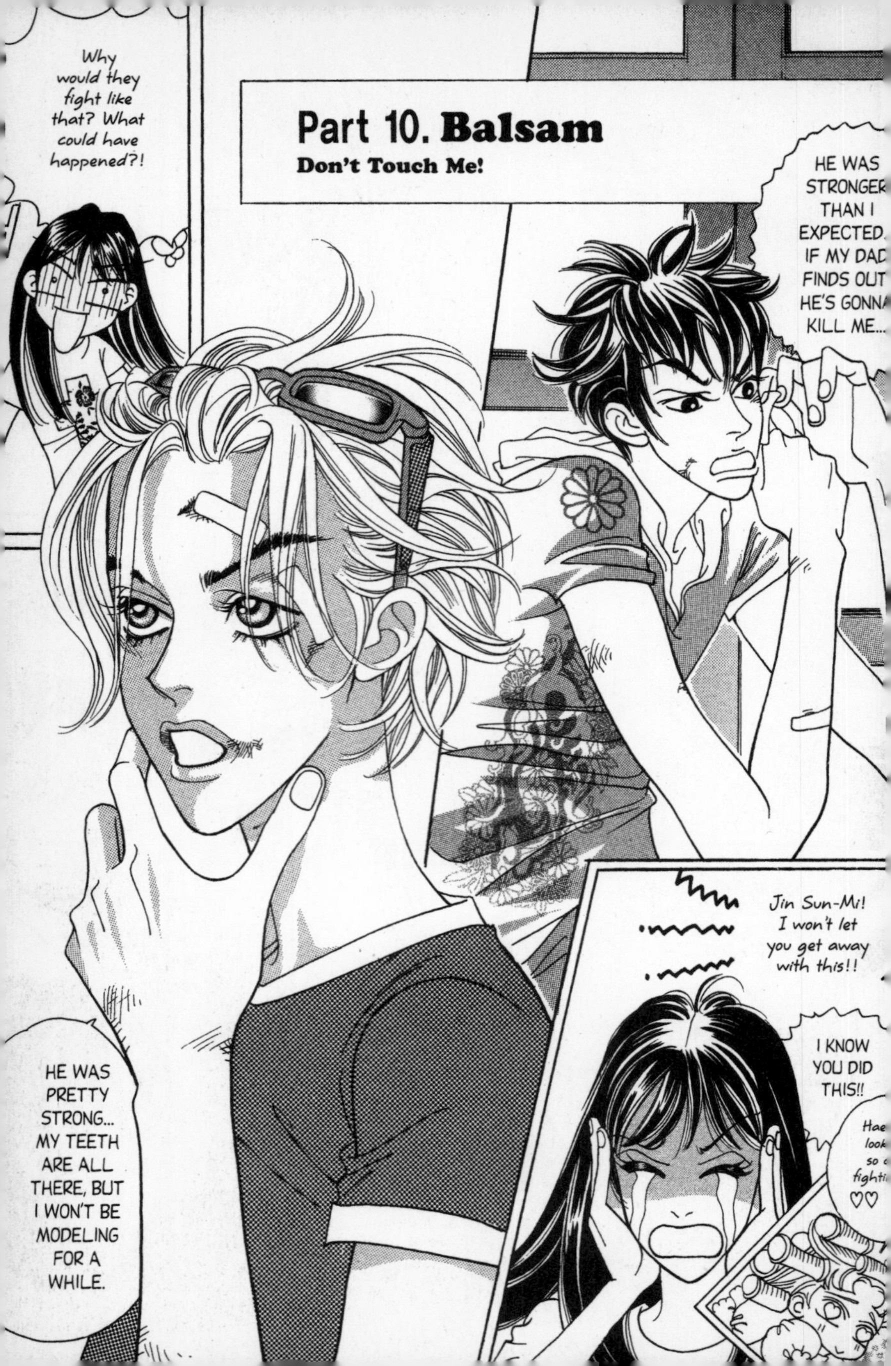
Why would they fight like that? What could have happened?!
Part 10. Balsam
Don't Touch Me!
HE WAS STRONGER THAN I EXPECTED. IF MY DAD FINDS OUT HE'S GONNA KILL ME...
HE WAS PRETTY STRONG... MY TEETH ARE ALL THERE, BUT I WON'T BE MODELING FOR A WHILE.
Jin Sun-Mi! I won't let you get away with this!!
I KNOW YOU DID THIS!!

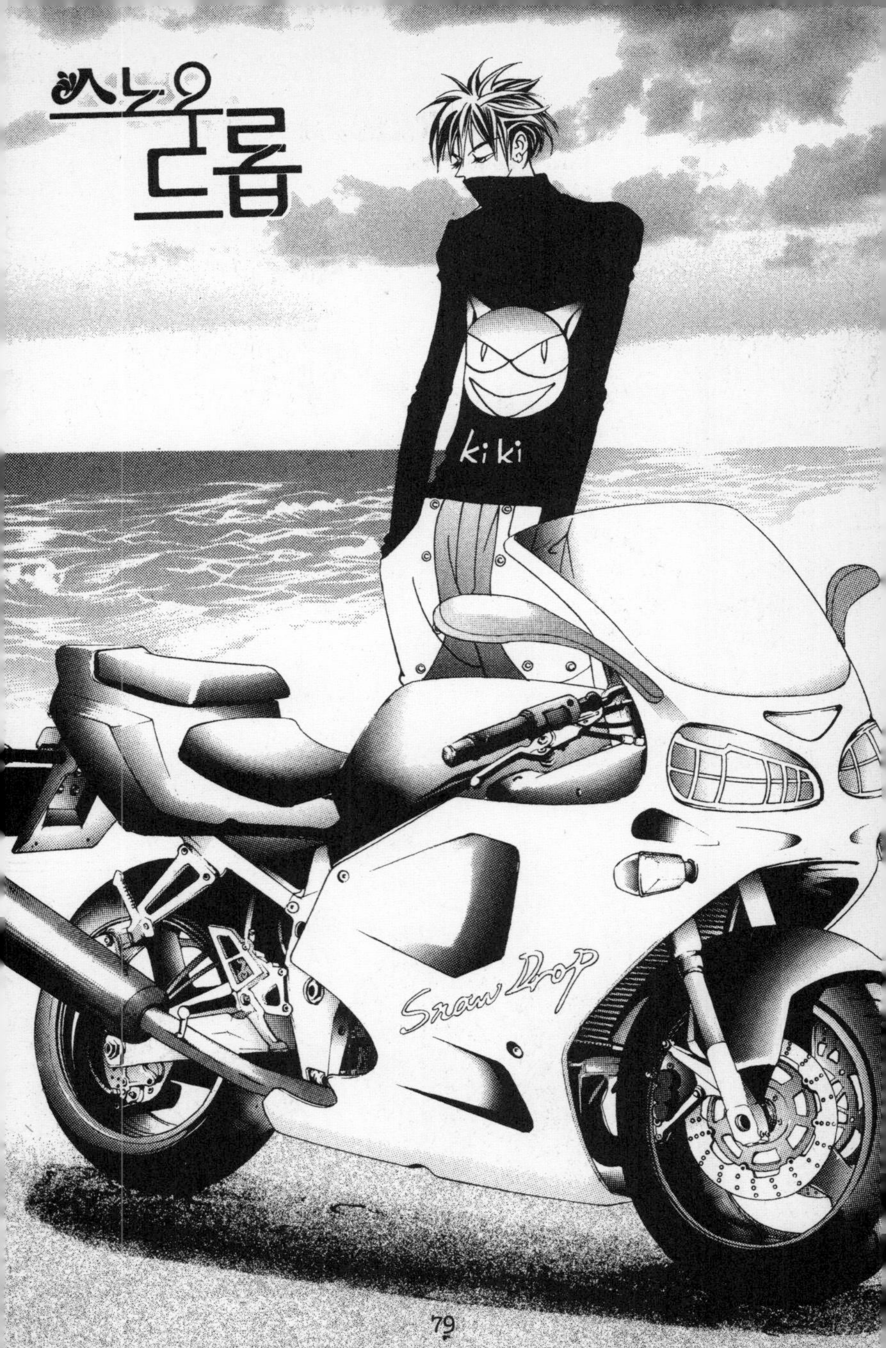
스노우 드롭
ki ki
Snow Drop

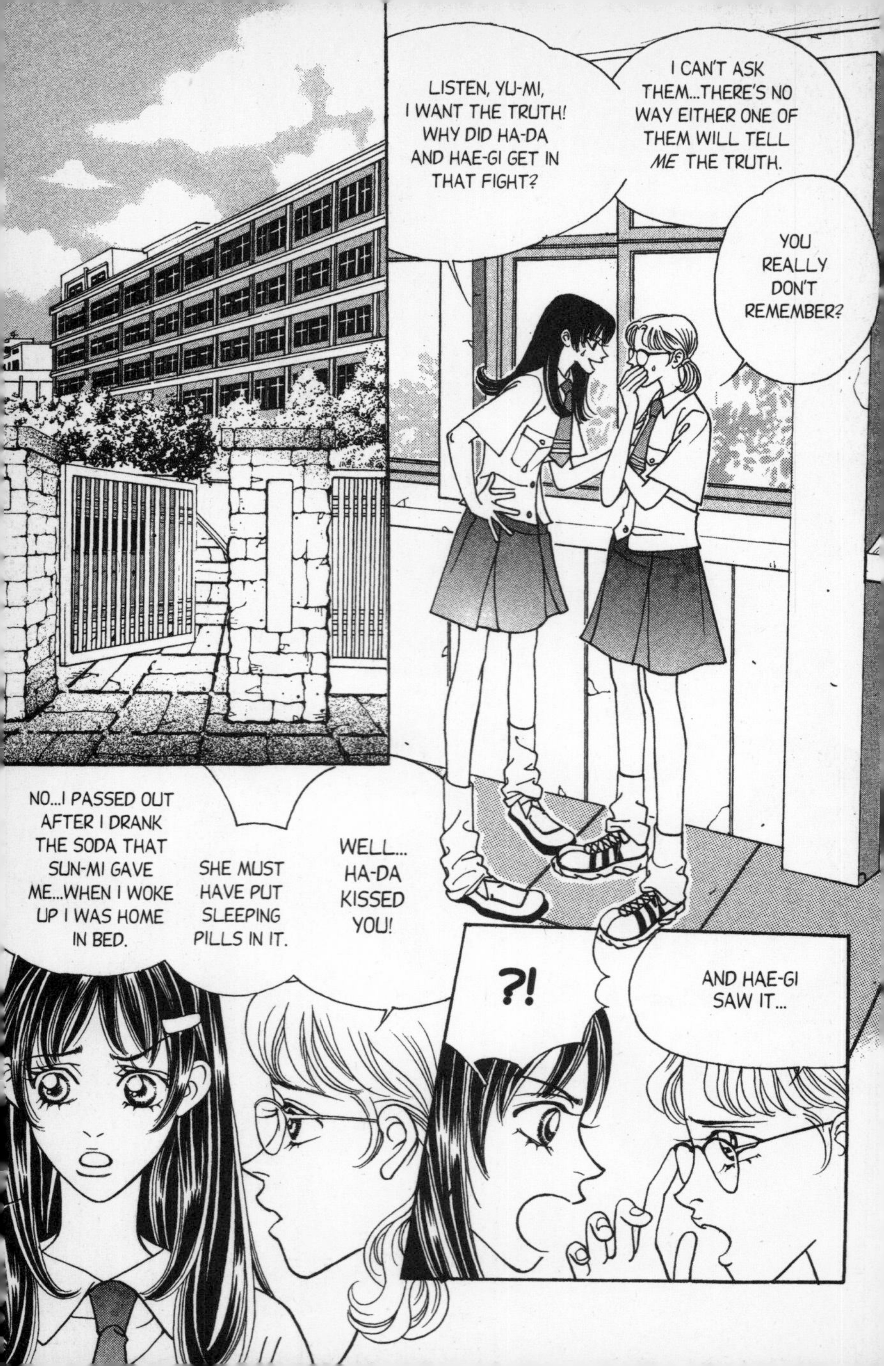
LISTEN, YU-MI, I WANT THE TRUTH! WHY DID HA-DA AND HAE-GI GET IN THAT FIGHT?
I CAN'T ASK THEM...THERE'S NO WAY EITHER ONE OF THEM WILL TELL *ME* THE TRUTH.
YOU REALLY DON'T REMEMBER?
NO...I PASSED OUT AFTER I DRANK THE SODA THAT SUN-MI GAVE ME...WHEN I WOKE UP I WAS HOME IN BED.
SHE MUST HAVE PUT SLEEPING PILLS IN IT.
WELL... HA-DA KISSED YOU!
?!
AND HAE-GI SAW IT...

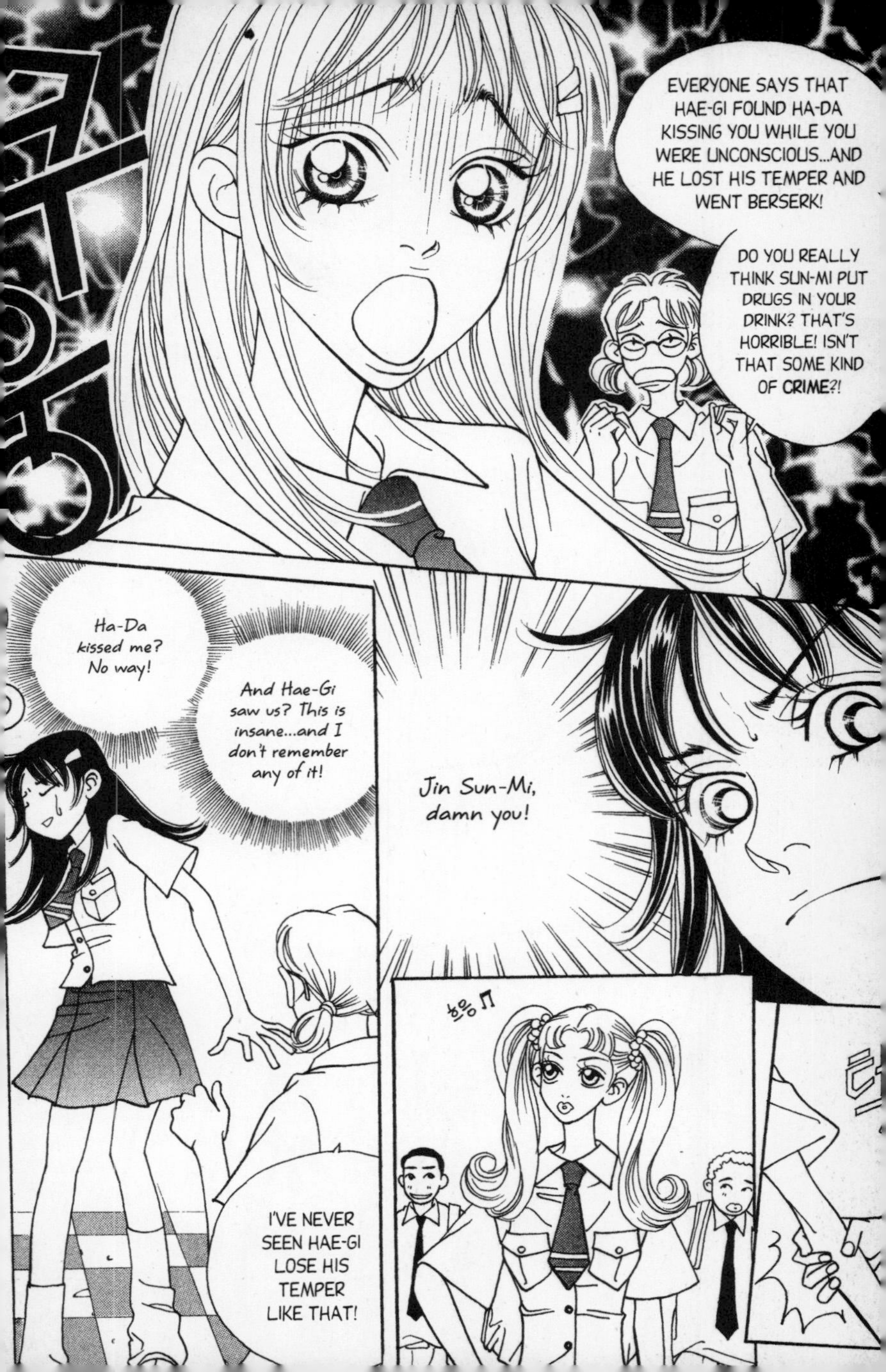
EVERYONE SAYS THAT HAE-GI FOUND HA-DA KISSING YOU WHILE YOU WERE UNCONSCIOUS...AND HE LOST HIS TEMPER AND WENT BERSERK!
DO YOU REALLY THINK SUN-MI PUT DRUGS IN YOUR DRINK? THAT'S HORRIBLE! ISN'T THAT SOME KIND OF CRIME?!
Ha-Da kissed me? No way!
And Hae-Gi saw us? This is insane...and I don't remember any of it!
I'VE NEVER SEEN HAE-GI LOSE HIS TEMPER LIKE THAT!
Jin Sun-Mi, damn you!

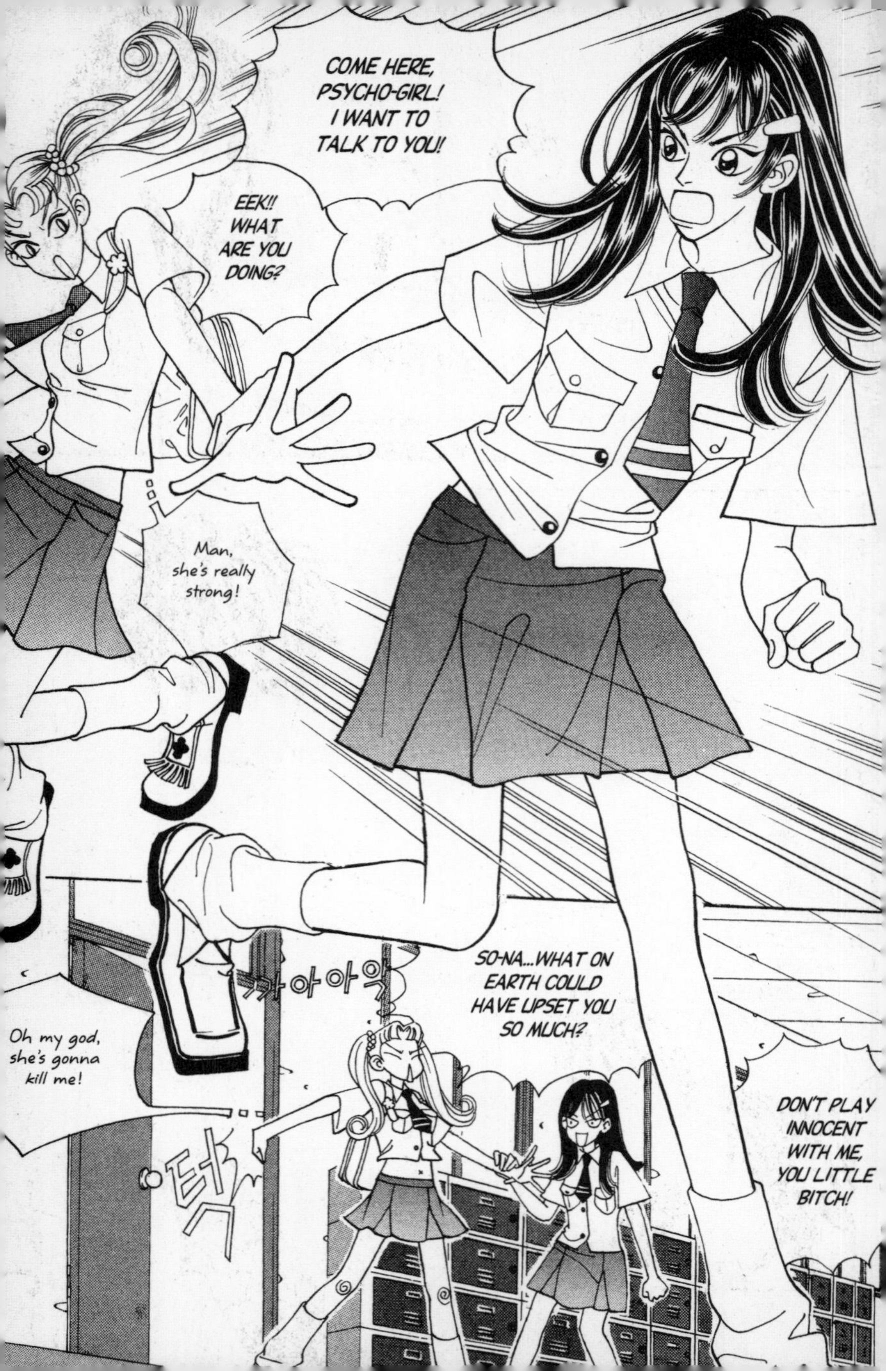
COME HERE, PSYCHO-GIRL! I WANT TO TALK TO YOU!
EEK!! WHAT ARE YOU DOING?
Man, she's really strong!
꺄아아악
Oh my god, she's gonna kill me!
SO-NA...WHAT ON EARTH COULD HAVE UPSET YOU SO MUCH?
턱
DON'T PLAY INNOCENT WITH ME, YOU LITTLE BITCH!

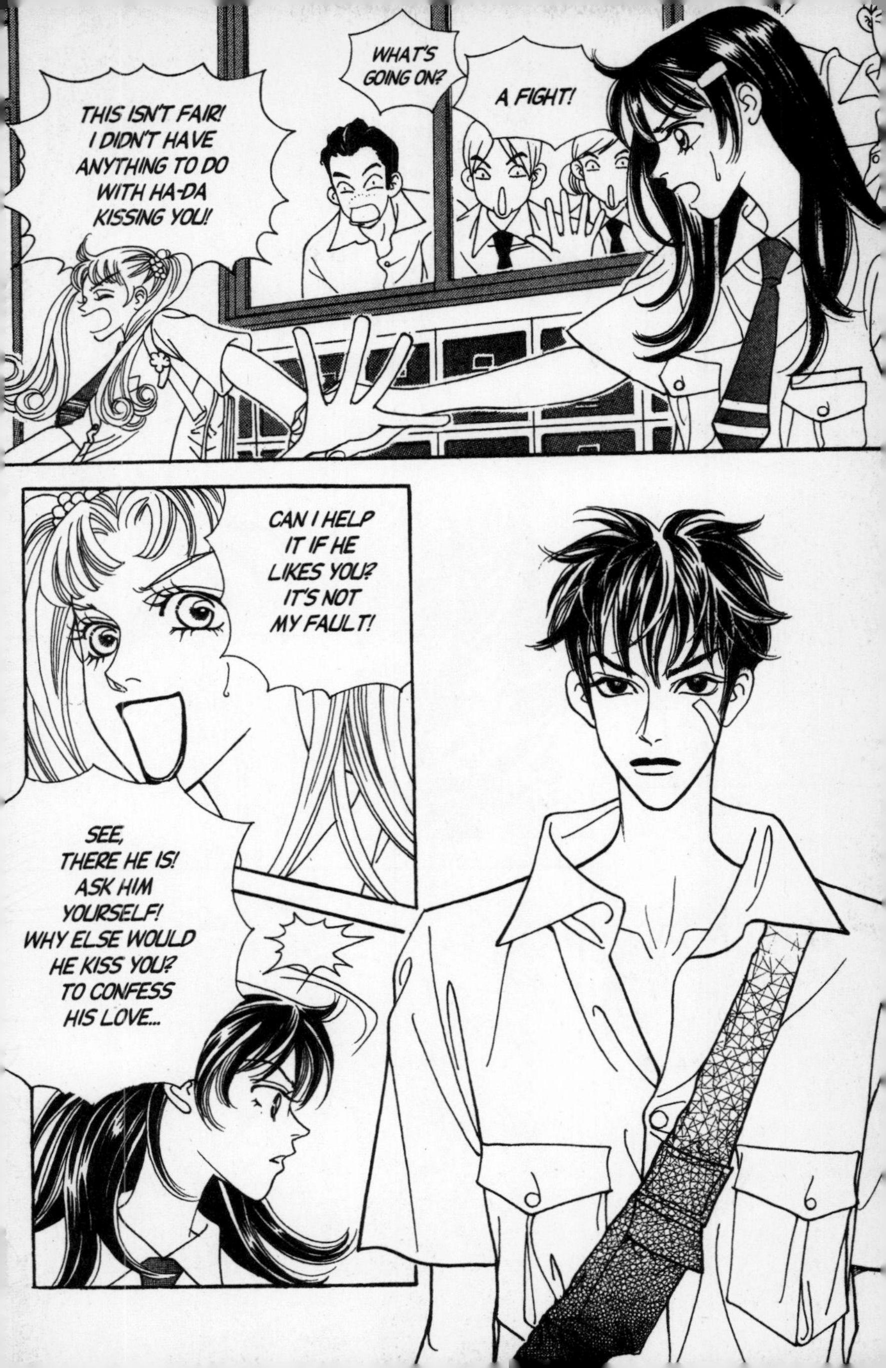
THIS ISN'T FAIR! I DIDN'T HAVE ANYTHING TO DO WITH HA-DA KISSING YOU!
WHAT'S GOING ON?
A FIGHT!
CAN I HELP IT IF HE LIKES YOU? IT'S NOT MY FAULT!
SEE, THERE HE IS! ASK HIM YOURSELF! WHY ELSE WOULD HE KISS YOU? TO CONFESS HIS LOVE...

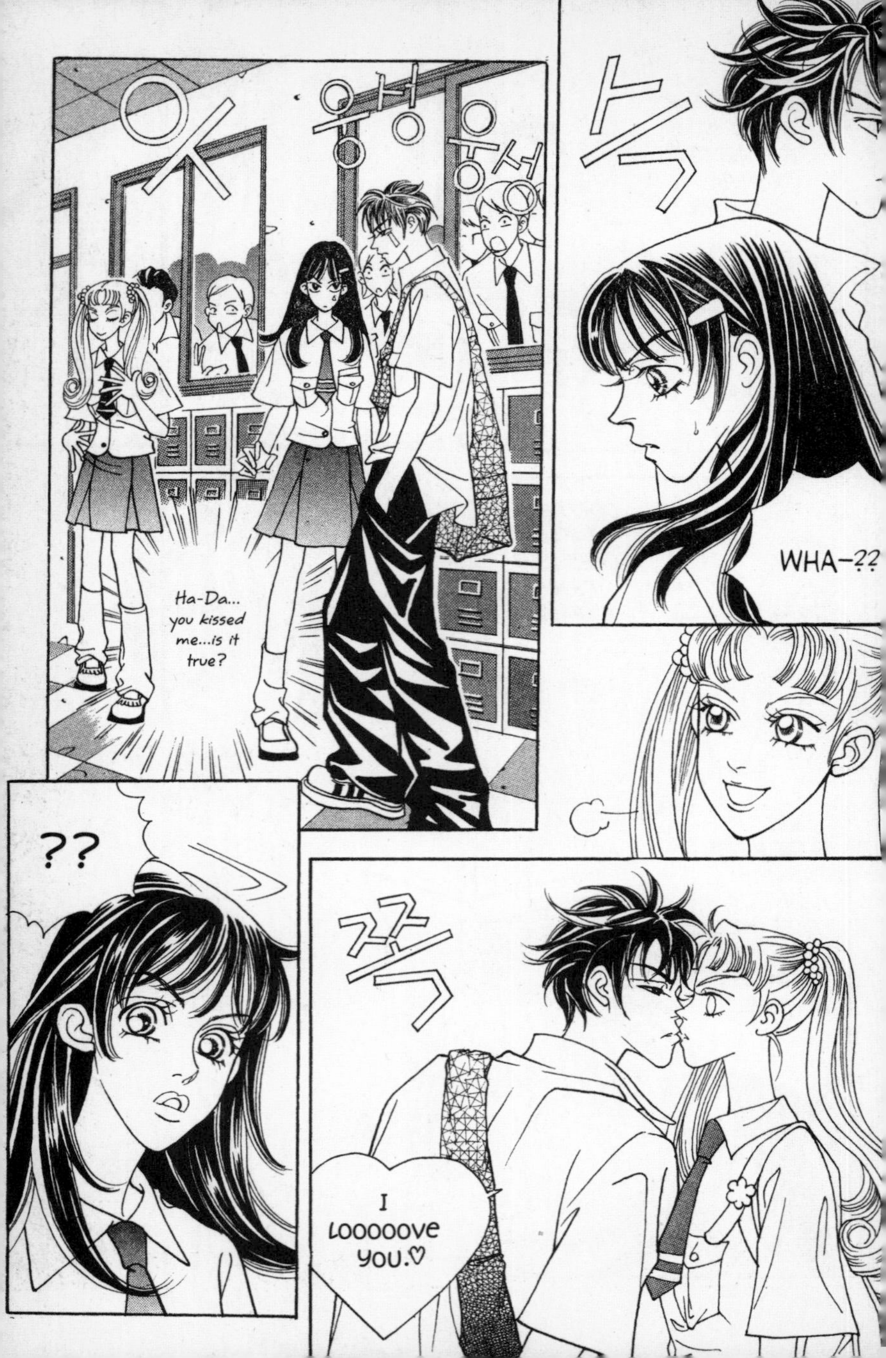
Ha-Da... you kissed me...is it true?
WHA-??
??
I LOOOOOVE YOU.♡

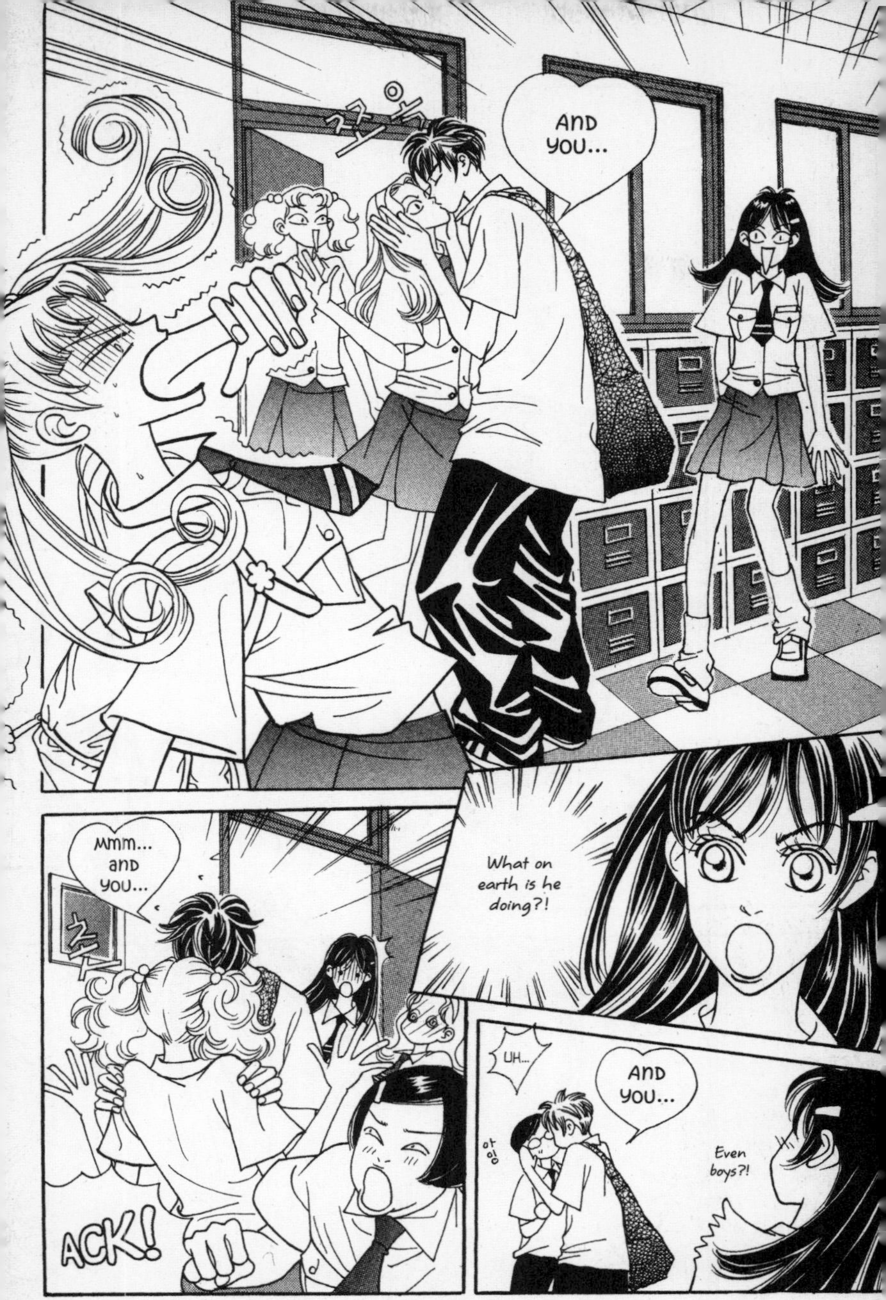
AND YOU...
Mmm... and you...
ACK!
What on earth is he doing?!
UH...
AND YOU...
Even boys?!

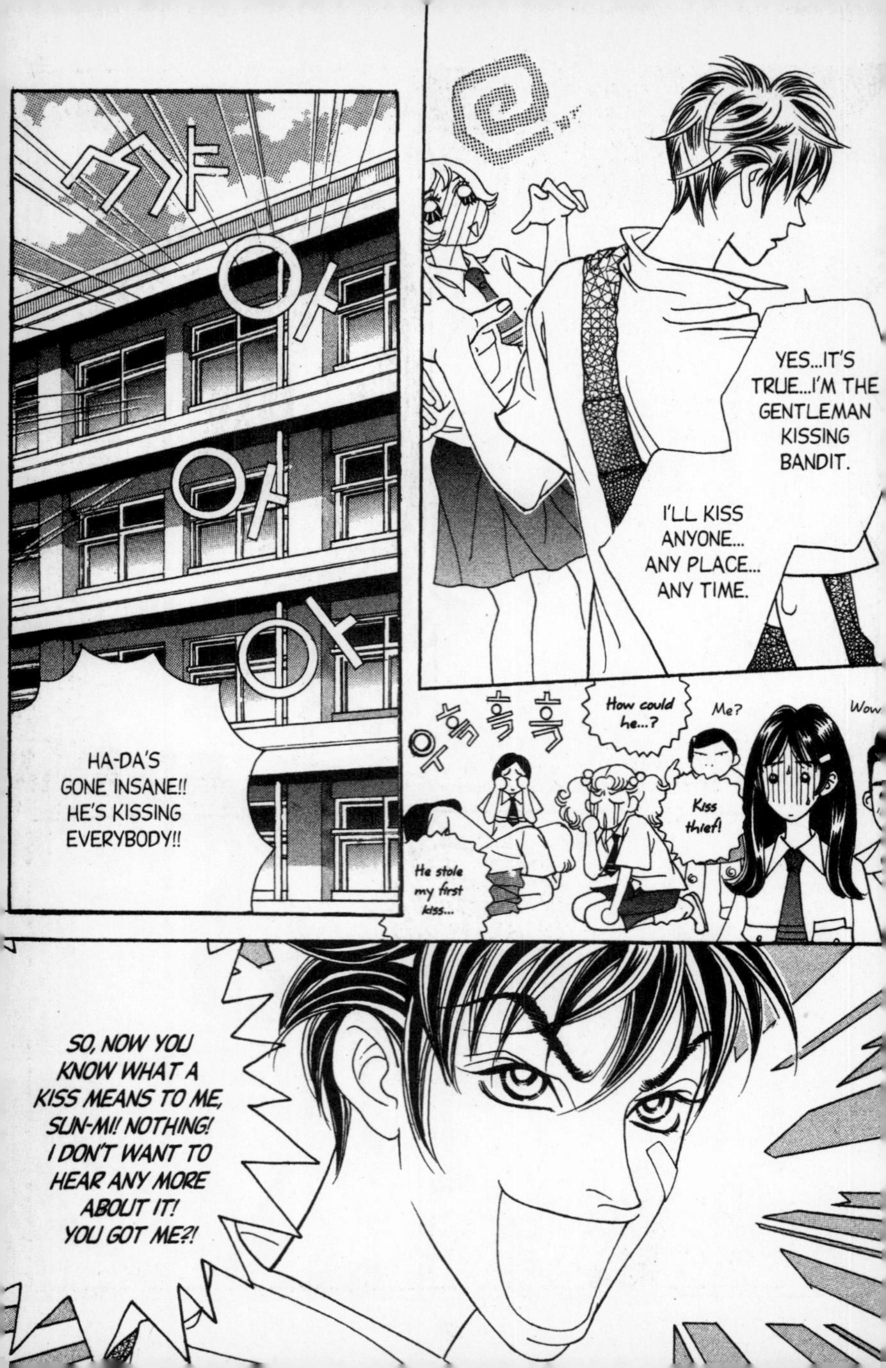
HA-DA'S GONE INSANE!! HE'S KISSING EVERYBODY!!
YES...IT'S TRUE...I'M THE GENTLEMAN KISSING BANDIT.
I'LL KISS ANYONE... ANY PLACE... ANY TIME.
How could he...?
Me?
Wow
Kiss thief!
He stole my first kiss...
SO, NOW YOU KNOW WHAT A KISS MEANS TO ME, SUN-MI! NOTHING! I DON'T WANT TO HEAR ANY MORE ABOUT IT! YOU GOT ME?!

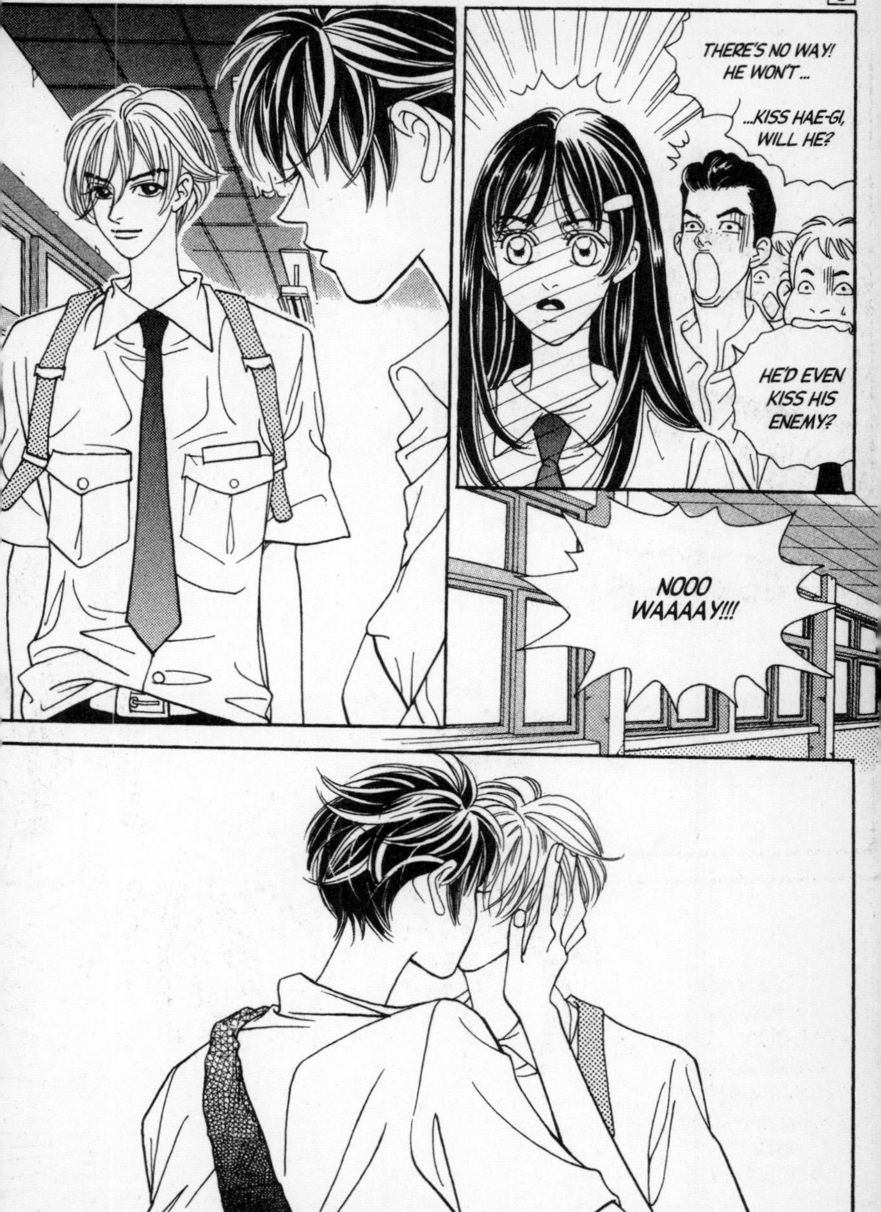
THERE'S NO WAY! HE WON'T...
...KISS HAE-GI, WILL HE?
HE'D EVEN KISS HIS ENEMY?
NOOO WAAAAY!!!

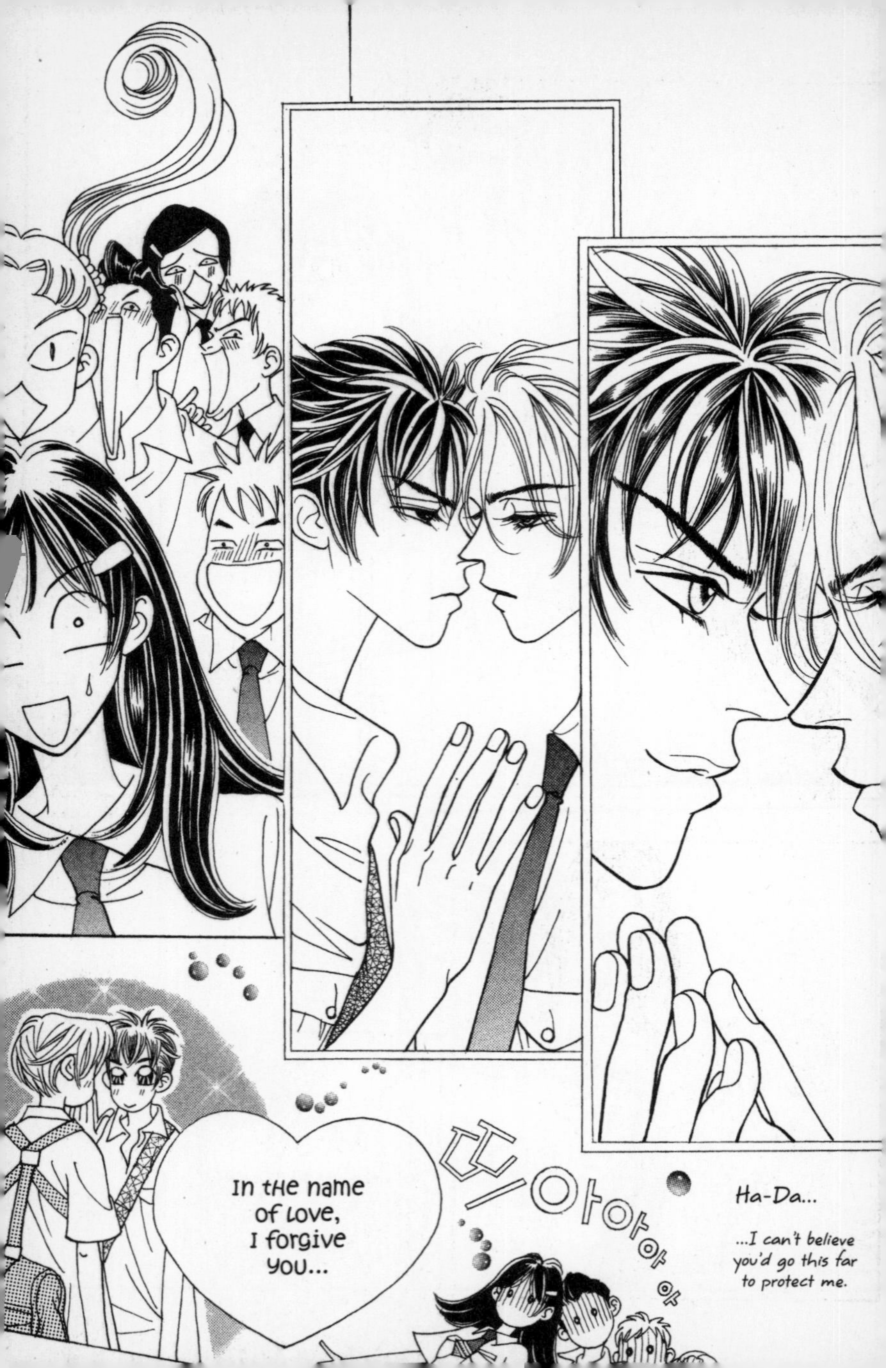
In the name of love, I forgive you...
Ha-Da...
...I can't believe you'd go this far to protect me.

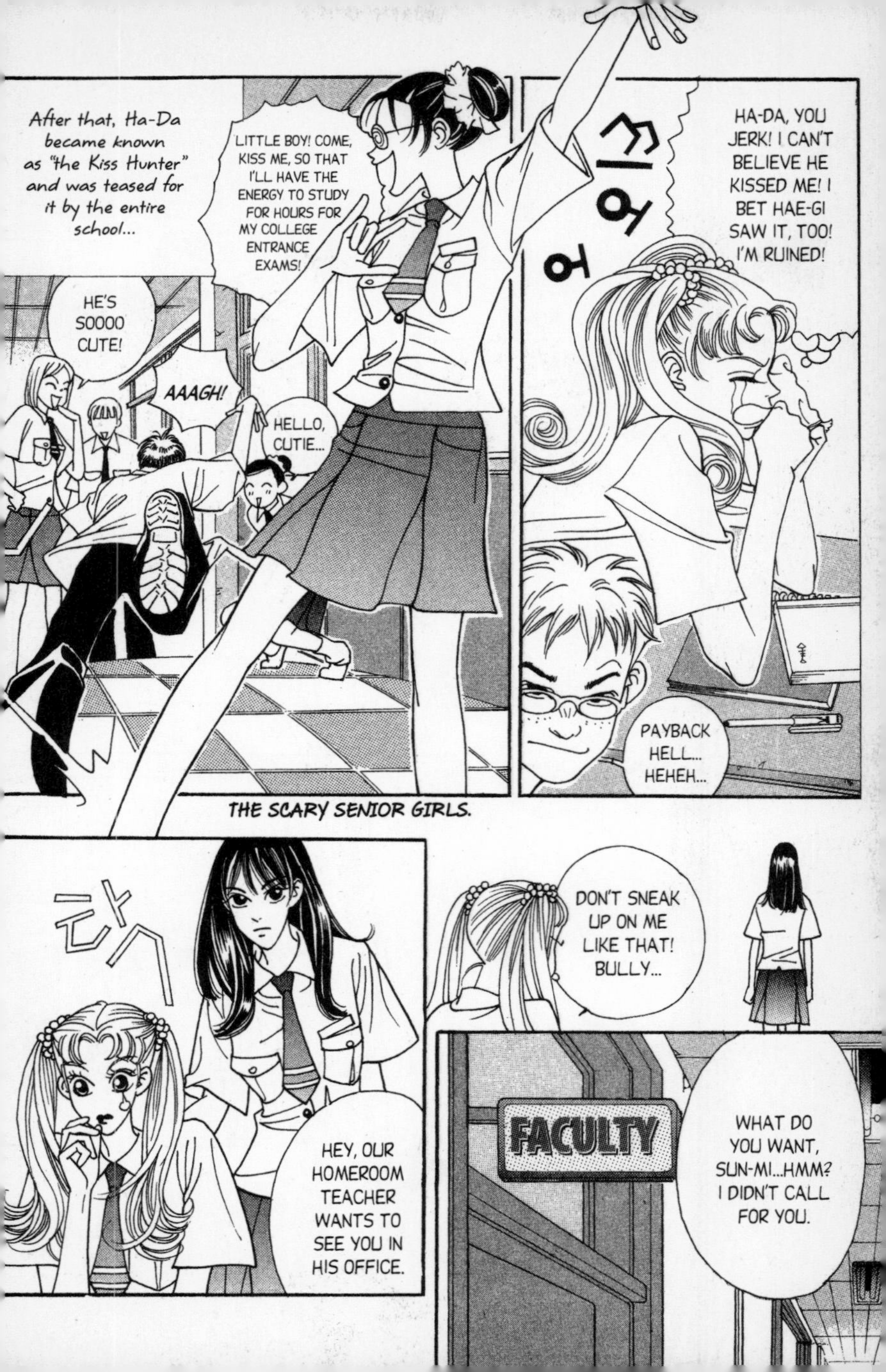
After that, Ha-Da became known as "the Kiss Hunter" and was teased for it by the entire school...
LITTLE BOY! COME, KISS ME, SO THAT I'LL HAVE THE ENERGY TO STUDY FOR HOURS FOR MY COLLEGE ENTRANCE EXAMS!
HE'S SOOOO CUTE!
AAAGH!
HELLO, CUTIE...
HA-DA, YOU JERK! I CAN'T BELIEVE HE KISSED ME! I BET HAE-GI SAW IT, TOO! I'M RUINED!
PAYBACK HELL... HEHEH...
THE SCARY SENIOR GIRLS.
HEY, OUR HOMEROOM TEACHER WANTS TO SEE YOU IN HIS OFFICE.
DON'T SNEAK UP ON ME LIKE THAT! BULLY...
FACULTY
WHAT DO YOU WANT, SUN-MI...HMM? I DIDN'T CALL FOR YOU.

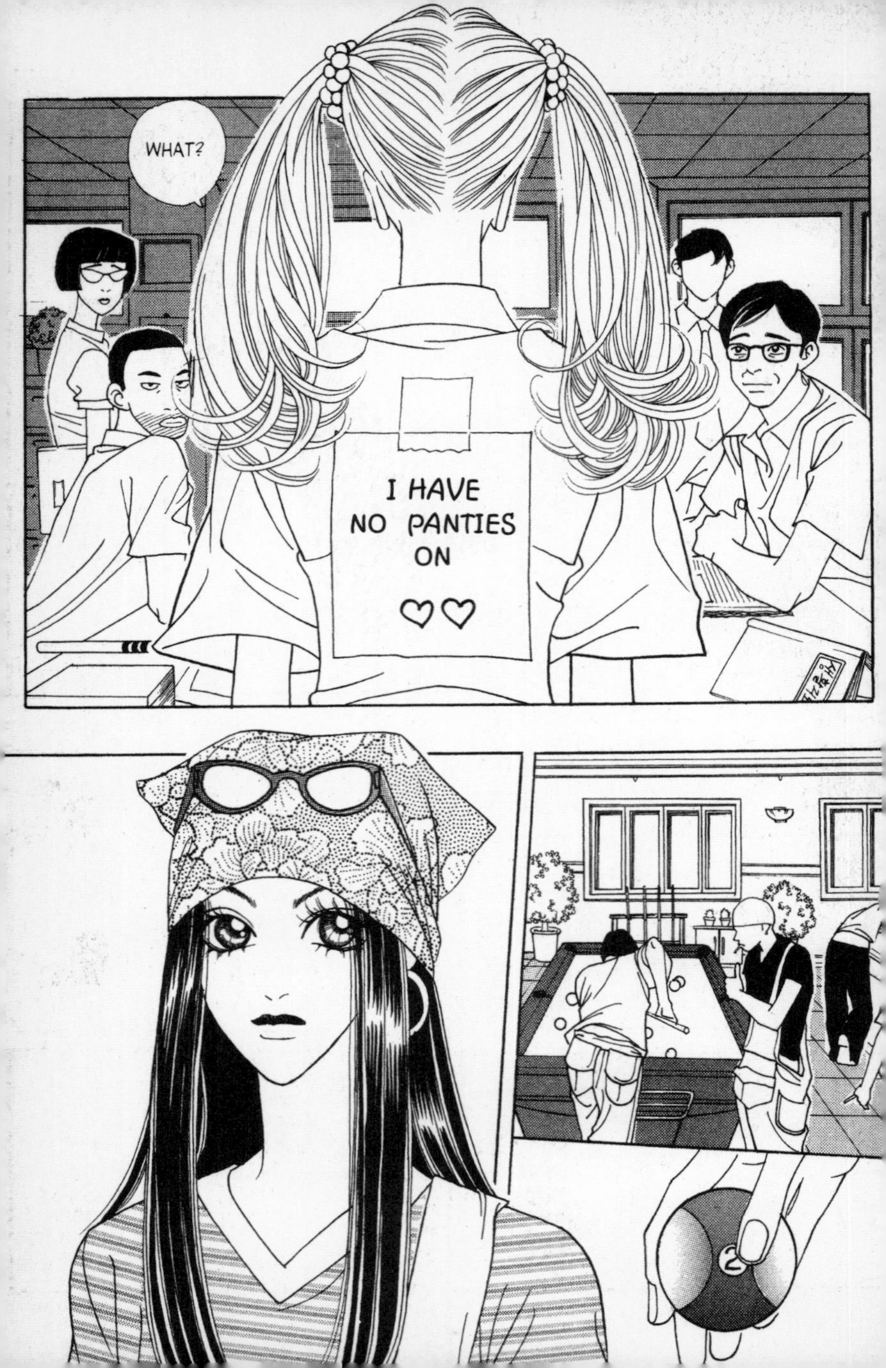
WHAT?
I HAVE NO PANTIES ON
♡♡

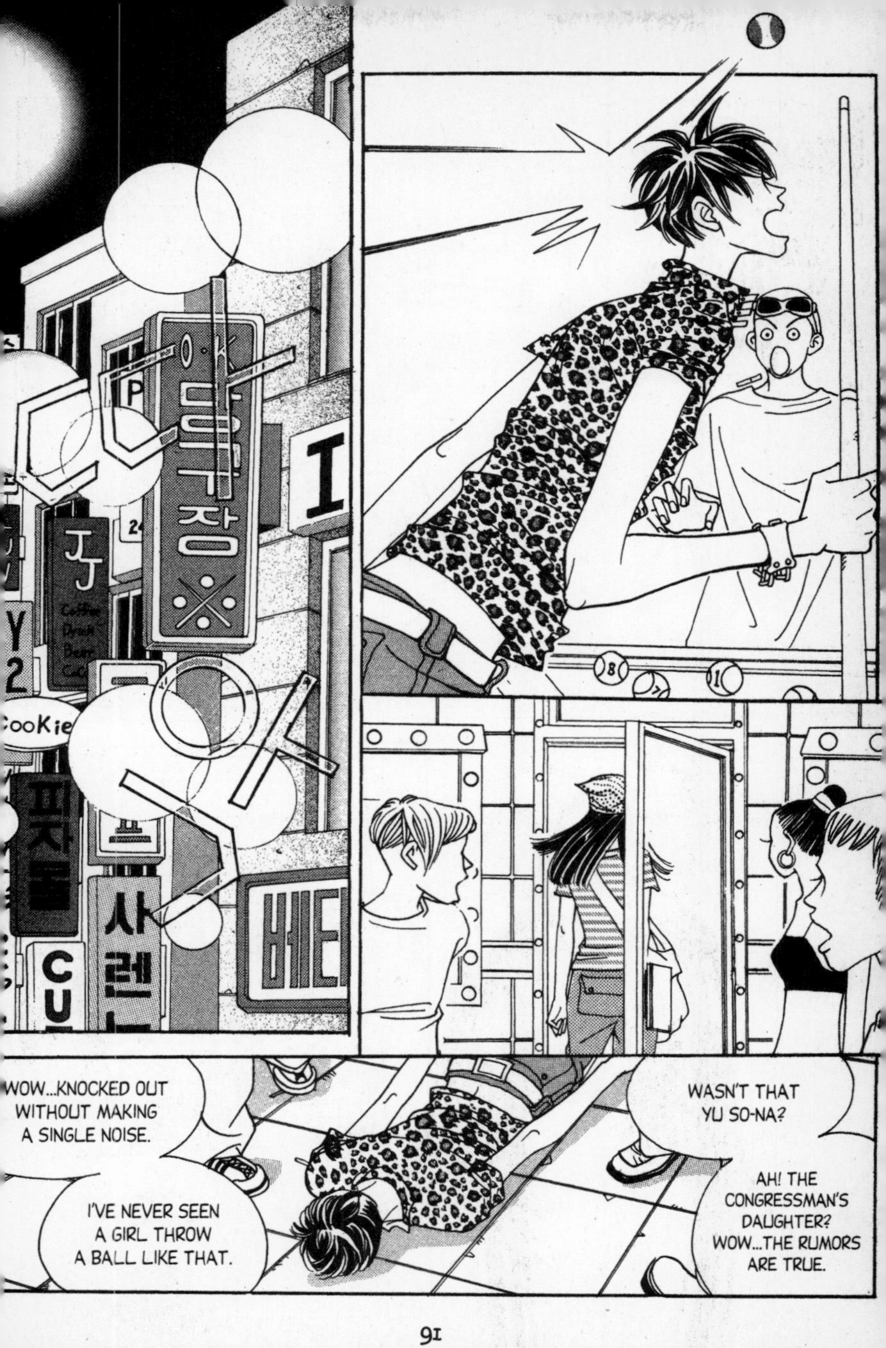
WOW...KNOCKED OUT WITHOUT MAKING A SINGLE NOISE.
I'VE NEVER SEEN A GIRL THROW A BALL LIKE THAT.
WASN'T THAT YU SO-NA?
AH! THE CONGRESSMAN'S DAUGHTER? WOW...THE RUMORS ARE TRUE.

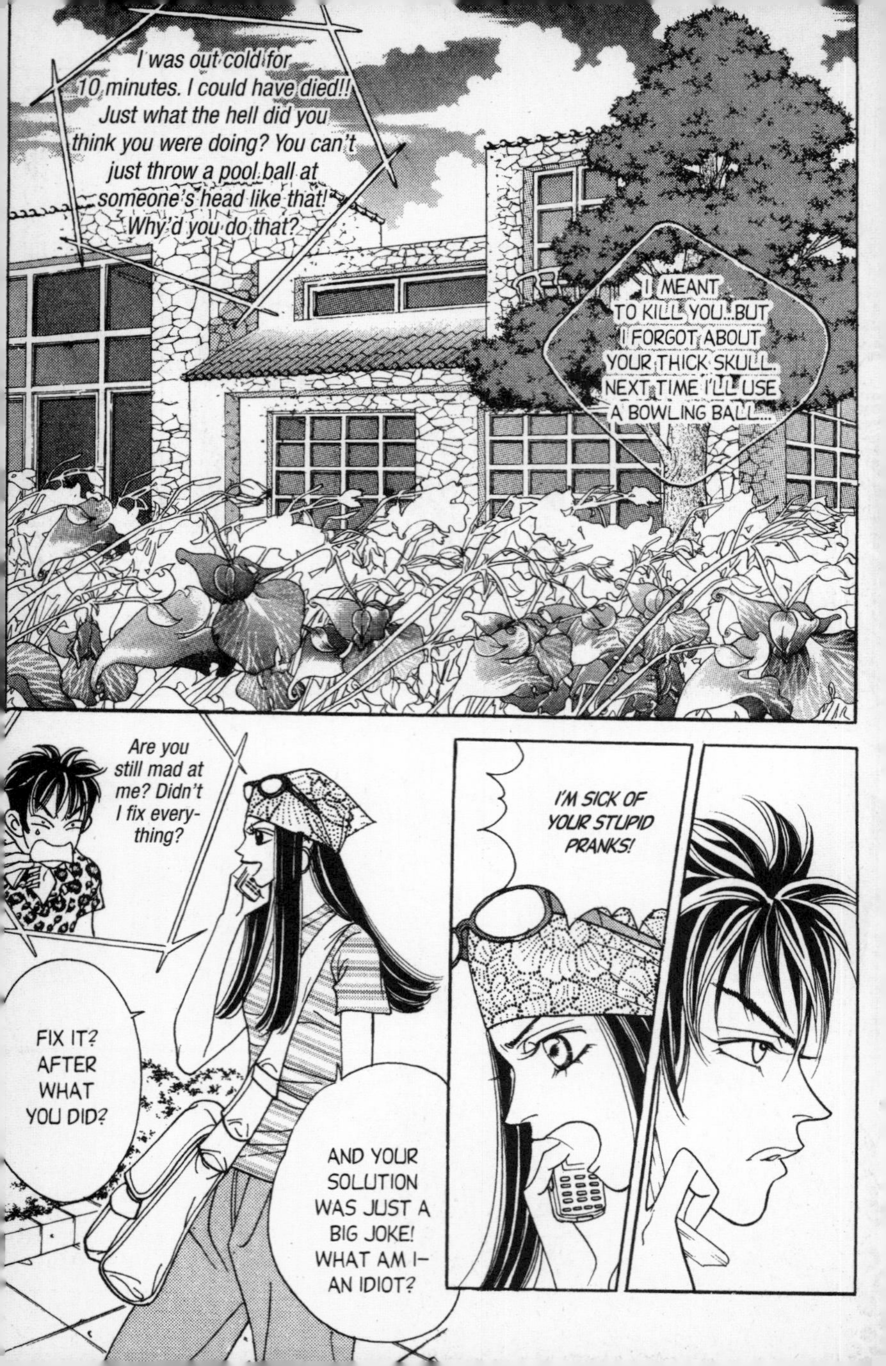
I was out cold for 10 minutes. I could have died!! Just what the hell did you think you were doing? You can't just throw a pool ball at someone's head like that! Why'd you do that?
I MEANT TO KILL YOU...BUT I FORGOT ABOUT YOUR THICK SKULL. NEXT TIME I'LL USE A BOWLING BALL...
Are you still mad at me? Didn't I fix every-thing?
FIX IT? AFTER WHAT YOU DID?
AND YOUR SOLUTION WAS JUST A BIG JOKE! WHAT AM I— AN IDIOT?
I'M SICK OF YOUR STUPID PRANKS!

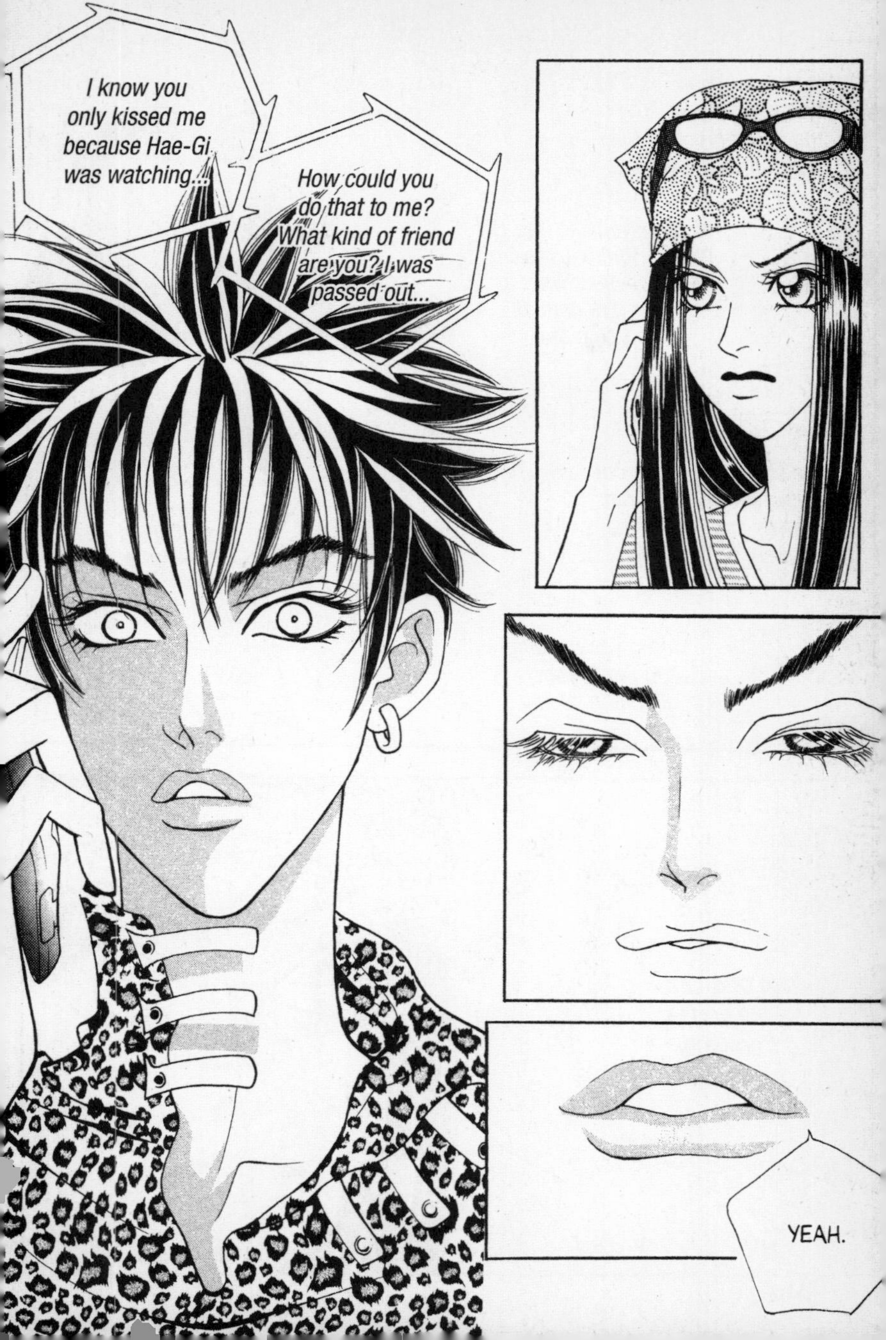
I know you only kissed me because Hae-Gi was watching...
How could you do that to me? What kind of friend are you? I was passed out...
YEAH.

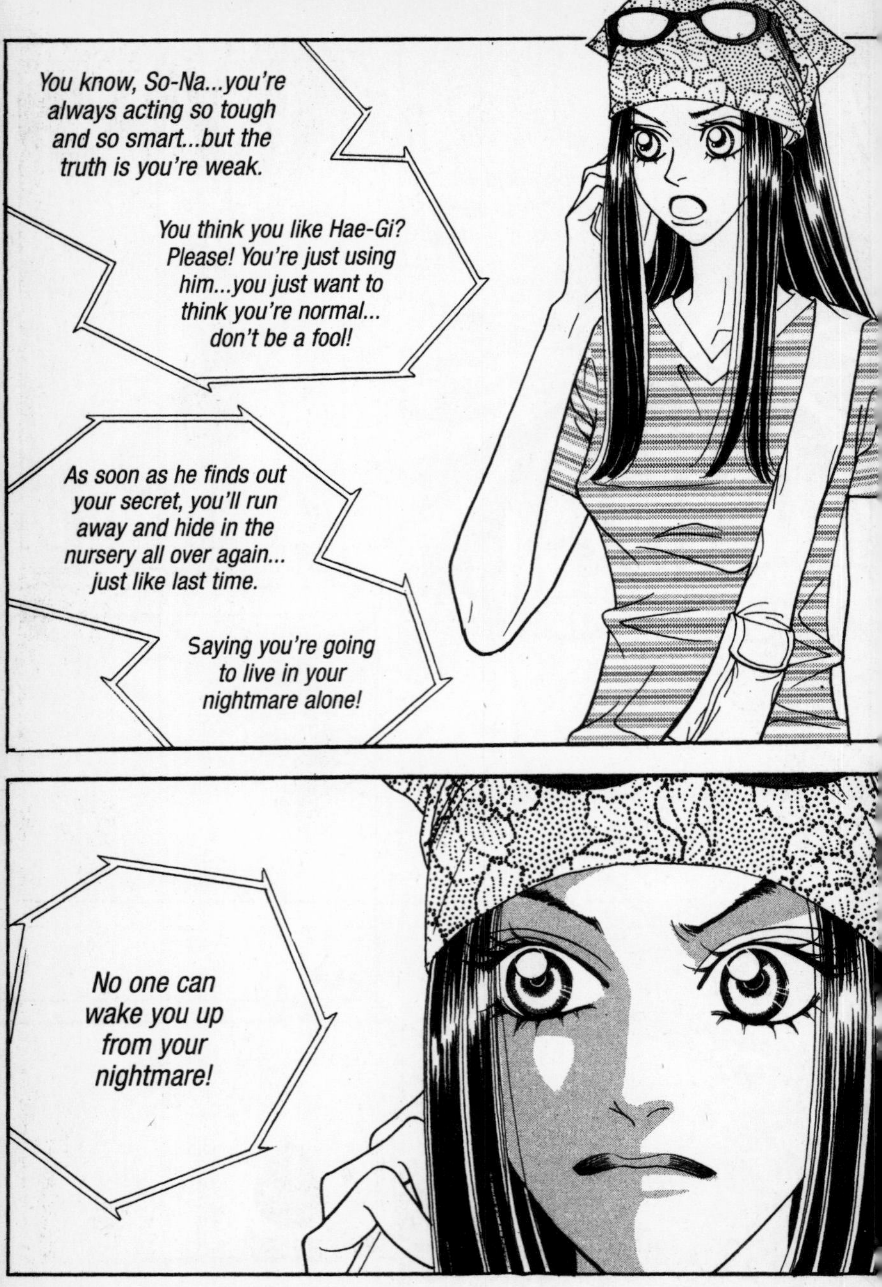
You know, So-Na...you're always acting so tough and so smart...but the truth is you're weak.
You think you like Hae-Gi? Please! You're just using him...you just want to think you're normal... don't be a fool!
As soon as he finds out your secret, you'll run away and hide in the nursery all over again... just like last time.
Saying you're going to live in your nightmare alone!
No one can wake you up from your nightmare!

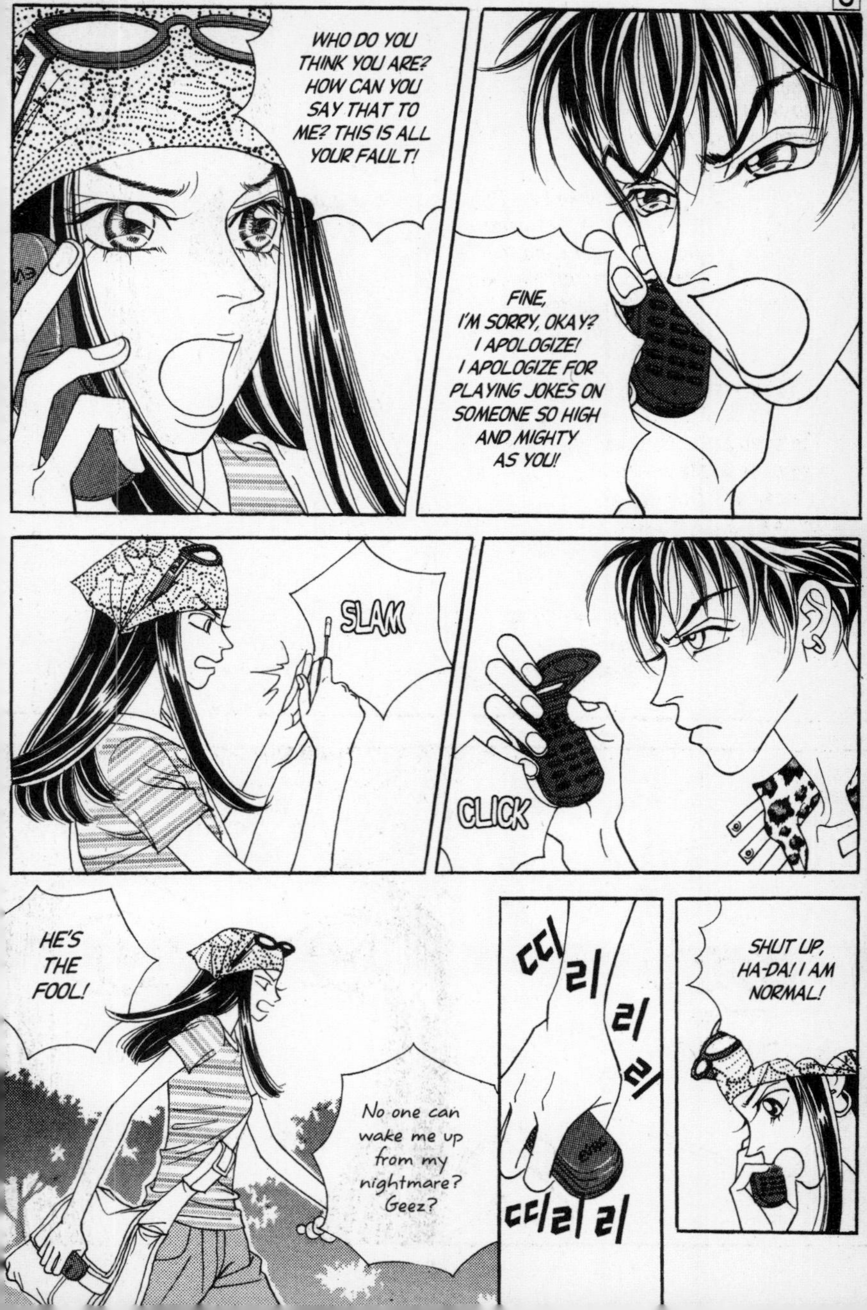
WHO DO YOU THINK YOU ARE? HOW CAN YOU SAY THAT TO ME? THIS IS ALL YOUR FAULT!
FINE, I'M SORRY, OKAY? I APOLOGIZE! I APOLOGIZE FOR PLAYING JOKES ON SOMEONE SO HIGH AND MIGHTY AS YOU!
SLAM
CLICK
HE'S THE FOOL!
No one can wake me up from my nightmare? Geez?
SHUT UP, HA-DA! I AM NORMAL!

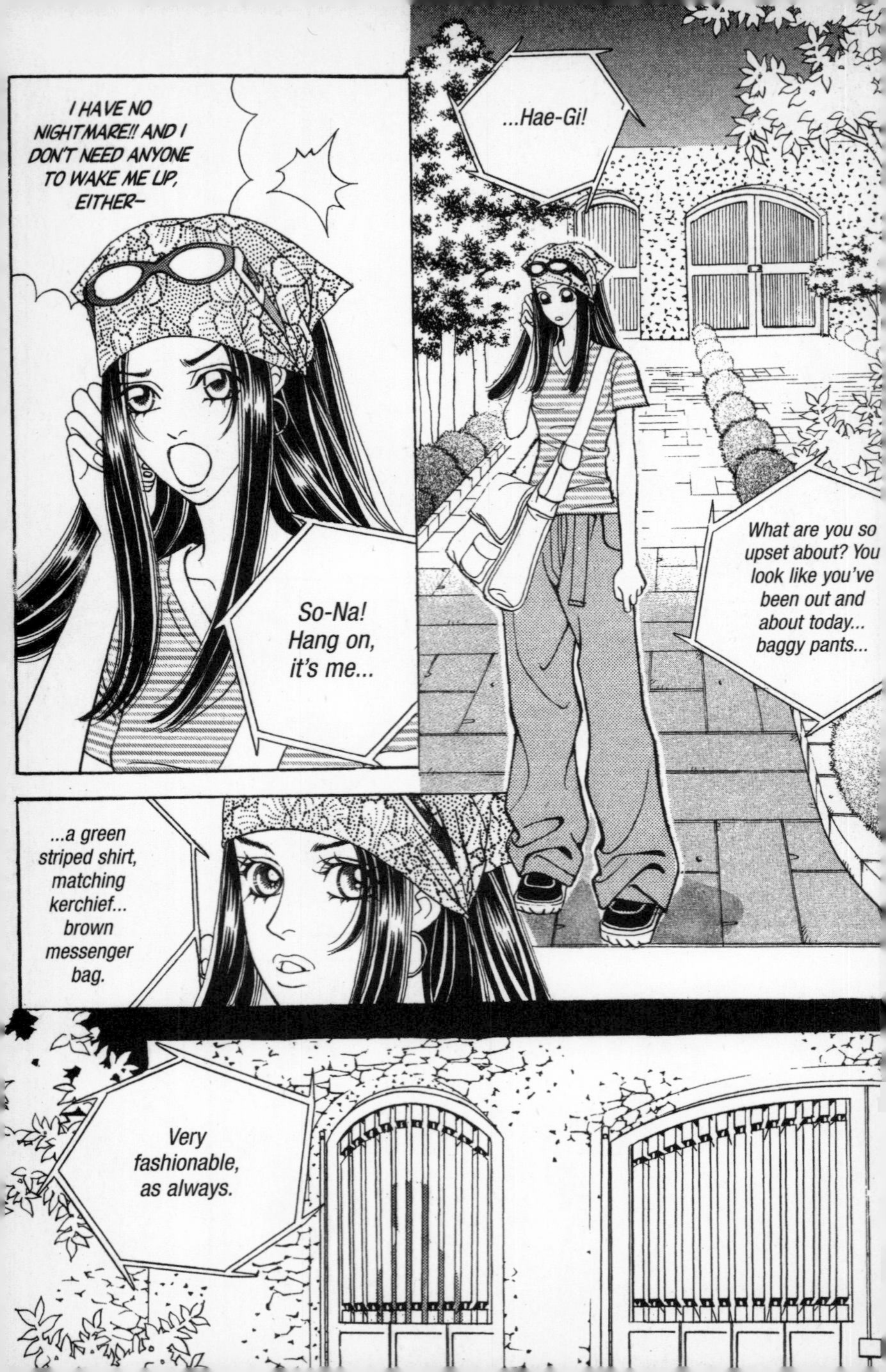
I HAVE NO NIGHTMARE!! AND I DON'T NEED ANYONE TO WAKE ME UP, EITHER–
So-Na! Hang on, it's me...
...a green striped shirt, matching kerchief... brown messenger bag.
...Hae-Gi!
What are you so upset about? You look like you've been out and about today... baggy pants...
Very fashionable, as always.

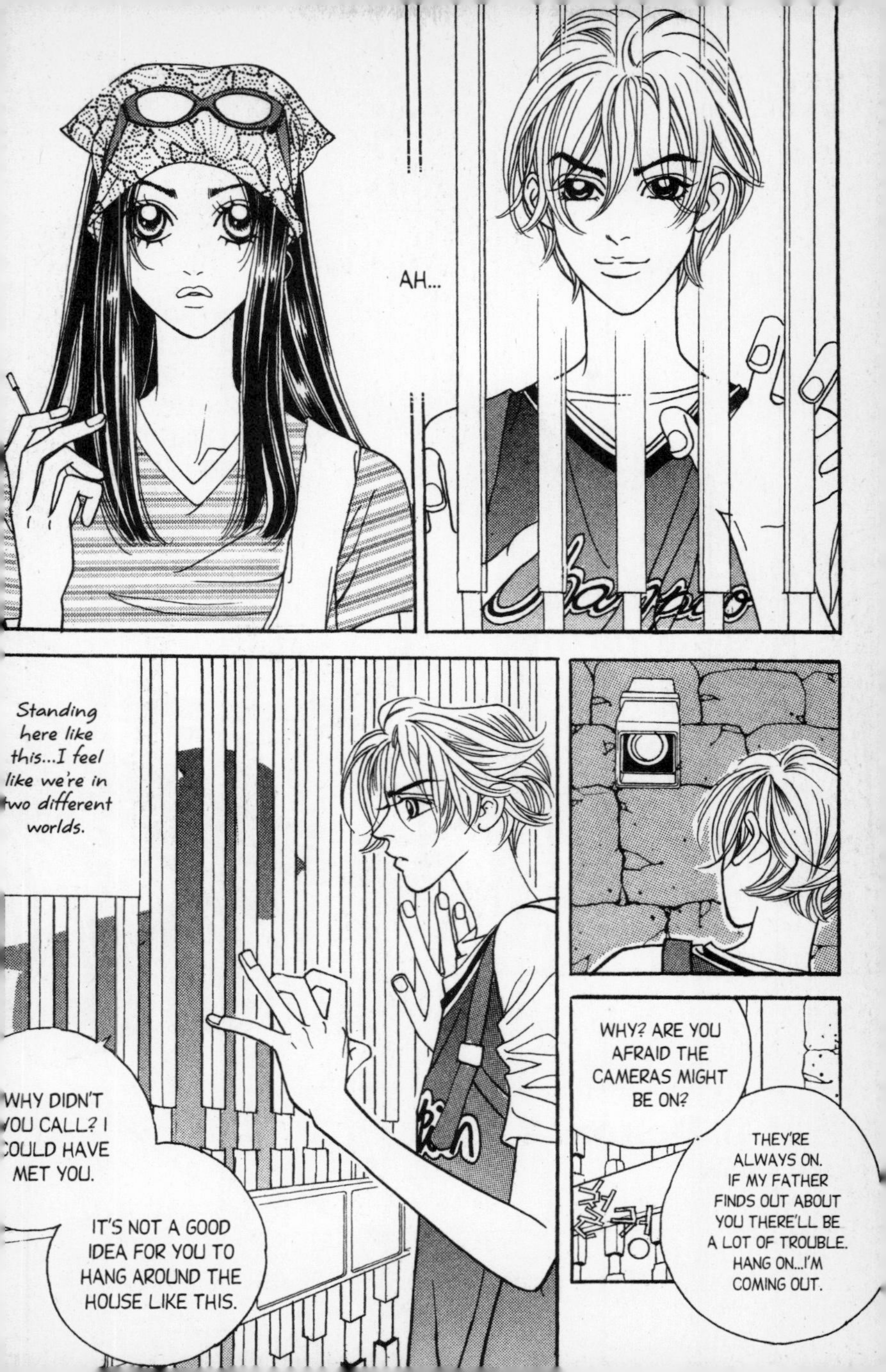
AH...
Standing here like this...I feel like we're in two different worlds.
WHY DIDN'T YOU CALL? I COULD HAVE MET YOU.
IT'S NOT A GOOD IDEA FOR YOU TO HANG AROUND THE HOUSE LIKE THIS.
WHY? ARE YOU AFRAID THE CAMERAS MIGHT BE ON?
THEY'RE ALWAYS ON. IF MY FATHER FINDS OUT ABOUT YOU THERE'LL BE A LOT OF TROUBLE. HANG ON...I'M COMING OUT.

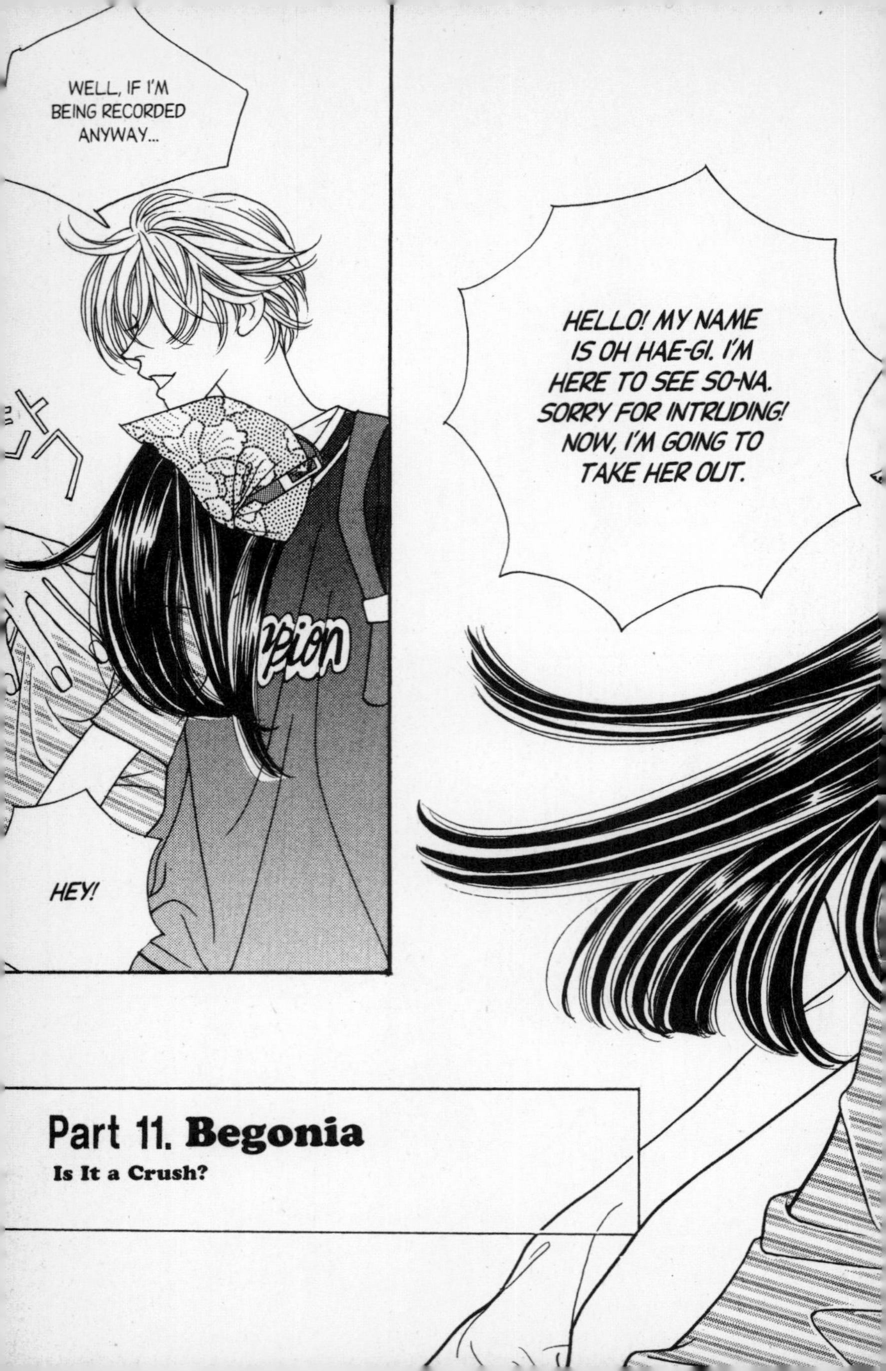
WELL, IF I'M BEING RECORDED ANYWAY...
HEY!
HELLO! MY NAME IS OH HAE-GI. I'M HERE TO SEE SO-NA. SORRY FOR INTRUDING! NOW, I'M GOING TO TAKE HER OUT.

## Part 11. Begonia

**Is It a Crush?**

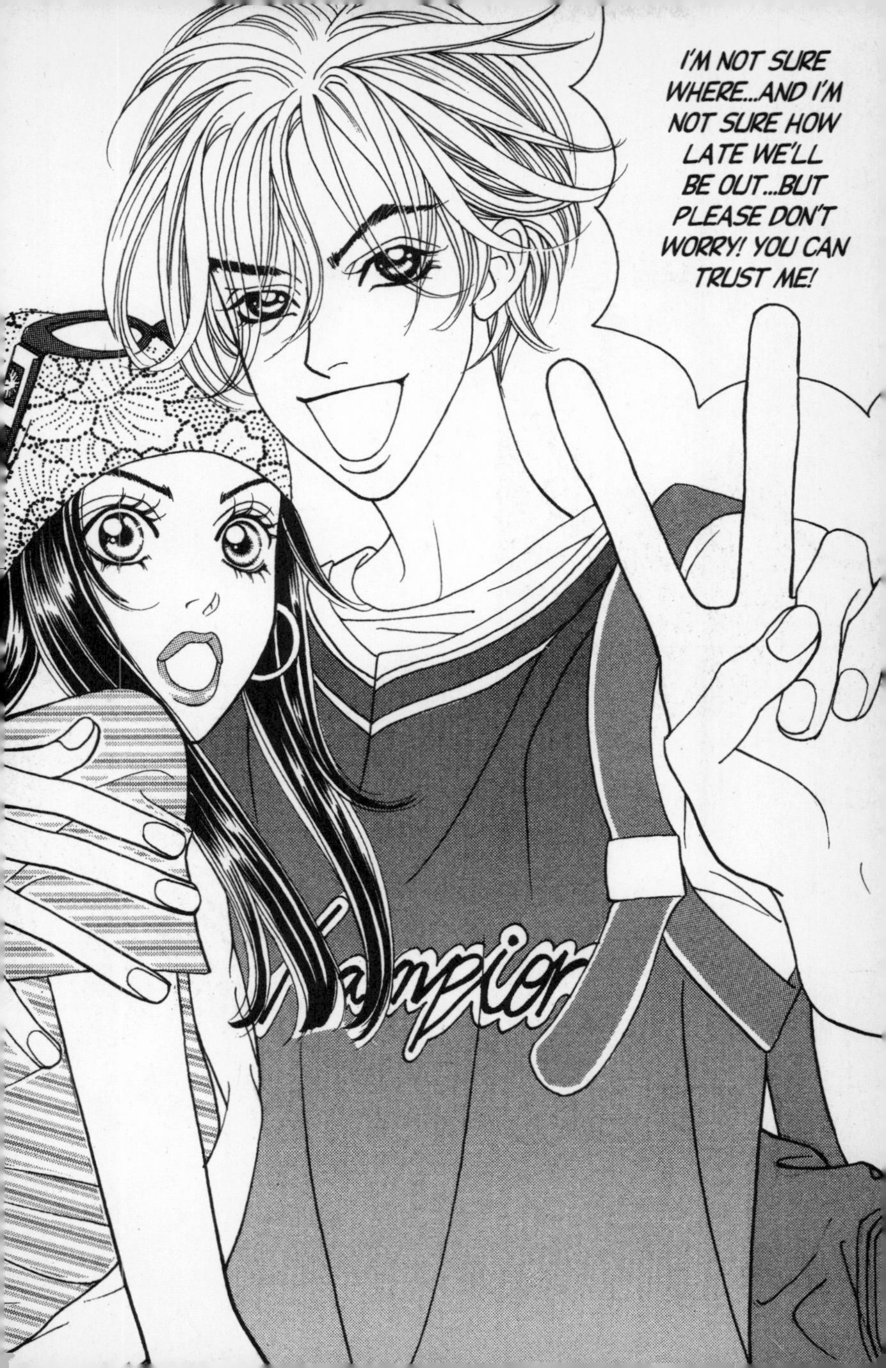
I'M NOT SURE WHERE...AND I'M NOT SURE HOW LATE WE'LL BE OUT...BUT PLEASE DON'T WORRY! YOU CAN TRUST ME!

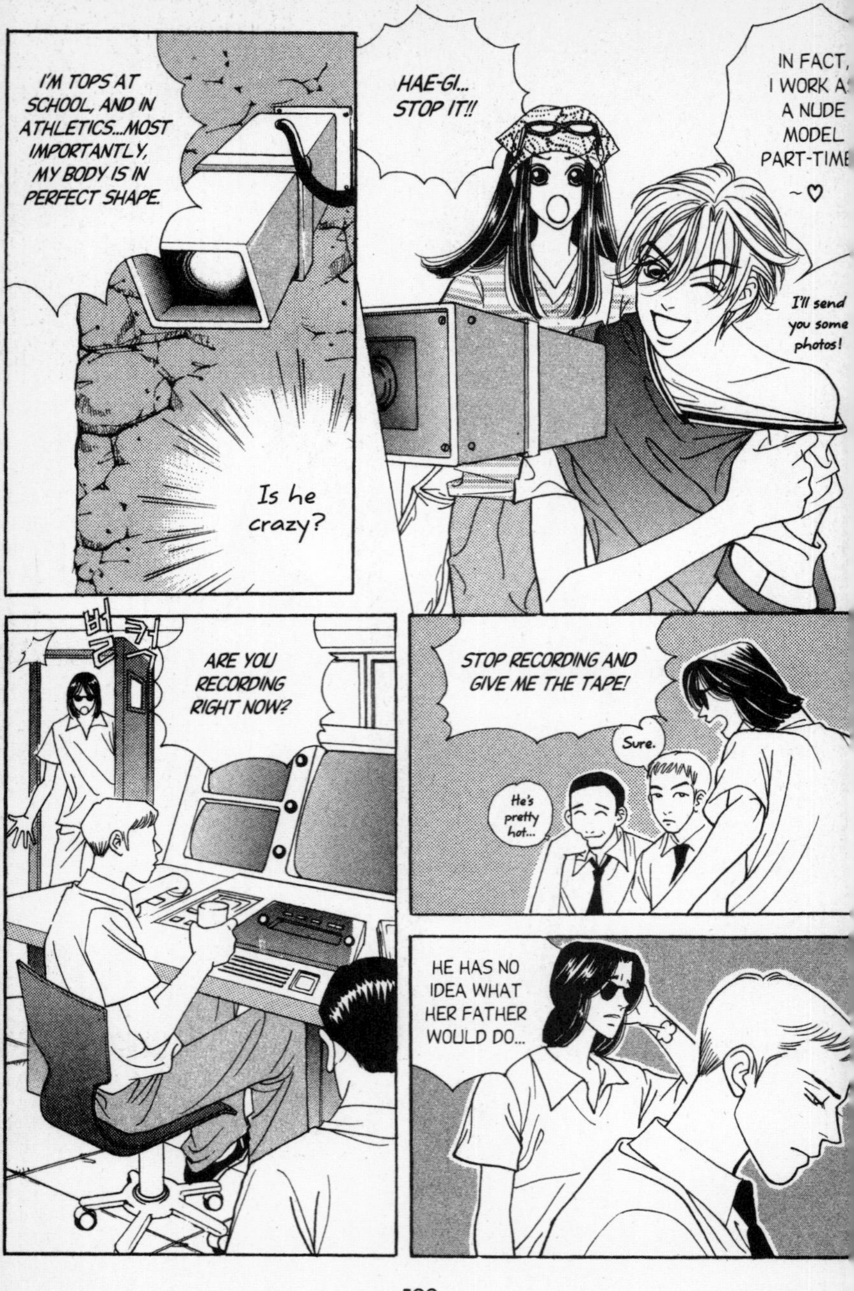

I'M TOPS AT SCHOOL, AND IN ATHLETICS...MOST IMPORTANTLY, MY BODY IS IN PERFECT SHAPE.
Is he crazy?
HAE-GI... STOP IT!!
IN FACT, I WORK AS A NUDE MODEL PART-TIME ~♡
I'll send you some photos!
ARE YOU RECORDING RIGHT NOW?
STOP RECORDING AND GIVE ME THE TAPE!
Sure.
He's pretty hot...
HE HAS NO IDEA WHAT HER FATHER WOULD DO...

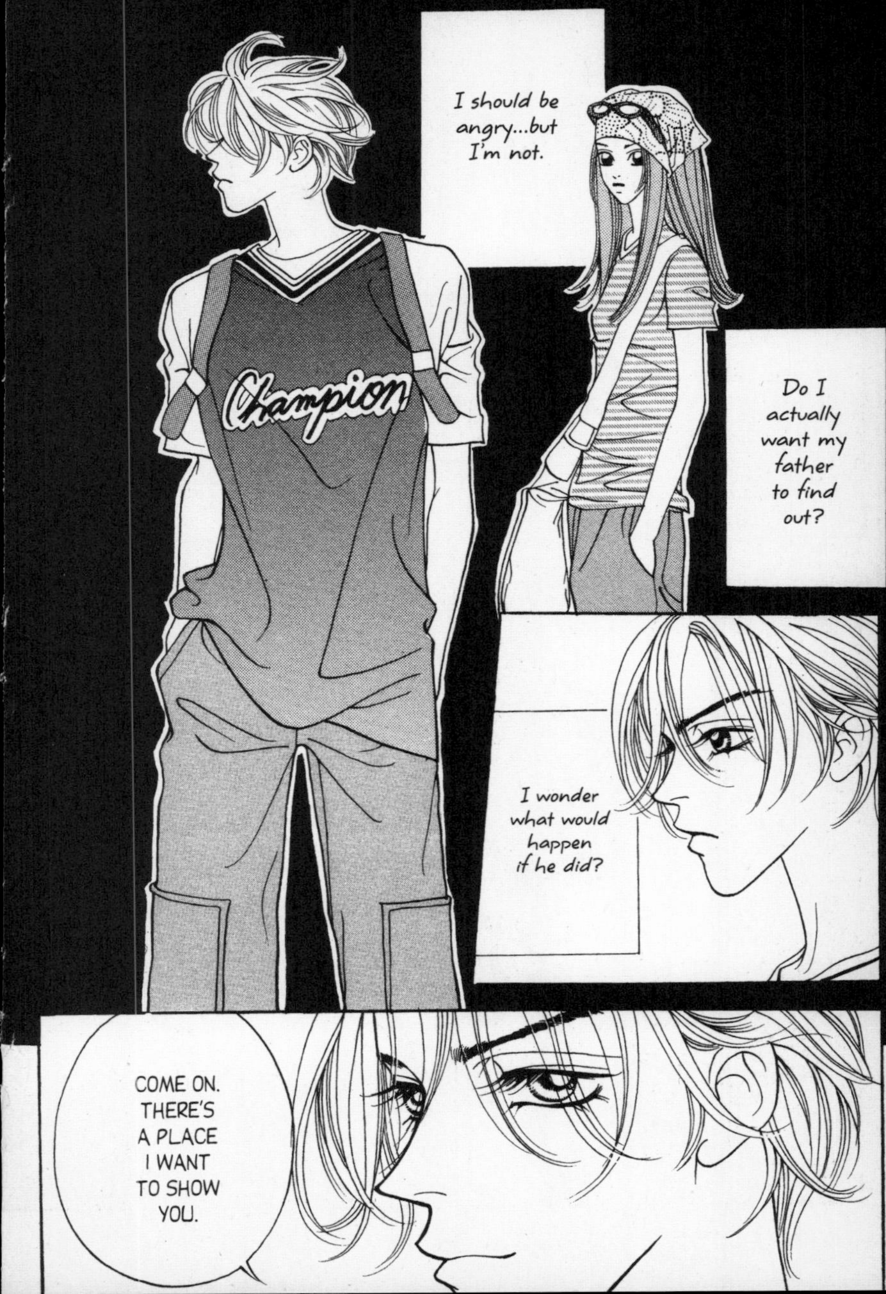
I should be angry...but I'm not.
Do I actually want my father to find out?
I wonder what would happen if he did?
COME ON. THERE'S A PLACE I WANT TO SHOW YOU.

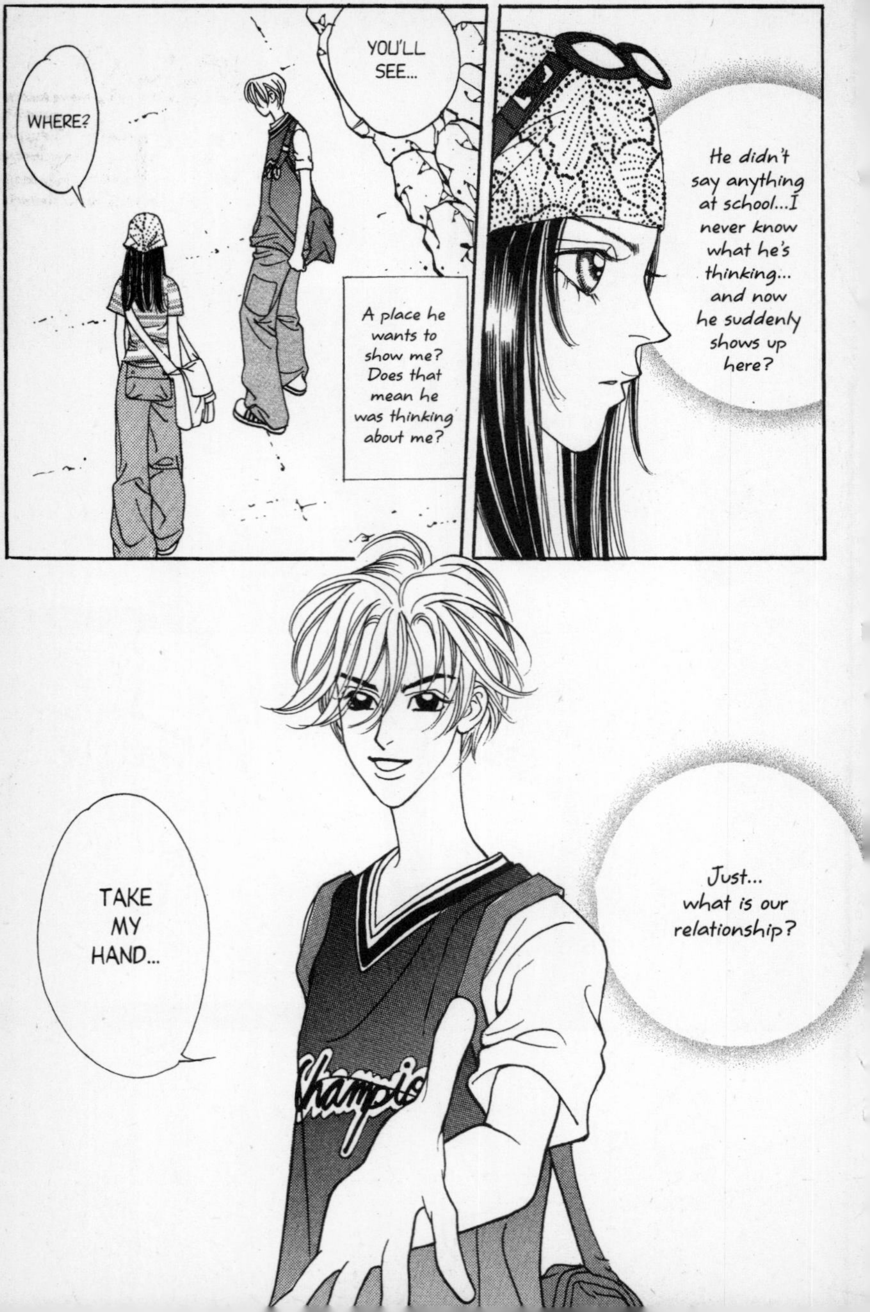
WHERE?
YOU'LL SEE...
A place he wants to show me? Does that mean he was thinking about me?
He didn't say anything at school...I never know what he's thinking... and now he suddenly shows up here?
TAKE MY HAND...
Just... what is our relationship?

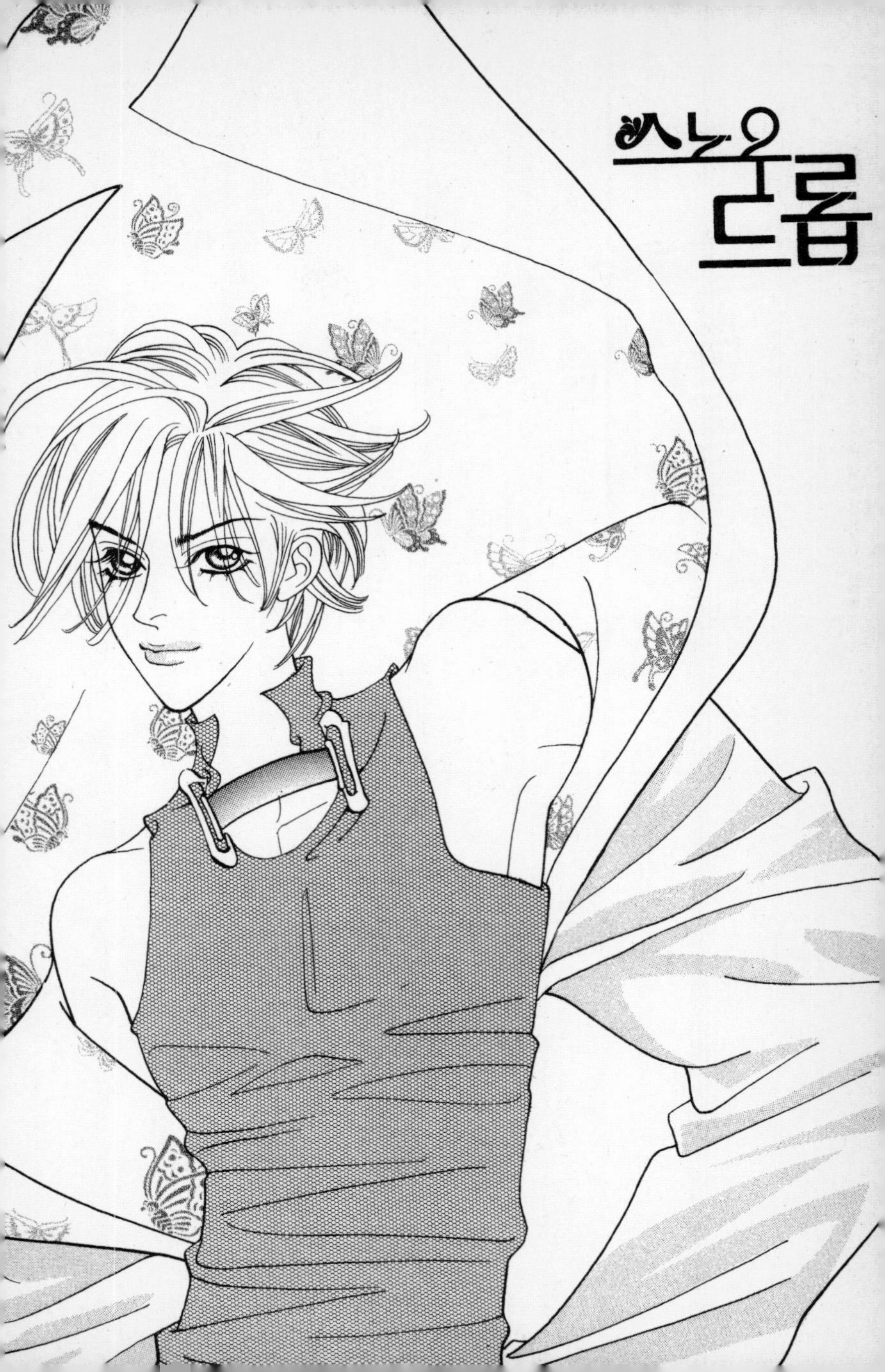
스노우 드롭

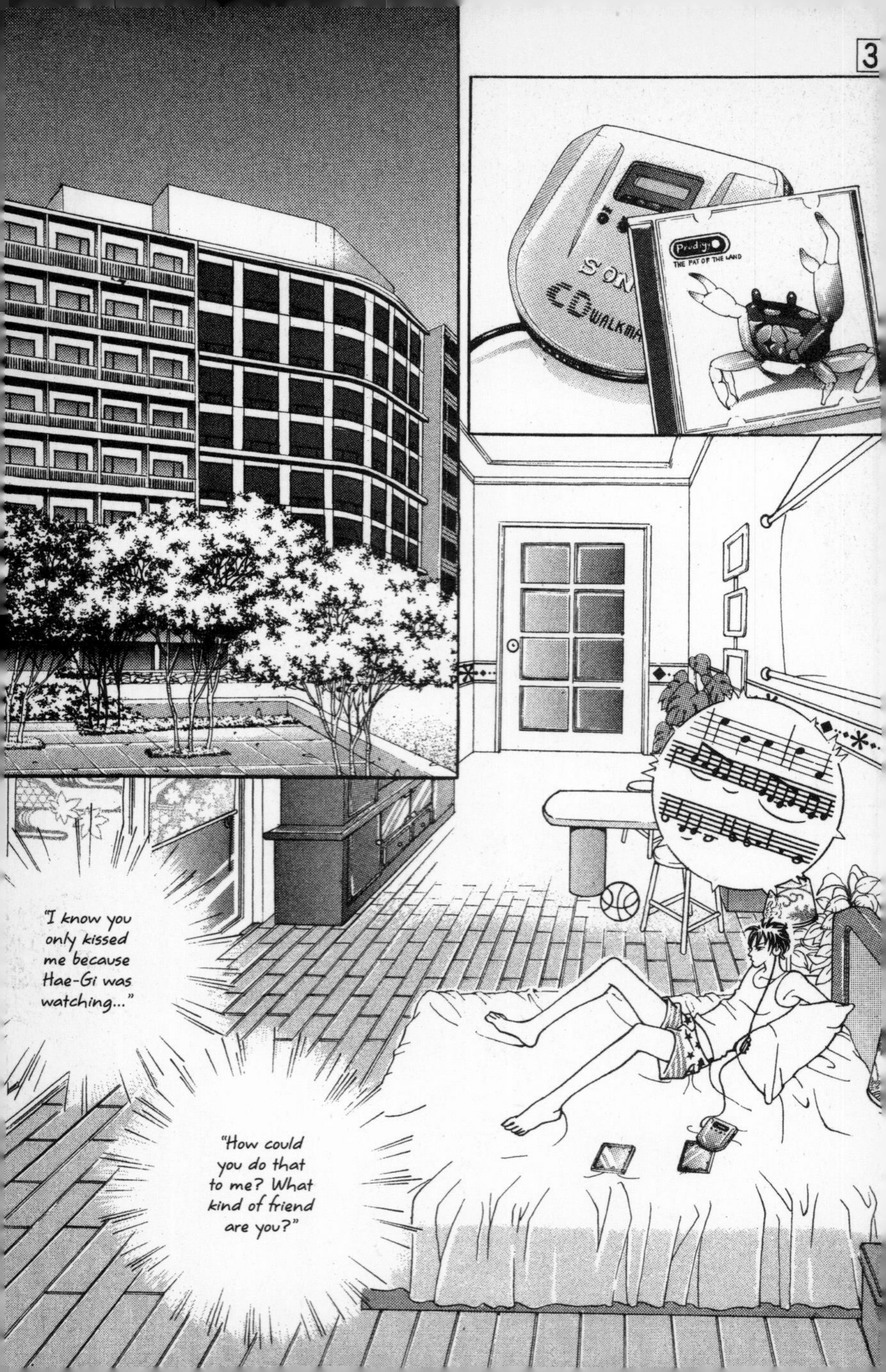
3
"I know you only kissed me because Hae-Gi was watching..."
"How could you do that to me? What kind of friend are you?"

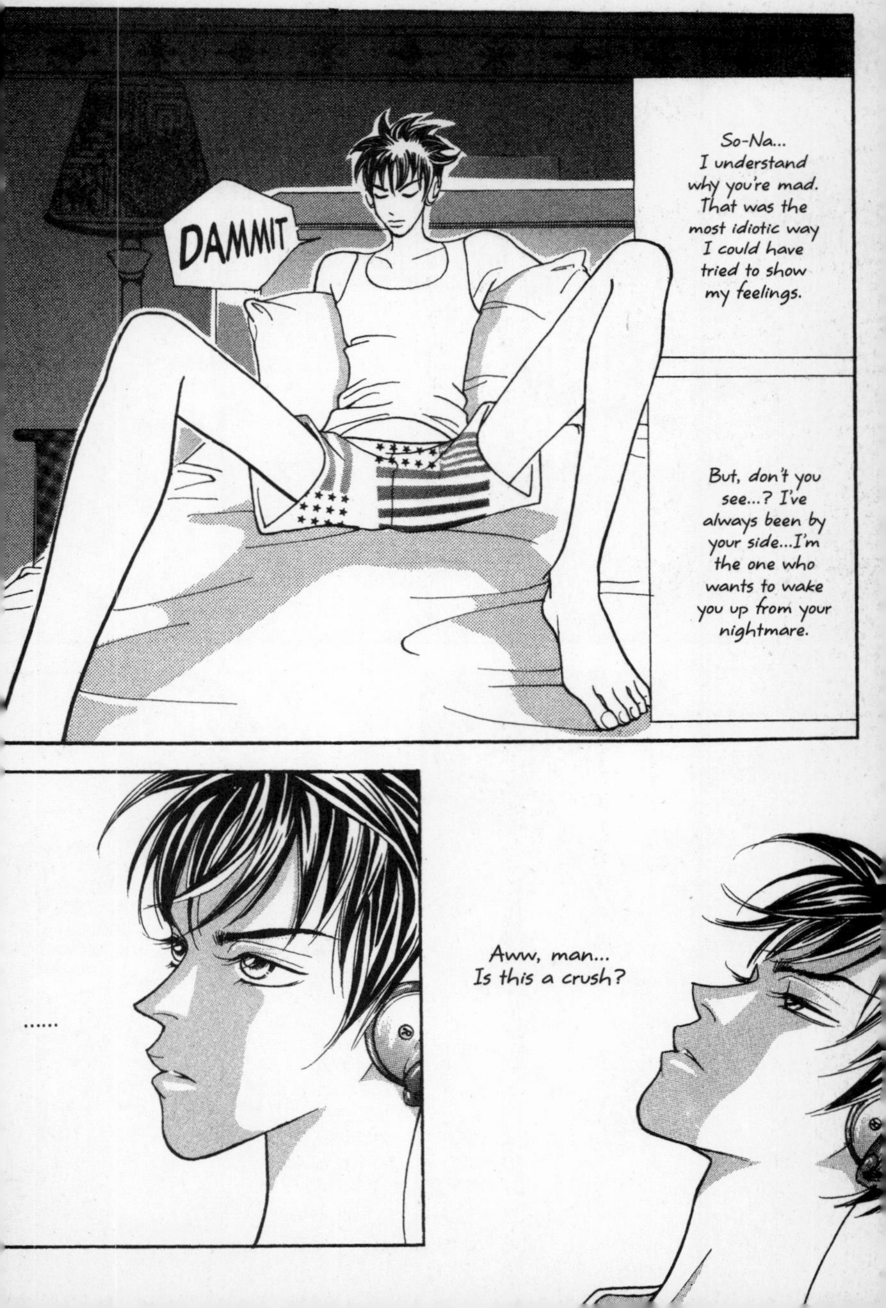
DAMMIT
So-Na... I understand why you're mad. That was the most idiotic way I could have tried to show my feelings.
But, don't you see...? I've always been by your side...I'm the one who wants to wake you up from your nightmare.
......
Aww, man... Is this a crush?

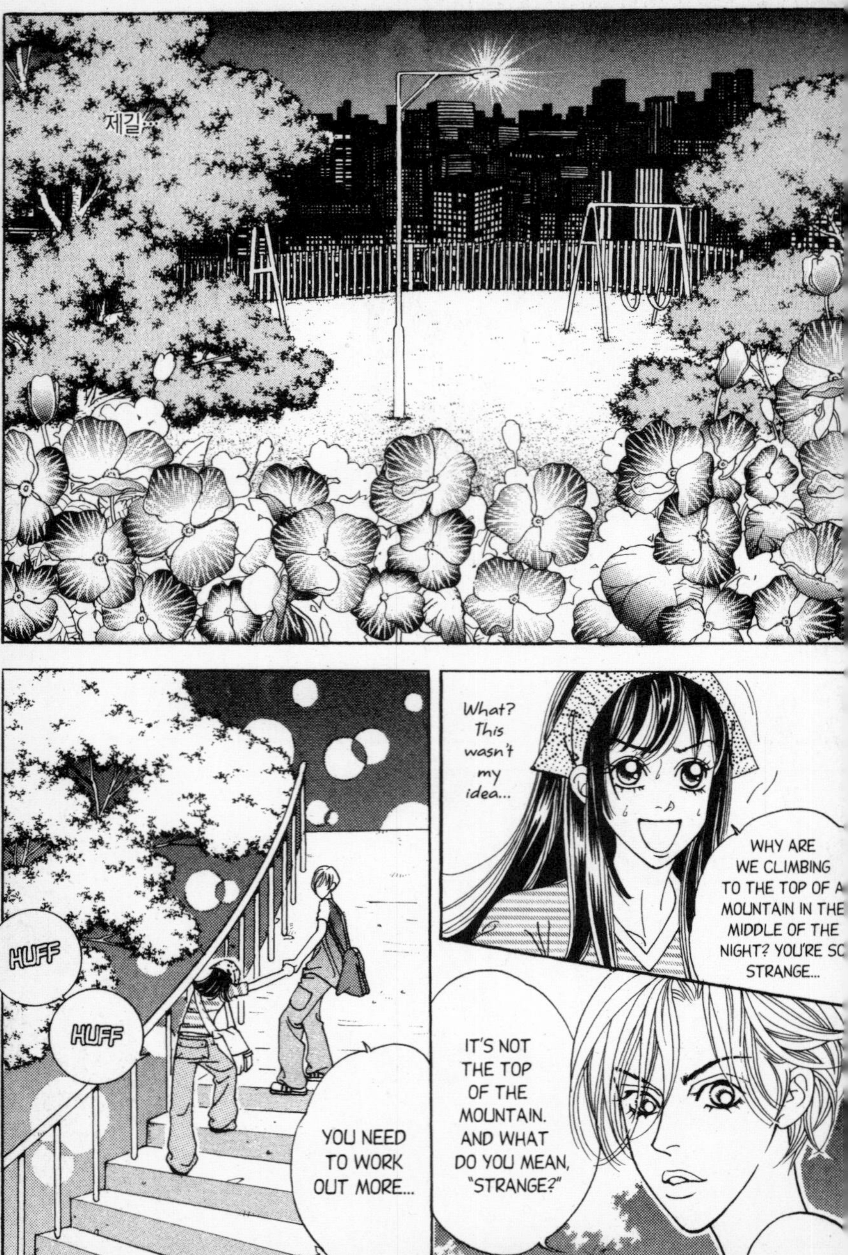

제길...
HUFF
HUFF
YOU NEED TO WORK OUT MORE...
What? This wasn't my idea...
WHY ARE WE CLIMBING TO THE TOP OF A MOUNTAIN IN THE MIDDLE OF THE NIGHT? YOU'RE SO STRANGE...
IT'S NOT THE TOP OF THE MOUNTAIN. AND WHAT DO YOU MEAN, "STRANGE?"

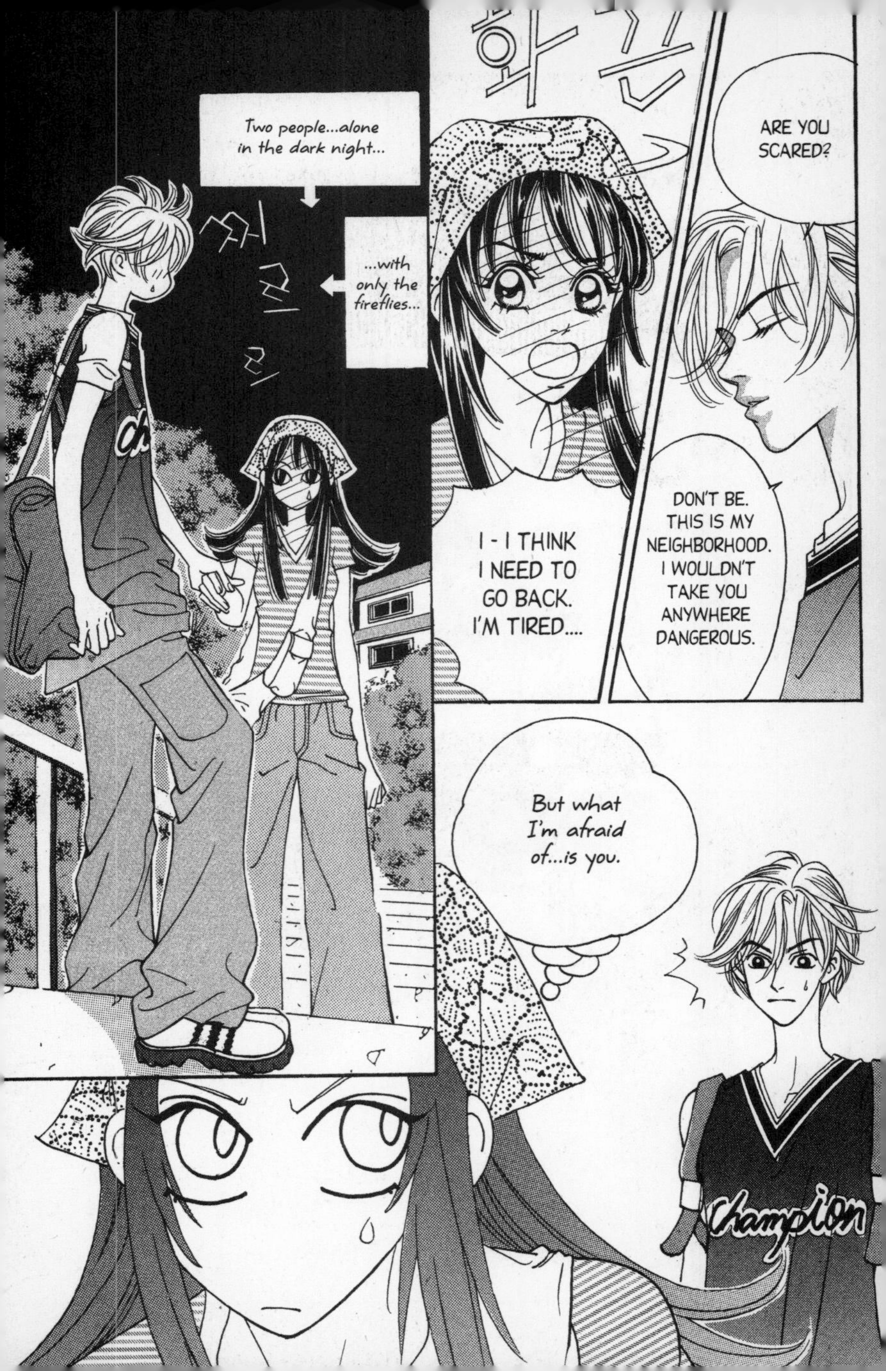
Two people...alone in the dark night...
...with only the fireflies...
화끈
ARE YOU SCARED?
I - I THINK I NEED TO GO BACK. I'M TIRED....
DON'T BE. THIS IS MY NEIGHBORHOOD. I WOULDN'T TAKE YOU ANYWHERE DANGEROUS.
But what I'm afraid of...is you.
Champion

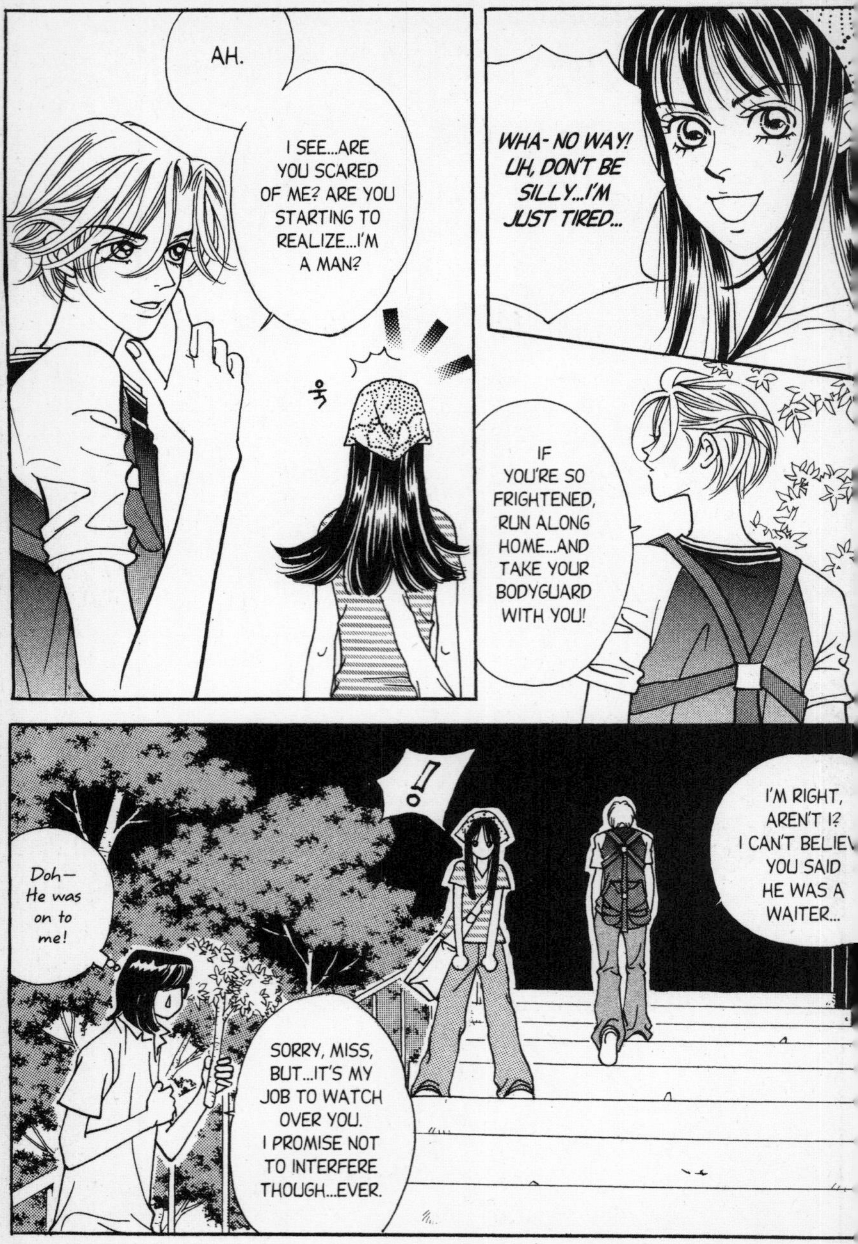
AH.
I SEE...ARE YOU SCARED OF ME? ARE YOU STARTING TO REALIZE...I'M A MAN?
WHA- NO WAY! UH, DON'T BE SILLY...I'M JUST TIRED...
IF YOU'RE SO FRIGHTENED, RUN ALONG HOME...AND TAKE YOUR BODYGUARD WITH YOU!
Doh— He was on to me!
!
I'M RIGHT, AREN'T I? I CAN'T BELIEV YOU SAID HE WAS A WAITER...
SORRY, MISS, BUT...IT'S MY JOB TO WATCH OVER YOU. I PROMISE NOT TO INTERFERE THOUGH...EVER.

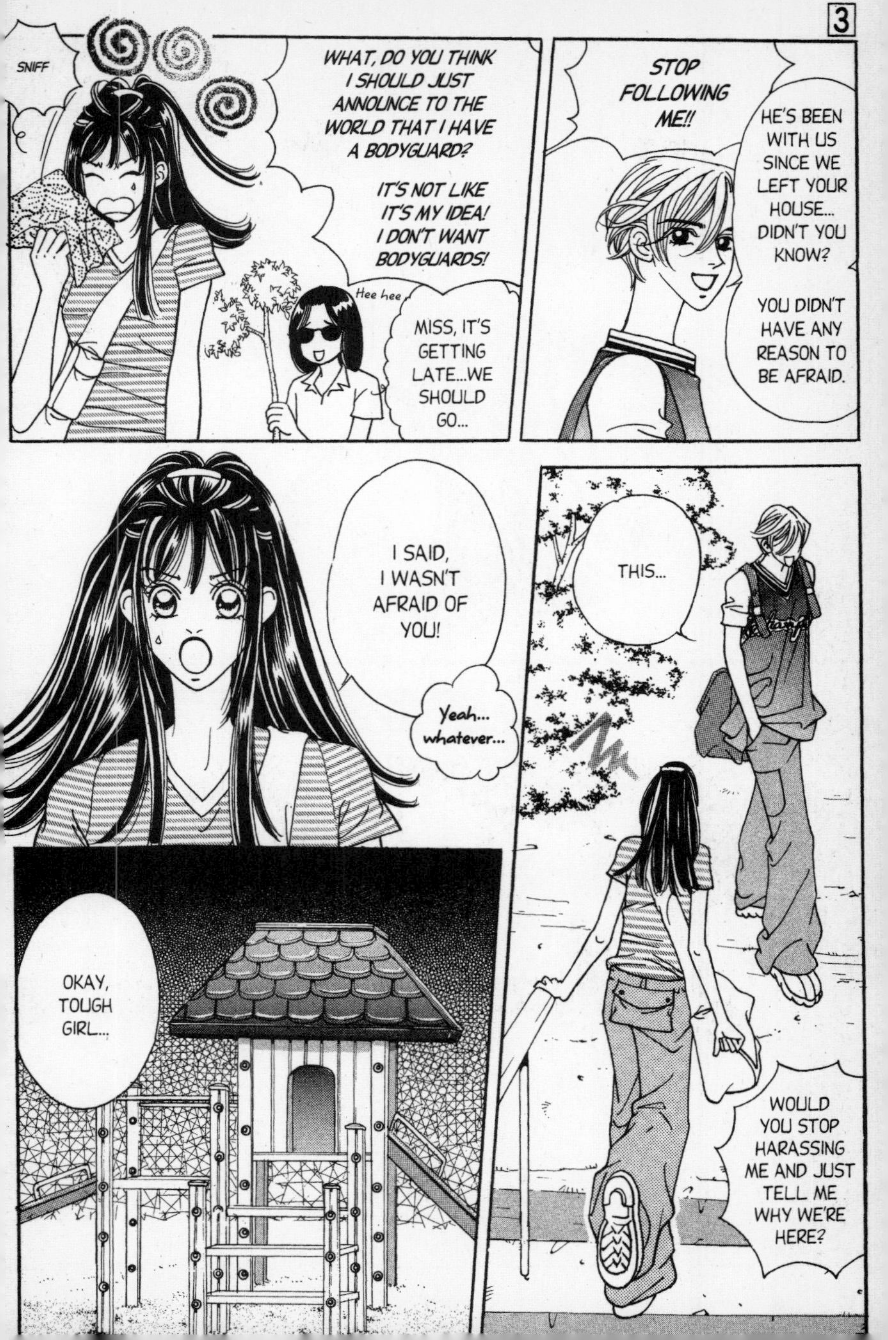
3
SNIFF
WHAT, DO YOU THINK I SHOULD JUST ANNOUNCE TO THE WORLD THAT I HAVE A BODYGUARD?
IT'S NOT LIKE IT'S MY IDEA! I DON'T WANT BODYGUARDS!
Hee hee
MISS, IT'S GETTING LATE...WE SHOULD GO...
STOP FOLLOWING ME!!
HE'S BEEN WITH US SINCE WE LEFT YOUR HOUSE... DIDN'T YOU KNOW?
YOU DIDN'T HAVE ANY REASON TO BE AFRAID.
I SAID, I WASN'T AFRAID OF YOU!
Yeah... whatever...
OKAY, TOUGH GIRL...
THIS...
WOULD YOU STOP HARASSING ME AND JUST TELL ME WHY WE'RE HERE?

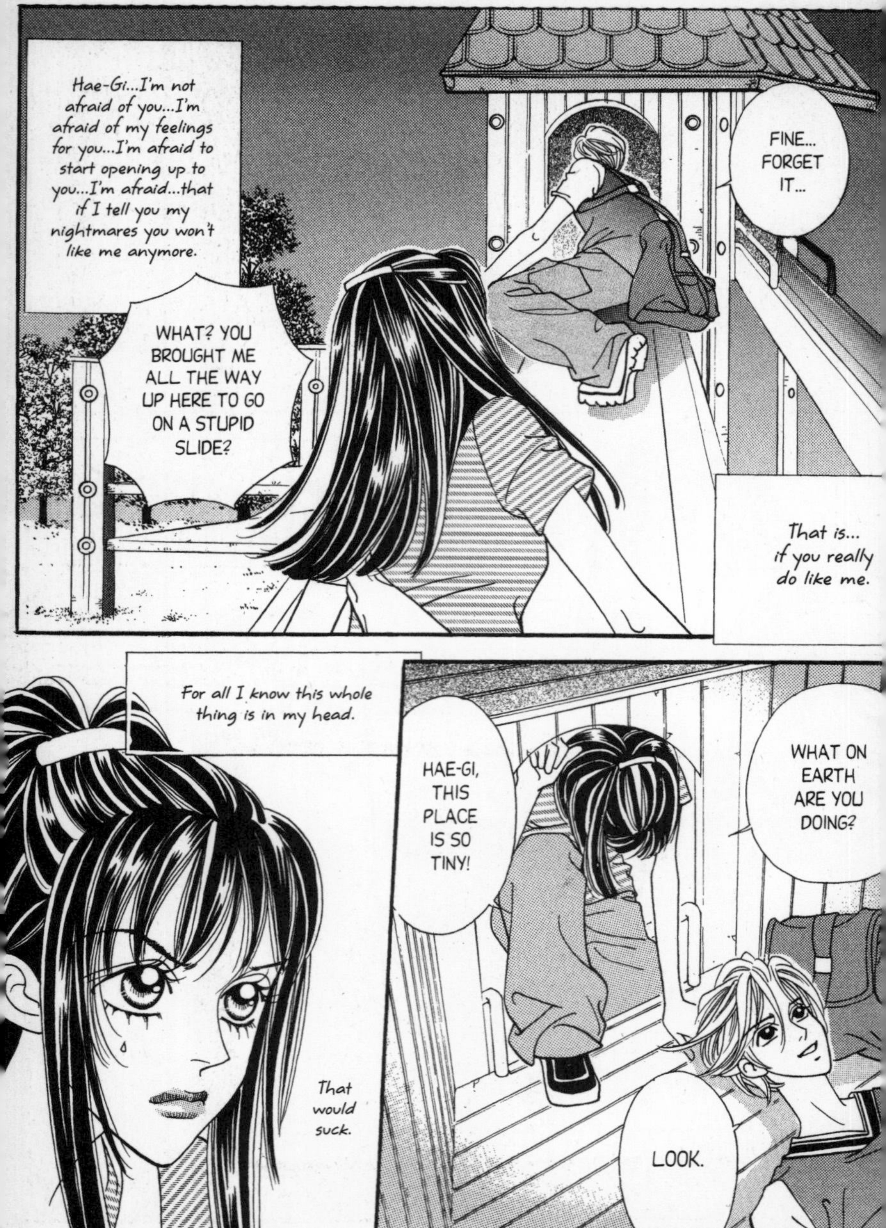
Hae-Gi...I'm not afraid of you...I'm afraid of my feelings for you...I'm afraid to start opening up to you...I'm afraid...that if I tell you my nightmares you won't like me anymore.
WHAT? YOU BROUGHT ME ALL THE WAY UP HERE TO GO ON A STUPID SLIDE?
FINE... FORGET IT...
That is... if you really do like me.
For all I know this whole thing is in my head.
That would suck.
HAE-GI, THIS PLACE IS SO TINY!
WHAT ON EARTH ARE YOU DOING?
LOOK.

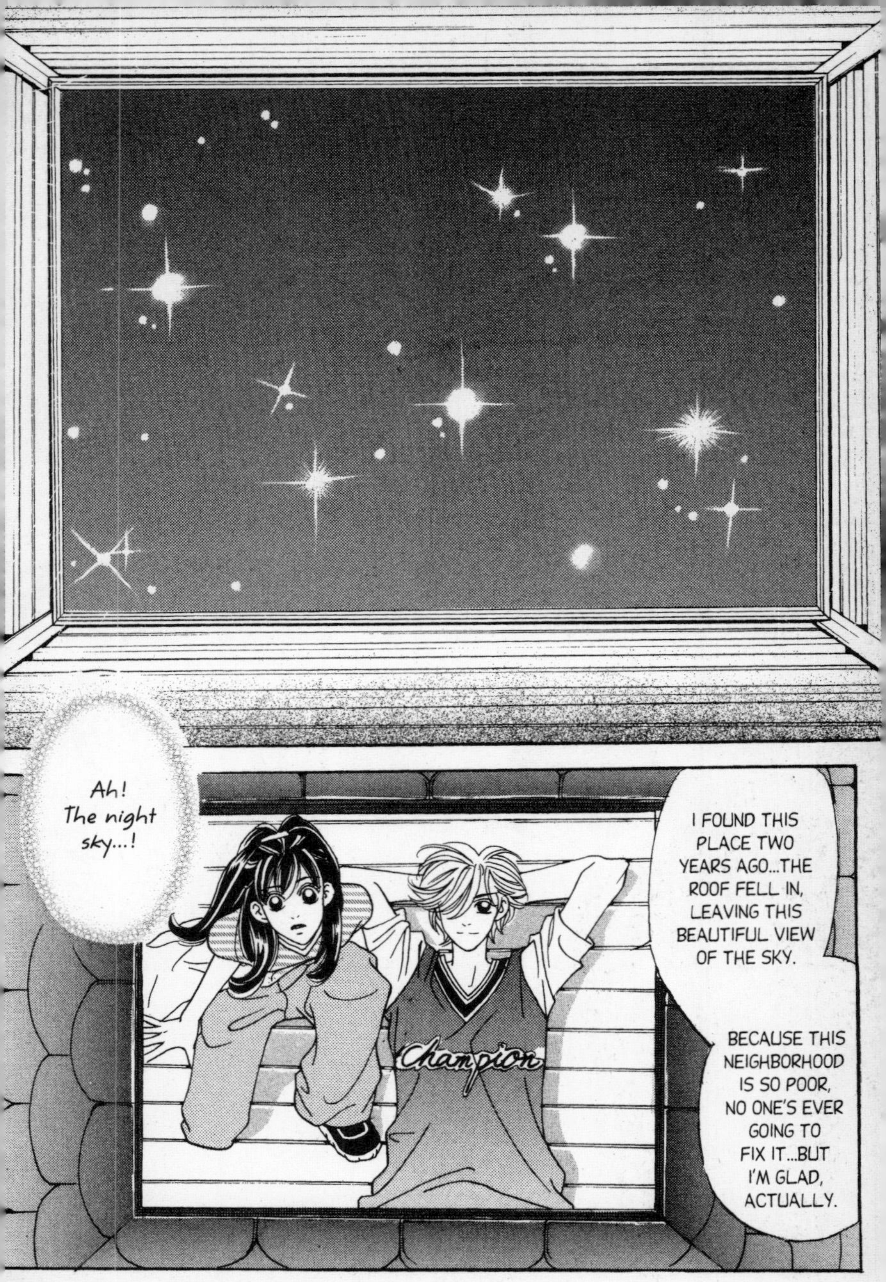
Ah! The night sky...!
I FOUND THIS PLACE TWO YEARS AGO...THE ROOF FELL IN, LEAVING THIS BEAUTIFUL VIEW OF THE SKY.
BECAUSE THIS NEIGHBORHOOD IS SO POOR, NO ONE'S EVER GOING TO FIX IT...BUT I'M GLAD, ACTUALLY.
Champion

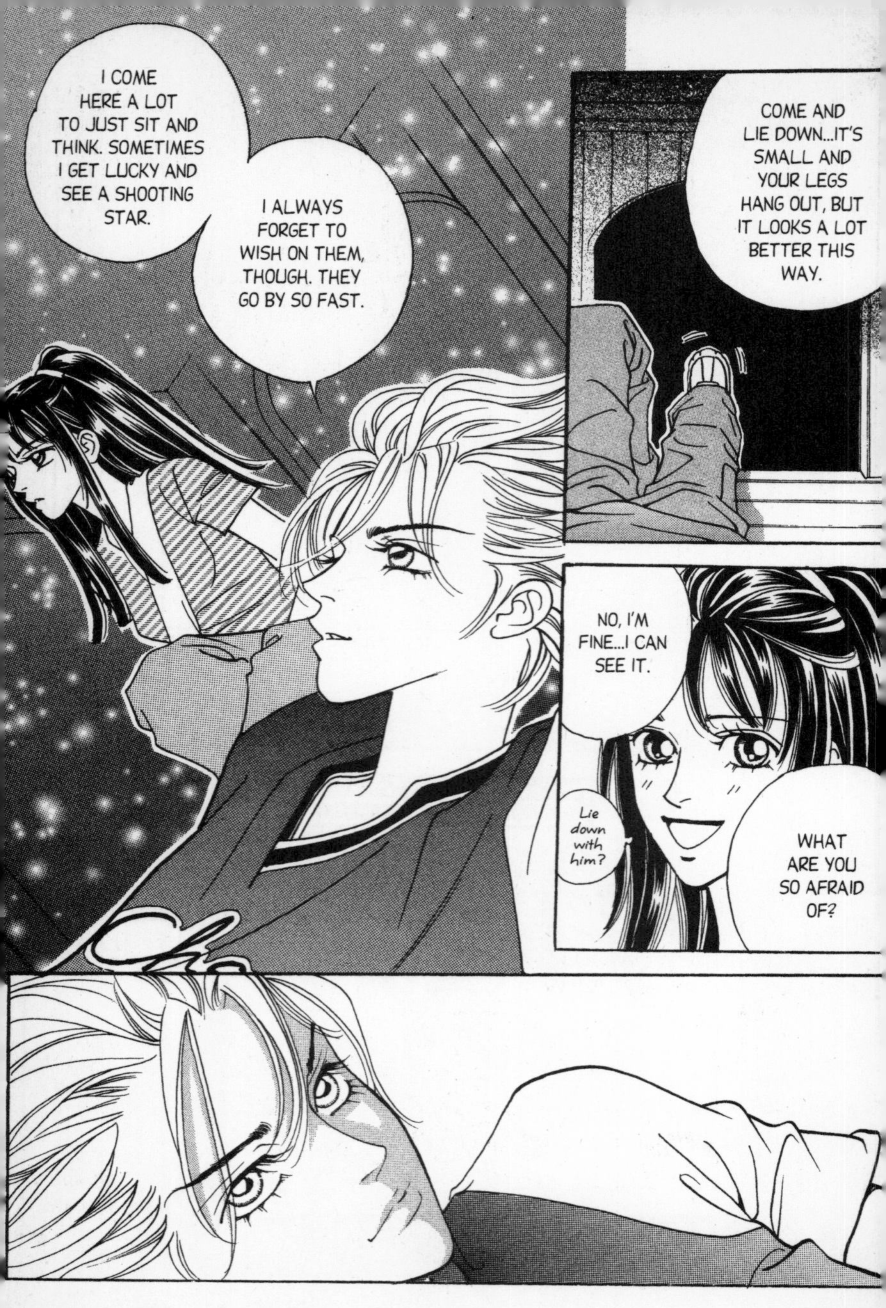
I COME HERE A LOT TO JUST SIT AND THINK. SOMETIMES I GET LUCKY AND SEE A SHOOTING STAR.
I ALWAYS FORGET TO WISH ON THEM, THOUGH. THEY GO BY SO FAST.
Cha
COME AND LIE DOWN...IT'S SMALL AND YOUR LEGS HANG OUT, BUT IT LOOKS A LOT BETTER THIS WAY.
NO, I'M FINE...I CAN SEE IT.
Lie down with him?
WHAT ARE YOU SO AFRAID OF?

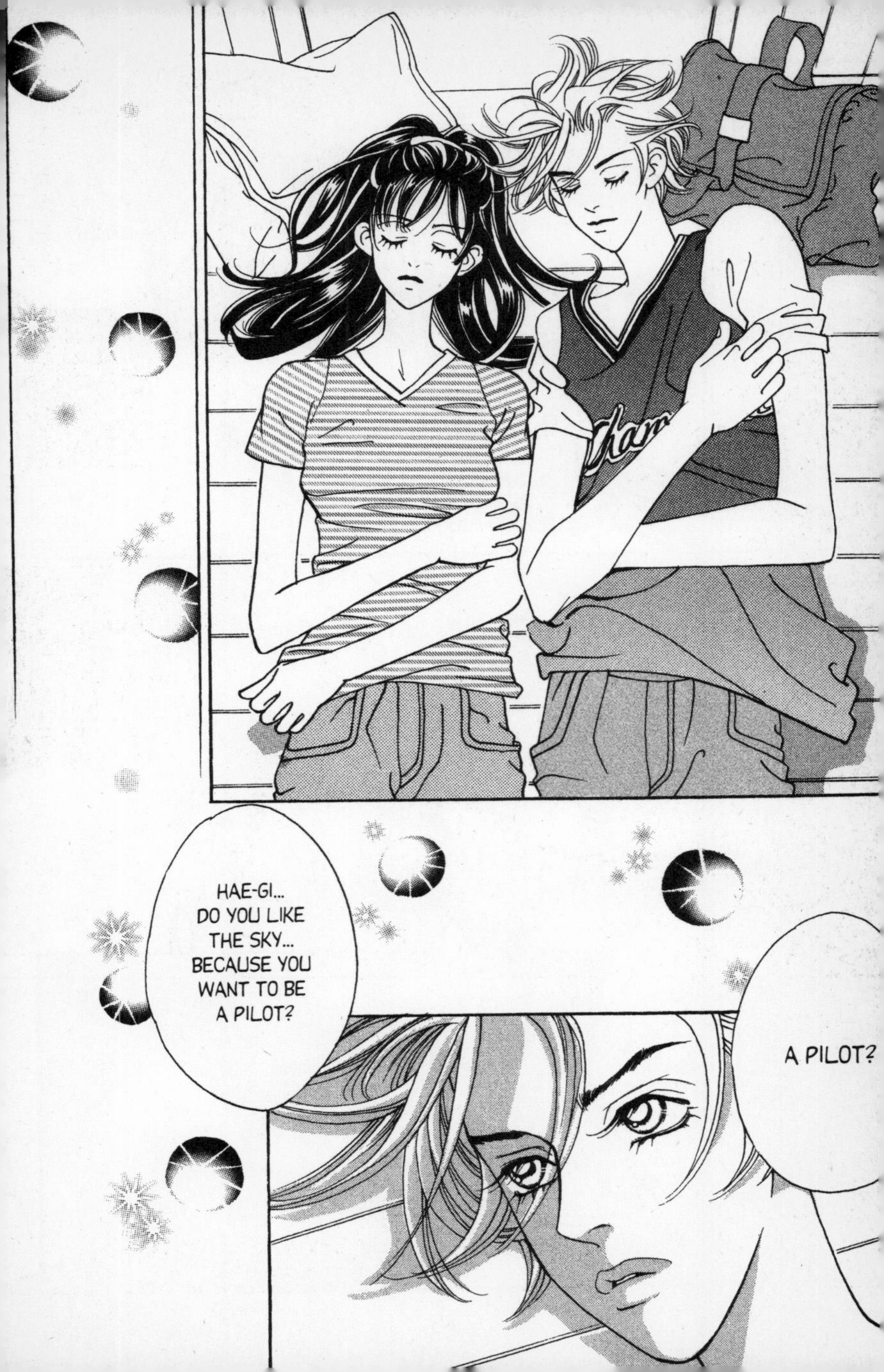
HAE-GI... DO YOU LIKE THE SKY... BECAUSE YOU WANT TO BE A PILOT?
A PILOT?

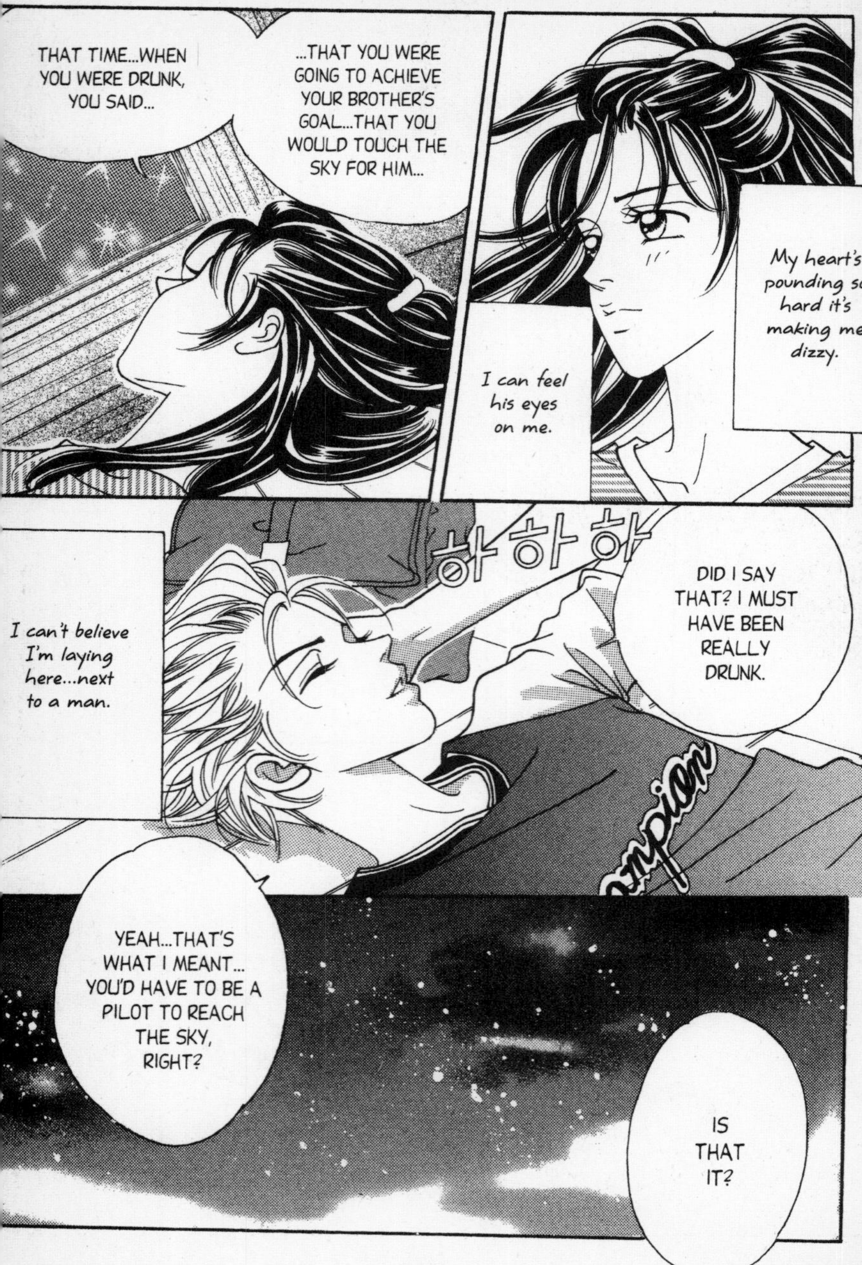
THAT TIME...WHEN YOU WERE DRUNK, YOU SAID...
...THAT YOU WERE GOING TO ACHIEVE YOUR BROTHER'S GOAL...THAT YOU WOULD TOUCH THE SKY FOR HIM...
My heart's pounding so hard it's making me dizzy.
I can feel his eyes on me.
I can't believe I'm laying here...next to a man.
하하하
DID I SAY THAT? I MUST HAVE BEEN REALLY DRUNK.
Champion
YEAH...THAT'S WHAT I MEANT... YOU'D HAVE TO BE A PILOT TO REACH THE SKY, RIGHT?
IS THAT IT?

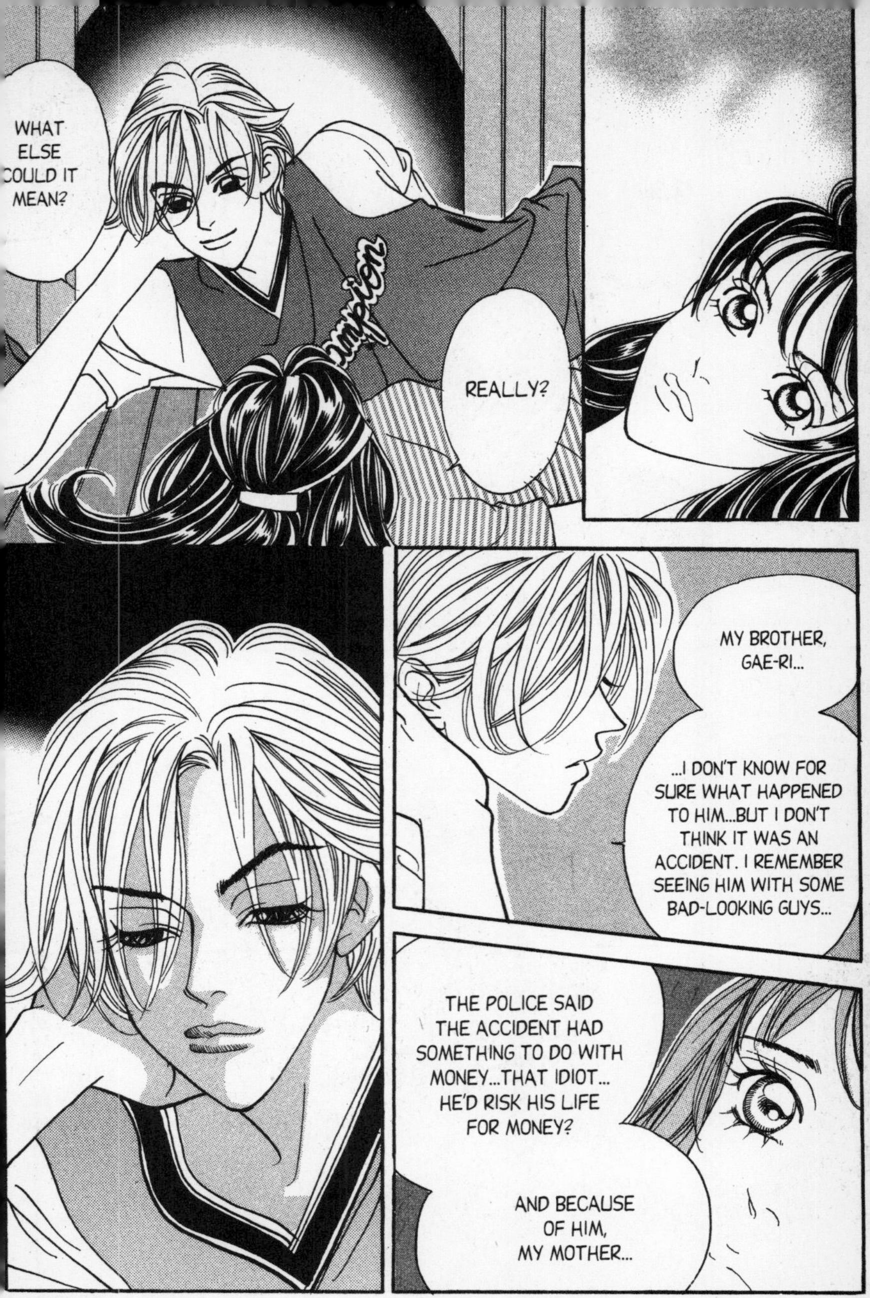
WHAT ELSE COULD IT MEAN?
REALLY?
MY BROTHER, GAE-RI...
...I DON'T KNOW FOR SURE WHAT HAPPENED TO HIM...BUT I DON'T THINK IT WAS AN ACCIDENT. I REMEMBER SEEING HIM WITH SOME BAD-LOOKING GUYS...
THE POLICE SAID THE ACCIDENT HAD SOMETHING TO DO WITH MONEY...THAT IDIOT... HE'D RISK HIS LIFE FOR MONEY?
AND BECAUSE OF HIM, MY MOTHER...

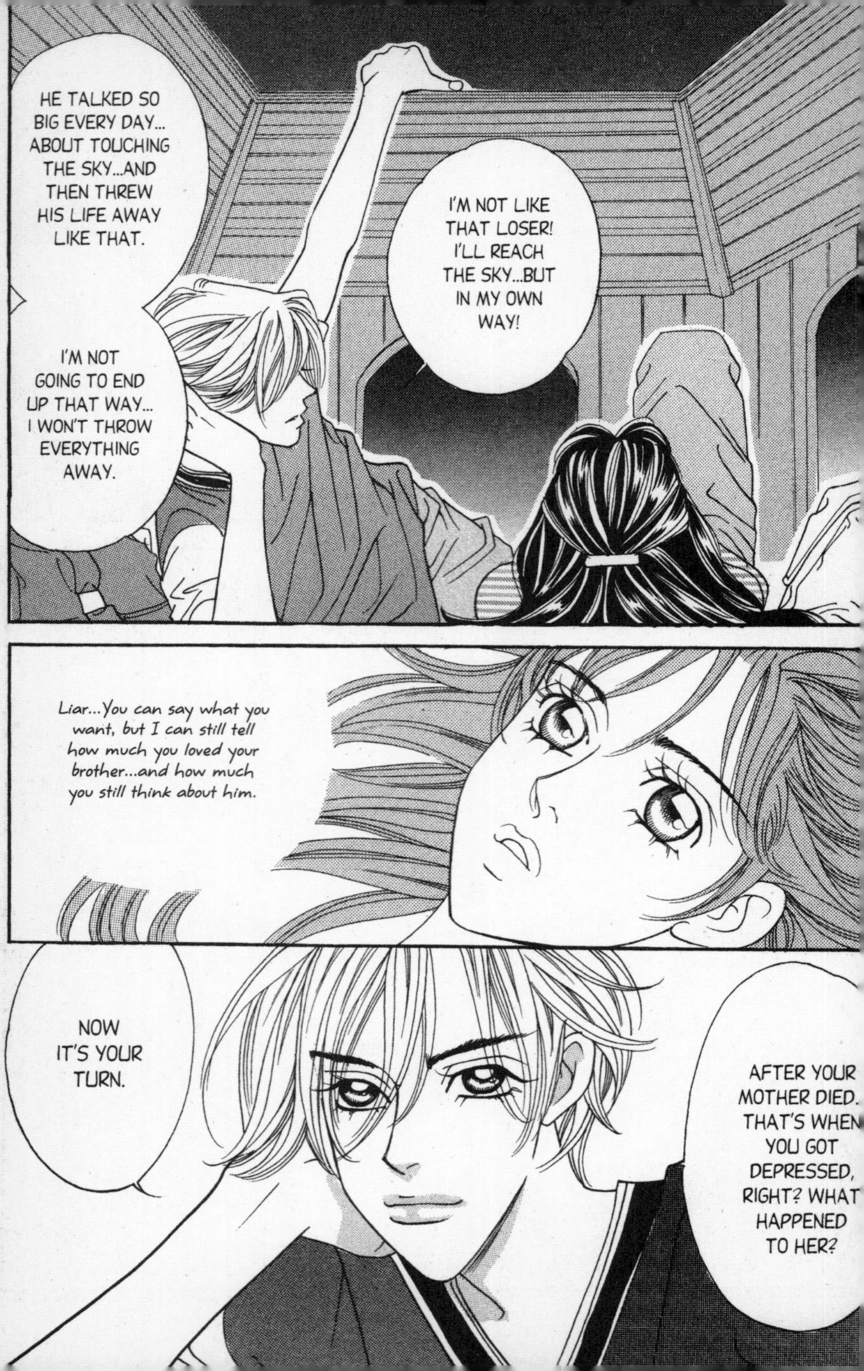
HE TALKED SO BIG EVERY DAY... ABOUT TOUCHING THE SKY...AND THEN THREW HIS LIFE AWAY LIKE THAT.
I'M NOT LIKE THAT LOSER! I'LL REACH THE SKY...BUT IN MY OWN WAY!
I'M NOT GOING TO END UP THAT WAY... I WON'T THROW EVERYTHING AWAY.
Liar...You can say what you want, but I can still tell how much you loved your brother...and how much you still think about him.
NOW IT'S YOUR TURN.
AFTER YOUR MOTHER DIED. THAT'S WHEN YOU GOT DEPRESSED, RIGHT? WHAT HAPPENED TO HER?

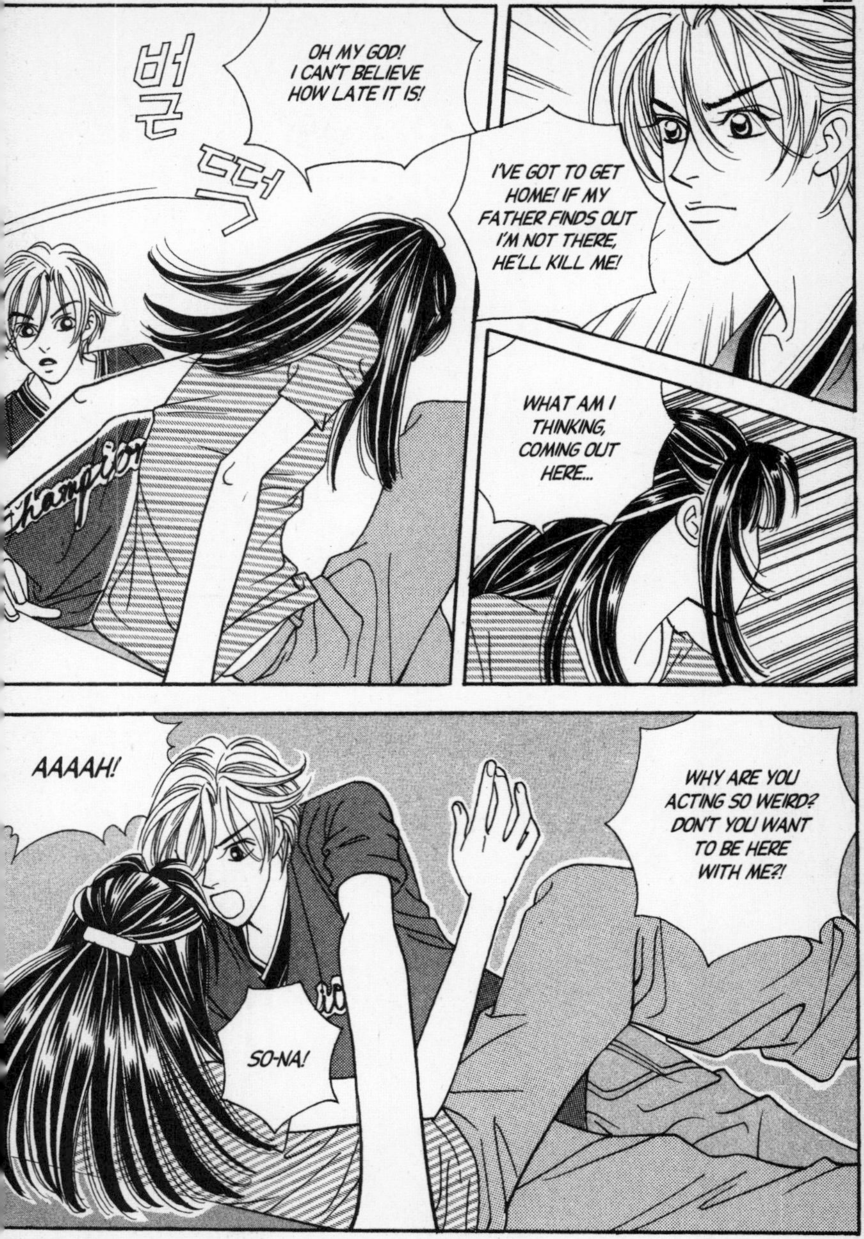
벌떡
OH MY GOD! I CAN'T BELIEVE HOW LATE IT IS!
I'VE GOT TO GET HOME! IF MY FATHER FINDS OUT I'M NOT THERE, HE'LL KILL ME!
WHAT AM I THINKING, COMING OUT HERE...
AAAAH!
SO-NA!
WHY ARE YOU ACTING SO WEIRD? DON'T YOU WANT TO BE HERE WITH ME?!

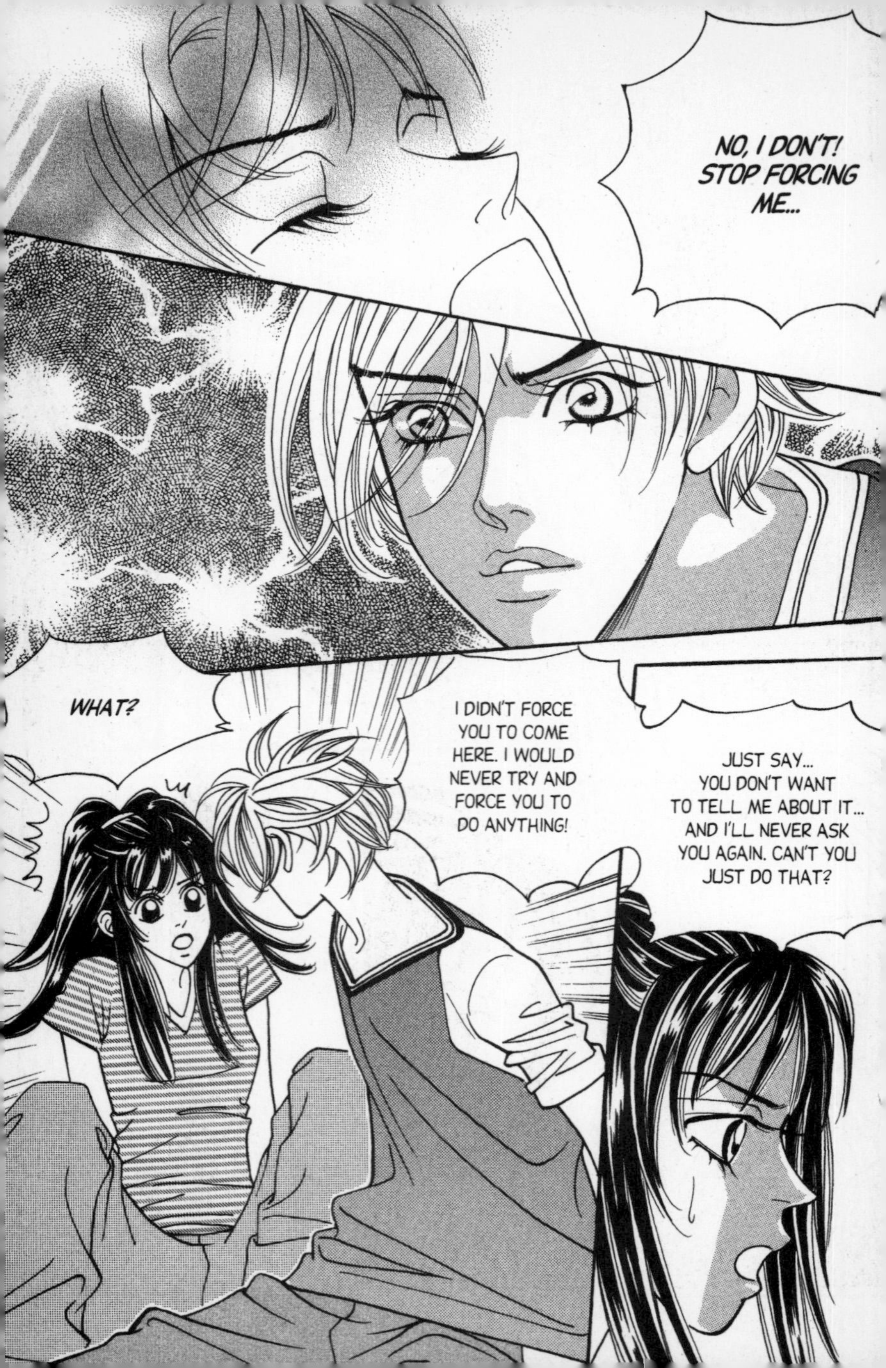
NO, I DON'T! STOP FORCING ME...
WHAT?
I DIDN'T FORCE YOU TO COME HERE. I WOULD NEVER TRY AND FORCE YOU TO DO ANYTHING!
JUST SAY... YOU DON'T WANT TO TELL ME ABOUT IT... AND I'LL NEVER ASK YOU AGAIN. CAN'T YOU JUST DO THAT?

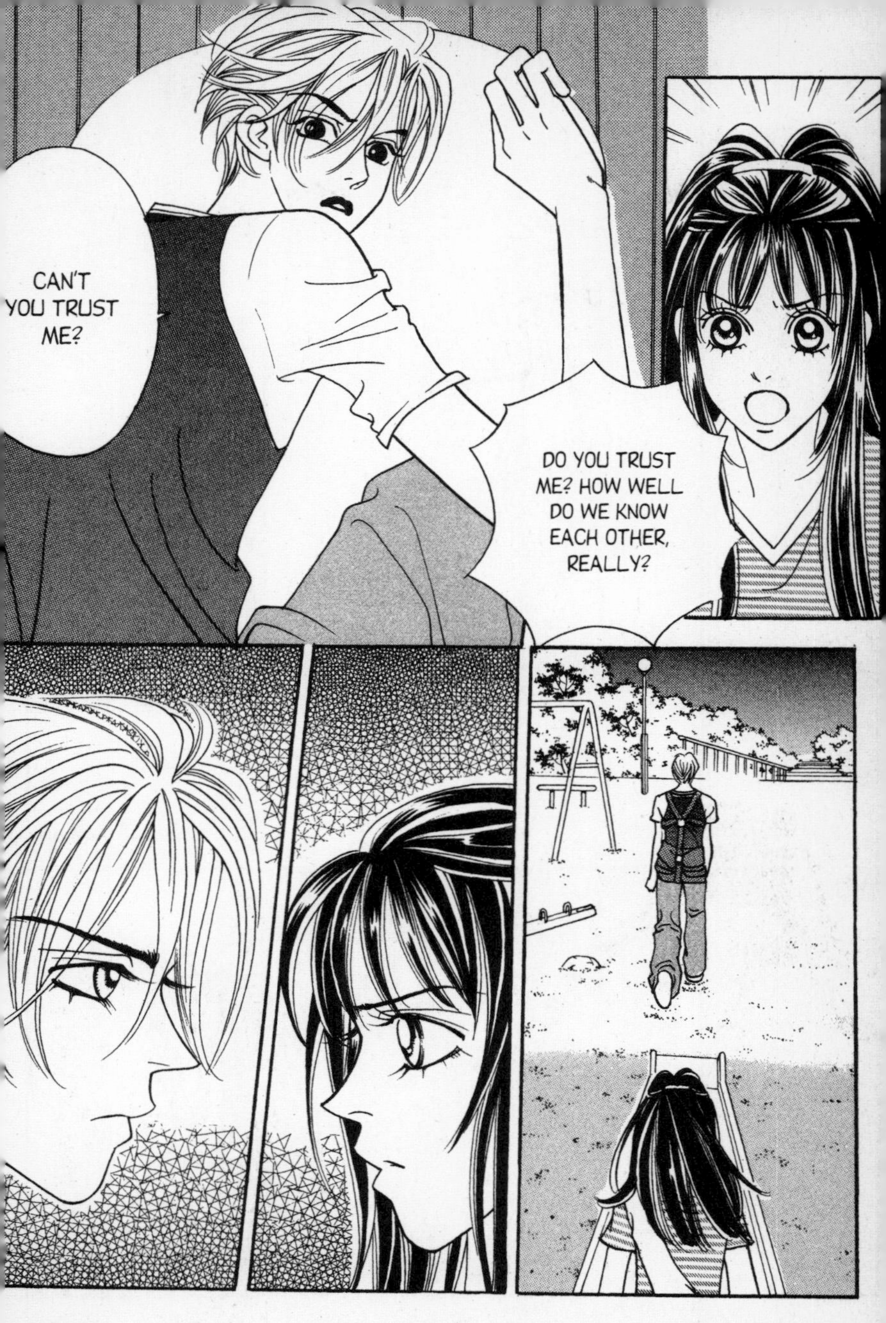
CAN'T YOU TRUST ME?
DO YOU TRUST ME? HOW WELL DO WE KNOW EACH OTHER, REALLY?

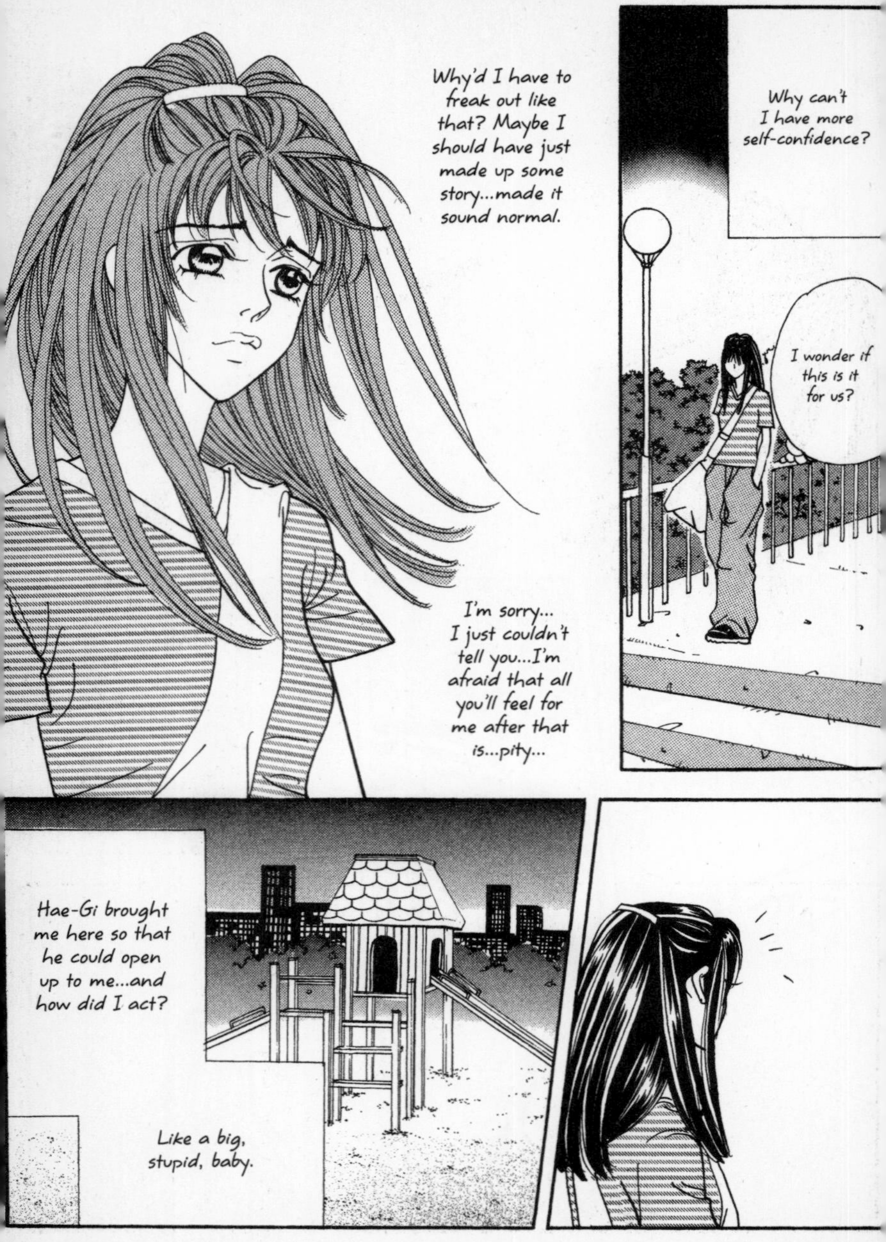
Why'd I have to freak out like that? Maybe I should have just made up some story...made it sound normal.
I'm sorry... I just couldn't tell you...I'm afraid that all you'll feel for me after that is...pity...
Why can't I have more self-confidence?
I wonder if this is it for us?
Hae-Gi brought me here so that he could open up to me...and how did I act?
Like a big, stupid, baby.

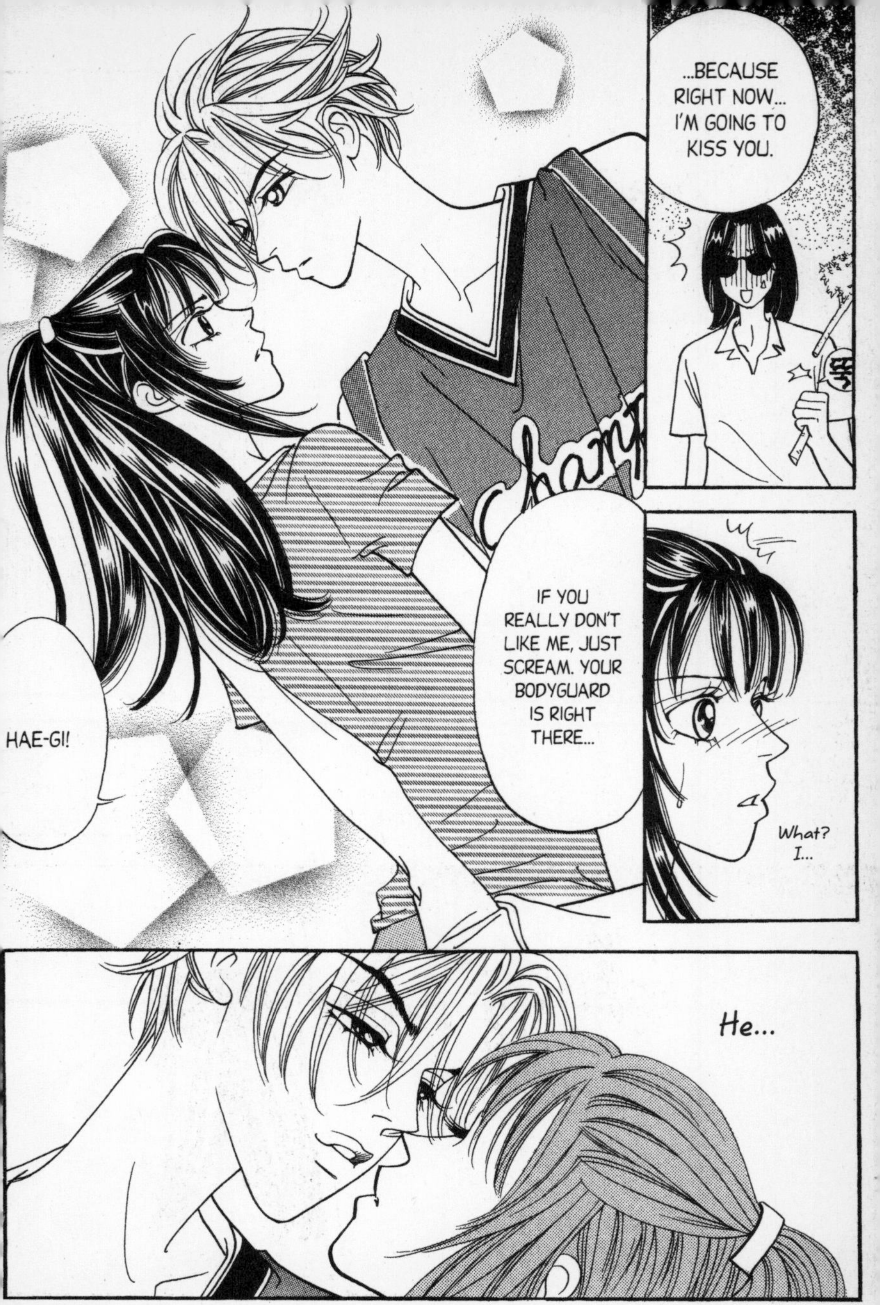
IF YOU REALLY DON'T LIKE ME, JUST SCREAM. YOUR BODYGUARD IS RIGHT THERE...
HAE-GI!
...BECAUSE RIGHT NOW... I'M GOING TO KISS YOU.
What? I...
He...

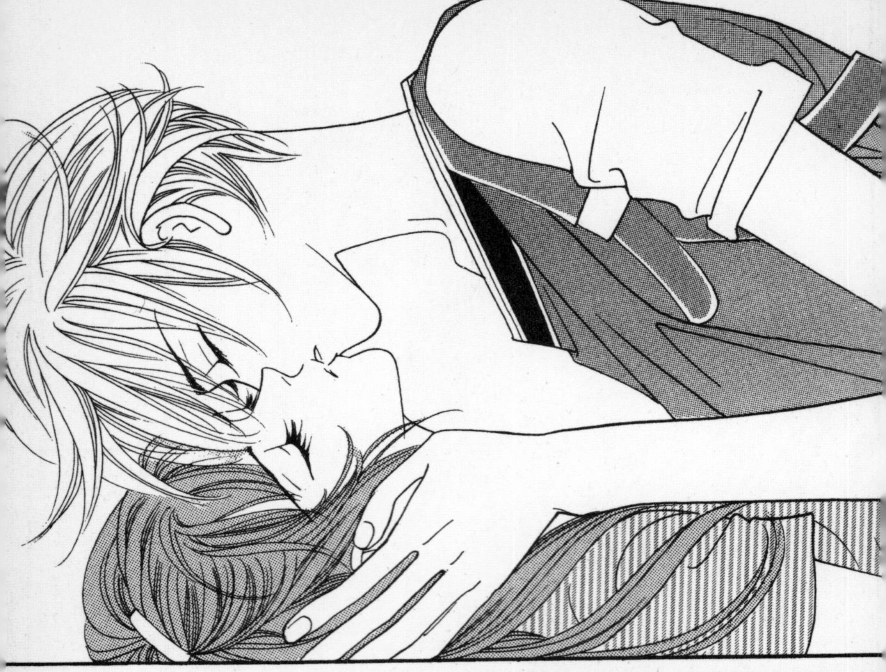

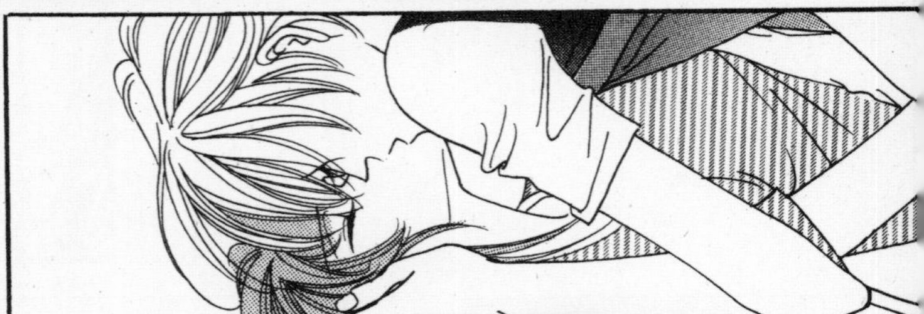

I...I can't even
make a sound...

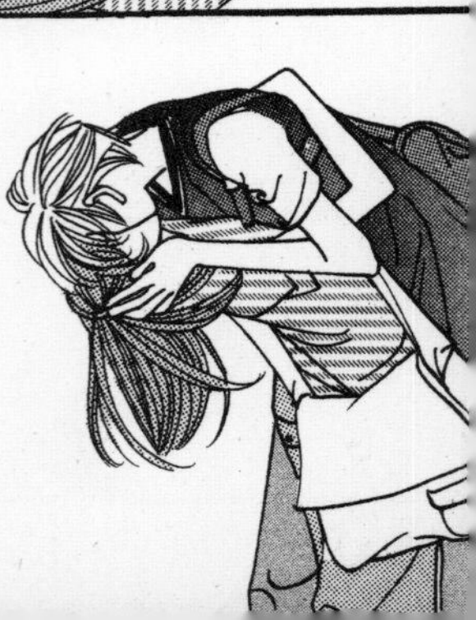

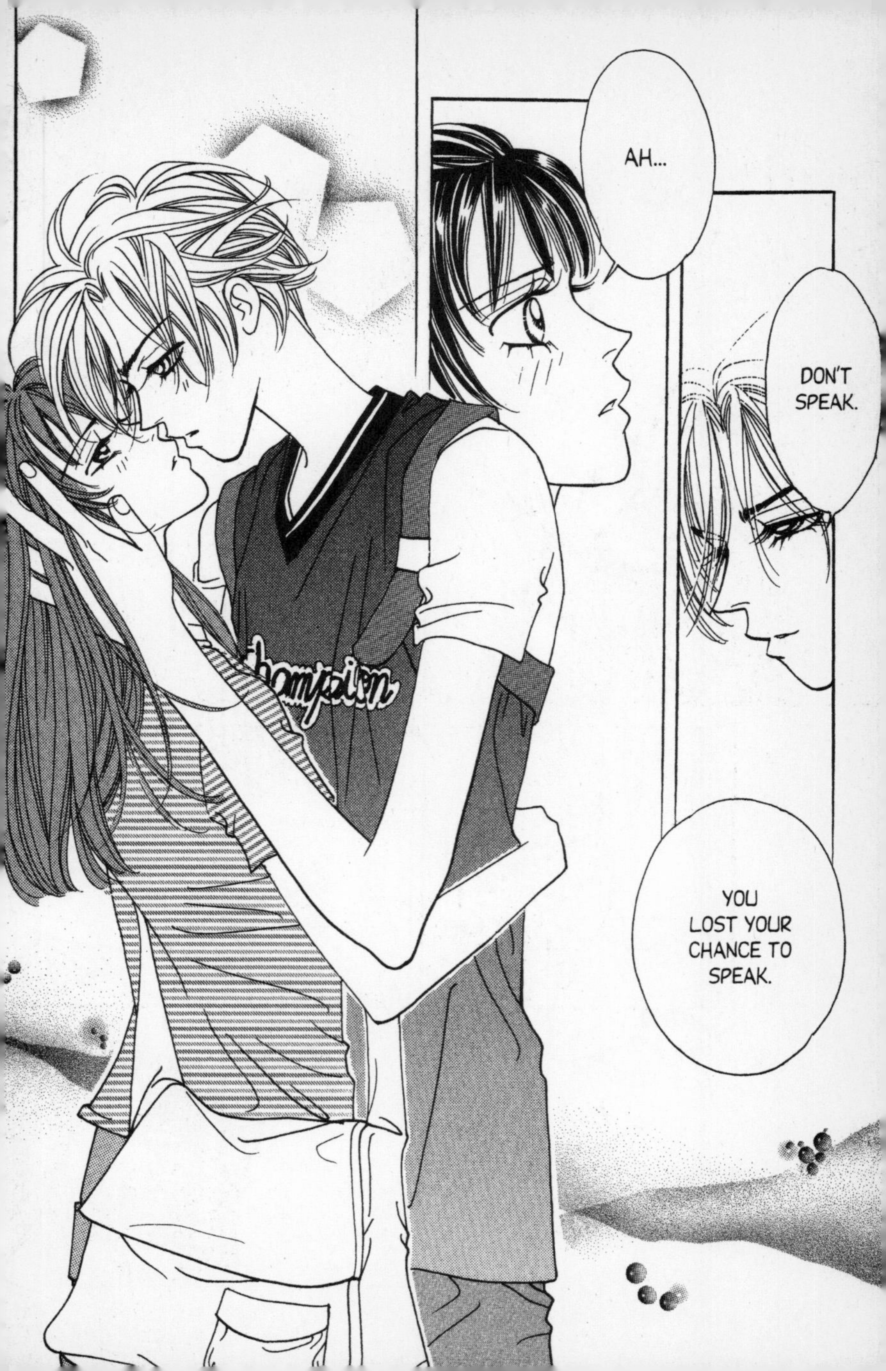
AH...
DON'T SPEAK.
YOU LOST YOUR CHANCE TO SPEAK.

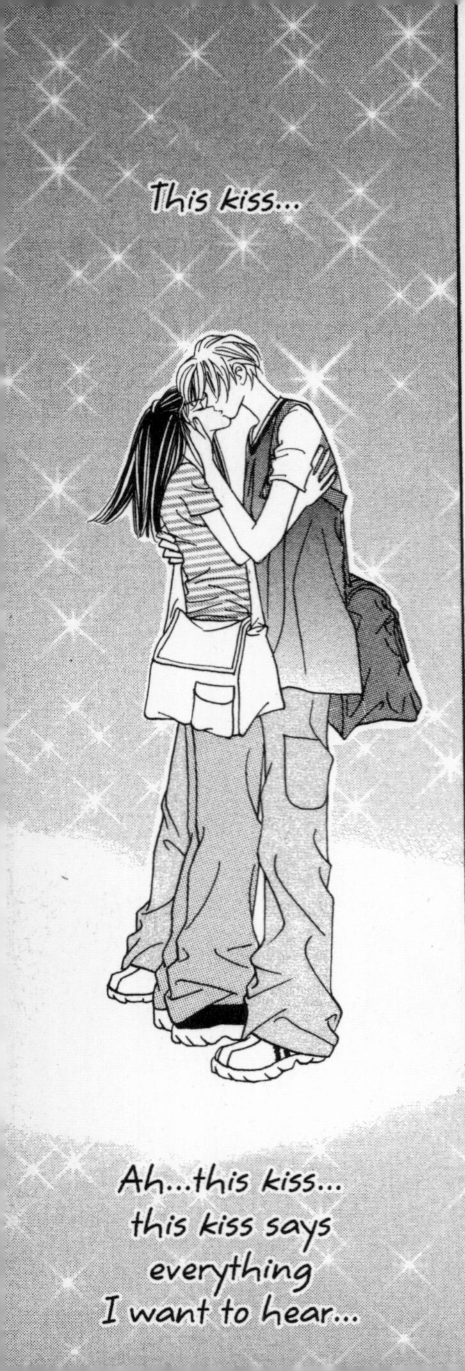
This kiss...
Ah...this kiss... this kiss says everything I want to hear...

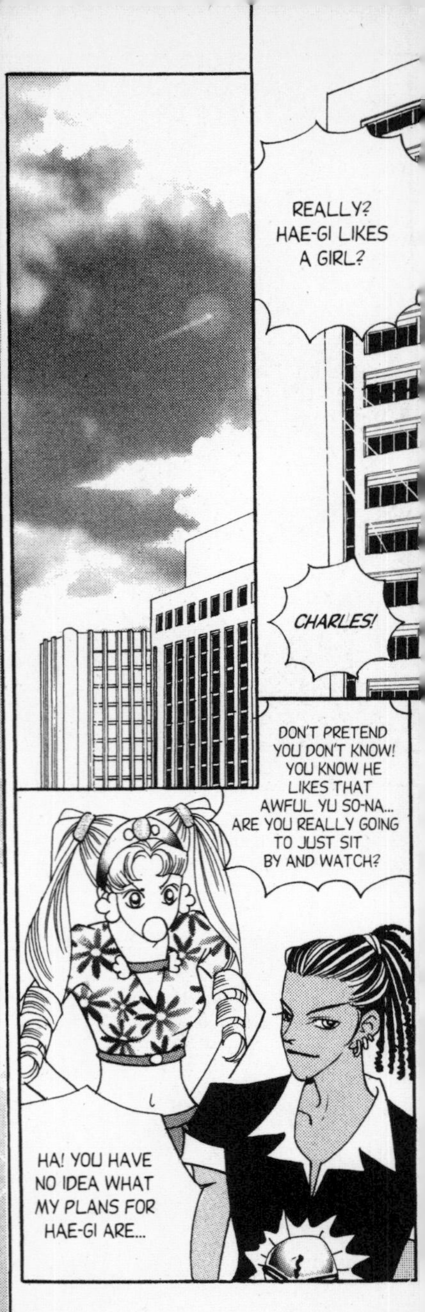
REALLY? HAE-GI LIKES A GIRL?
CHARLES!
DON'T PRETEND YOU DON'T KNOW! YOU KNOW HE LIKES THAT AWFUL YU SO-NA... ARE YOU REALLY GOING TO JUST SIT BY AND WATCH?
HA! YOU HAVE NO IDEA WHAT MY PLANS FOR HAE-GI ARE...

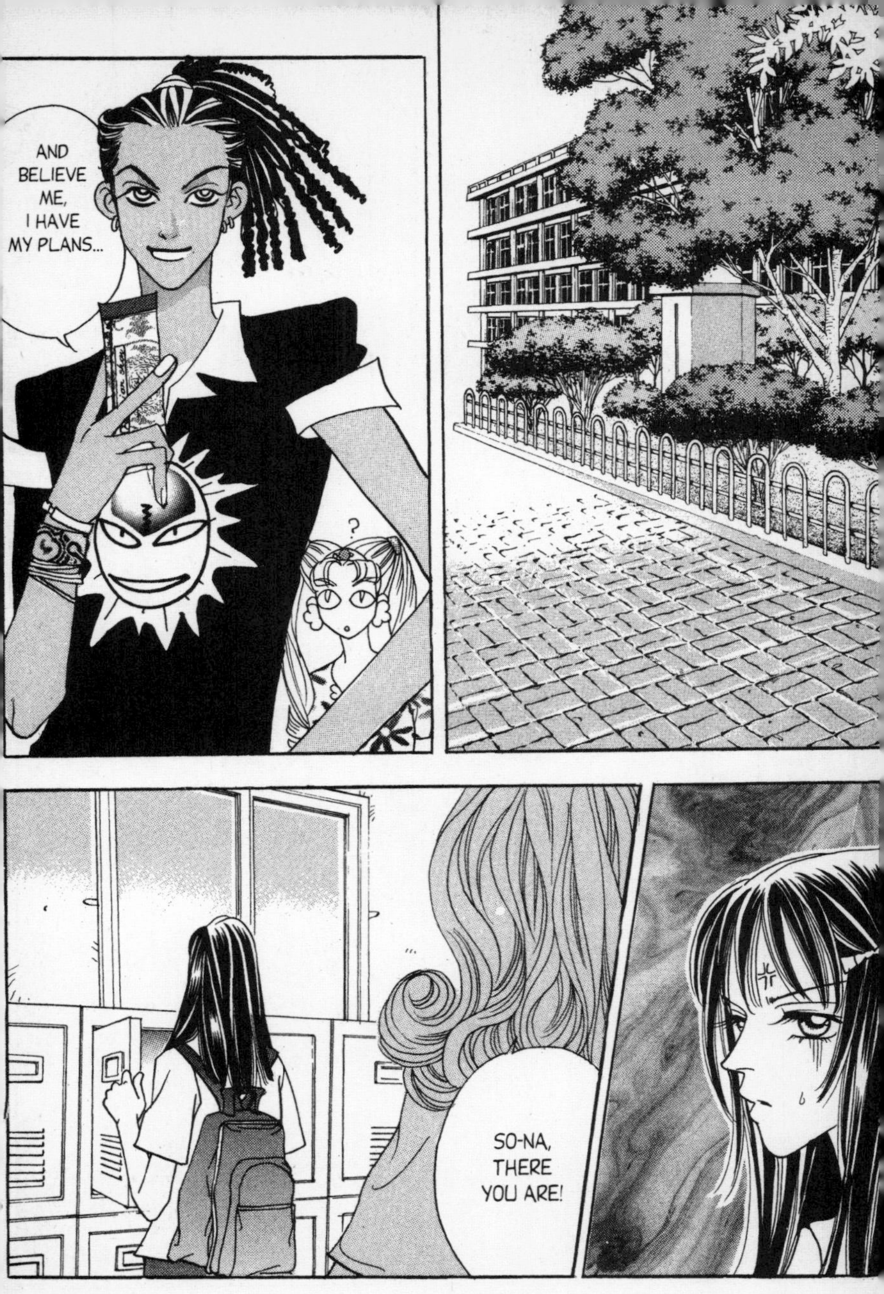
AND BELIEVE ME, I HAVE MY PLANS...
?
SO-NA, THERE YOU ARE!

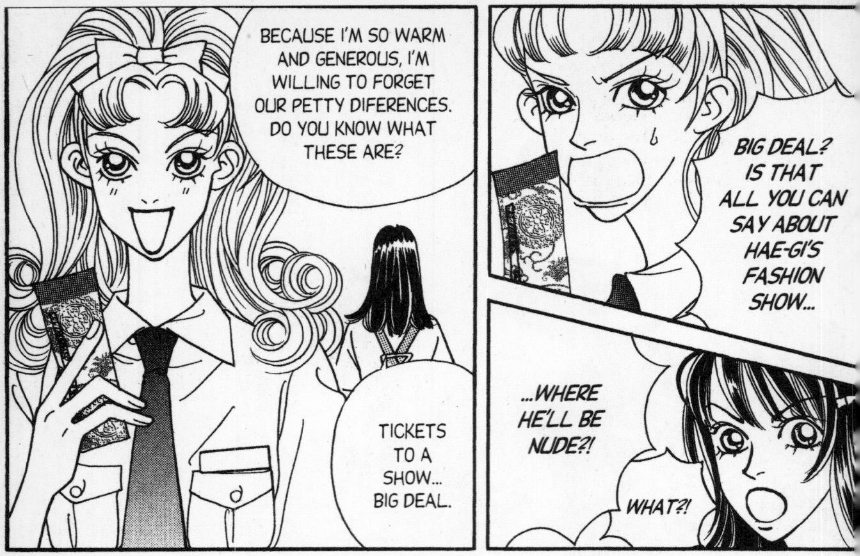
BECAUSE I'M SO WARM AND GENEROUS, I'M WILLING TO FORGET OUR PETTY DIFERENCES. DO YOU KNOW WHAT THESE ARE?
TICKETS TO A SHOW... BIG DEAL.
BIG DEAL? IS THAT ALL YOU CAN SAY ABOUT HAE-GI'S FASHION SHOW...
...WHERE HE'LL BE NUDE?!
WHAT?!

A NUDE FASHION SHOW?!

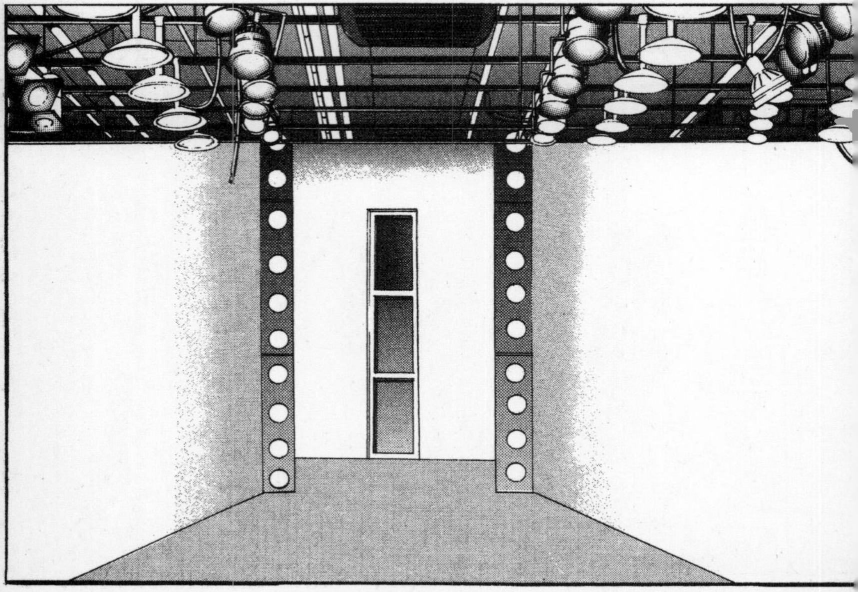

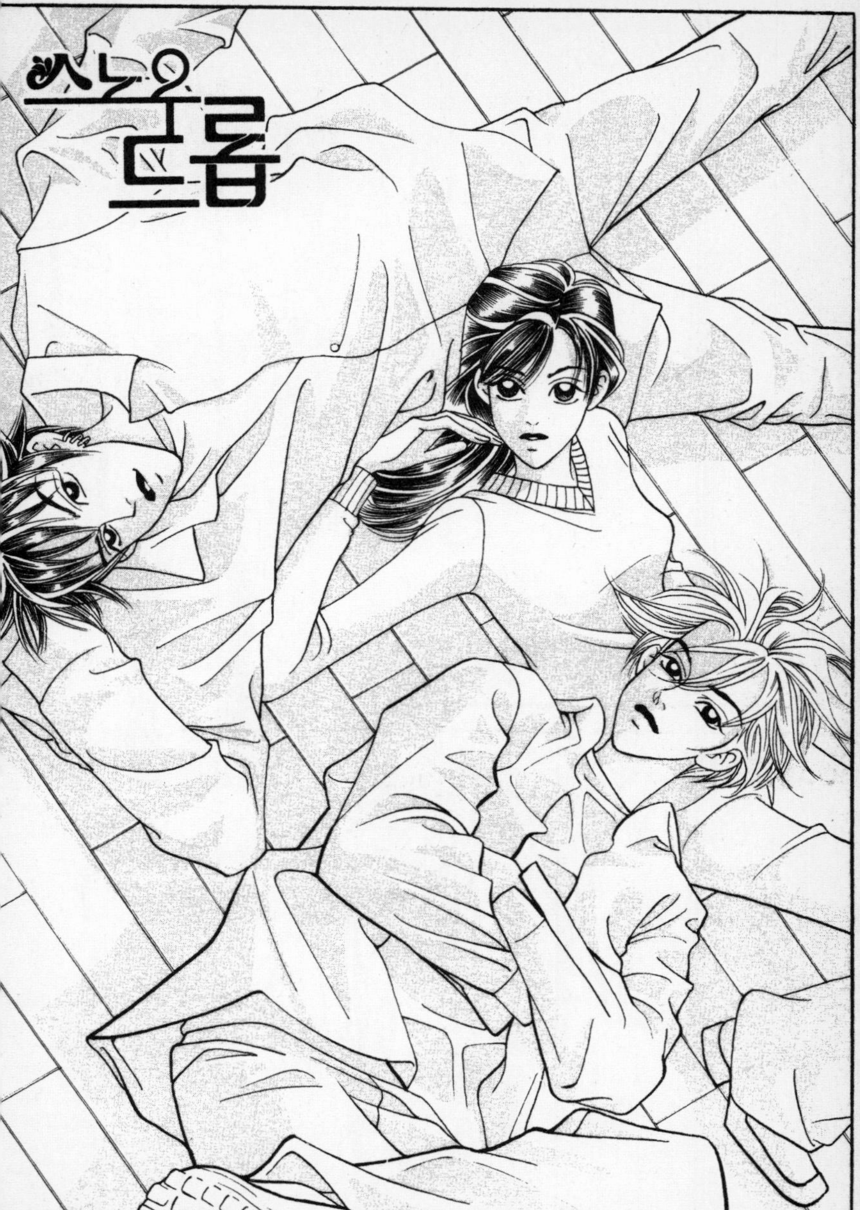
스노우 드롭

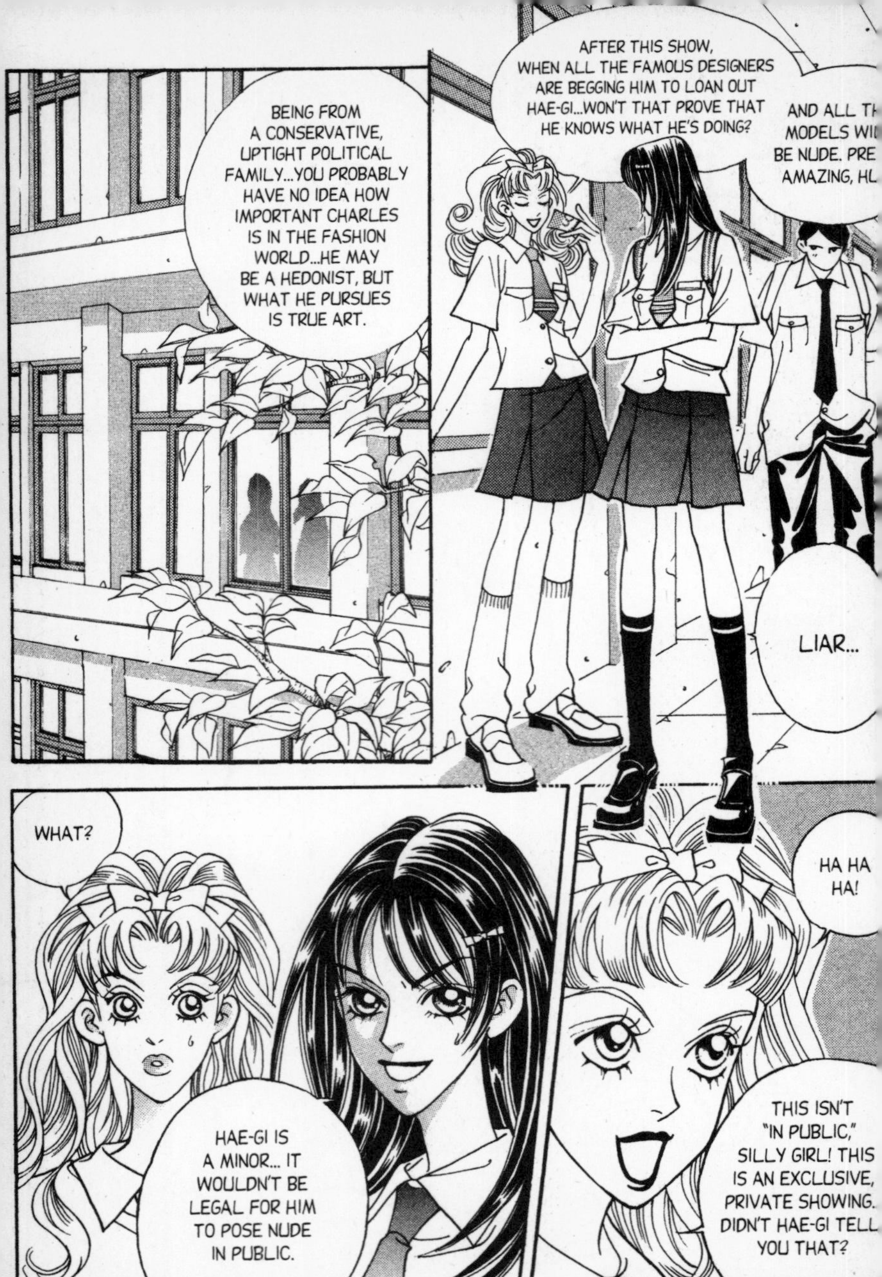
BEING FROM A CONSERVATIVE, UPTIGHT POLITICAL FAMILY...YOU PROBABLY HAVE NO IDEA HOW IMPORTANT CHARLES IS IN THE FASHION WORLD...HE MAY BE A HEDONIST, BUT WHAT HE PURSUES IS TRUE ART.
AFTER THIS SHOW, WHEN ALL THE FAMOUS DESIGNERS ARE BEGGING HIM TO LOAN OUT HAE-GI...WON'T THAT PROVE THAT HE KNOWS WHAT HE'S DOING?
AND ALL TH MODELS WI BE NUDE. PRE AMAZING, HU
LIAR...
WHAT?
HAE-GI IS A MINOR... IT WOULDN'T BE LEGAL FOR HIM TO POSE NUDE IN PUBLIC.
HA HA HA!
THIS ISN'T "IN PUBLIC," SILLY GIRL! THIS IS AN EXCLUSIVE, PRIVATE SHOWING. DIDN'T HAE-GI TELL YOU THAT?

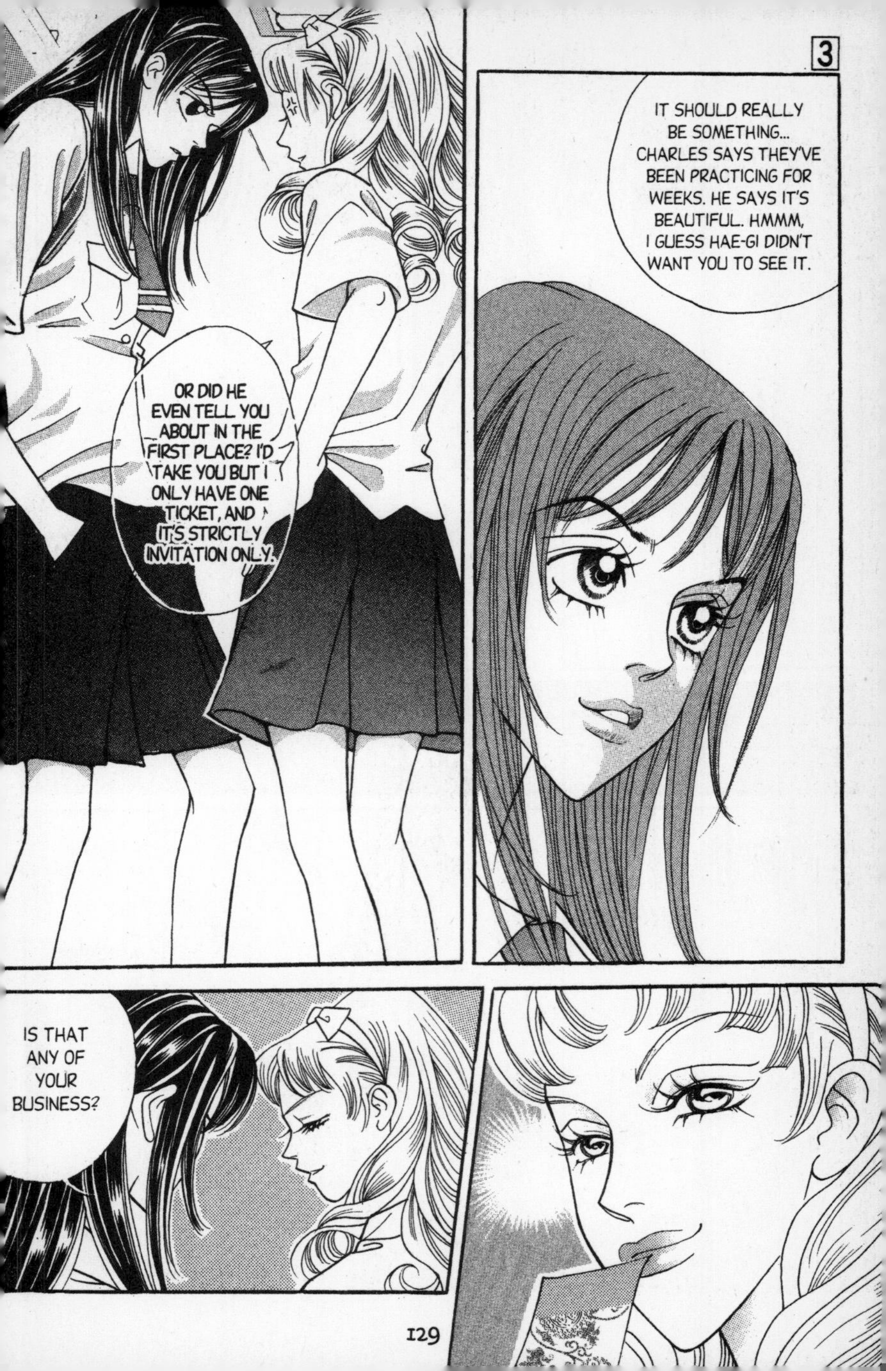
3
IT SHOULD REALLY BE SOMETHING... CHARLES SAYS THEY'VE BEEN PRACTICING FOR WEEKS. HE SAYS IT'S BEAUTIFUL. HMMM, I GUESS HAE-GI DIDN'T WANT YOU TO SEE IT.
OR DID HE EVEN TELL YOU ABOUT IN THE FIRST PLACE? I'D TAKE YOU BUT I ONLY HAVE ONE TICKET, AND IT'S STRICTLY INVITATION ONLY.
IS THAT ANY OF YOUR BUSINESS?

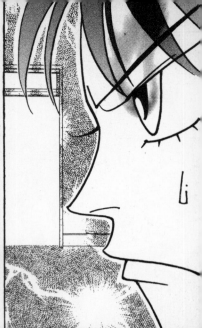

BUT SHE'S RIGHT!
I DIDN'T KNOW ABOUT IT!!!

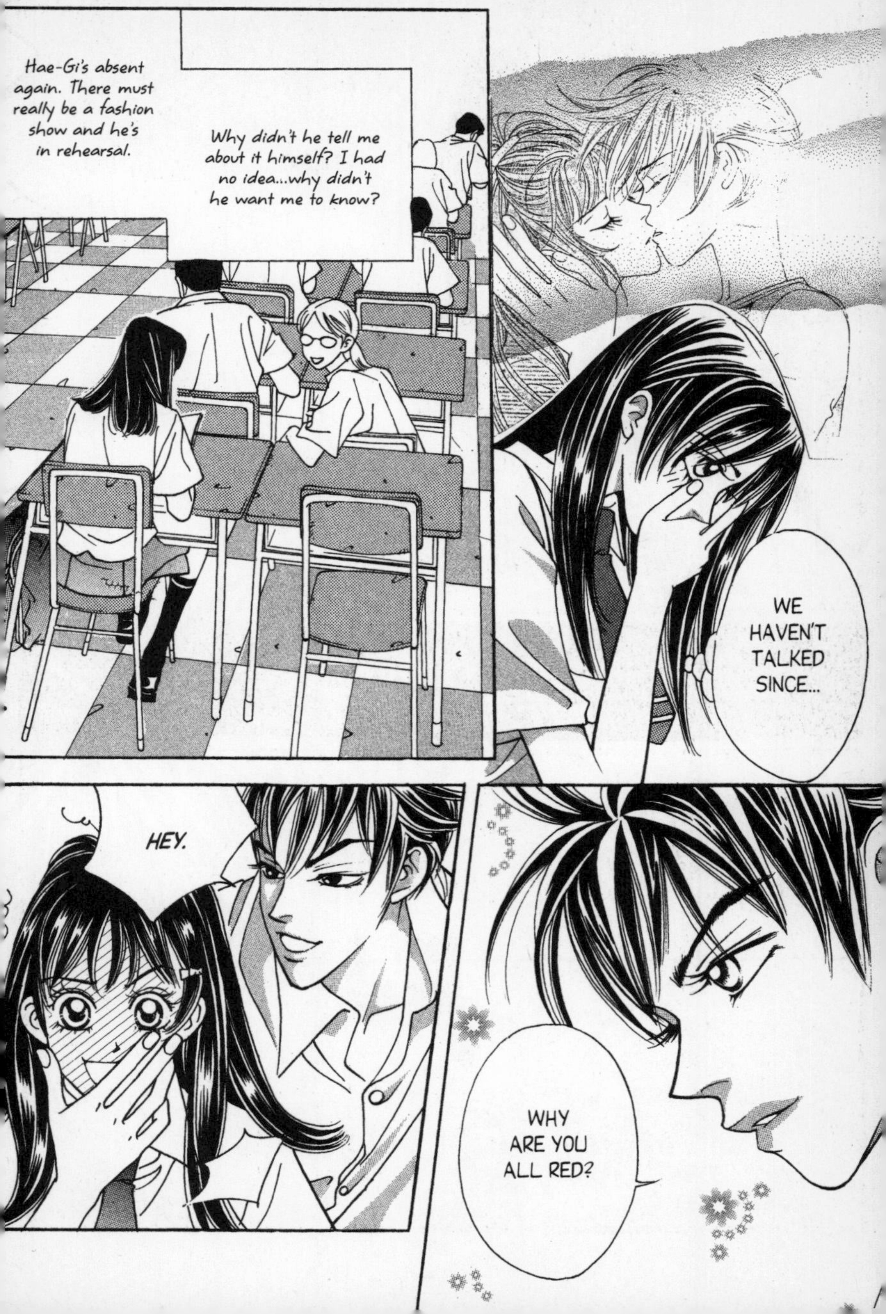
Hae-Gi's absent again. There must really be a fashion show and he's in rehearsal.
Why didn't he tell me about it himself? I had no idea...why didn't he want me to know?
WE HAVEN'T TALKED SINCE...
HEY.
WHY ARE YOU ALL RED?

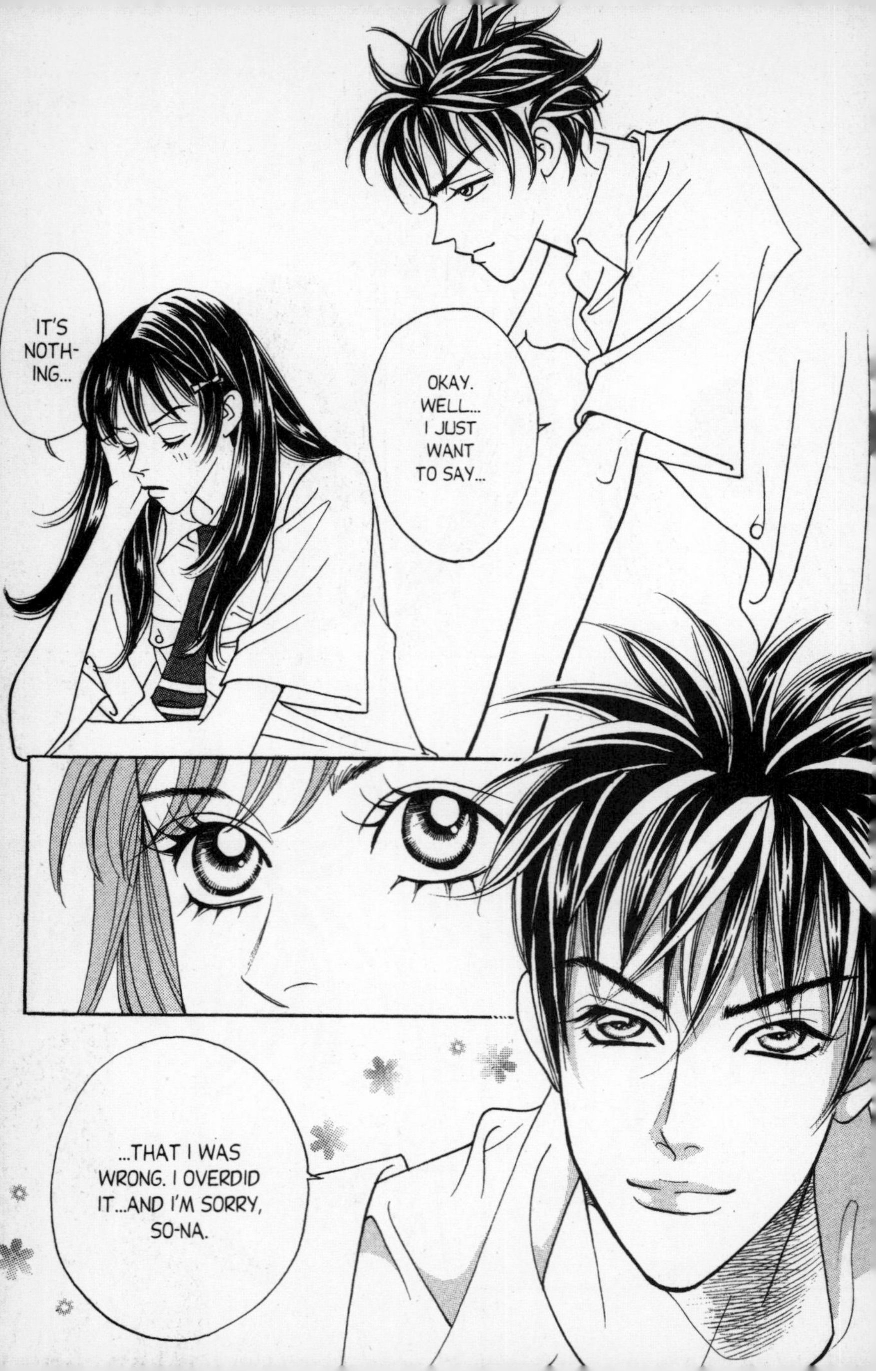
IT'S NOTH- ING...
OKAY. WELL... I JUST WANT TO SAY...
...THAT I WAS WRONG. I OVERDID IT...AND I'M SORRY, SO-NA.

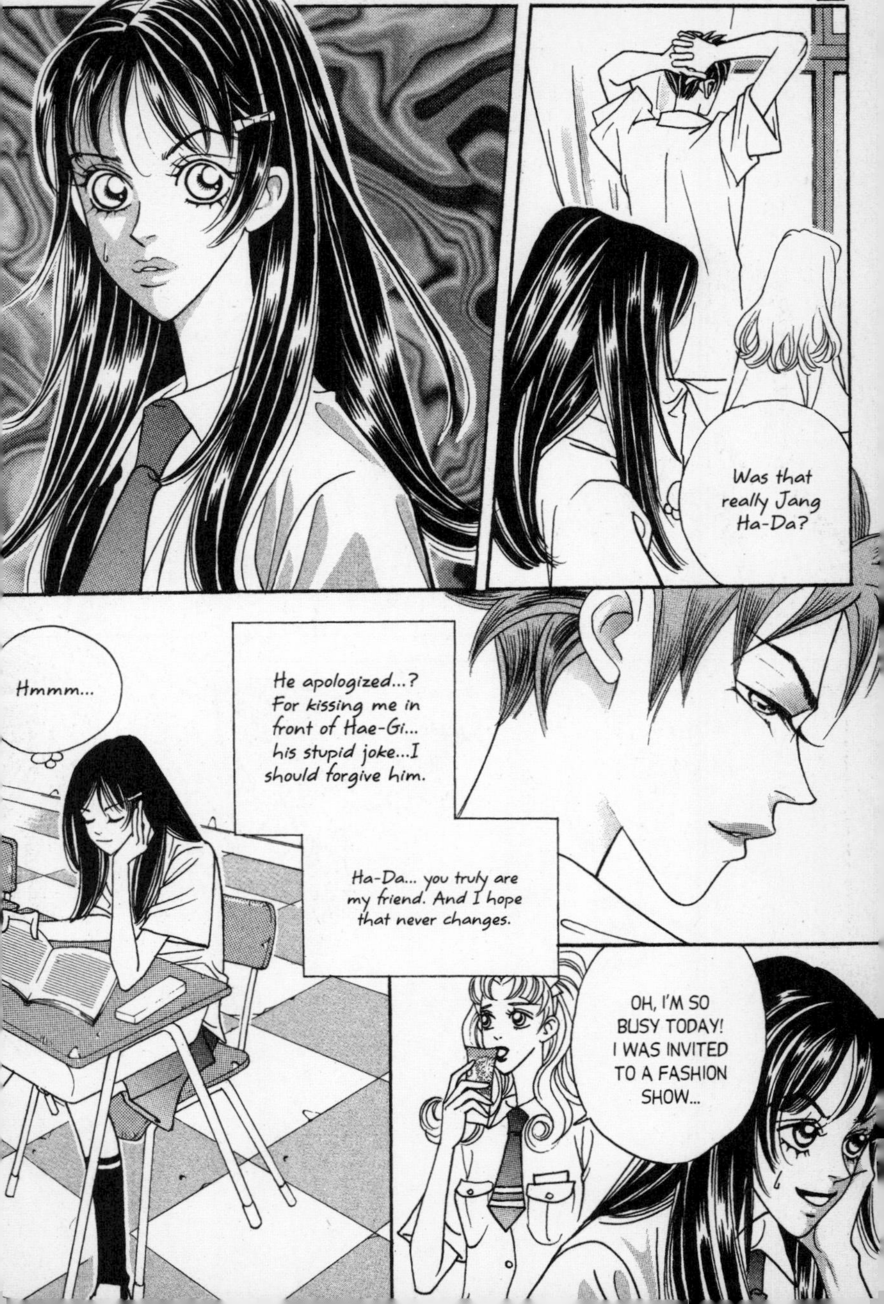
Was that really Jang Ha-Da?
Hmmm...
He apologized...? For kissing me in front of Hae-Gi... his stupid joke...I should forgive him.
Ha-Da... you truly are my friend. And I hope that never changes.
OH, I'M SO BUSY TODAY! I WAS INVITED TO A FASHION SHOW...

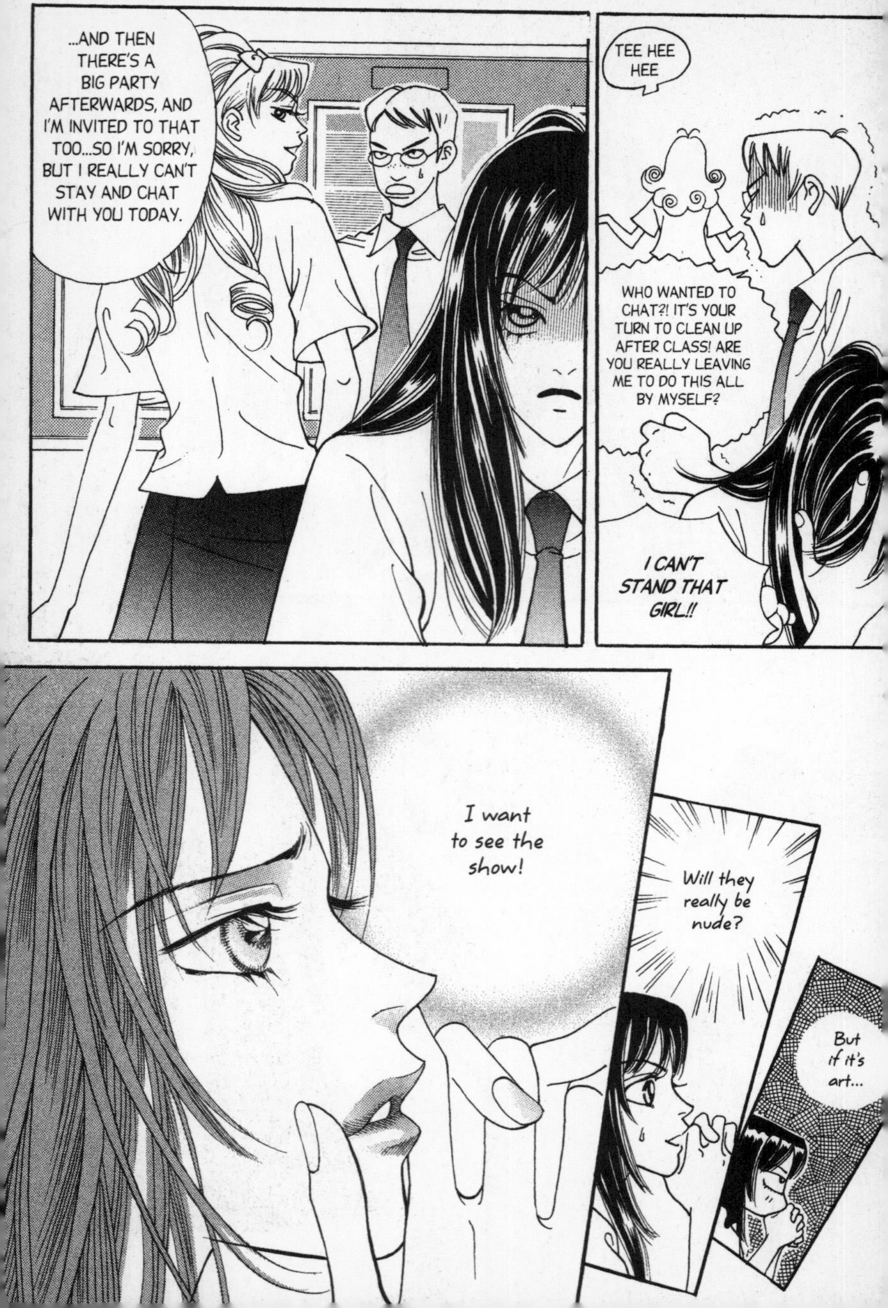
...AND THEN THERE'S A BIG PARTY AFTERWARDS, AND I'M INVITED TO THAT TOO...SO I'M SORRY, BUT I REALLY CAN'T STAY AND CHAT WITH YOU TODAY.
TEE HEE HEE
WHO WANTED TO CHAT?! IT'S YOUR TURN TO CLEAN UP AFTER CLASS! ARE YOU REALLY LEAVING ME TO DO THIS ALL BY MYSELF?
I CAN'T STAND THAT GIRL!!
I want to see the show!
Will they really be nude?
But if it's art...

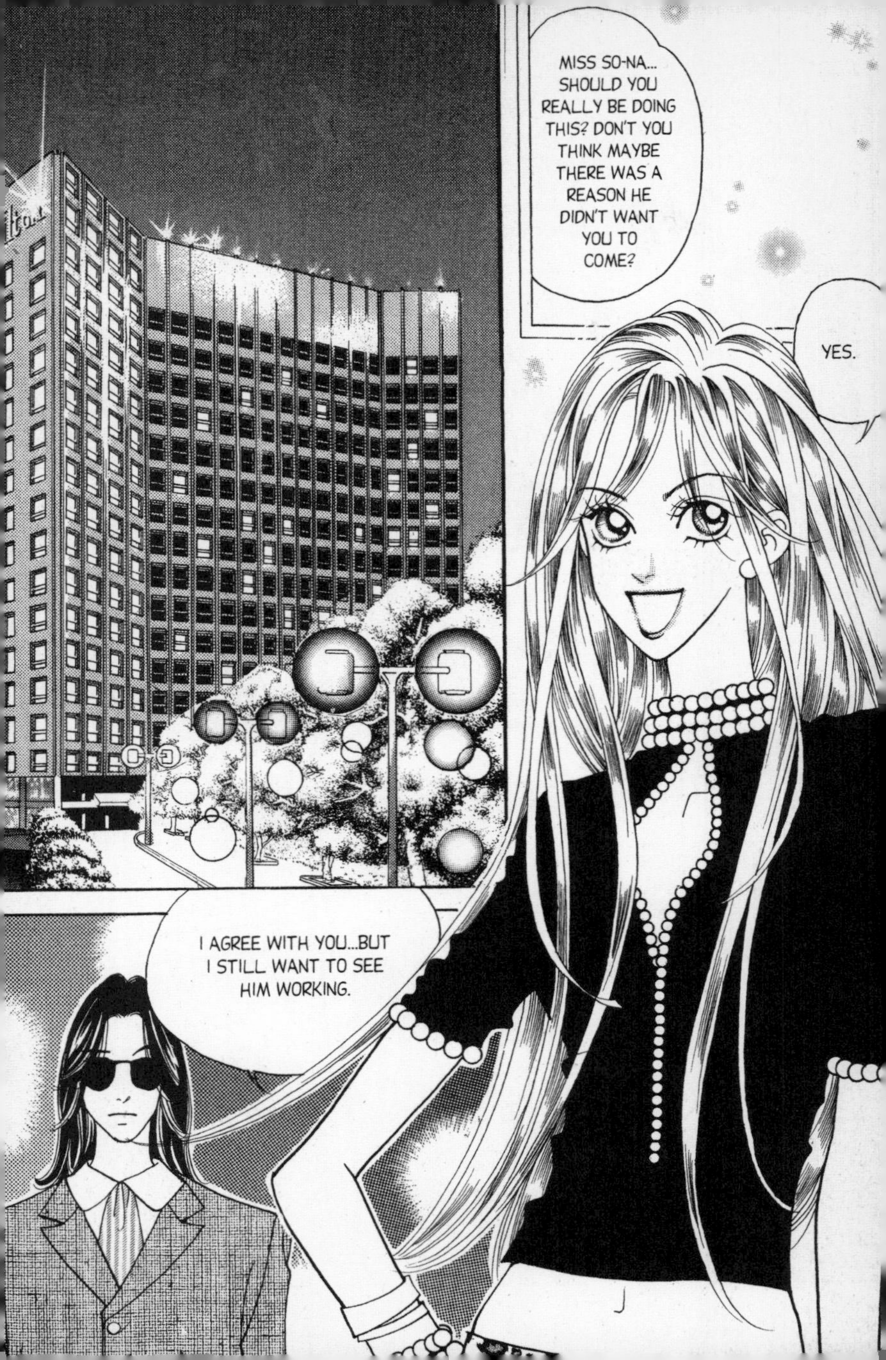
MISS SO-NA... SHOULD YOU REALLY BE DOING THIS? DON'T YOU THINK MAYBE THERE WAS A REASON HE DIDN'T WANT YOU TO COME?
YES.
I AGREE WITH YOU...BUT I STILL WANT TO SEE HIM WORKING.

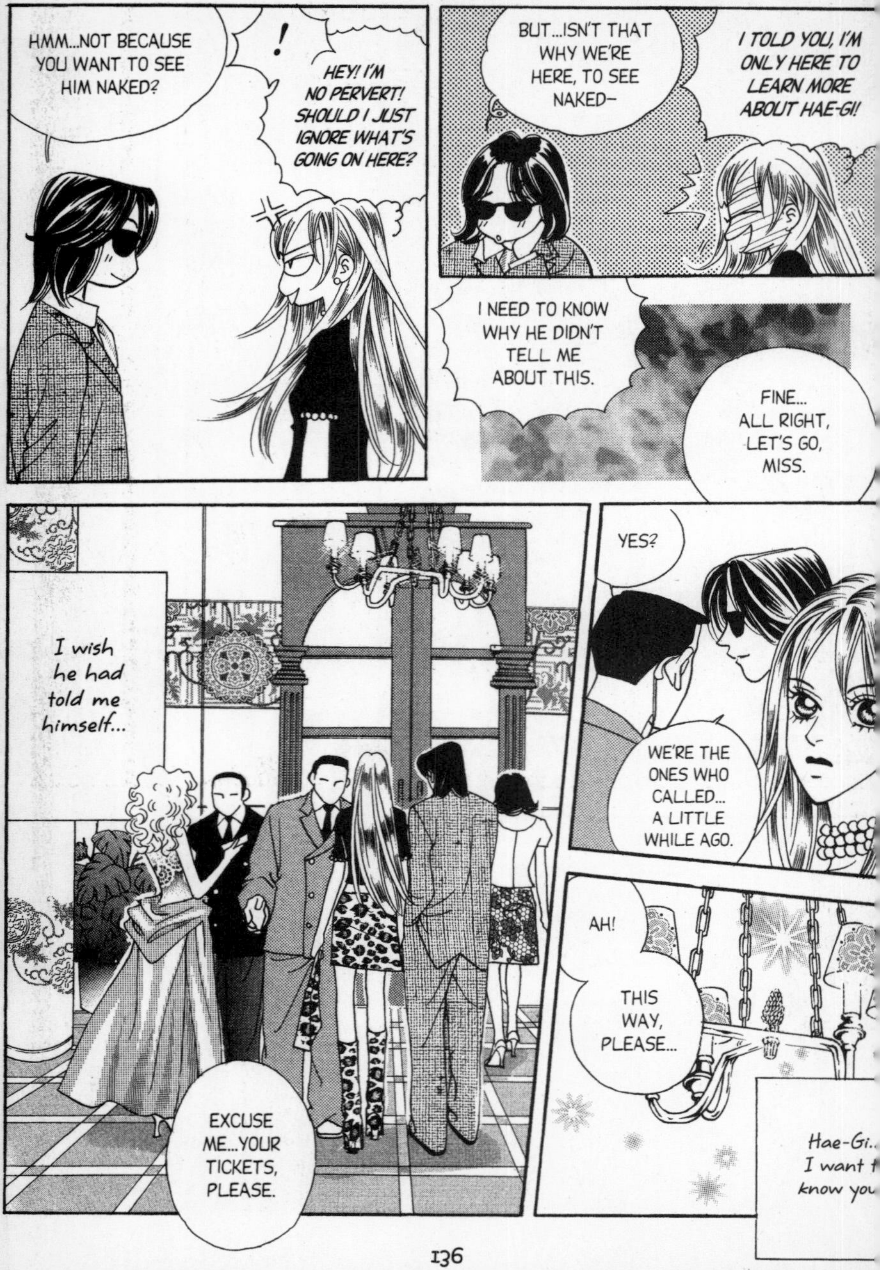
HMM...NOT BECAUSE YOU WANT TO SEE HIM NAKED?
!
HEY! I'M NO PERVERT! SHOULD I JUST IGNORE WHAT'S GOING ON HERE?
BUT...ISN'T THAT WHY WE'RE HERE, TO SEE NAKED–
I TOLD YOU, I'M ONLY HERE TO LEARN MORE ABOUT HAE-GI!
I NEED TO KNOW WHY HE DIDN'T TELL ME ABOUT THIS.
FINE... ALL RIGHT, LET'S GO, MISS.
I wish he had told me himself...
EXCUSE ME...YOUR TICKETS, PLEASE.
YES?
WE'RE THE ONES WHO CALLED... A LITTLE WHILE AGO.
AH!
THIS WAY, PLEASE...
Hae-Gi..
I want t
know you

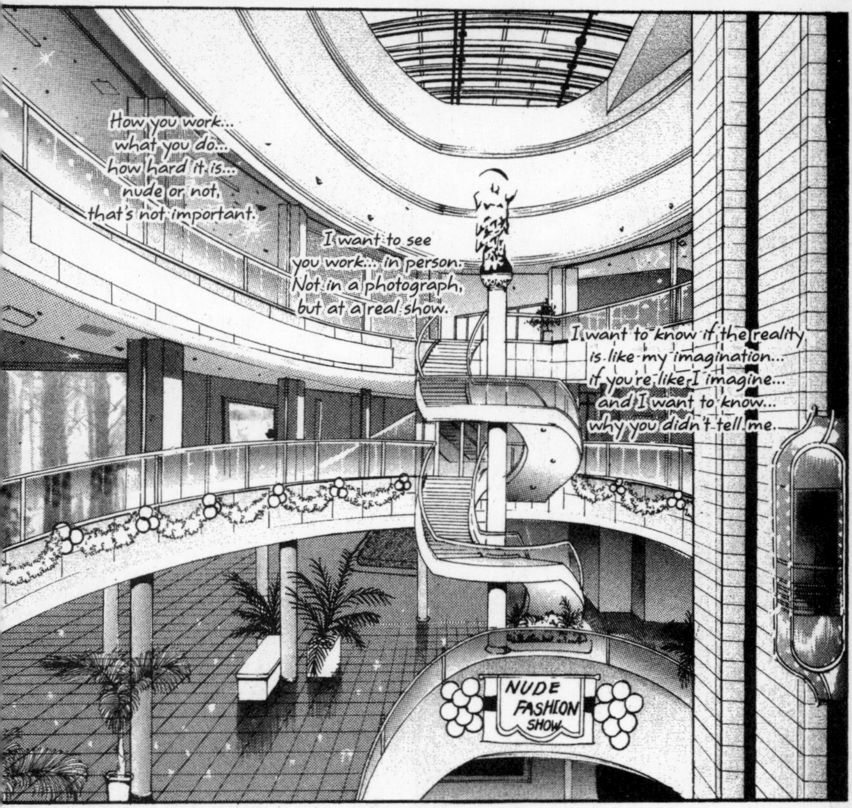
How you work... what you do... how hard it is... nude or not, that's not important.
I want to see you work... in person. Not in a photograph, but at a real show.
I want to know if the reality is like my imagination... if you're like I imagine... and I want to know... why you didn't tell me.
NUDE FASHION SHOW

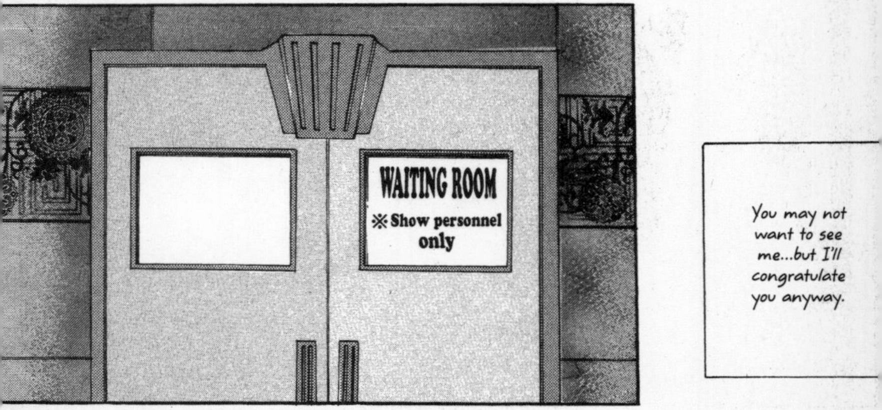
WAITING ROOM
※ Show personnel only
You may not want to see me...but I'll congratulate you anyway.

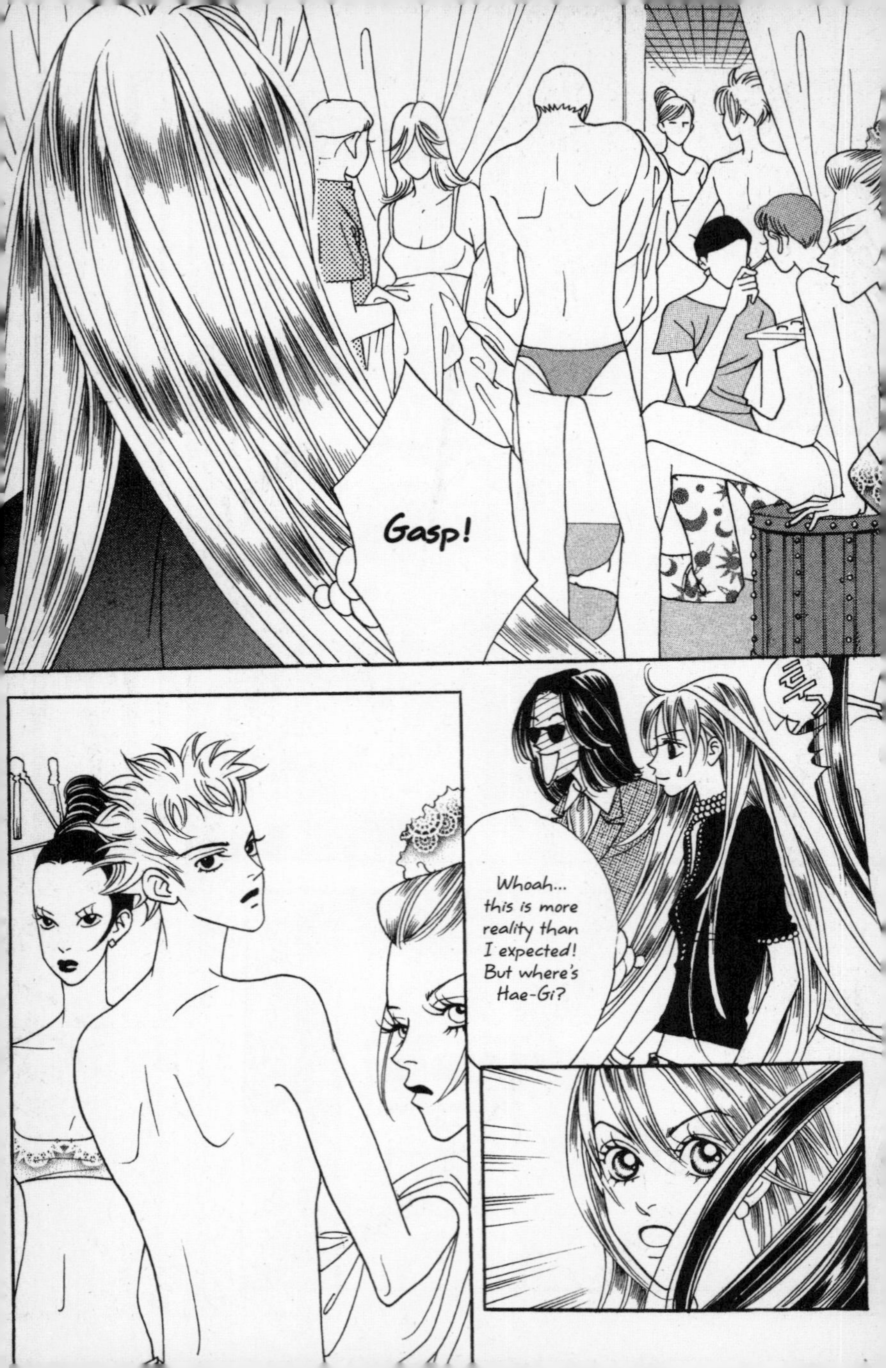
Gasp!
Whoah... this is more reality than I expected! But where's Hae-Gi?

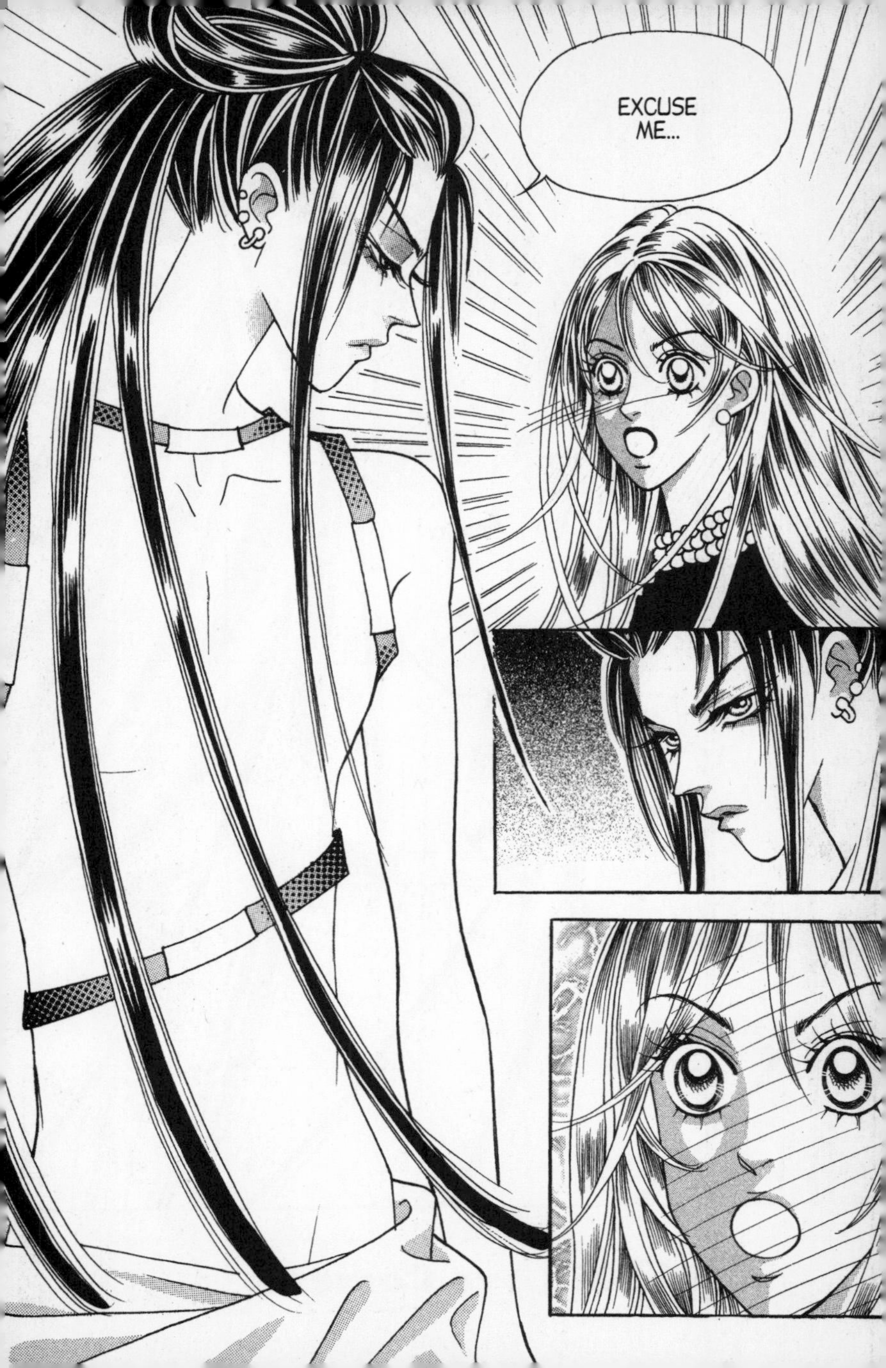
EXCUSE ME...

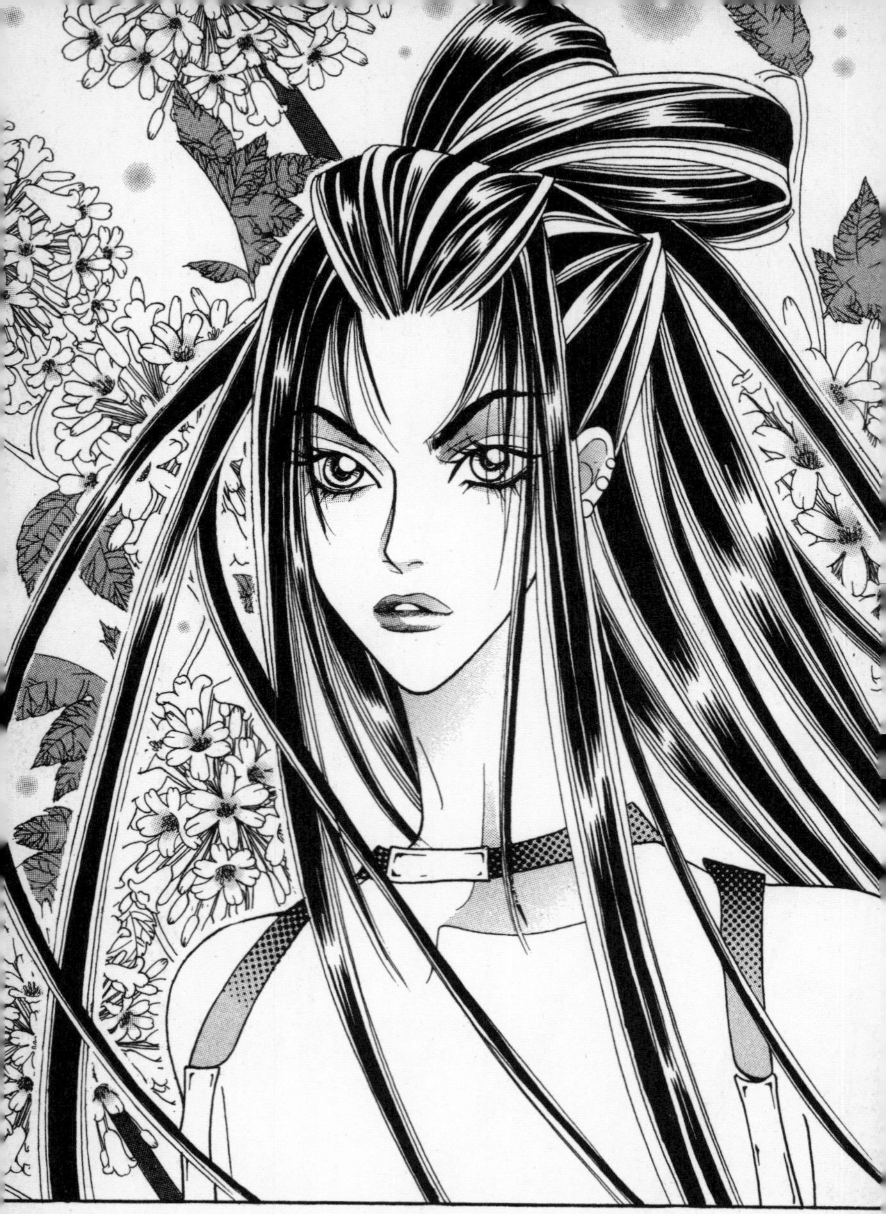

## Part 12. **If Love Comes...**

**African Lily**

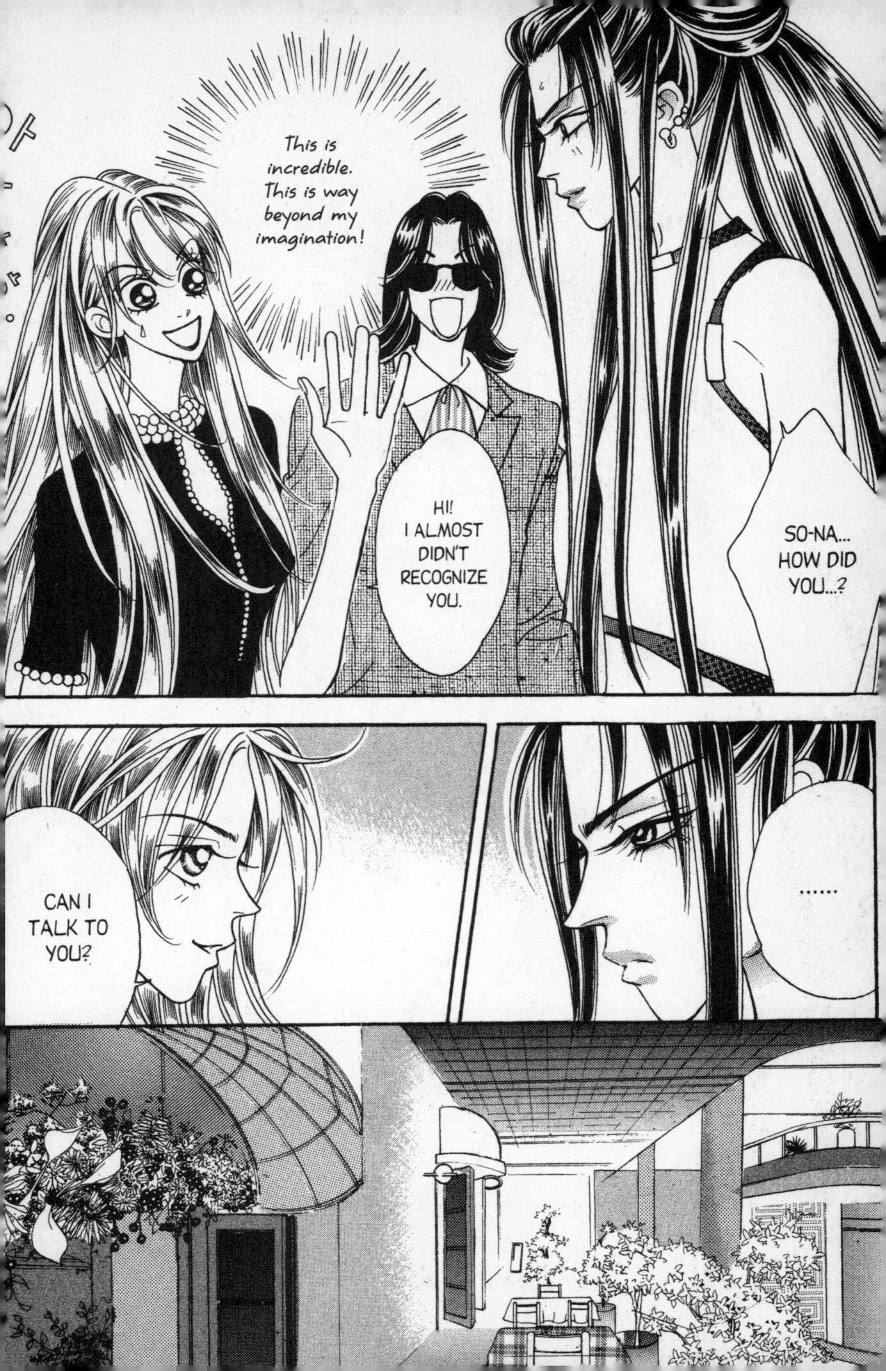
This is incredible. This is way beyond my imagination!
HI! I ALMOST DIDN'T RECOGNIZE YOU.
SO-NA... HOW DID YOU...?
CAN I TALK TO YOU?
......

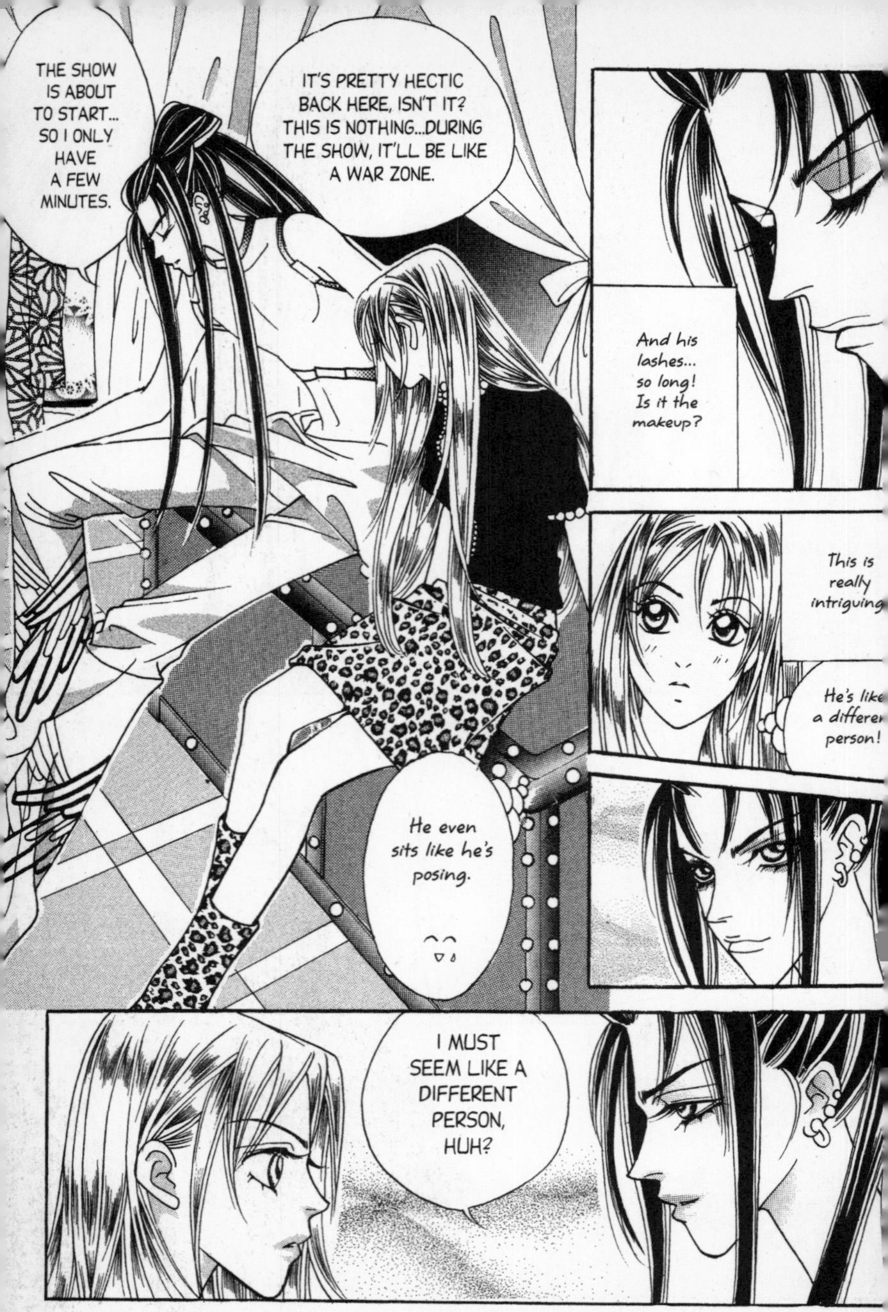
THE SHOW IS ABOUT TO START... SO I ONLY HAVE A FEW MINUTES.
IT'S PRETTY HECTIC BACK HERE, ISN'T IT? THIS IS NOTHING...DURING THE SHOW, IT'LL BE LIKE A WAR ZONE.
He even sits like he's posing.
And his lashes... so long! Is it the makeup?
This is really intriguing
He's like a differen person!
I MUST SEEM LIKE A DIFFERENT PERSON, HUH?

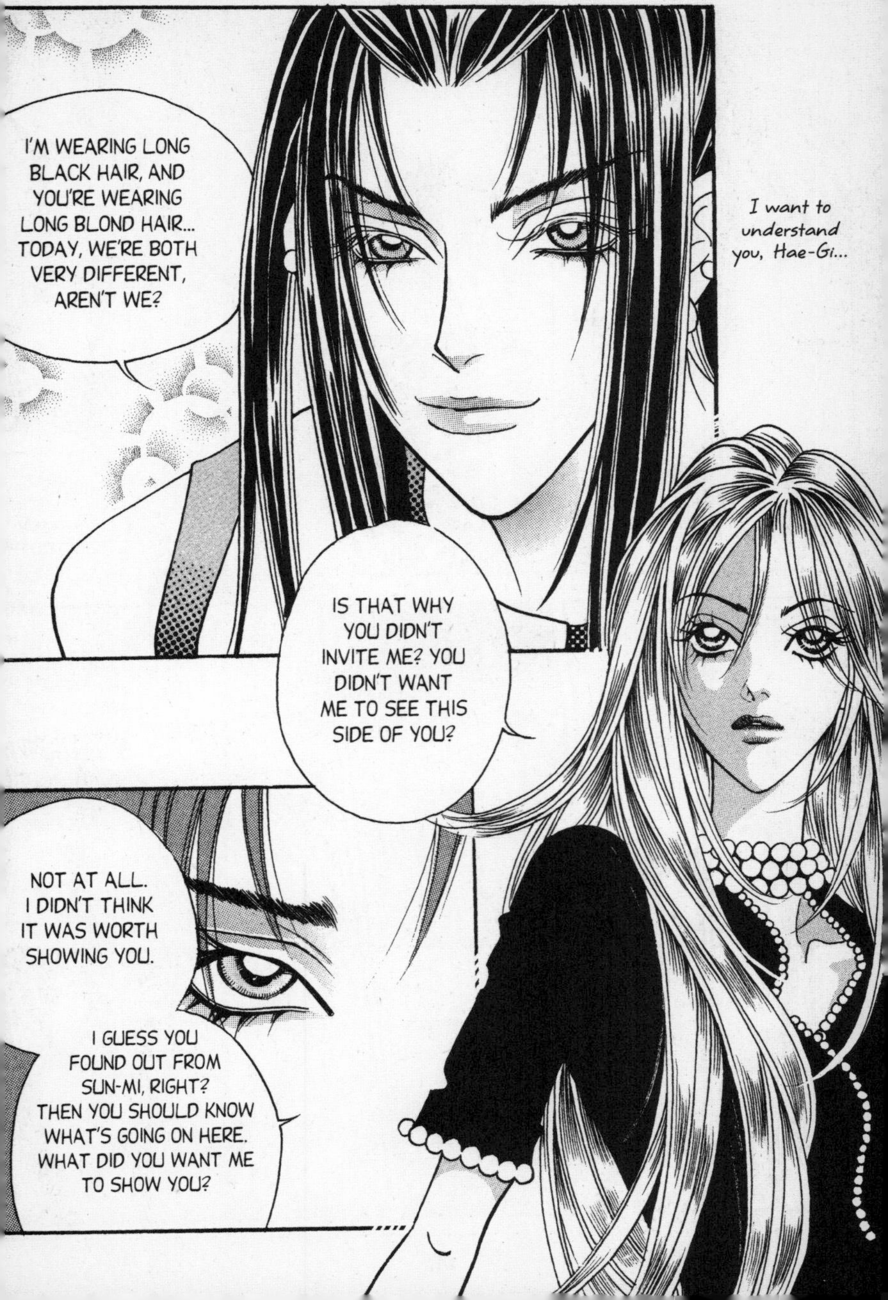
I'M WEARING LONG BLACK HAIR, AND YOU'RE WEARING LONG BLOND HAIR... TODAY, WE'RE BOTH VERY DIFFERENT, AREN'T WE?
I want to understand you, Hae-Gi...
IS THAT WHY YOU DIDN'T INVITE ME? YOU DIDN'T WANT ME TO SEE THIS SIDE OF YOU?
NOT AT ALL. I DIDN'T THINK IT WAS WORTH SHOWING YOU.
I GUESS YOU FOUND OUT FROM SUN-MI, RIGHT? THEN YOU SHOULD KNOW WHAT'S GOING ON HERE. WHAT DID YOU WANT ME TO SHOW YOU?

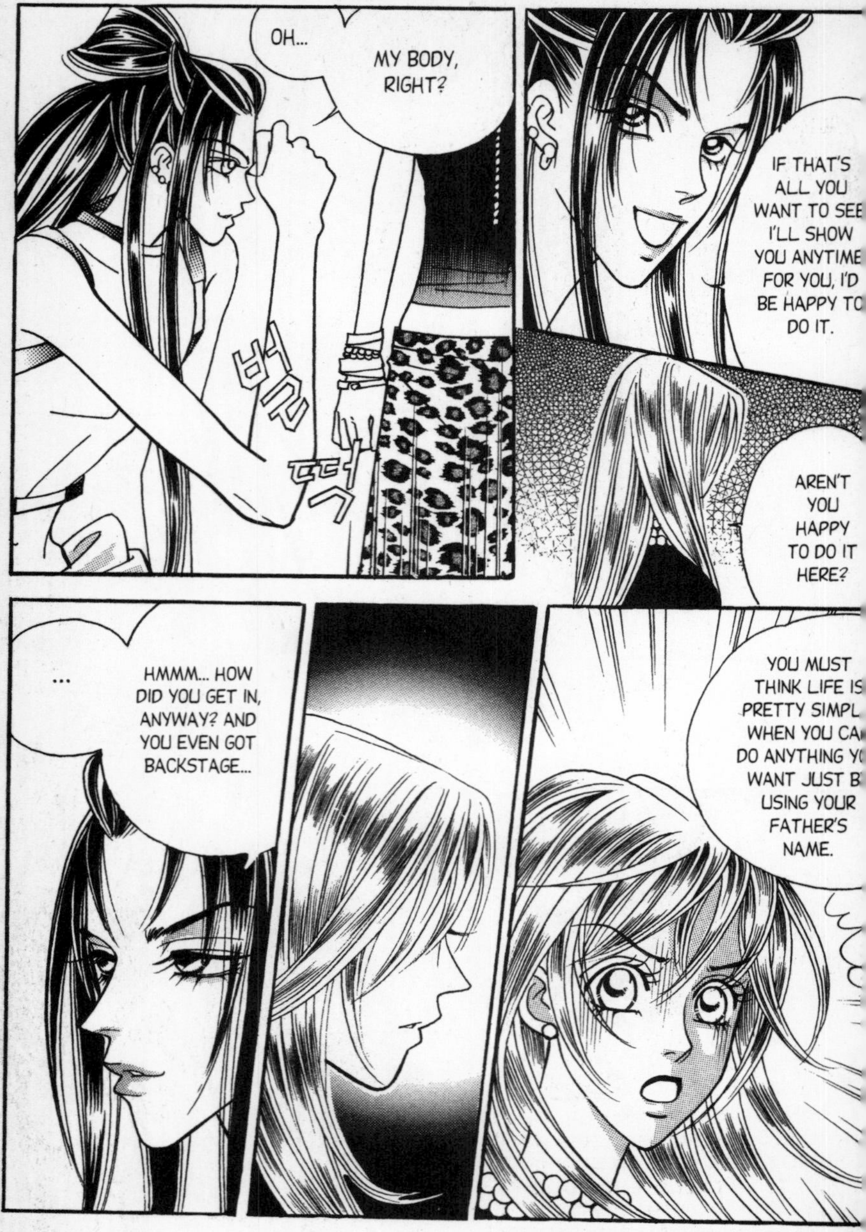
OH...
MY BODY, RIGHT?
IF THAT'S ALL YOU WANT TO SEE I'LL SHOW YOU ANYTIME FOR YOU, I'D BE HAPPY TO DO IT.
AREN'T YOU HAPPY TO DO IT HERE?
...
HMMM... HOW DID YOU GET IN, ANYWAY? AND YOU EVEN GOT BACKSTAGE...
YOU MUST THINK LIFE IS PRETTY SIMPL WHEN YOU CA DO ANYTHING Y WANT JUST B USING YOUR FATHER'S NAME.

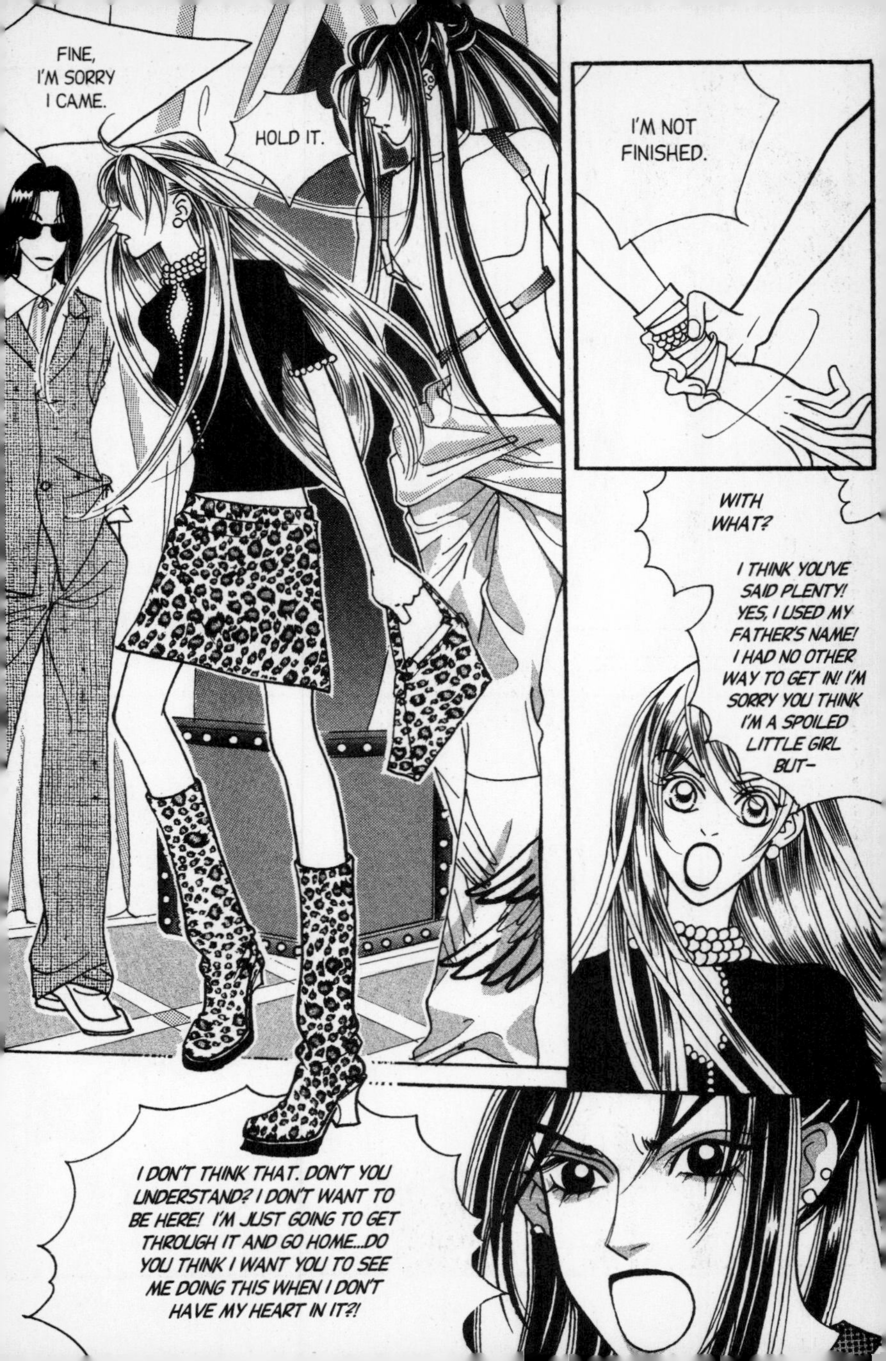

FINE, I'M SORRY I CAME.
HOLD IT.
I'M NOT FINISHED.
WITH WHAT?
I THINK YOU'VE SAID PLENTY! YES, I USED MY FATHER'S NAME! I HAD NO OTHER WAY TO GET IN! I'M SORRY YOU THINK I'M A SPOILED LITTLE GIRL BUT–
I DON'T THINK THAT. DON'T YOU UNDERSTAND? I DON'T WANT TO BE HERE! I'M JUST GOING TO GET THROUGH IT AND GO HOME...DO YOU THINK I WANT YOU TO SEE ME DOING THIS WHEN I DON'T HAVE MY HEART IN IT?!

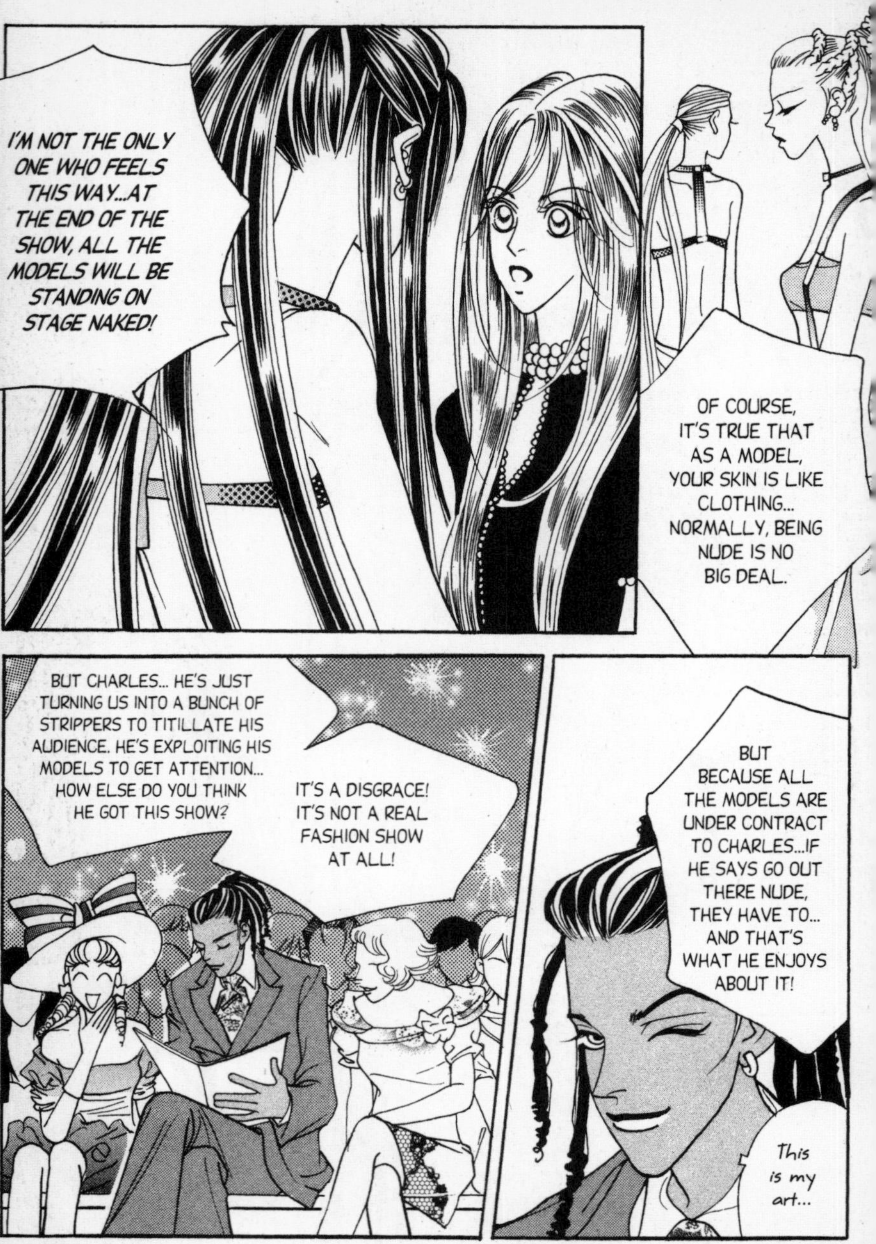
I'M NOT THE ONLY ONE WHO FEELS THIS WAY...AT THE END OF THE SHOW, ALL THE MODELS WILL BE STANDING ON STAGE NAKED!
OF COURSE, IT'S TRUE THAT AS A MODEL, YOUR SKIN IS LIKE CLOTHING... NORMALLY, BEING NUDE IS NO BIG DEAL.
BUT CHARLES... HE'S JUST TURNING US INTO A BUNCH OF STRIPPERS TO TITILLATE HIS AUDIENCE. HE'S EXPLOITING HIS MODELS TO GET ATTENTION... HOW ELSE DO YOU THINK HE GOT THIS SHOW?
IT'S A DISGRACE! IT'S NOT A REAL FASHION SHOW AT ALL!
BUT BECAUSE ALL THE MODELS ARE UNDER CONTRACT TO CHARLES...IF HE SAYS GO OUT THERE NUDE, THEY HAVE TO... AND THAT'S WHAT HE ENJOYS ABOUT IT!
This is my art...

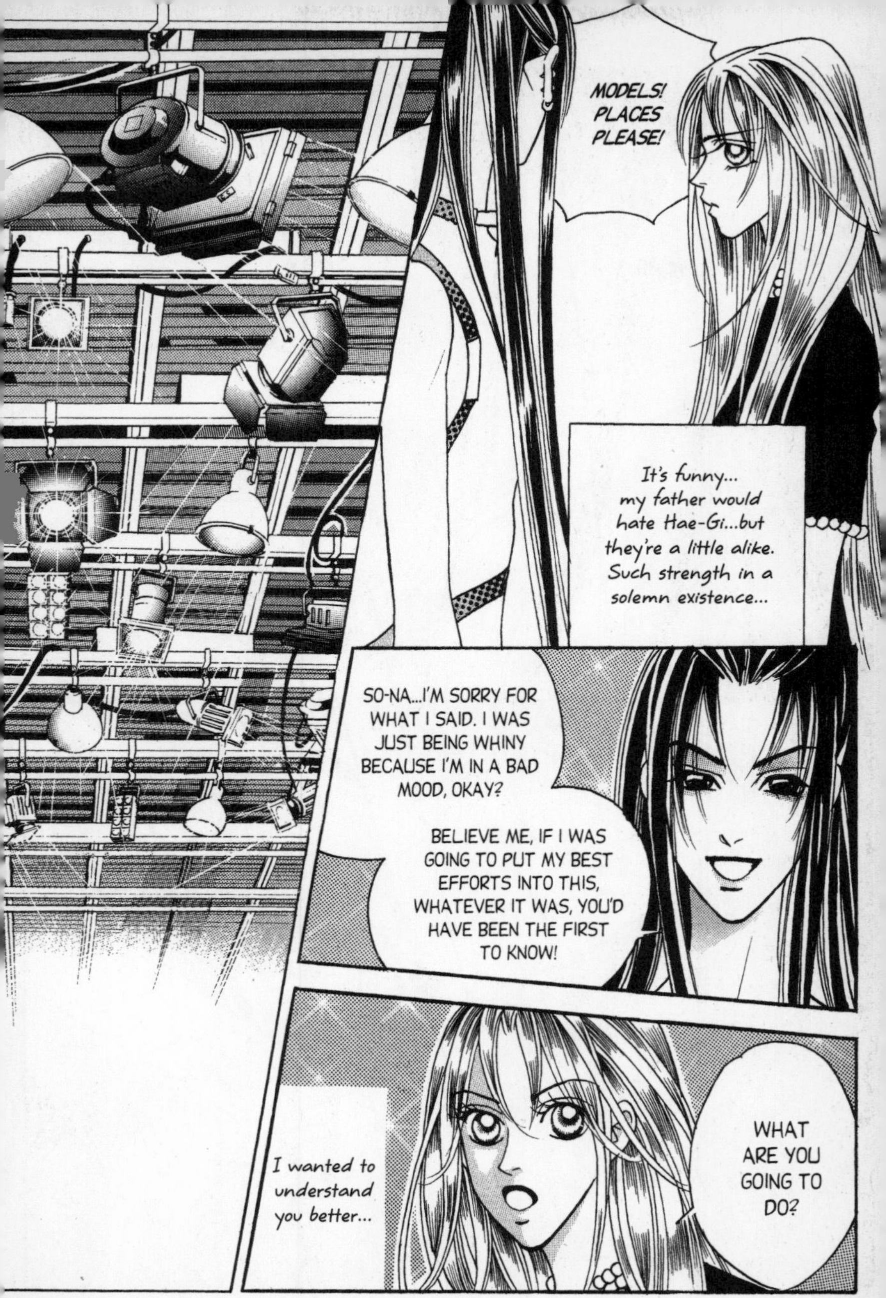
MODELS! PLACES PLEASE!
It's funny... my father would hate Hae-Gi...but they're a little alike. Such strength in a solemn existence...
SO-NA...I'M SORRY FOR WHAT I SAID. I WAS JUST BEING WHINY BECAUSE I'M IN A BAD MOOD, OKAY?
BELIEVE ME, IF I WAS GOING TO PUT MY BEST EFFORTS INTO THIS, WHATEVER IT WAS, YOU'D HAVE BEEN THE FIRST TO KNOW!
I wanted to understand you better...
WHAT ARE YOU GOING TO DO?

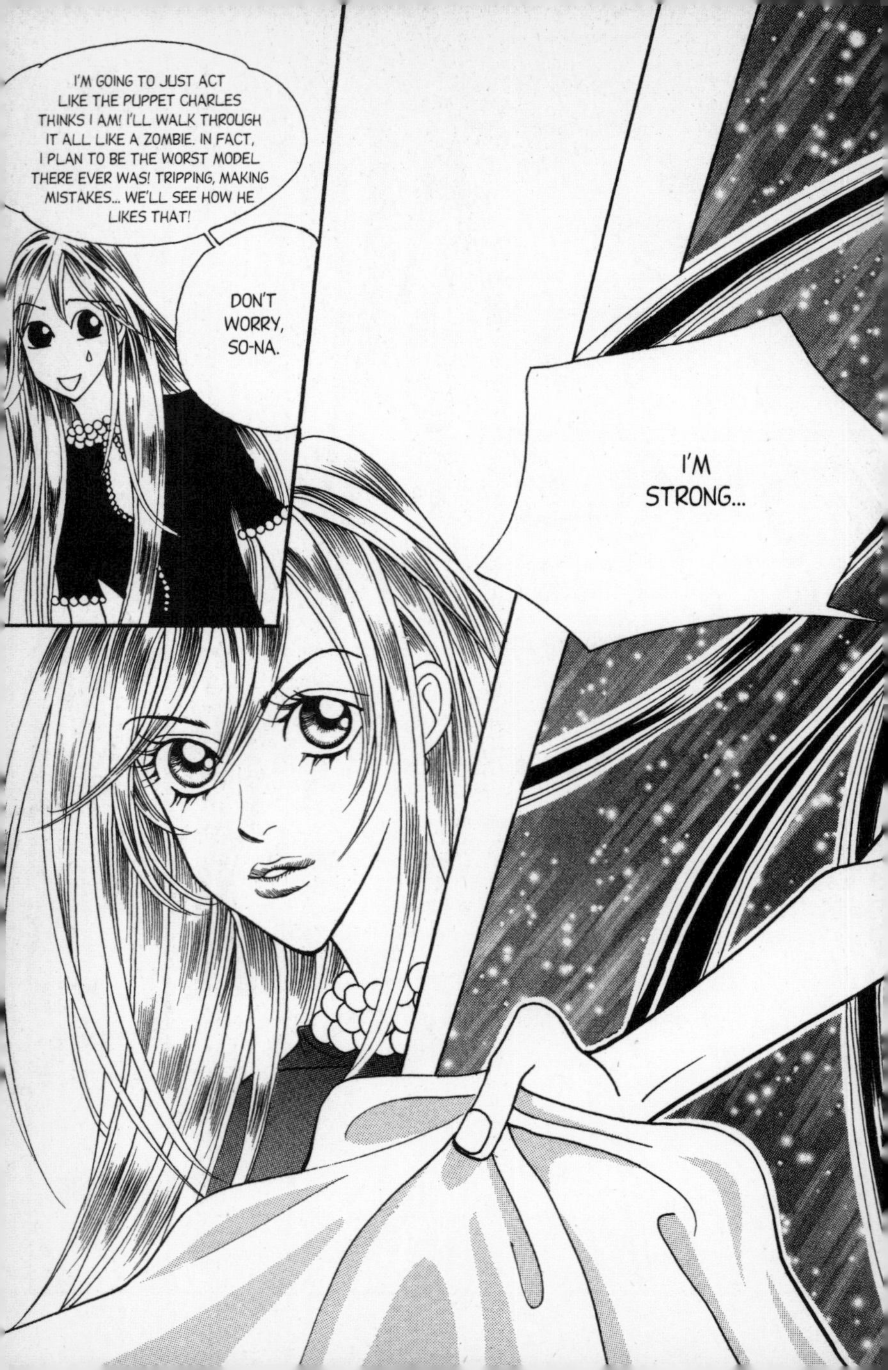
I'M GOING TO JUST ACT LIKE THE PUPPET CHARLES THINKS I AM! I'LL WALK THROUGH IT ALL LIKE A ZOMBIE. IN FACT, I PLAN TO BE THE WORST MODEL THERE EVER WAS! TRIPPING, MAKING MISTAKES... WE'LL SEE HOW HE LIKES THAT!
DON'T WORRY, SO-NA.
I'M STRONG...

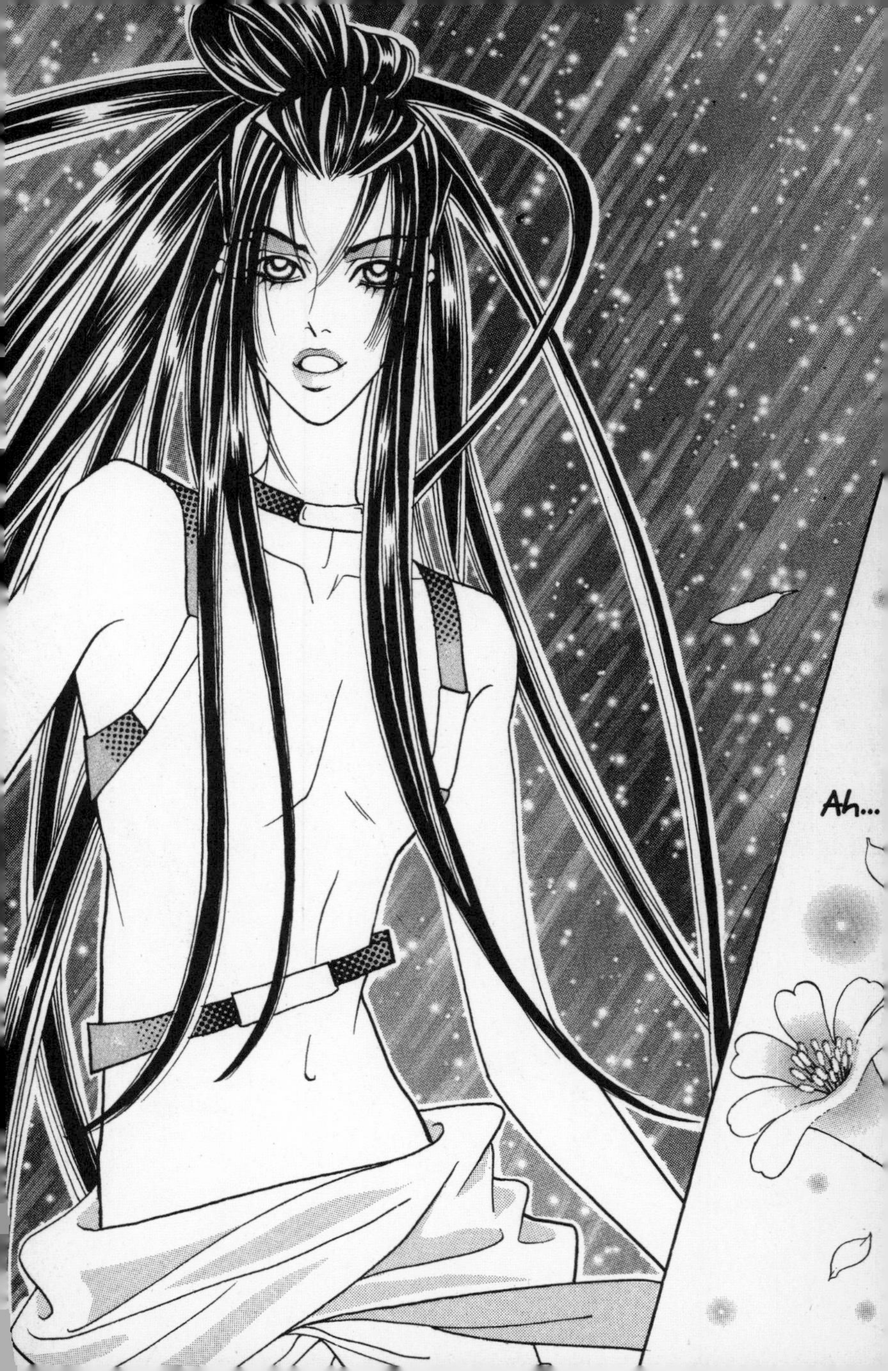
Ah...

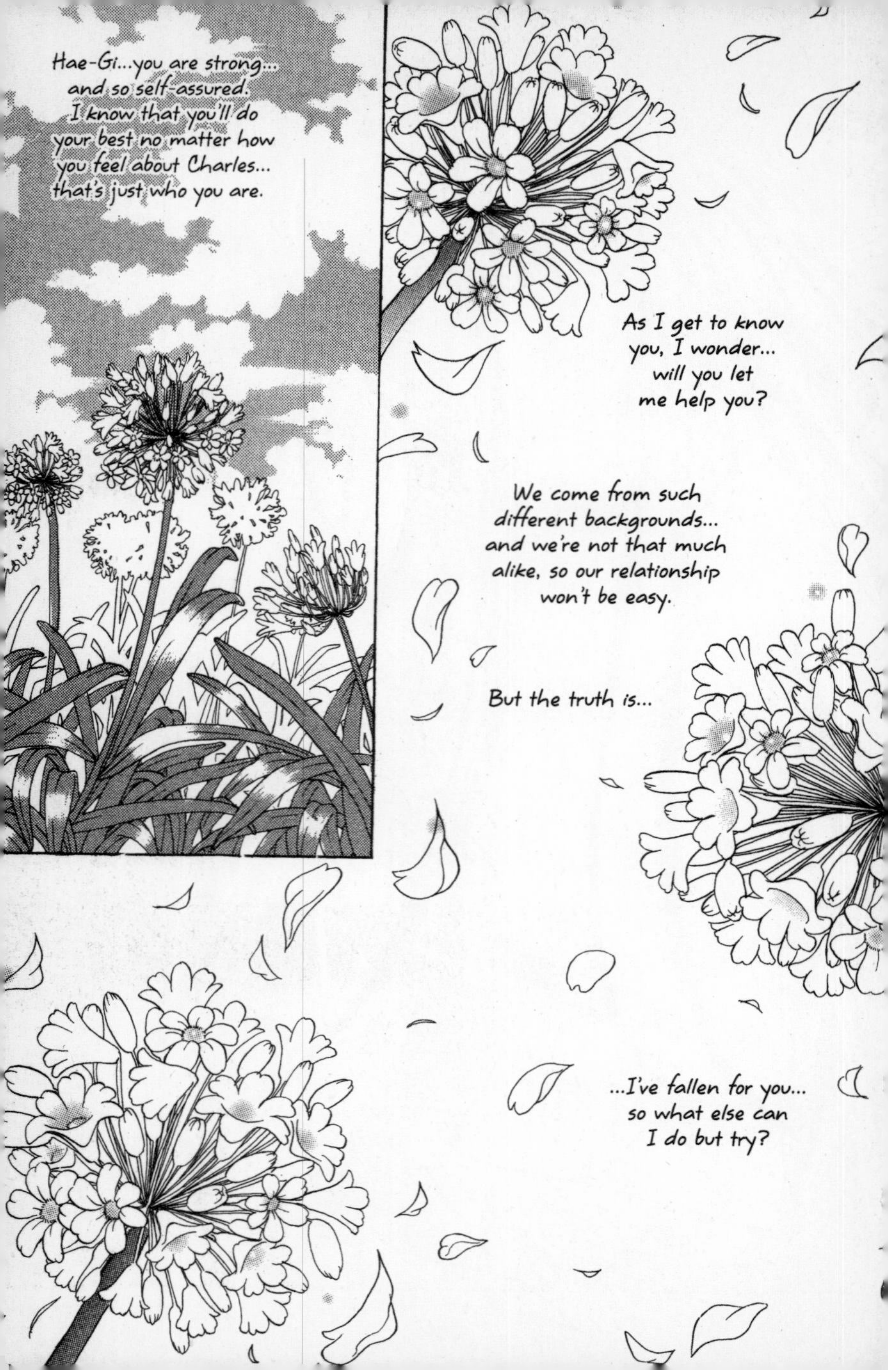
Hae-Gi...you are strong... and so self-assured. I know that you'll do your best no matter how you feel about Charles... that's just who you are.
As I get to know you, I wonder... will you let me help you?
We come from such different backgrounds... and we're not that much alike, so our relationship won't be easy.
But the truth is...
...I've fallen for you... so what else can I do but try?

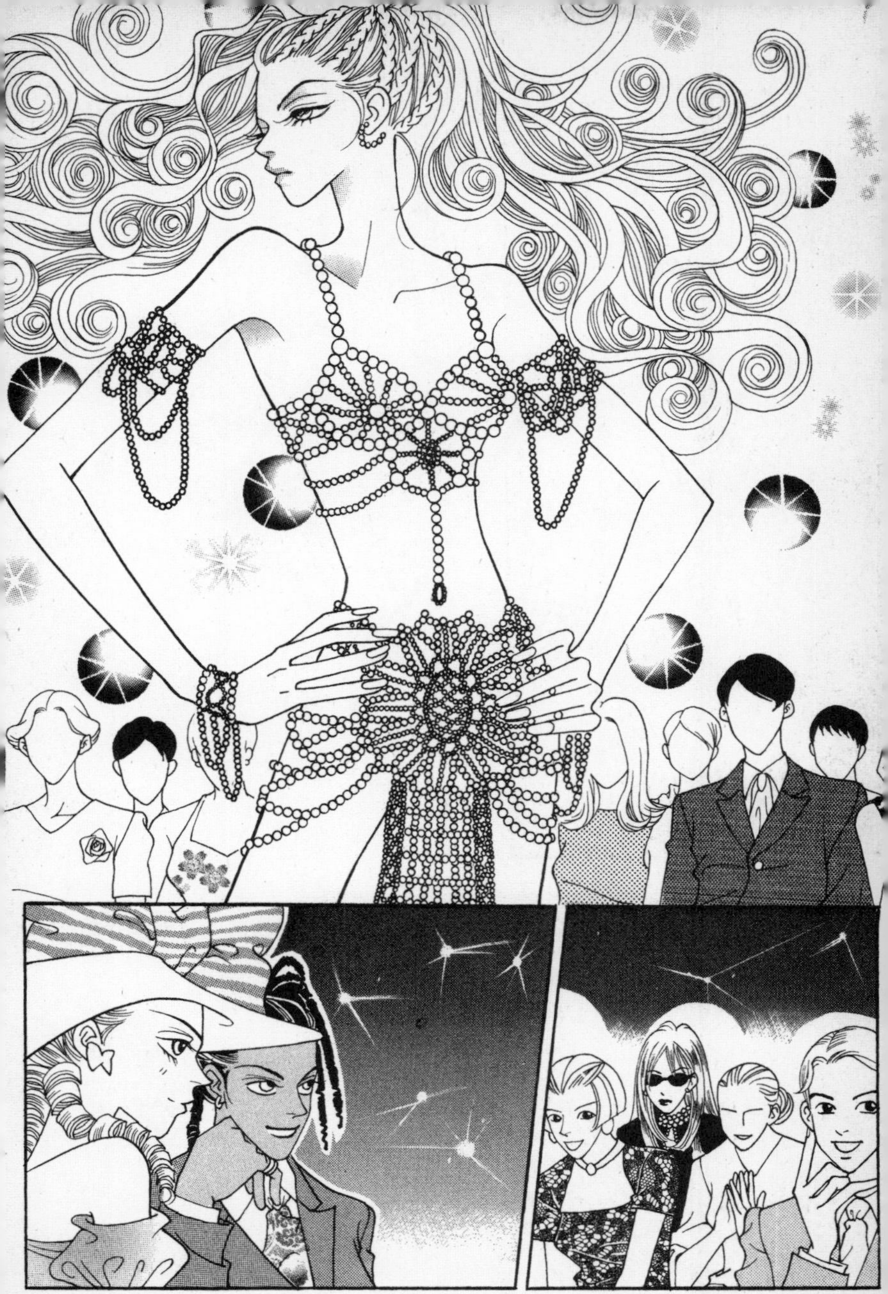

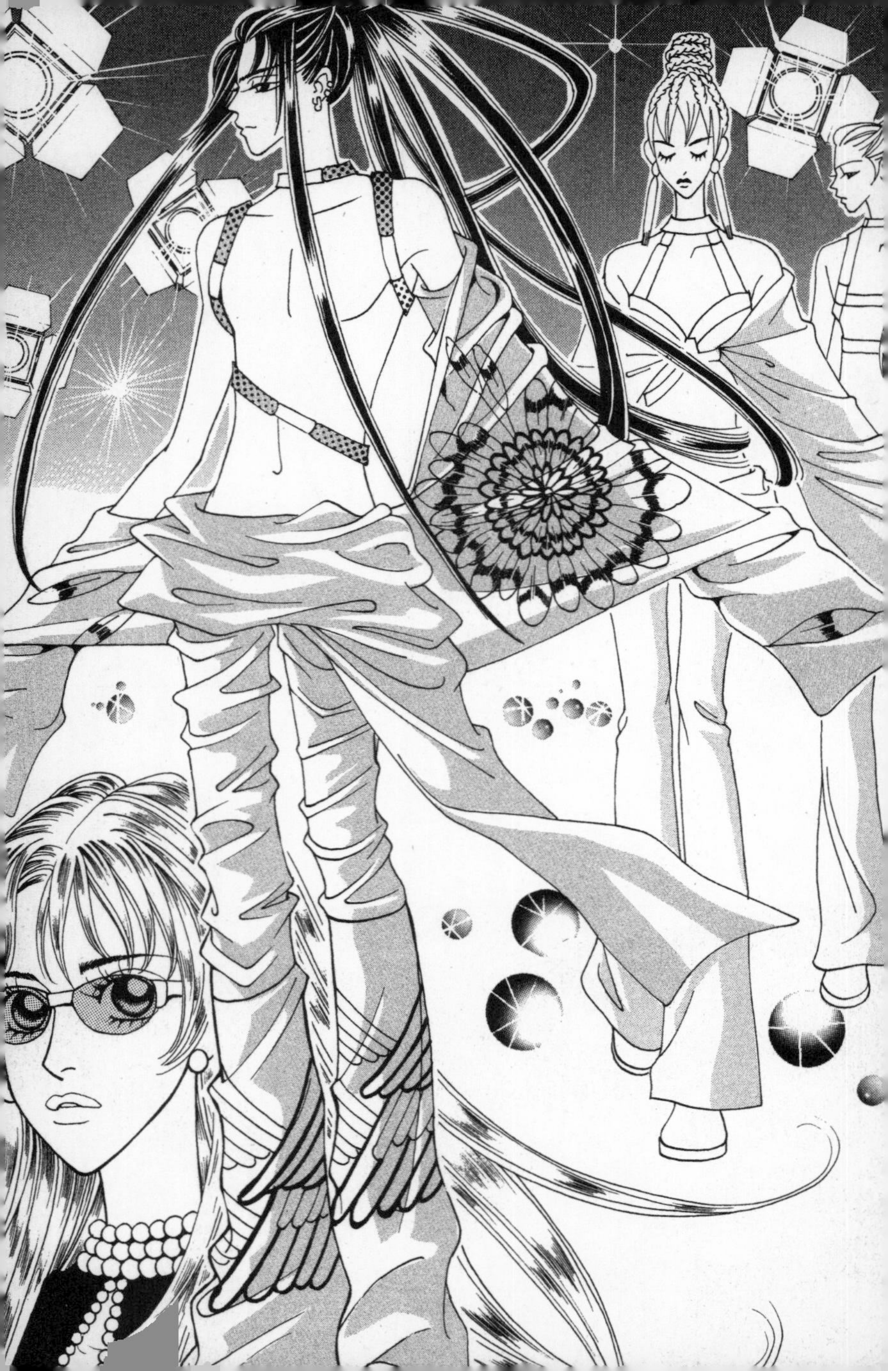

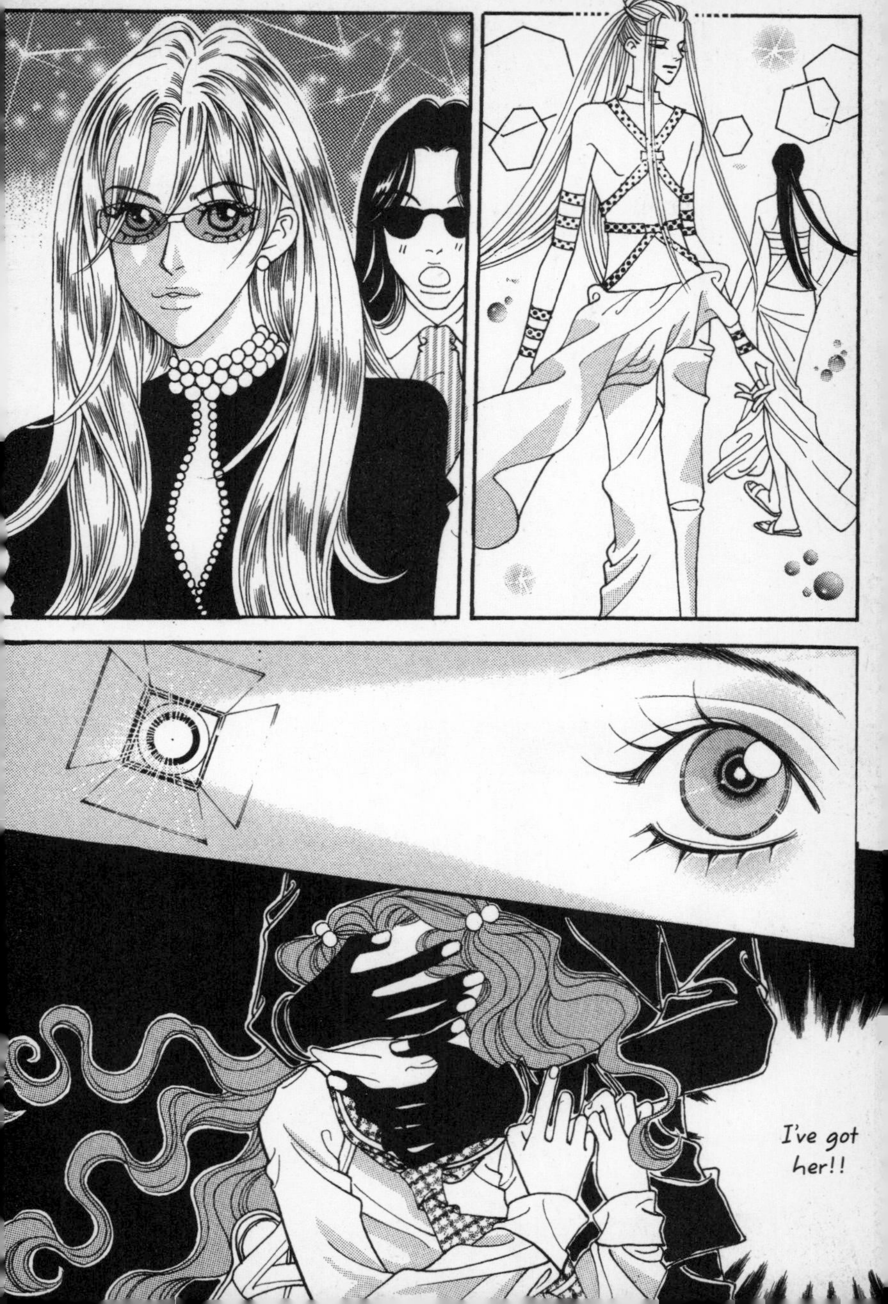
I've got her!!

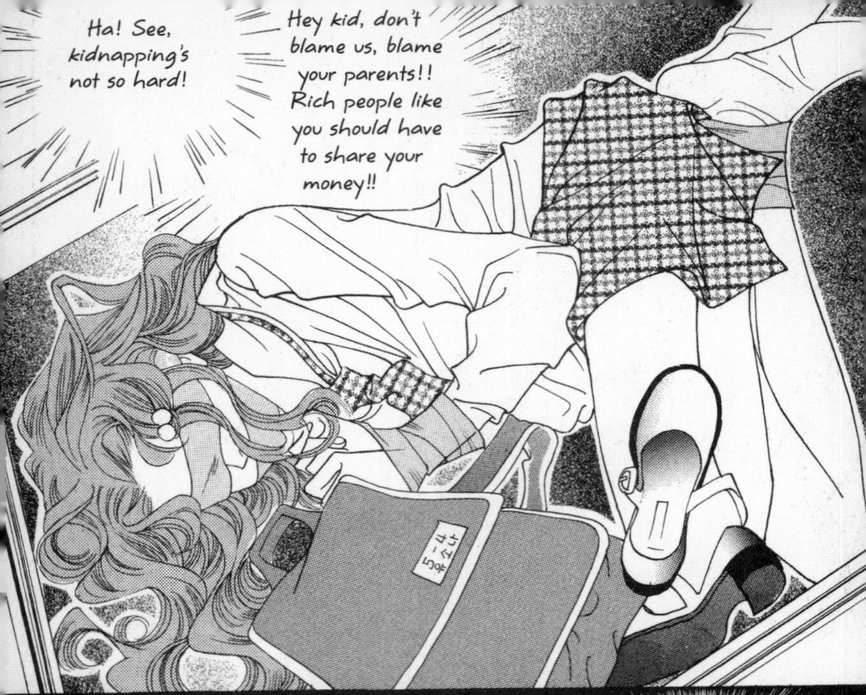
Ha! See, kidnapping's not so hard!
Hey kid, don't blame us, blame your parents!! Rich people like you should have to share your money!!
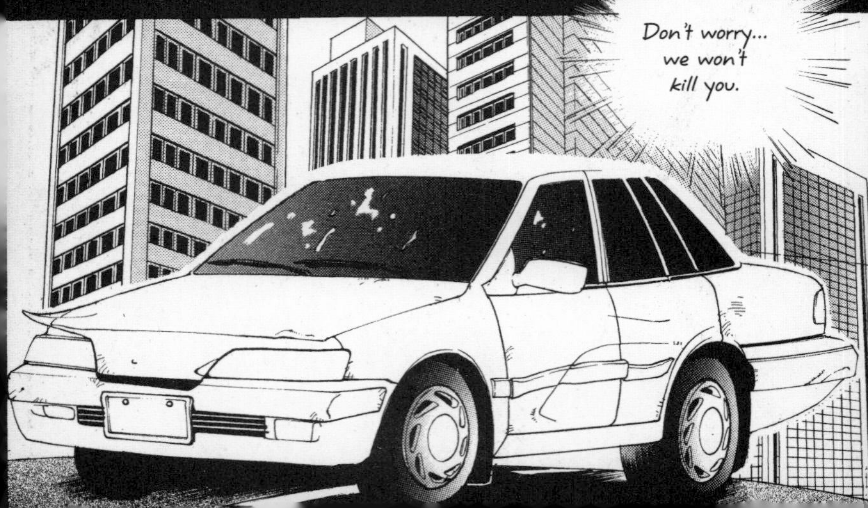
Don't worry... we won't kill you.

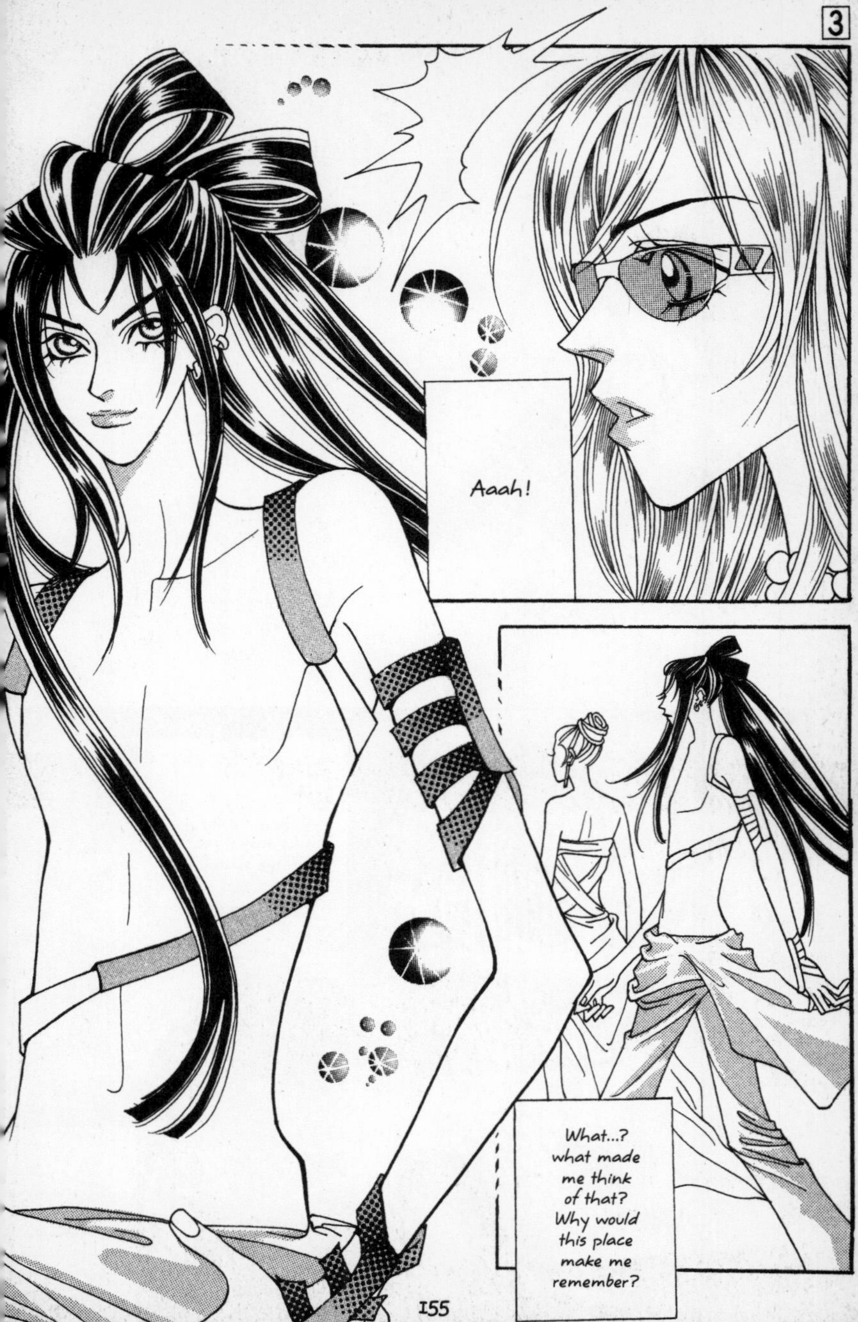
3
Aaah!
What...?
what made
me think
of that?
Why would
this place
make me
remember?

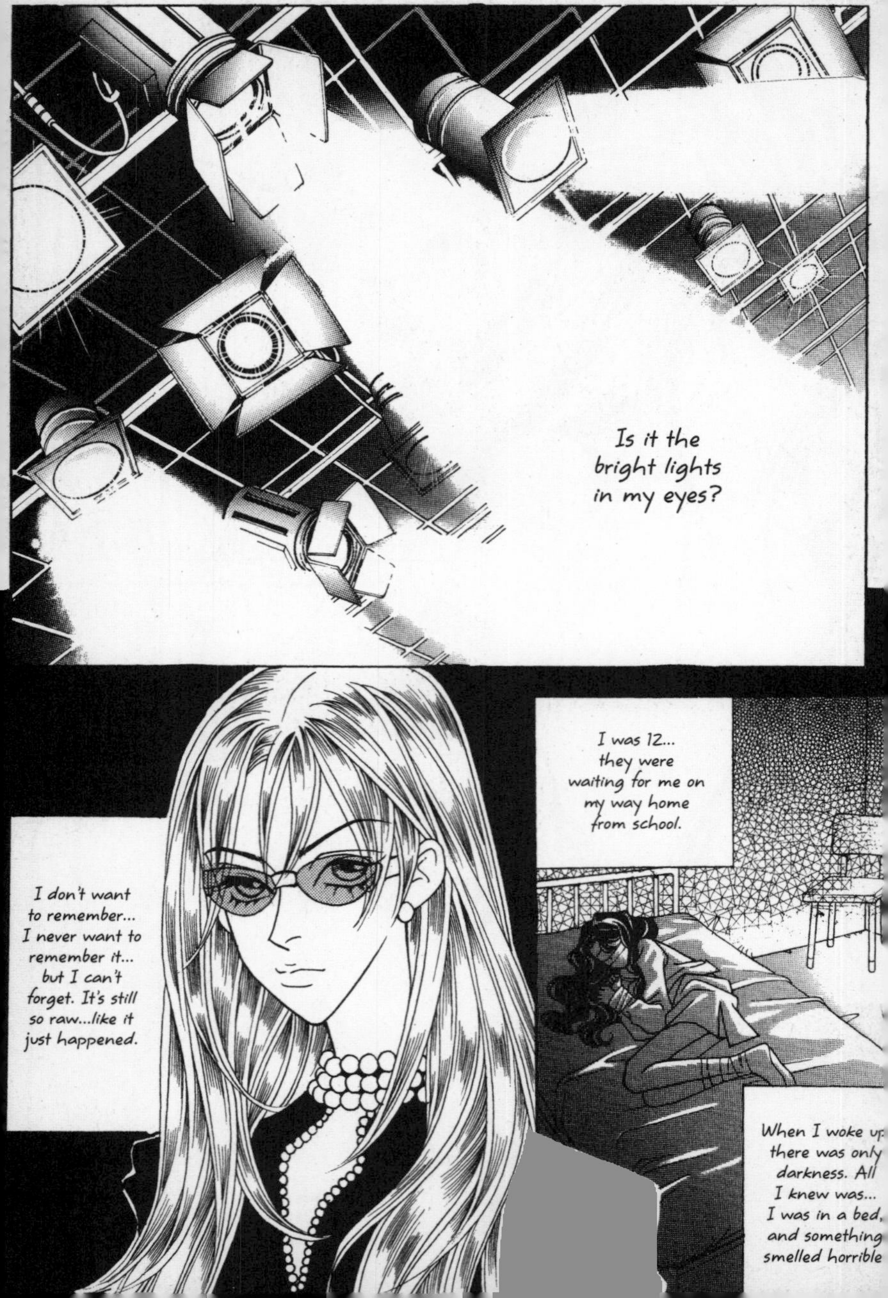
Is it the bright lights in my eyes?
I don't want to remember... I never want to remember it... but I can't forget. It's still so raw...like it just happened.
I was 12... they were waiting for me on my way home from school.
When I woke up there was only darkness. All I knew was... I was in a bed, and something smelled horrible

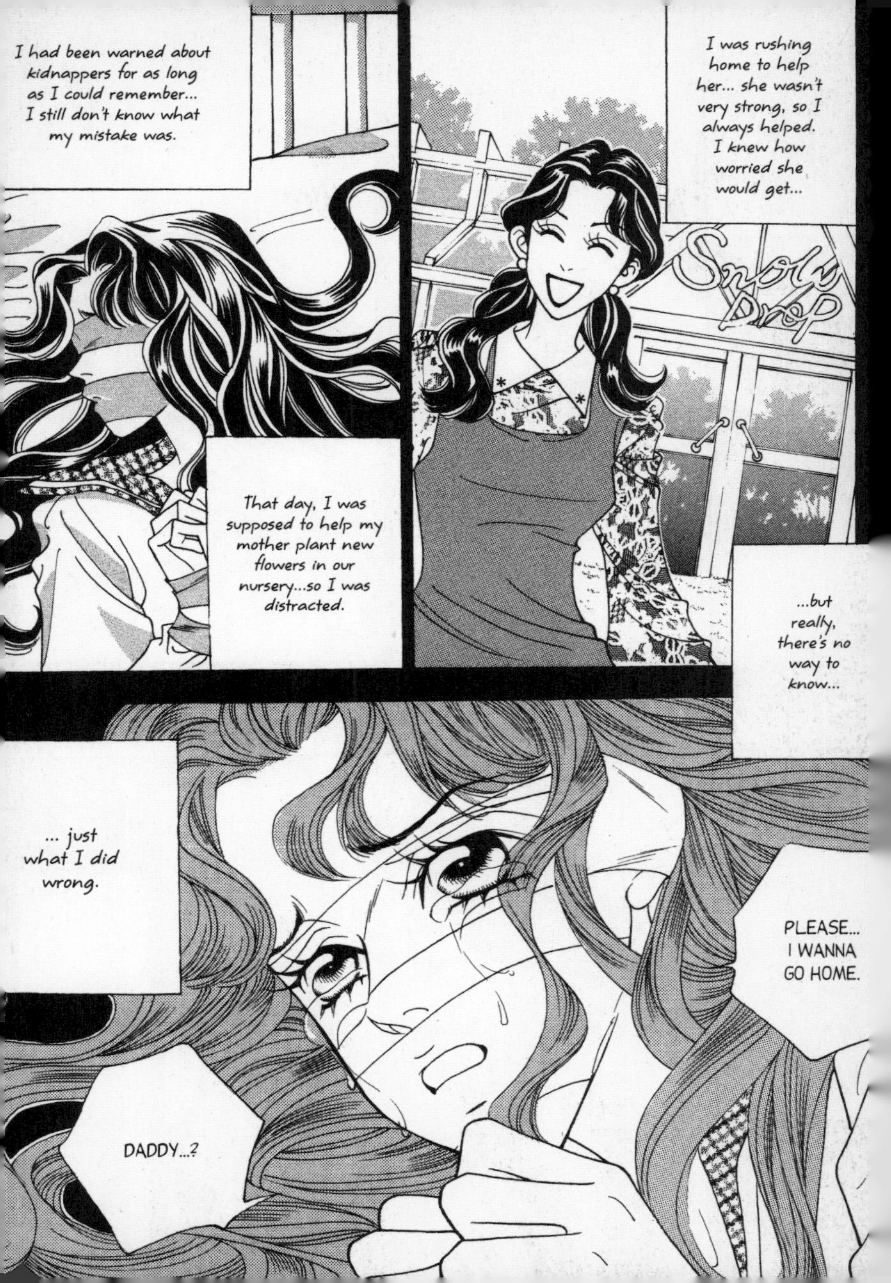
I had been warned about kidnappers for as long as I could remember... I still don't know what my mistake was.
That day, I was supposed to help my mother plant new flowers in our nursery...so I was distracted.
I was rushing home to help her... she wasn't very strong, so I always helped. I knew how worried she would get...
...but really, there's no way to know...
... just what I did wrong.
PLEASE... I WANNA GO HOME.
DADDY...?

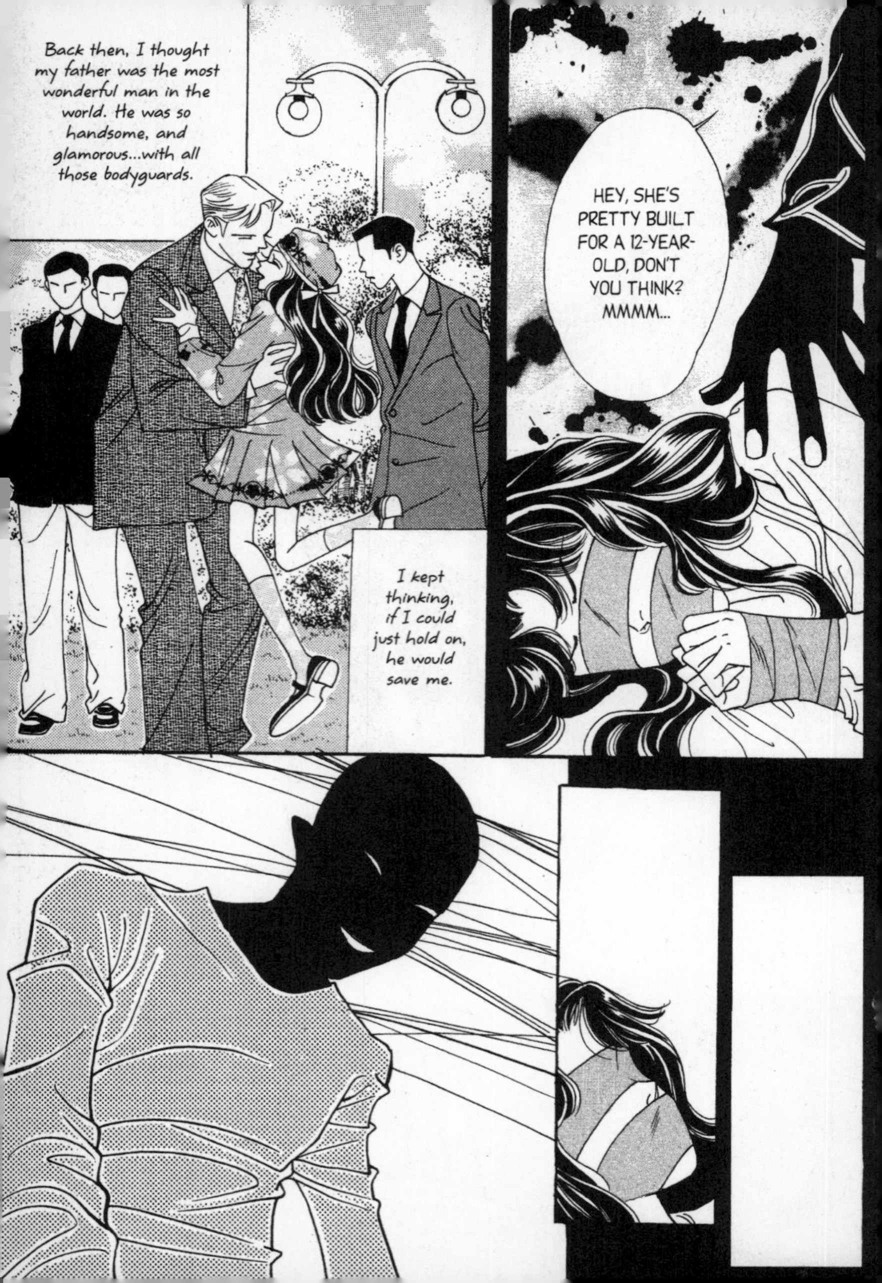
Back then, I thought my father was the most wonderful man in the world. He was so handsome, and glamorous...with all those bodyguards.
I kept thinking, if I could just hold on, he would save me.
HEY, SHE'S PRETTY BUILT FOR A 12-YEAR-OLD, DON'T YOU THINK? MMMM...

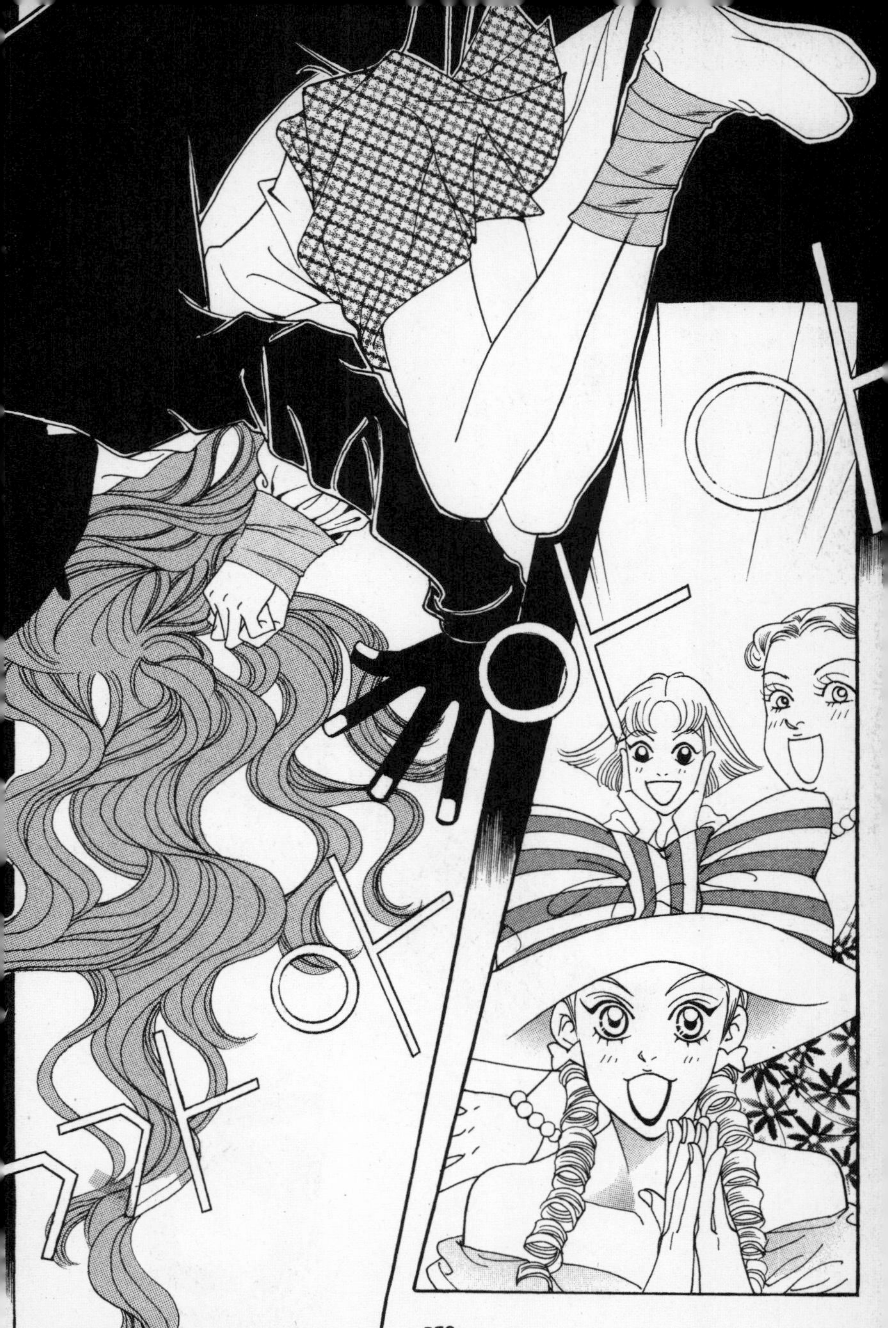

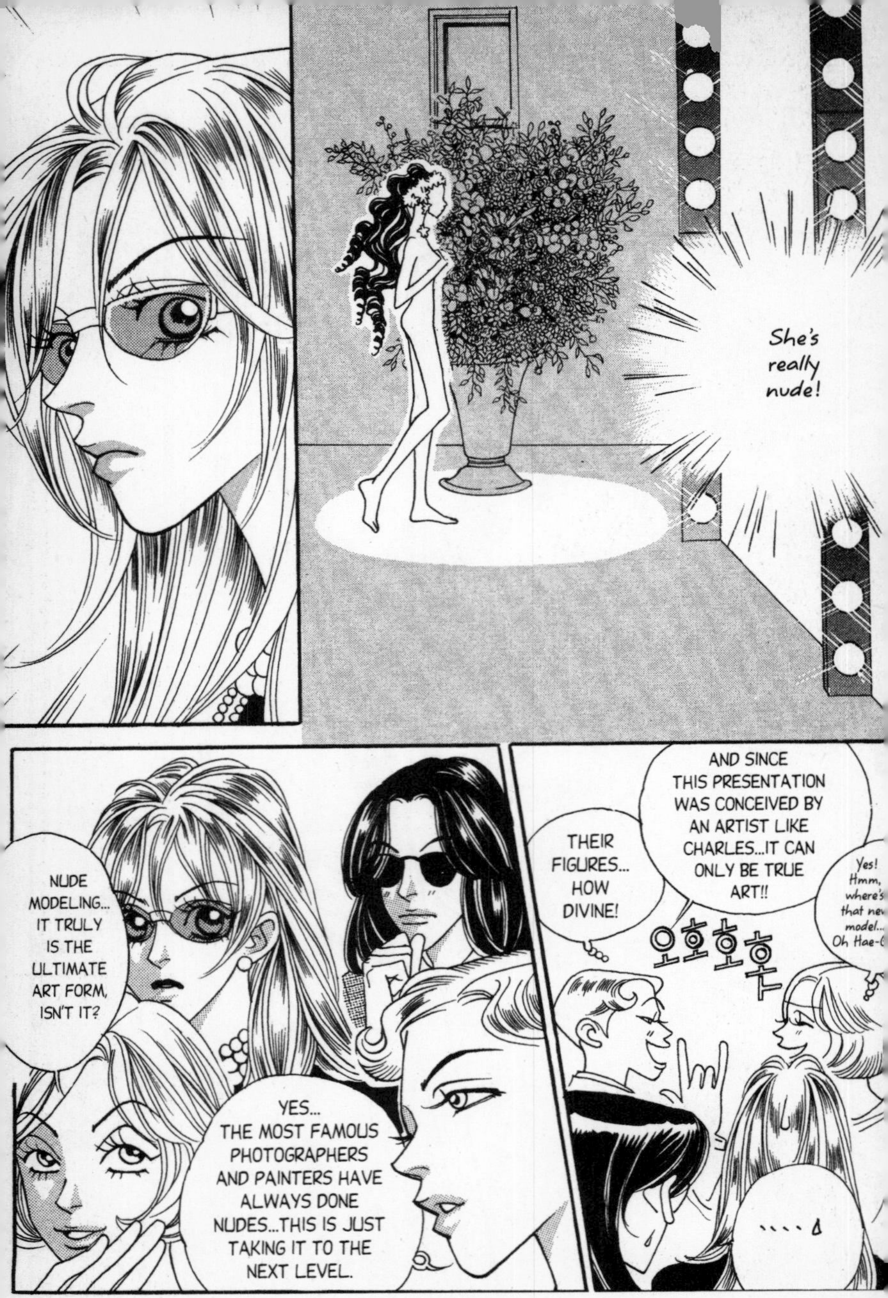
She's really nude!
NUDE MODELING... IT TRULY IS THE ULTIMATE ART FORM, ISN'T IT?
YES... THE MOST FAMOUS PHOTOGRAPHERS AND PAINTERS HAVE ALWAYS DONE NUDES...THIS IS JUST TAKING IT TO THE NEXT LEVEL.
THEIR FIGURES... HOW DIVINE!
AND SINCE THIS PRESENTATION WAS CONCEIVED BY AN ARTIST LIKE CHARLES...IT CAN ONLY BE TRUE ART!!
오호호호
Yes! Hmm, where's that new model... Oh Hae-

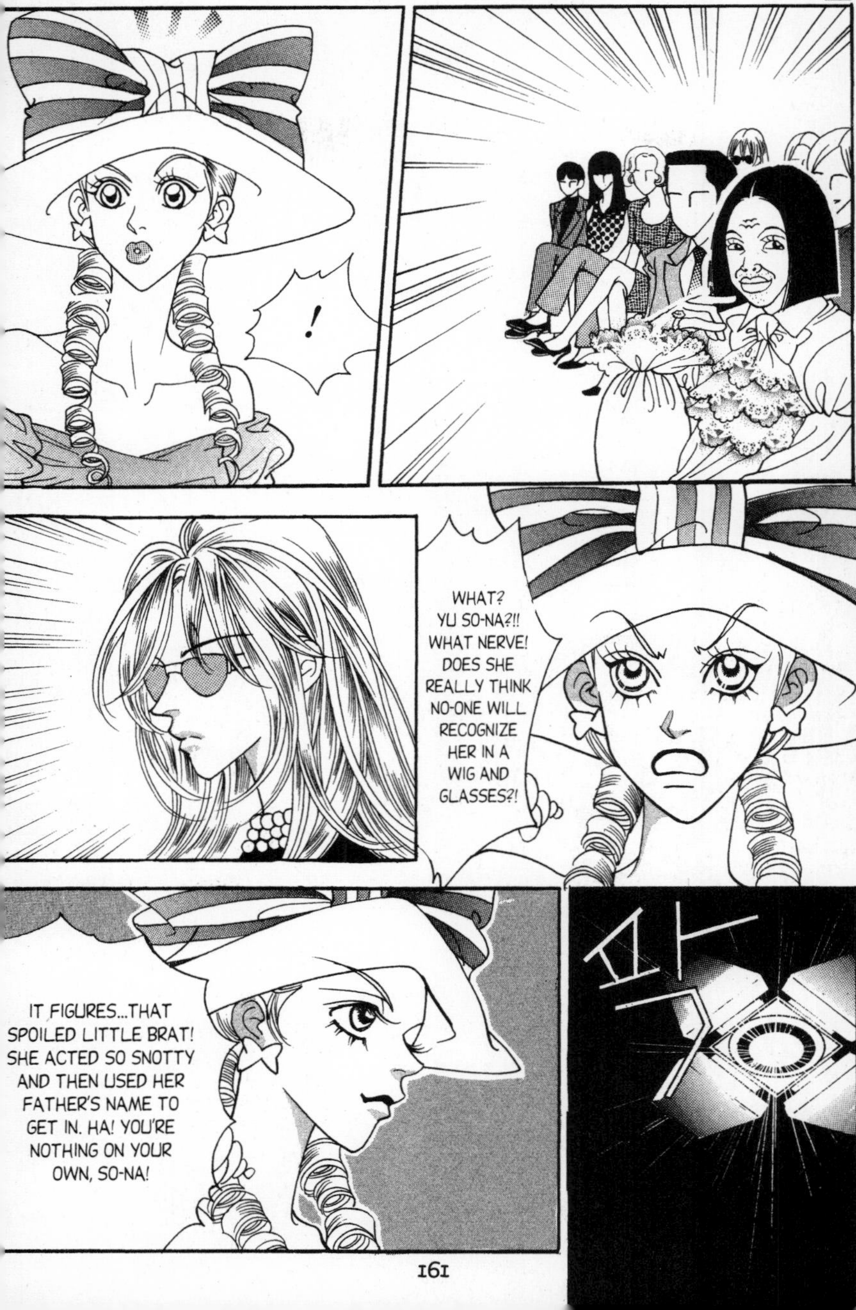
!
WHAT? YU SO-NA?!! WHAT NERVE! DOES SHE REALLY THINK NO-ONE WILL RECOGNIZE HER IN A WIG AND GLASSES?!
IT FIGURES...THAT SPOILED LITTLE BRAT! SHE ACTED SO SNOTTY AND THEN USED HER FATHER'S NAME TO GET IN. HA! YOU'RE NOTHING ON YOUR OWN, SO-NA!

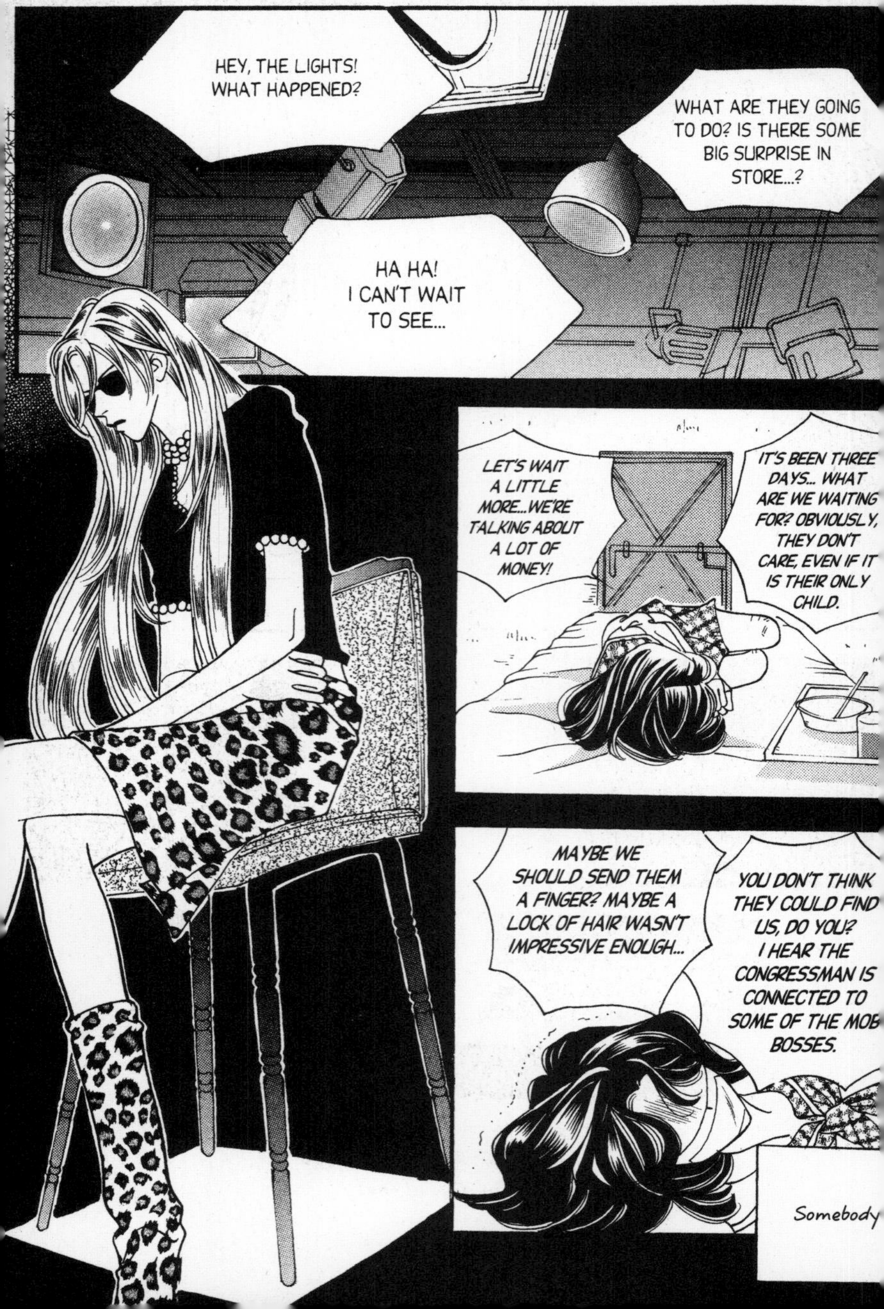
HEY, THE LIGHTS! WHAT HAPPENED?
WHAT ARE THEY GOING TO DO? IS THERE SOME BIG SURPRISE IN STORE...?
HA HA! I CAN'T WAIT TO SEE...
LET'S WAIT A LITTLE MORE...WE'RE TALKING ABOUT A LOT OF MONEY!
IT'S BEEN THREE DAYS... WHAT ARE WE WAITING FOR? OBVIOUSLY, THEY DON'T CARE, EVEN IF IT IS THEIR ONLY CHILD.
MAYBE WE SHOULD SEND THEM A FINGER? MAYBE A LOCK OF HAIR WASN'T IMPRESSIVE ENOUGH...
YOU DON'T THINK THEY COULD FIND US, DO YOU? I HEAR THE CONGRESSMAN IS CONNECTED TO SOME OF THE MOB BOSSES.
Somebody

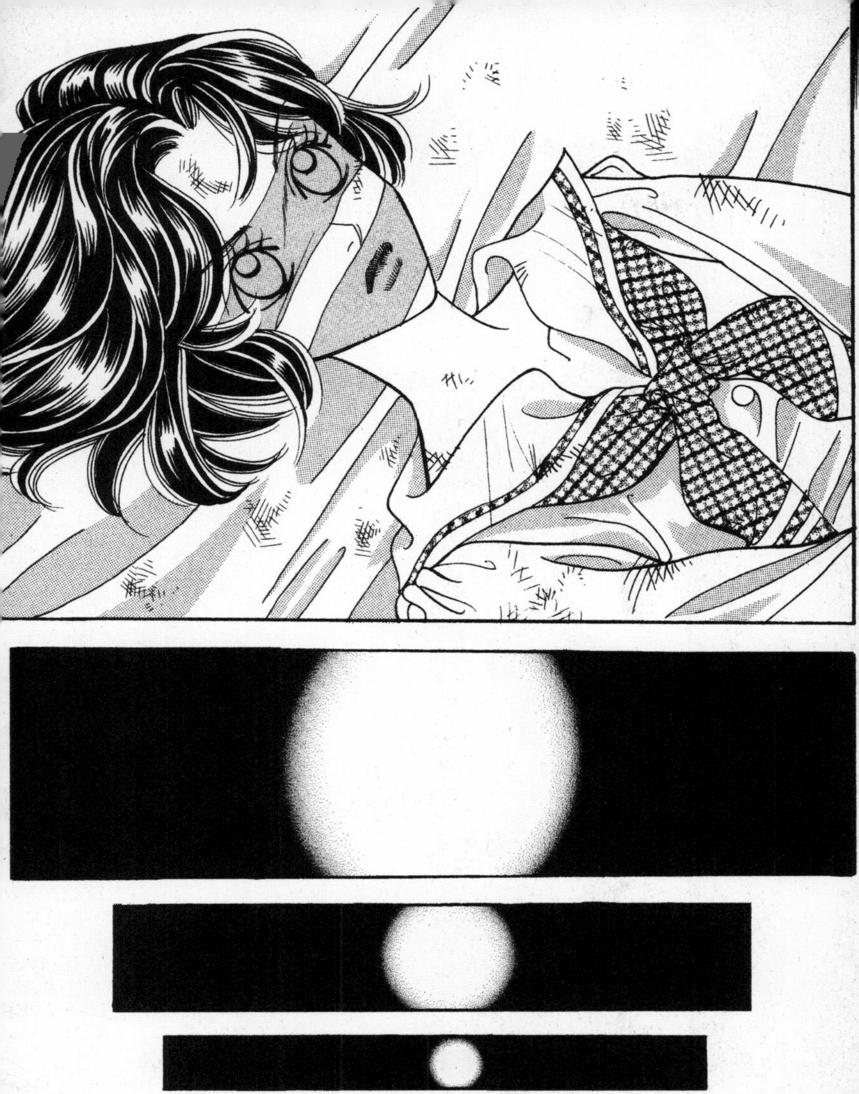

...please kill these people
and save me.

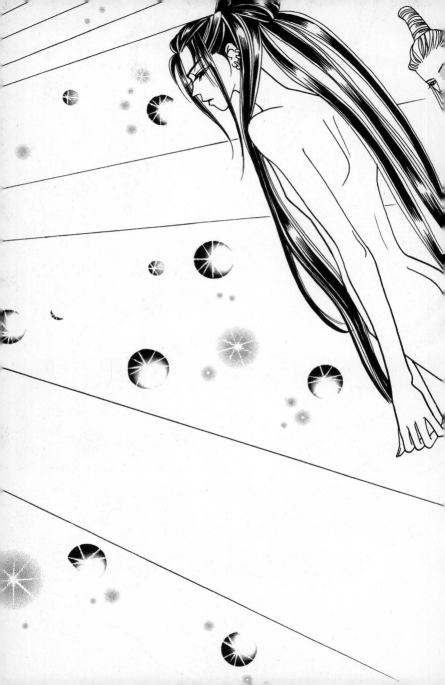

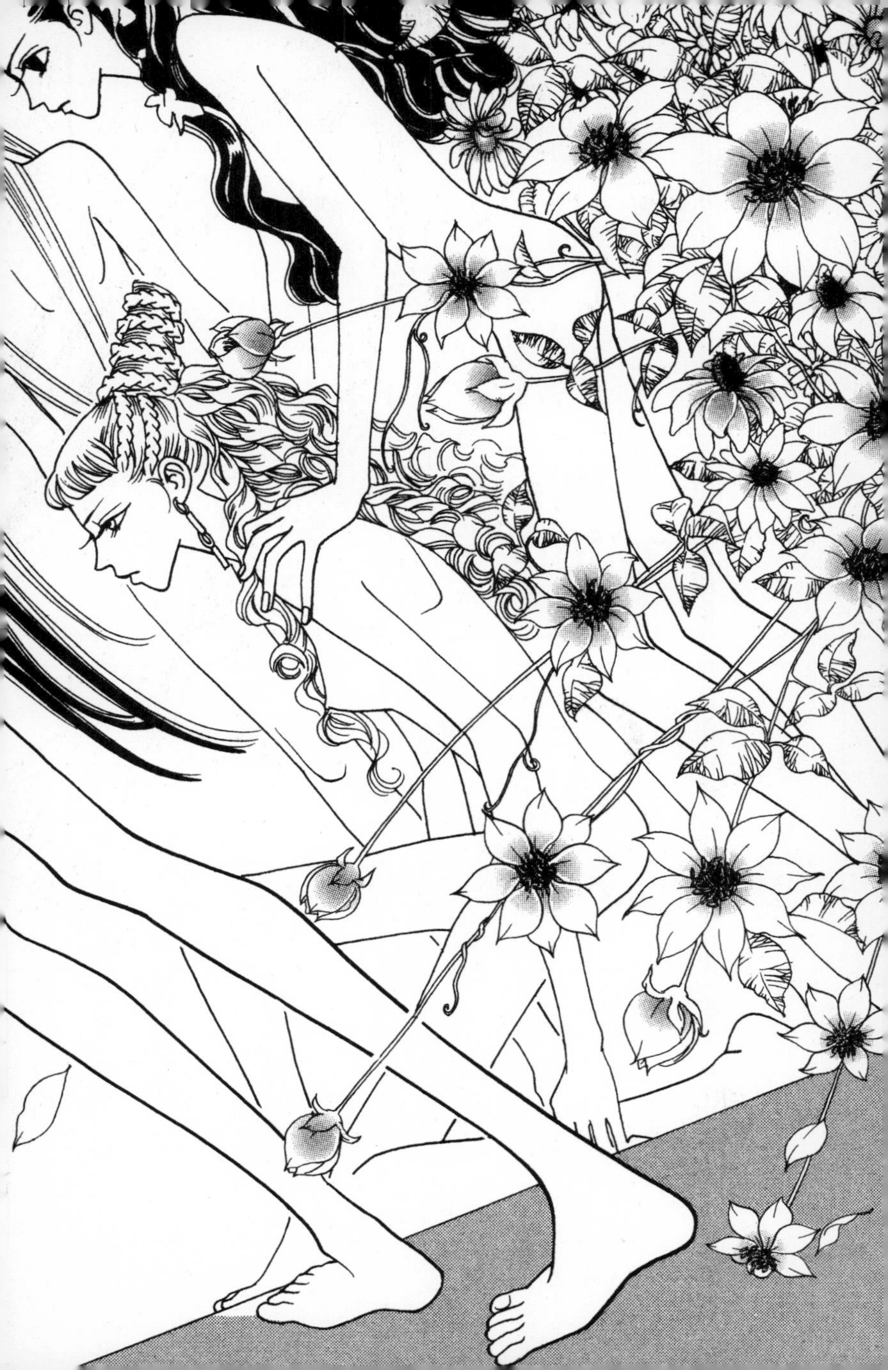

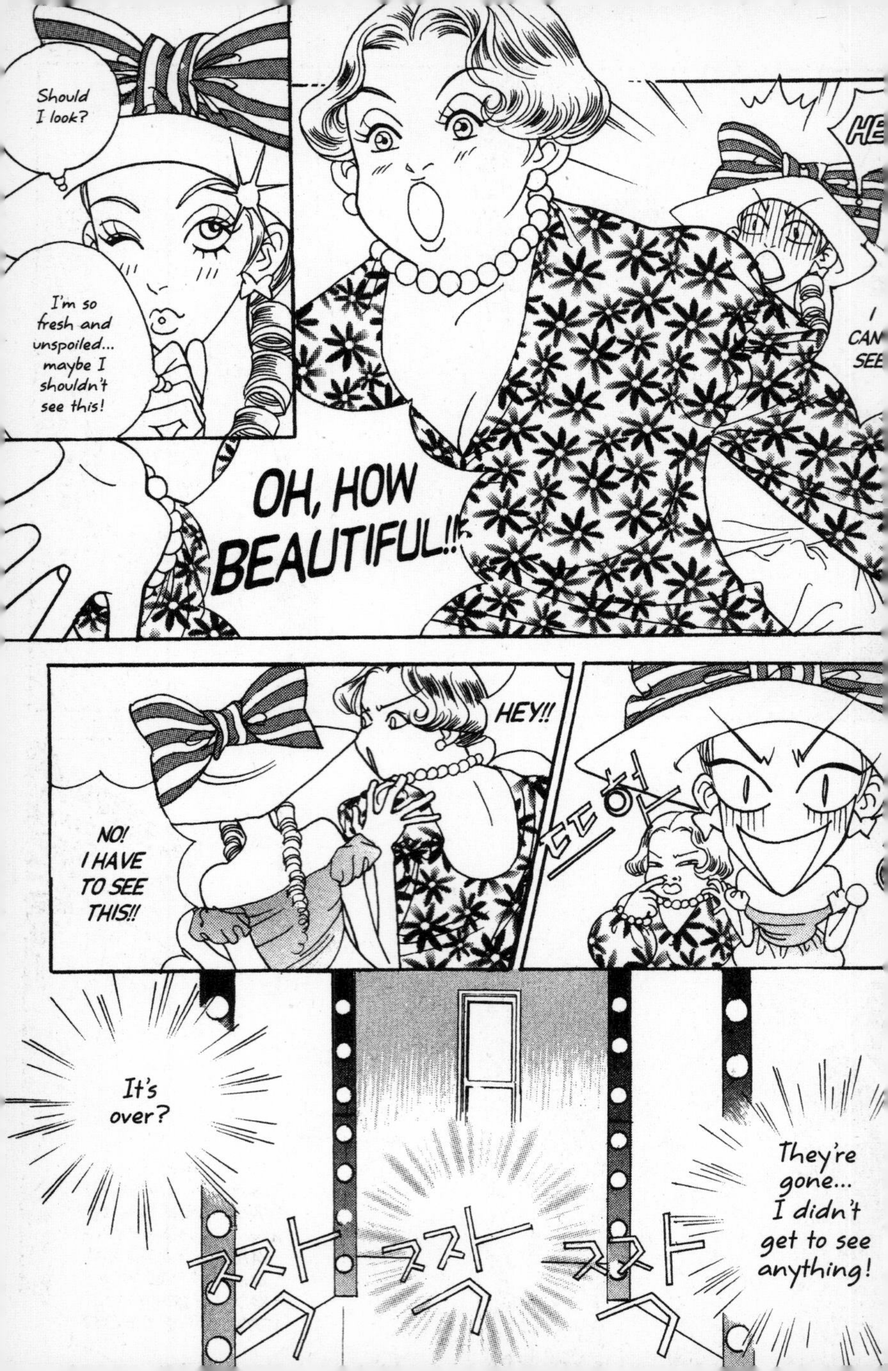
HE
I CAN SEE
OH, HOW BEAUTIFUL!!
Should I look?
I'm so fresh and unspoiled... maybe I shouldn't see this!
HEY!!
NO! I HAVE TO SEE THIS!!
They're gone... I didn't get to see anything!
It's over?

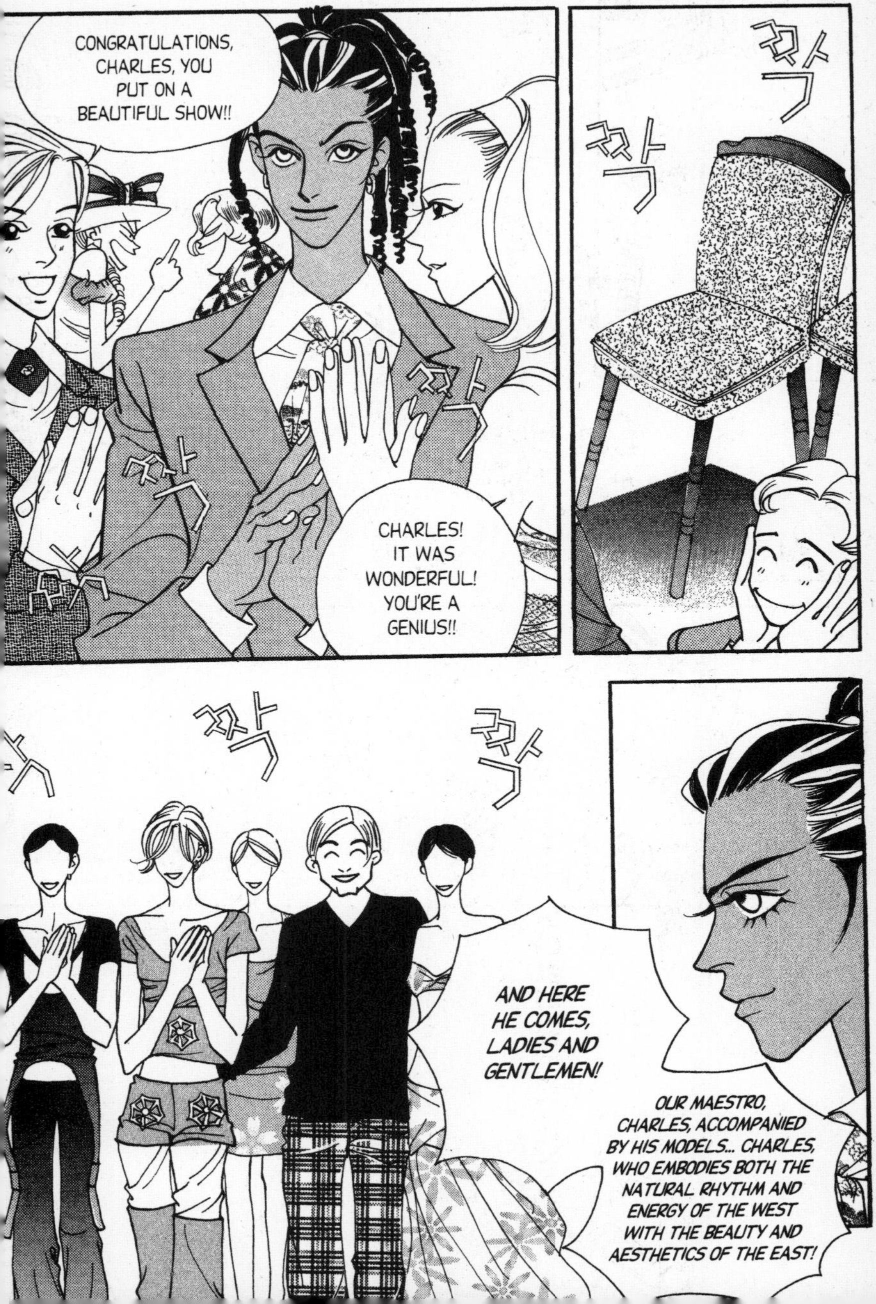
CONGRATULATIONS, CHARLES, YOU PUT ON A BEAUTIFUL SHOW!!
CHARLES! IT WAS WONDERFUL! YOU'RE A GENIUS!!
AND HERE HE COMES, LADIES AND GENTLEMEN!
OUR MAESTRO, CHARLES, ACCOMPANIED BY HIS MODELS... CHARLES, WHO EMBODIES BOTH THE NATURAL RHYTHM AND ENERGY OF THE WEST WITH THE BEAUTY AND AESTHETICS OF THE EAST!

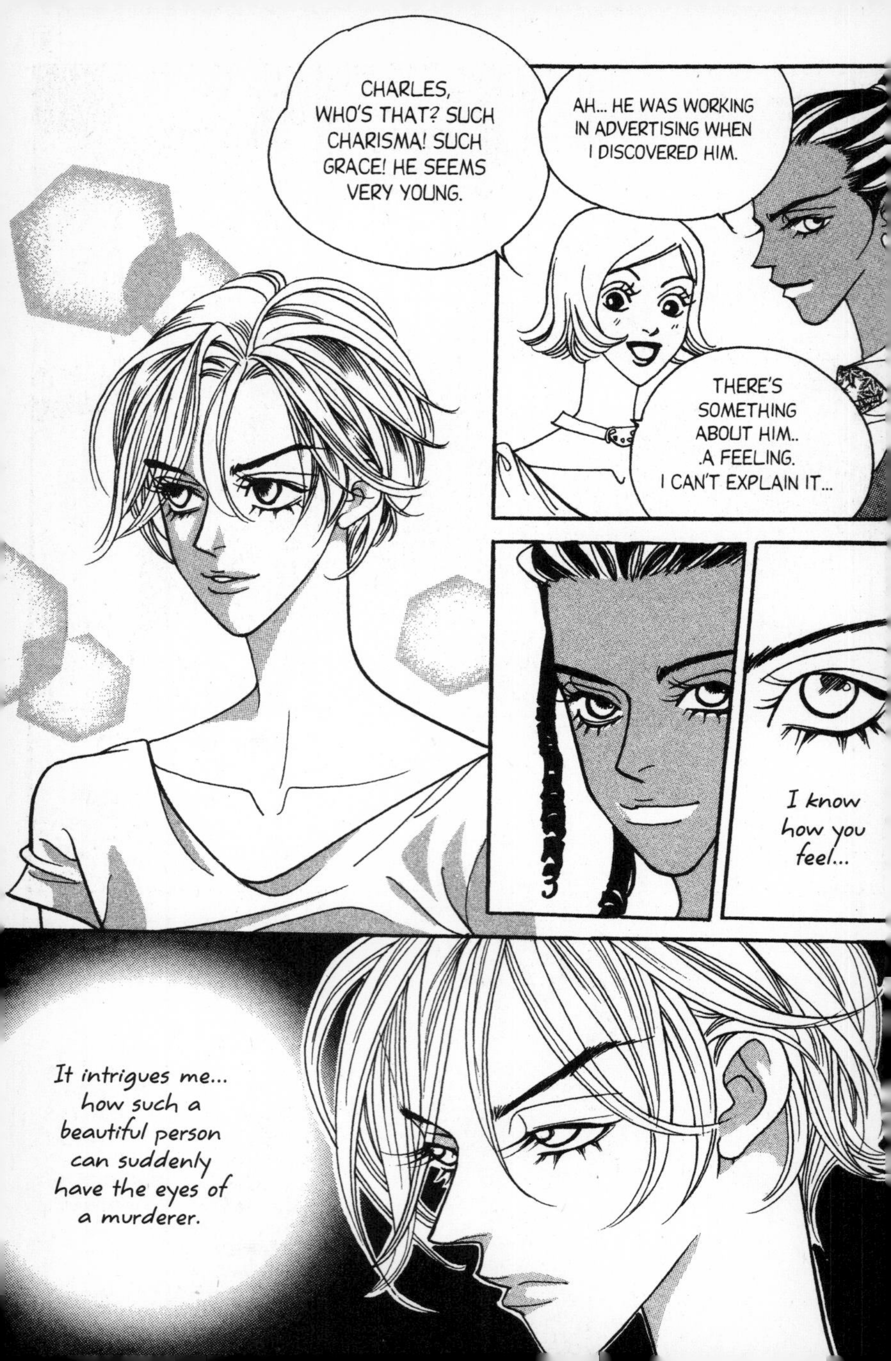
CHARLES, WHO'S THAT? SUCH CHARISMA! SUCH GRACE! HE SEEMS VERY YOUNG.
AH... HE WAS WORKING IN ADVERTISING WHEN I DISCOVERED HIM.
THERE'S SOMETHING ABOUT HIM.. .A FEELING. I CAN'T EXPLAIN IT...
I know how you feel...
It intrigues me... how such a beautiful person can suddenly have the eyes of a murderer.

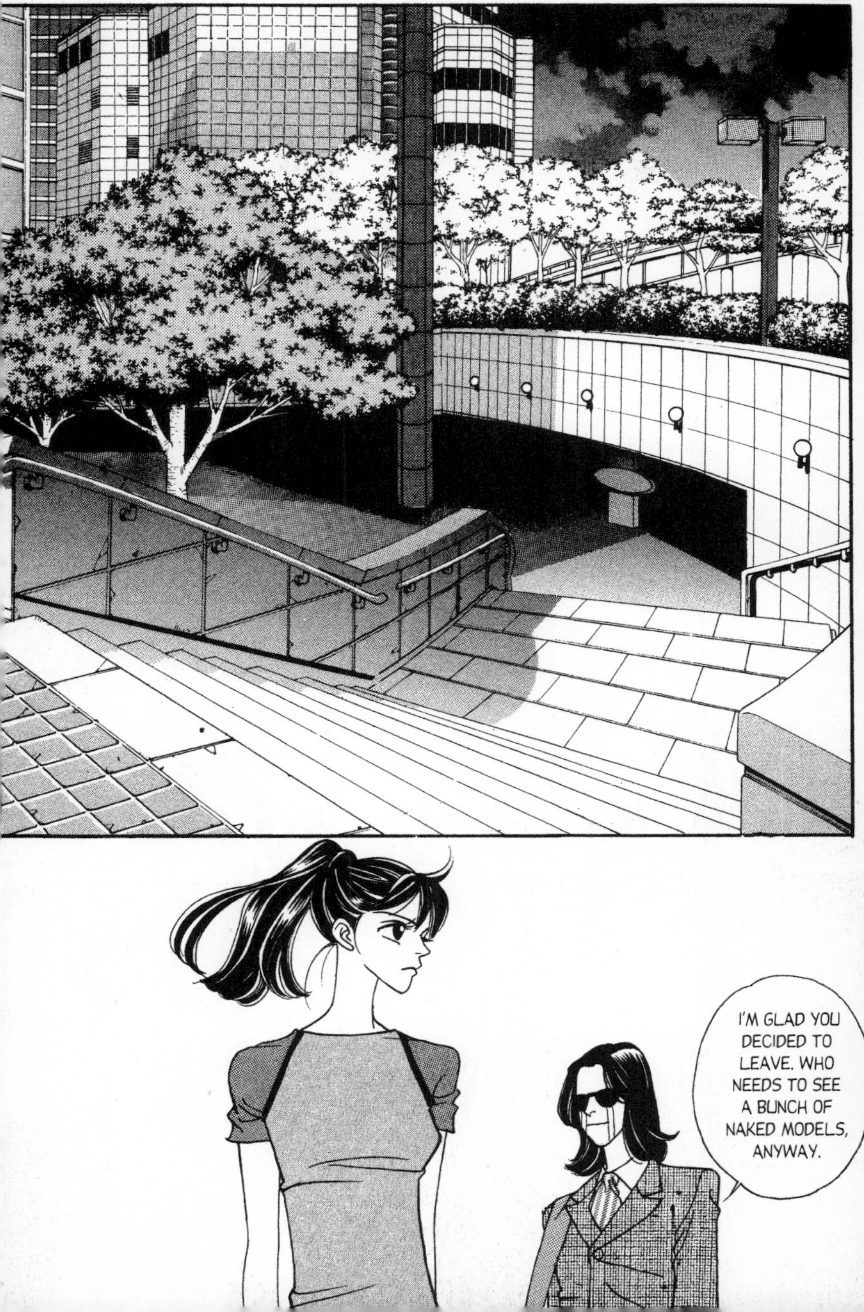
I'M GLAD YOU DECIDED TO LEAVE. WHO NEEDS TO SEE A BUNCH OF NAKED MODELS, ANYWAY.

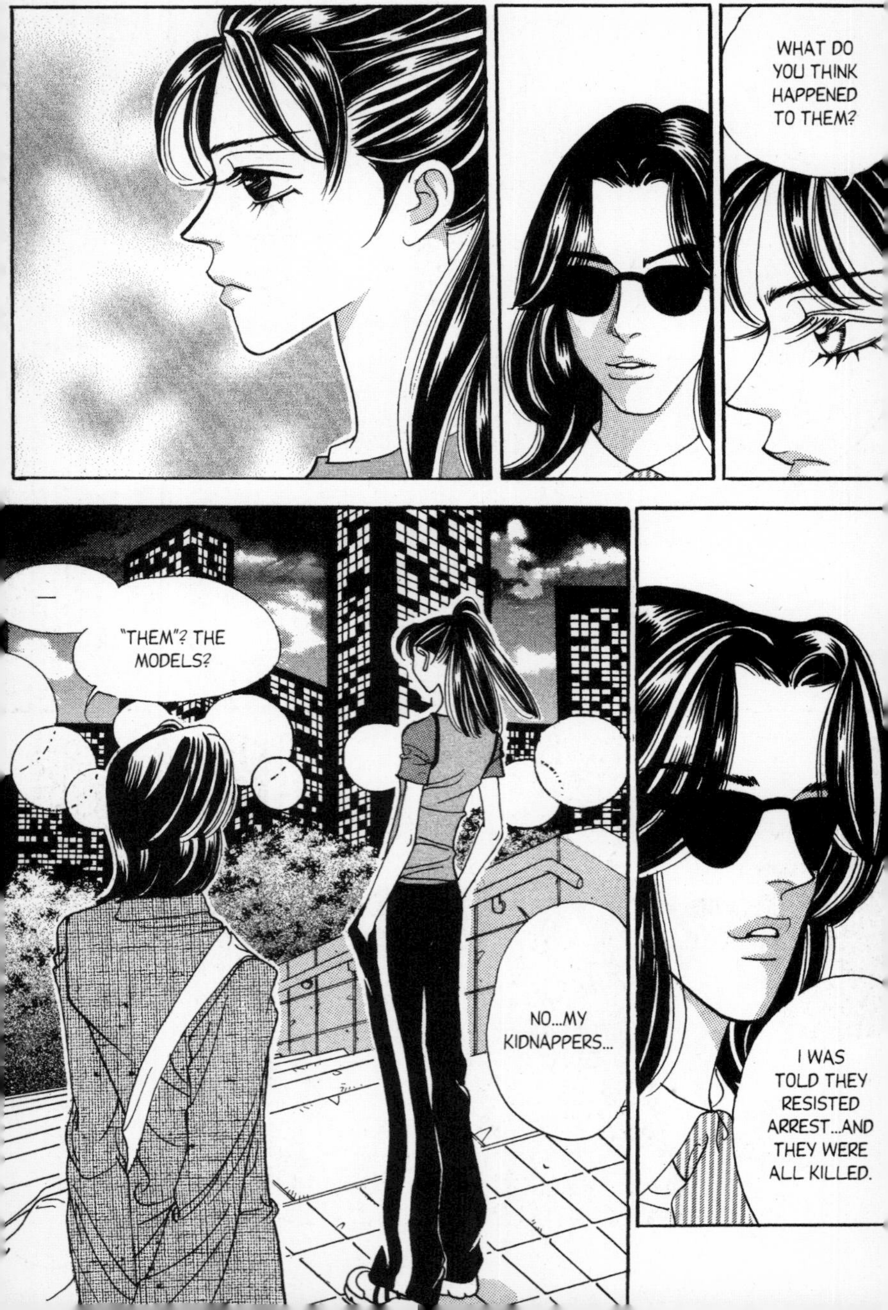
WHAT DO YOU THINK HAPPENED TO THEM?
"THEM"? THE MODELS?
NO...MY KIDNAPPERS...
I WAS TOLD THEY RESISTED ARREST...AND THEY WERE ALL KILLED.

DO YOU THINK THEY *LEFT* FAMILIES?

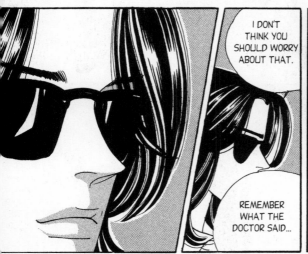

I DON'T THINK YOU SHOULD WORRY ABOUT THAT.

REMEMBER WHAT THE DOCTOR SAID...

THEY SAID THEY NEEDED MONEY FOR THEIR FAMILY.

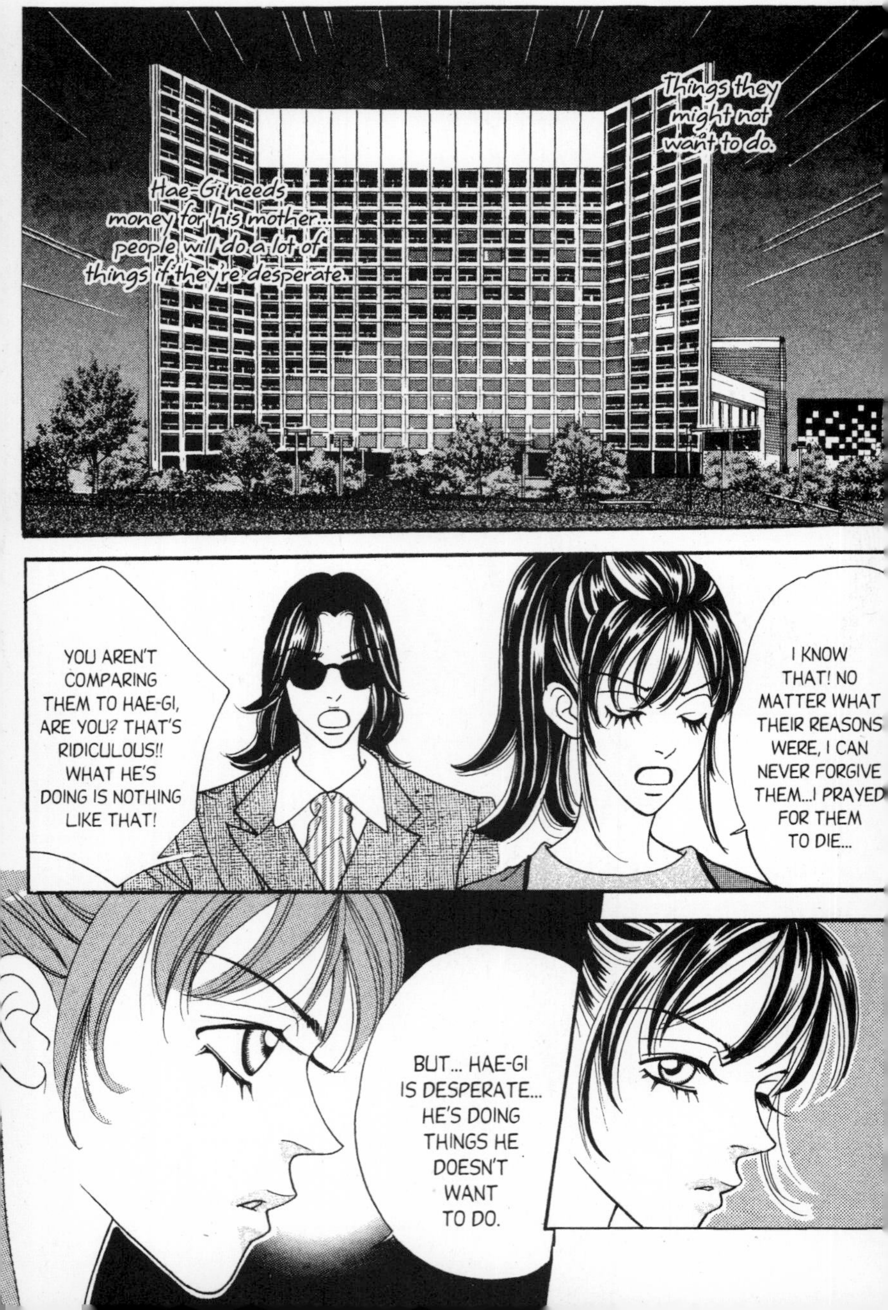
Hae-Gi needs money for his mother... people will do a lot of things if they're desperate.
Things they might not want to do.
YOU AREN'T COMPARING THEM TO HAE-GI, ARE YOU? THAT'S RIDICULOUS!! WHAT HE'S DOING IS NOTHING LIKE THAT!
I KNOW THAT! NO MATTER WHAT THEIR REASONS WERE, I CAN NEVER FORGIVE THEM...I PRAYED FOR THEM TO DIE...
BUT... HAE-GI IS DESPERATE... HE'S DOING THINGS HE DOESN'T WANT TO DO.

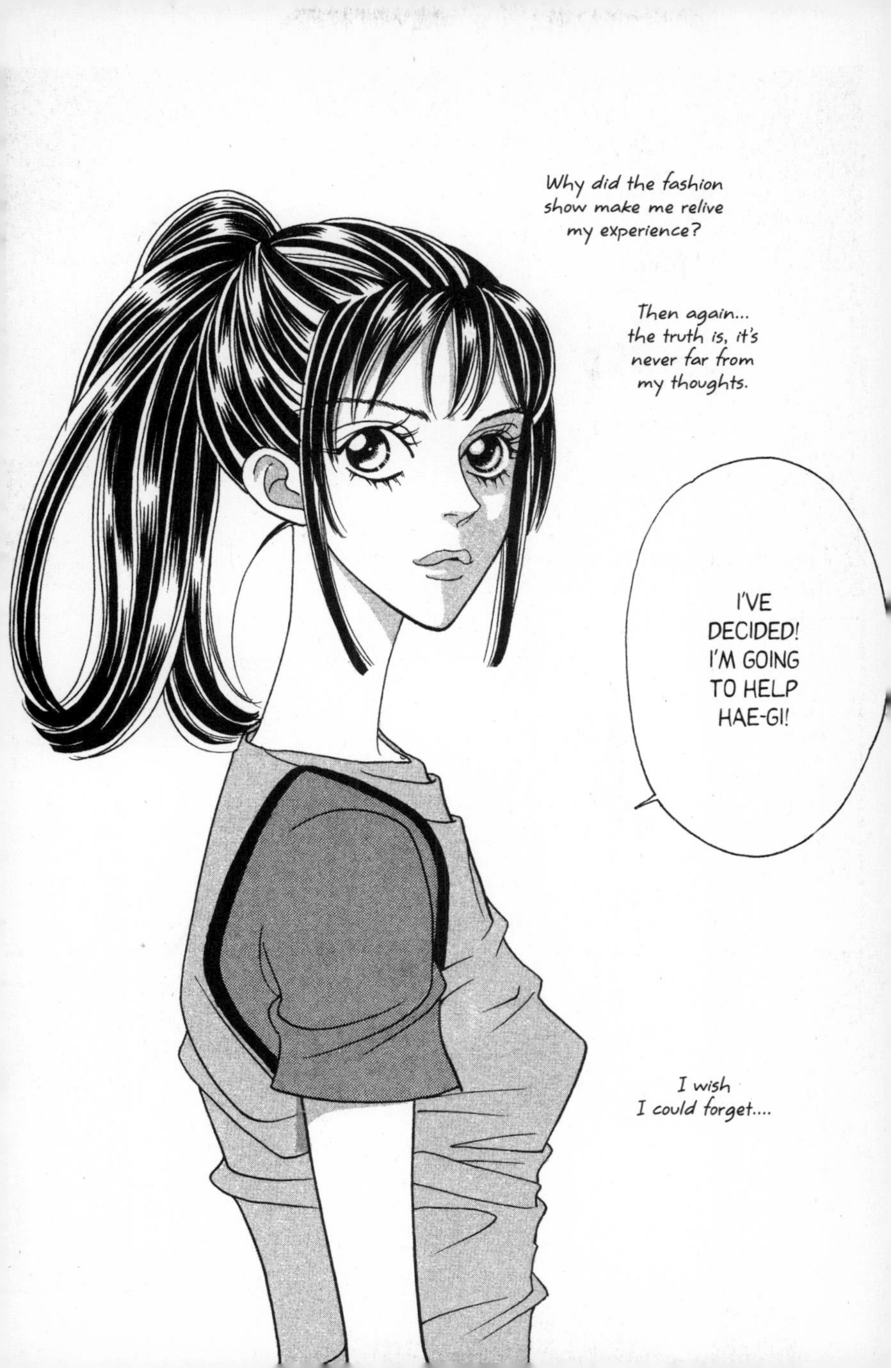
Why did the fashion show make me relive my experience?
Then again... the truth is, it's never far from my thoughts.
I'VE DECIDED! I'M GOING TO HELP HAE-GI!
I wish I could forget....

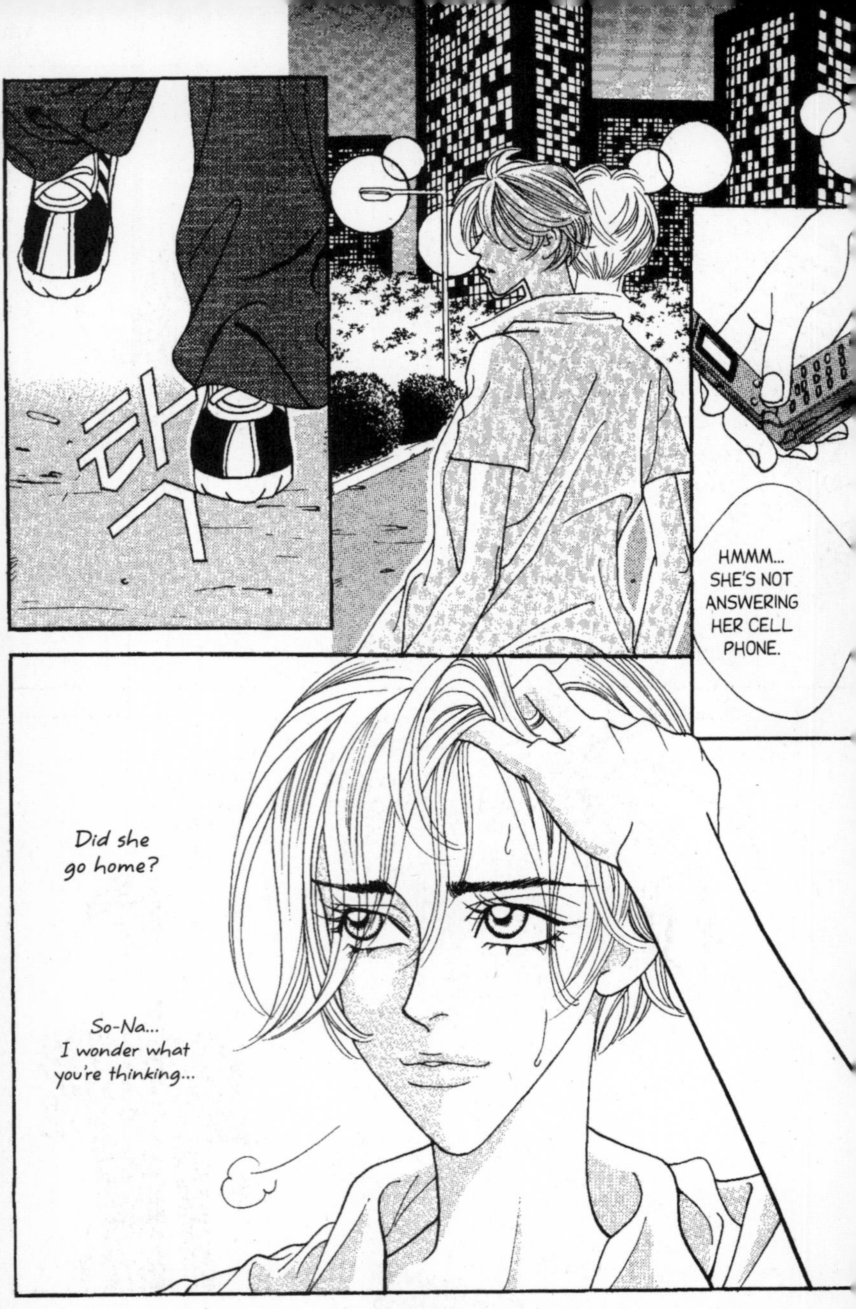
탓
HMMM... SHE'S NOT ANSWERING HER CELL PHONE.
Did she go home?
So-Na... I wonder what you're thinking...

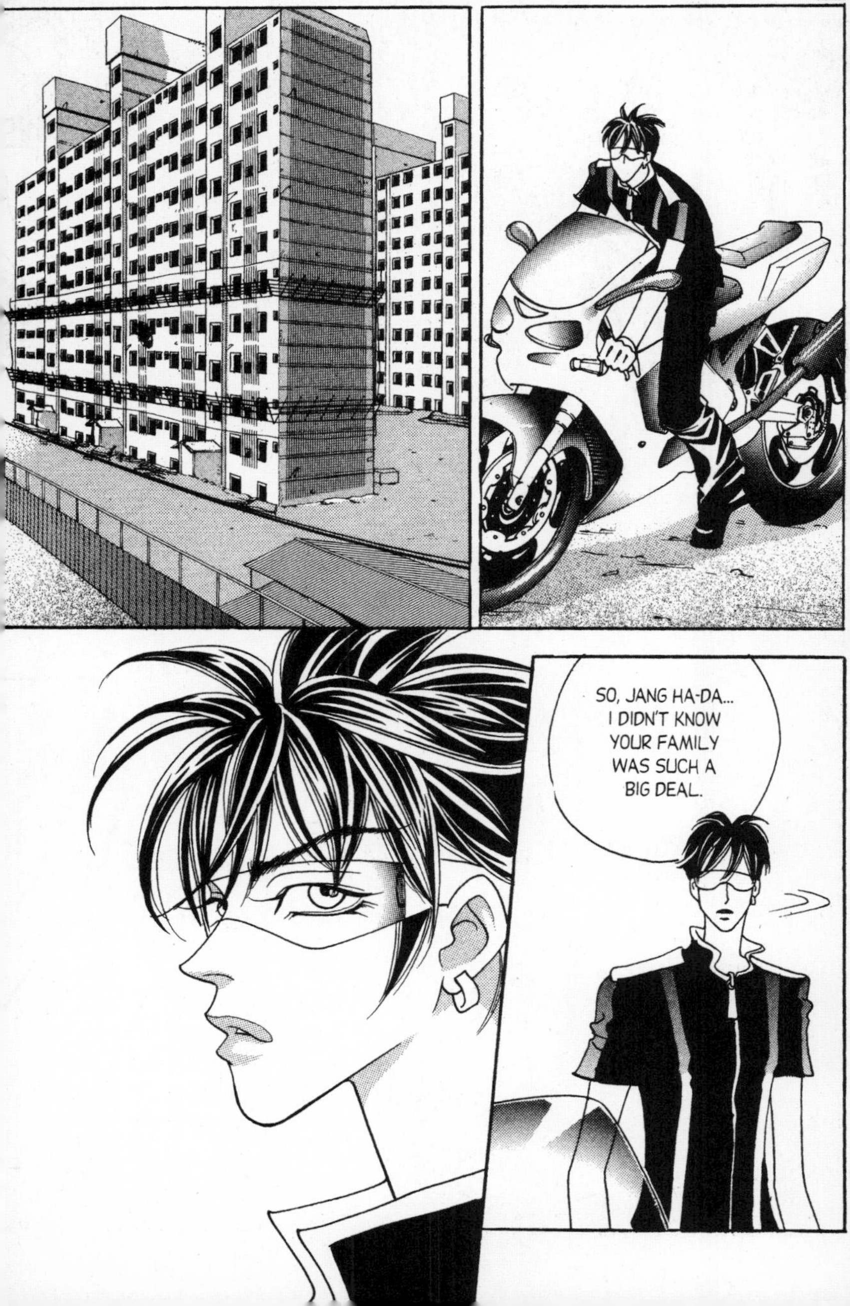
SO, JANG HA-DA...
I DIDN'T KNOW
YOUR FAMILY
WAS SUCH A
BIG DEAL.

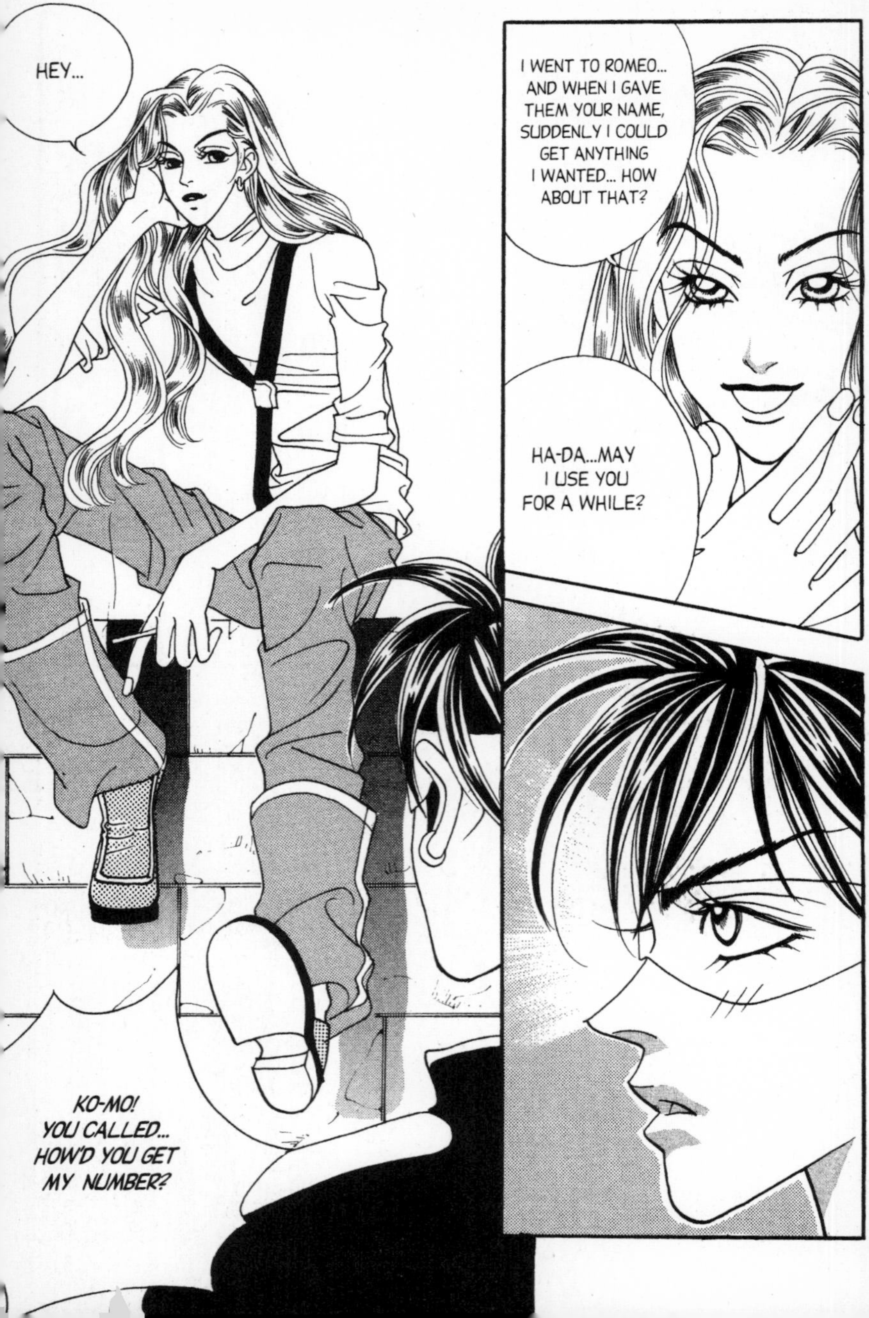
HEY...
KO-MO! YOU CALLED... HOW'D YOU GET MY NUMBER?
I WENT TO ROMEO... AND WHEN I GAVE THEM YOUR NAME, SUDDENLY I COULD GET ANYTHING I WANTED... HOW ABOUT THAT?
HA-DA...MAY I USE YOU FOR A WHILE?

# Part 13. Chrysanthemum

## A Truthful Person

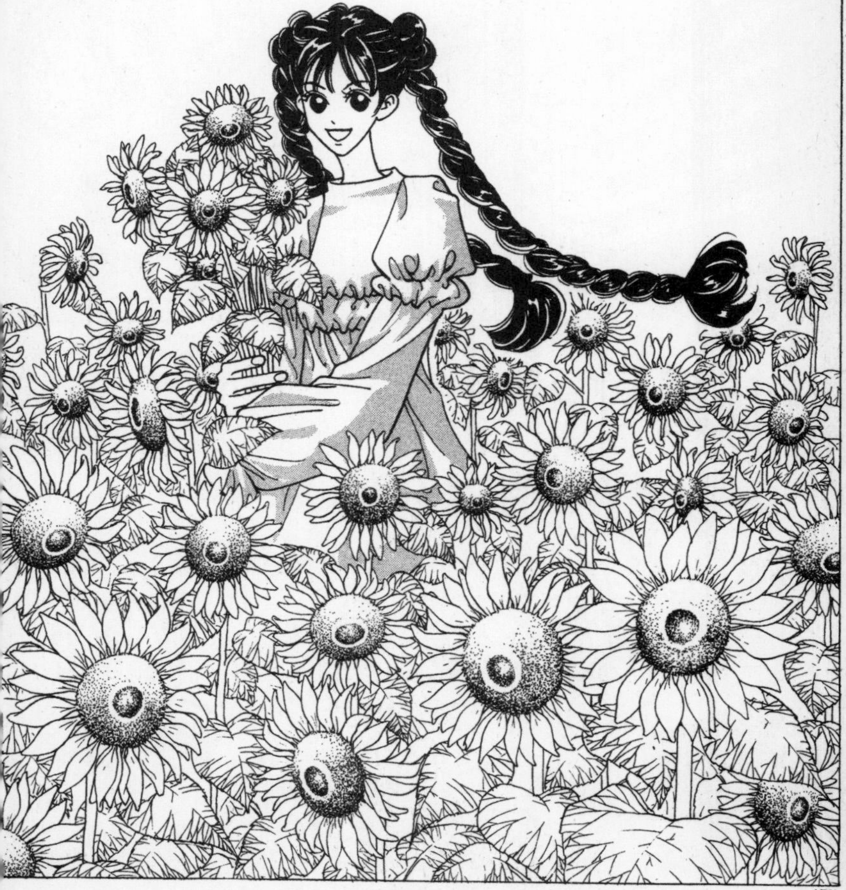

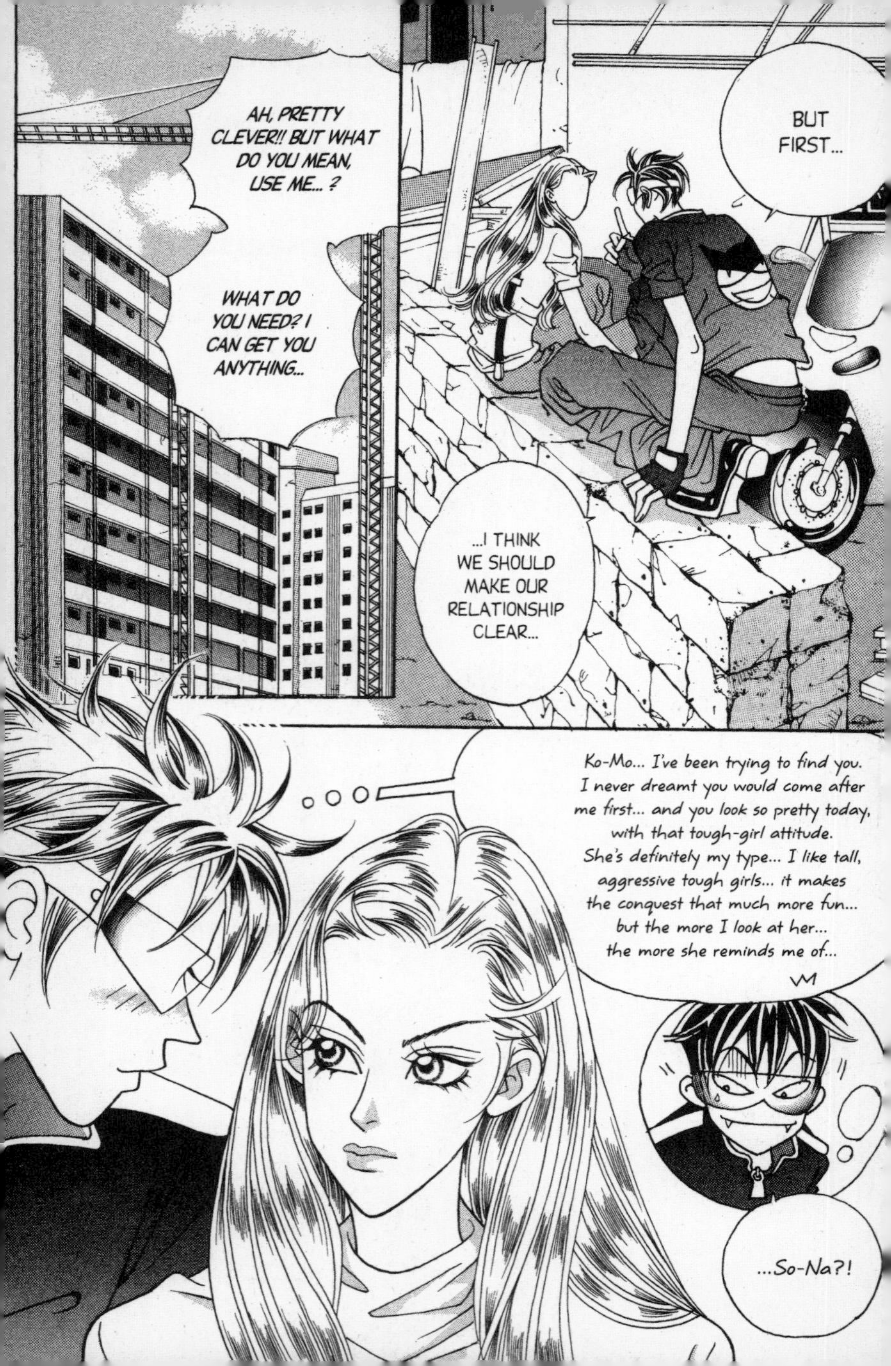
AH, PRETTY CLEVER!! BUT WHAT DO YOU MEAN, USE ME... ?
WHAT DO YOU NEED? I CAN GET YOU ANYTHING...
BUT FIRST...
...I THINK WE SHOULD MAKE OUR RELATIONSHIP CLEAR...
Ko-Mo... I've been trying to find you. I never dreamt you would come after me first... and you look so pretty today, with that tough-girl attitude. She's definitely my type... I like tall, aggressive tough girls... it makes the conquest that much more fun... but the more I look at her... the more she reminds me of...
...So-Na?!

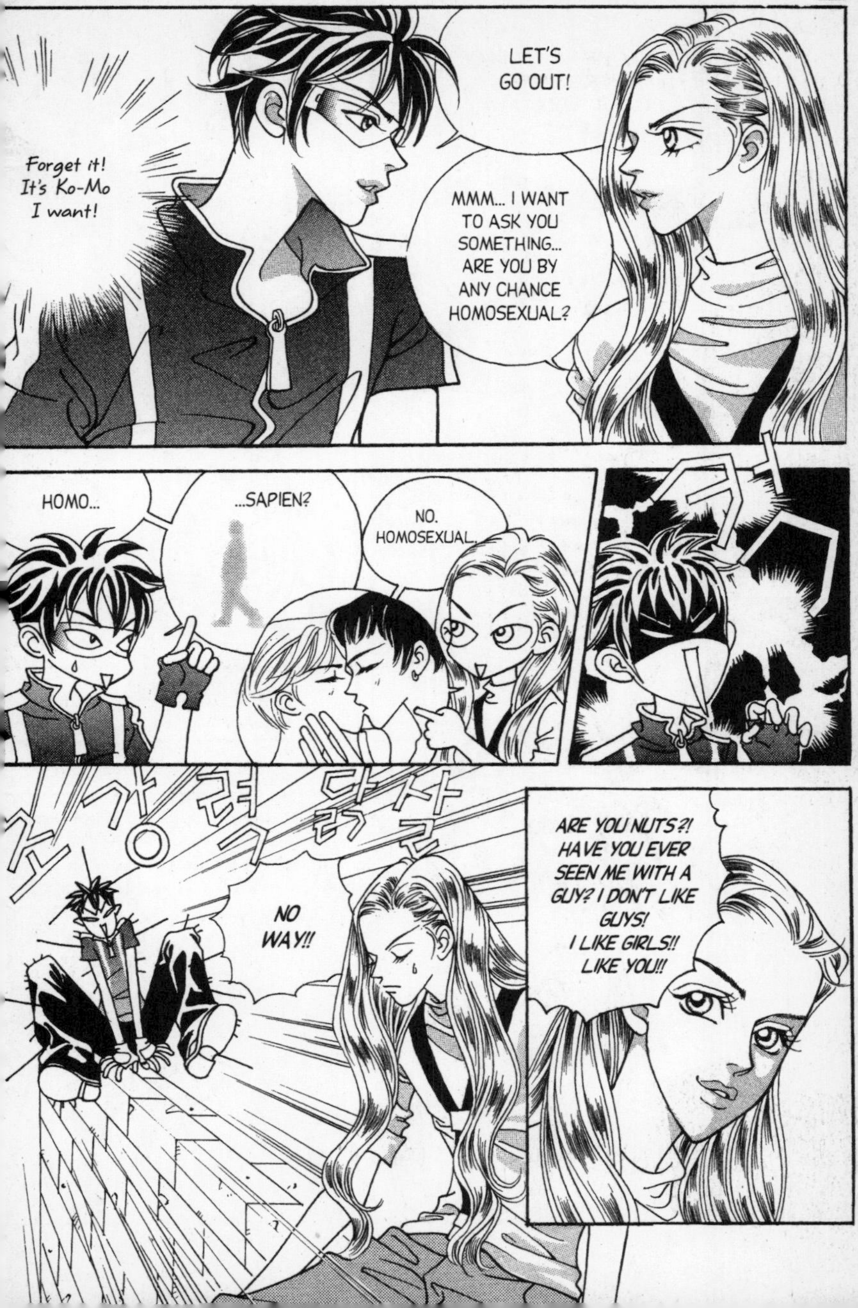
Forget it! It's Ko-Mo I want!
LET'S GO OUT!
MMM... I WANT TO ASK YOU SOMETHING... ARE YOU BY ANY CHANCE HOMOSEXUAL?
HOMO...
...SAPIEN?
NO. HOMOSEXUAL.
NO WAY!!
ARE YOU NUTS?! HAVE YOU EVER SEEN ME WITH A GUY? I DON'T LIKE GUYS! I LIKE GIRLS!! LIKE YOU!!

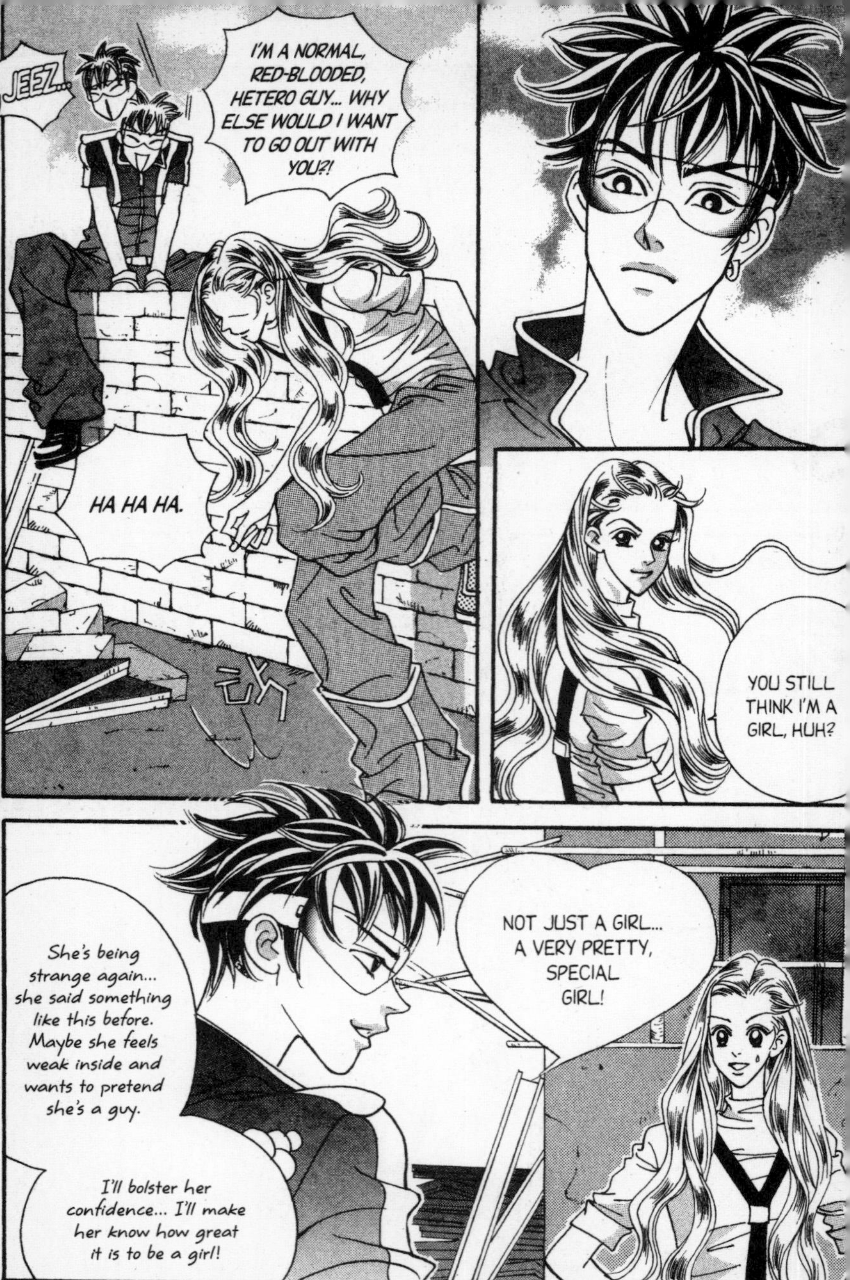
JEEZ...
I'M A NORMAL, RED-BLOODED, HETERO GUY... WHY ELSE WOULD I WANT TO GO OUT WITH YOU?!
HA HA HA.
YOU STILL THINK I'M A GIRL, HUH?
NOT JUST A GIRL... A VERY PRETTY, SPECIAL GIRL!
She's being strange again... she said something like this before. Maybe she feels weak inside and wants to pretend she's a guy.
I'll bolster her confidence... I'll make her know how great it is to be a girl!

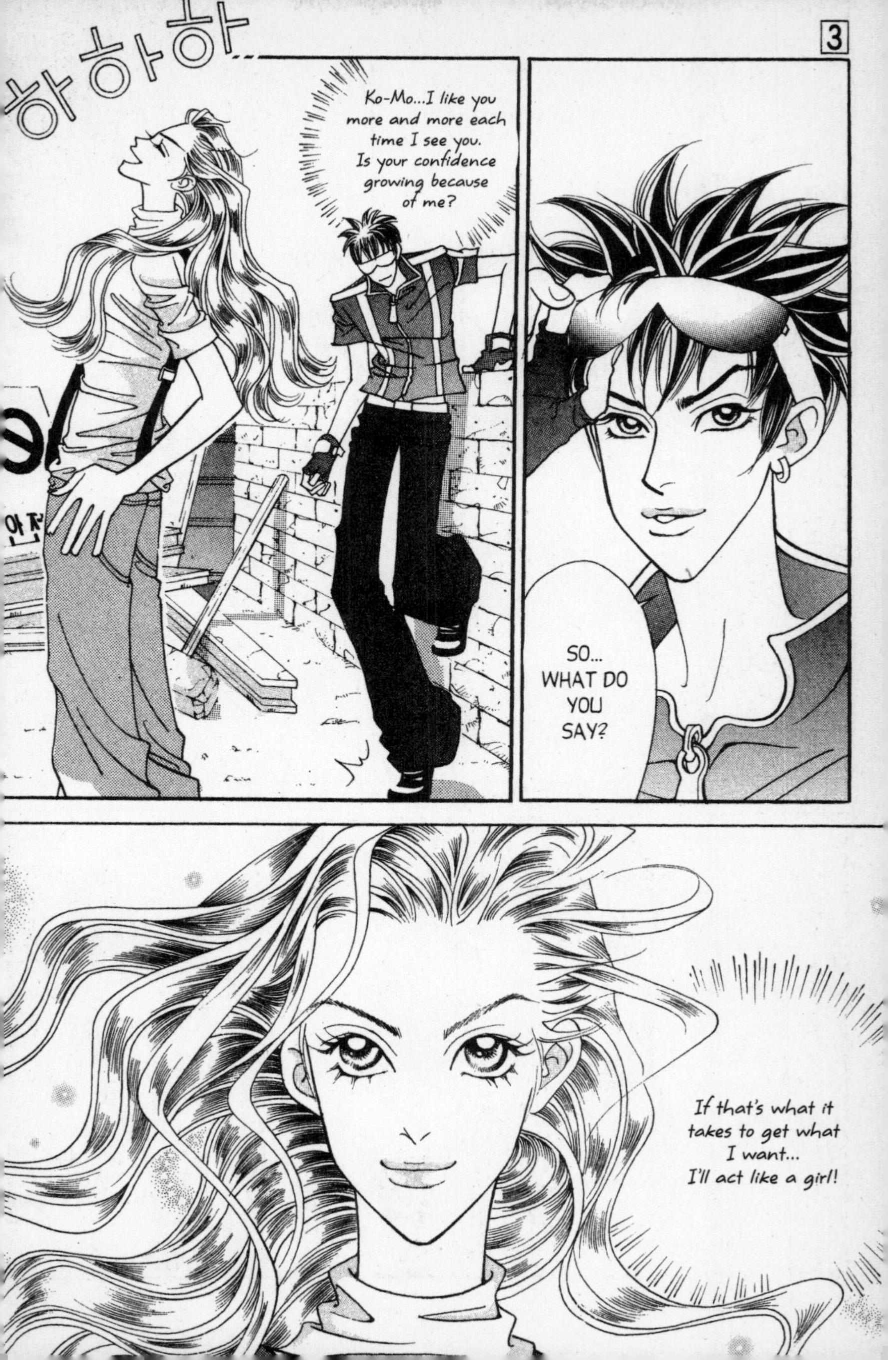
3
하하하...
Ko-Mo...I like you more and more each time I see you. Is your confidence growing because of me?
SO... WHAT DO YOU SAY?
If that's what it takes to get what I want... I'll act like a girl!

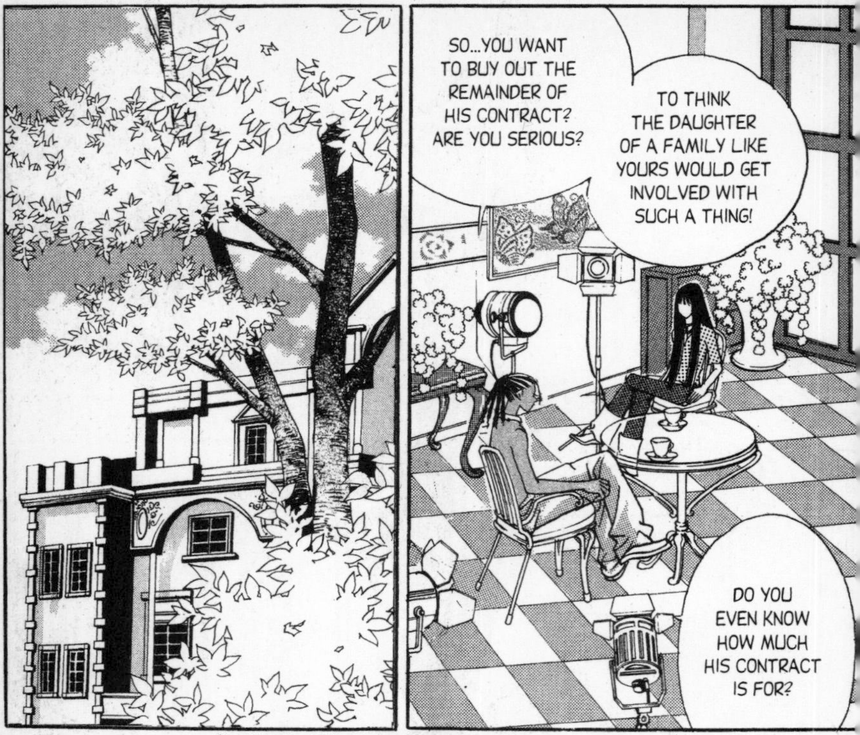
SO...YOU WANT TO BUY OUT THE REMAINDER OF HIS CONTRACT? ARE YOU SERIOUS?
TO THINK THE DAUGHTER OF A FAMILY LIKE YOURS WOULD GET INVOLVED WITH SUCH A THING!
DO YOU EVEN KNOW HOW MUCH HIS CONTRACT IS FOR?

*EDITOR'S NOTE: AROUND $100,000

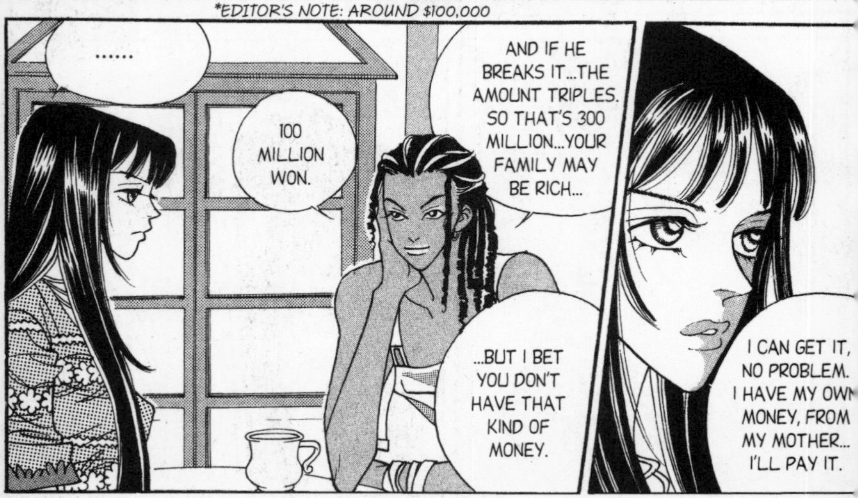
......
100 MILLION WON.
AND IF HE BREAKS IT...THE AMOUNT TRIPLES. SO THAT'S 300 MILLION...YOUR FAMILY MAY BE RICH...
...BUT I BET YOU DON'T HAVE THAT KIND OF MONEY.
I CAN GET IT, NO PROBLEM. I HAVE MY OWN MONEY, FROM MY MOTHER... I'LL PAY IT.

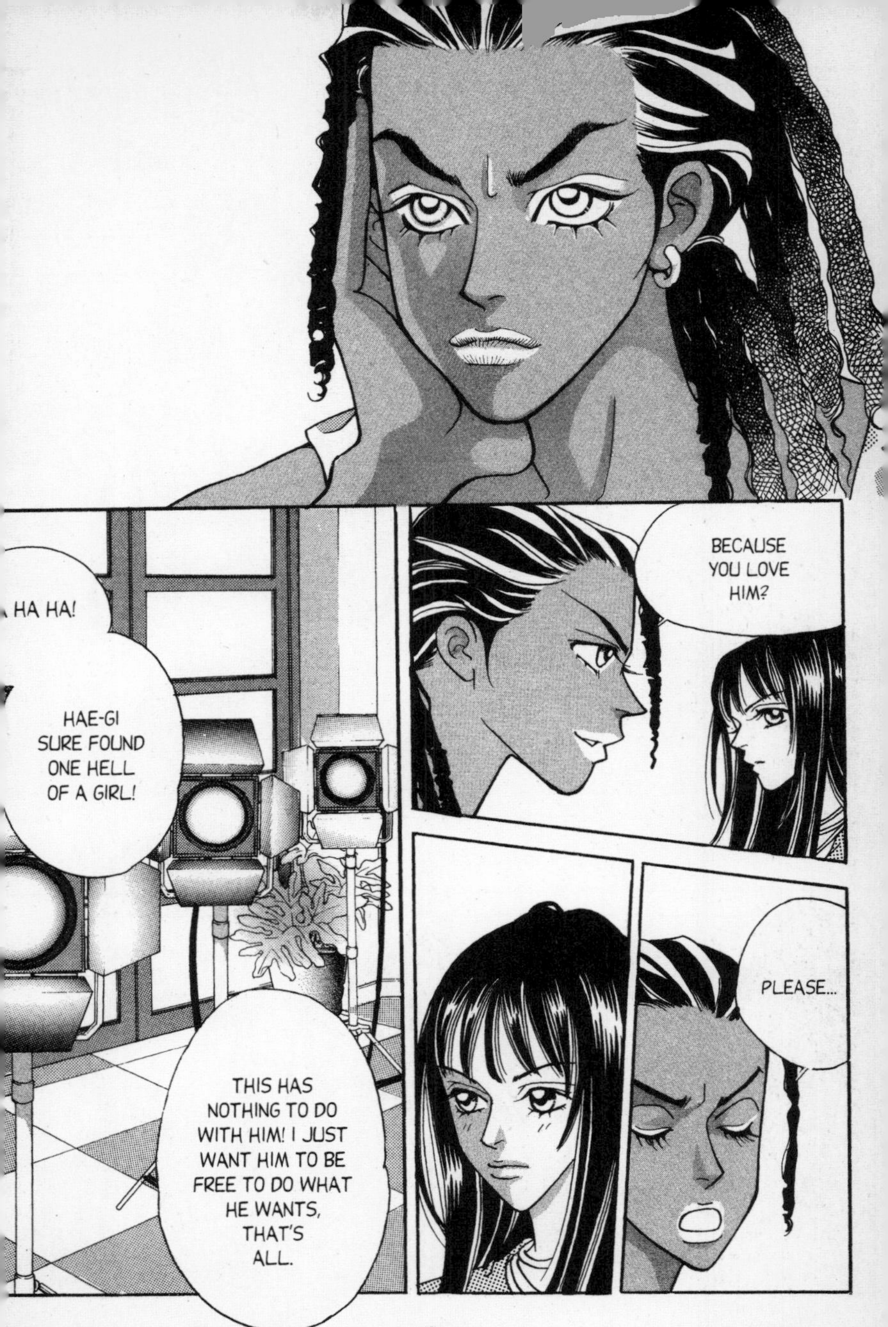
HA HA!
HAE-GI SURE FOUND ONE HELL OF A GIRL!
THIS HAS NOTHING TO DO WITH HIM! I JUST WANT HIM TO BE FREE TO DO WHAT HE WANTS, THAT'S ALL.
BECAUSE YOU LOVE HIM?
PLEASE...

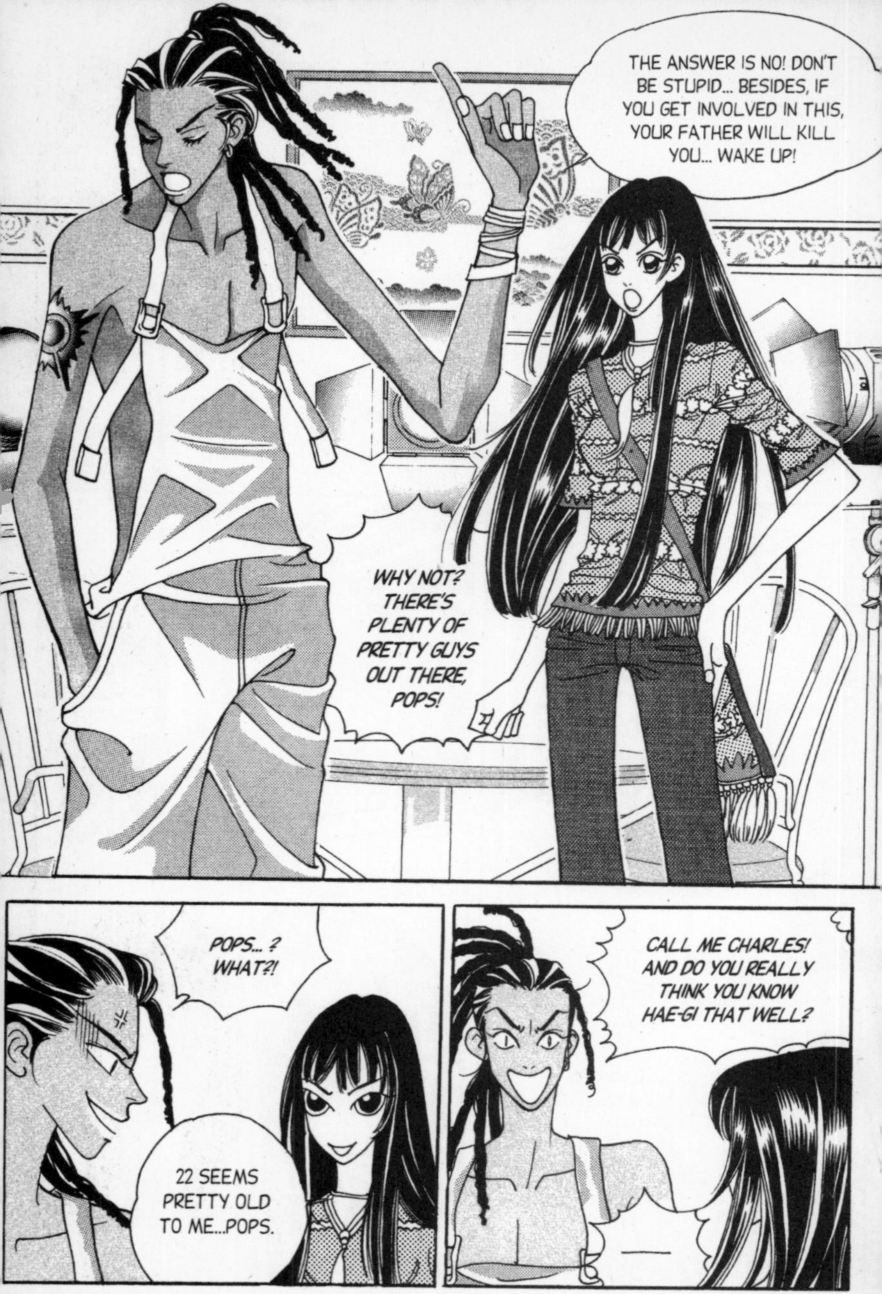
THE ANSWER IS NO! DON'T BE STUPID... BESIDES, IF YOU GET INVOLVED IN THIS, YOUR FATHER WILL KILL YOU... WAKE UP!
WHY NOT? THERE'S PLENTY OF PRETTY GUYS OUT THERE, POPS!
POPS... ? WHAT?!
22 SEEMS PRETTY OLD TO ME...POPS.
CALL ME CHARLES! AND DO YOU REALLY THINK YOU KNOW HAE-GI THAT WELL?

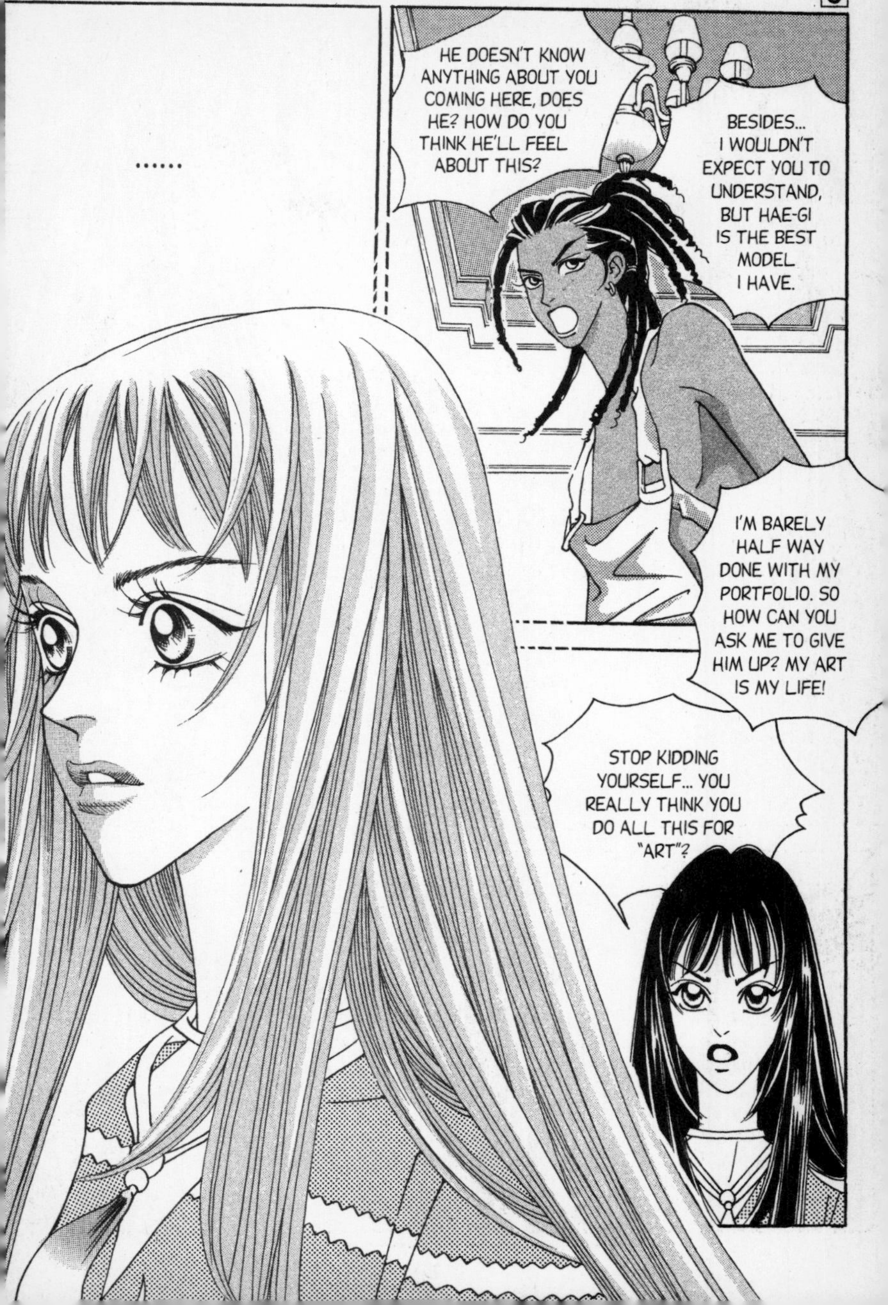
......
HE DOESN'T KNOW ANYTHING ABOUT YOU COMING HERE, DOES HE? HOW DO YOU THINK HE'LL FEEL ABOUT THIS?
BESIDES... I WOULDN'T EXPECT YOU TO UNDERSTAND, BUT HAE-GI IS THE BEST MODEL I HAVE.
I'M BARELY HALF WAY DONE WITH MY PORTFOLIO. SO HOW CAN YOU ASK ME TO GIVE HIM UP? MY ART IS MY LIFE!
STOP KIDDING YOURSELF... YOU REALLY THINK YOU DO ALL THIS FOR "ART"?

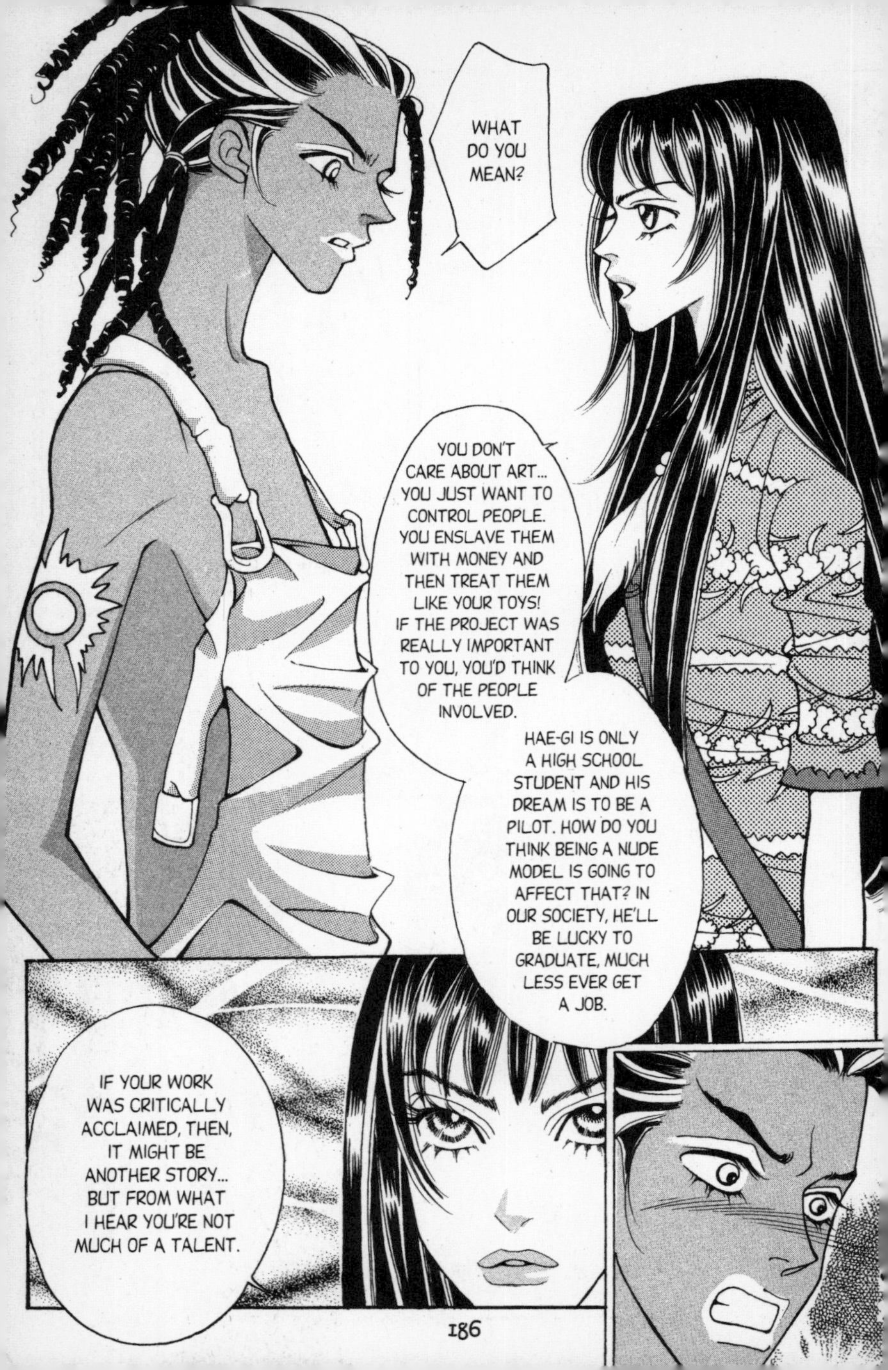
WHAT DO YOU MEAN?
YOU DON'T CARE ABOUT ART... YOU JUST WANT TO CONTROL PEOPLE. YOU ENSLAVE THEM WITH MONEY AND THEN TREAT THEM LIKE YOUR TOYS! IF THE PROJECT WAS REALLY IMPORTANT TO YOU, YOU'D THINK OF THE PEOPLE INVOLVED.
HAE-GI IS ONLY A HIGH SCHOOL STUDENT AND HIS DREAM IS TO BE A PILOT. HOW DO YOU THINK BEING A NUDE MODEL IS GOING TO AFFECT THAT? IN OUR SOCIETY, HE'LL BE LUCKY TO GRADUATE, MUCH LESS EVER GET A JOB.
IF YOUR WORK WAS CRITICALLY ACCLAIMED, THEN, IT MIGHT BE ANOTHER STORY... BUT FROM WHAT I HEAR YOU'RE NOT MUCH OF A TALENT.

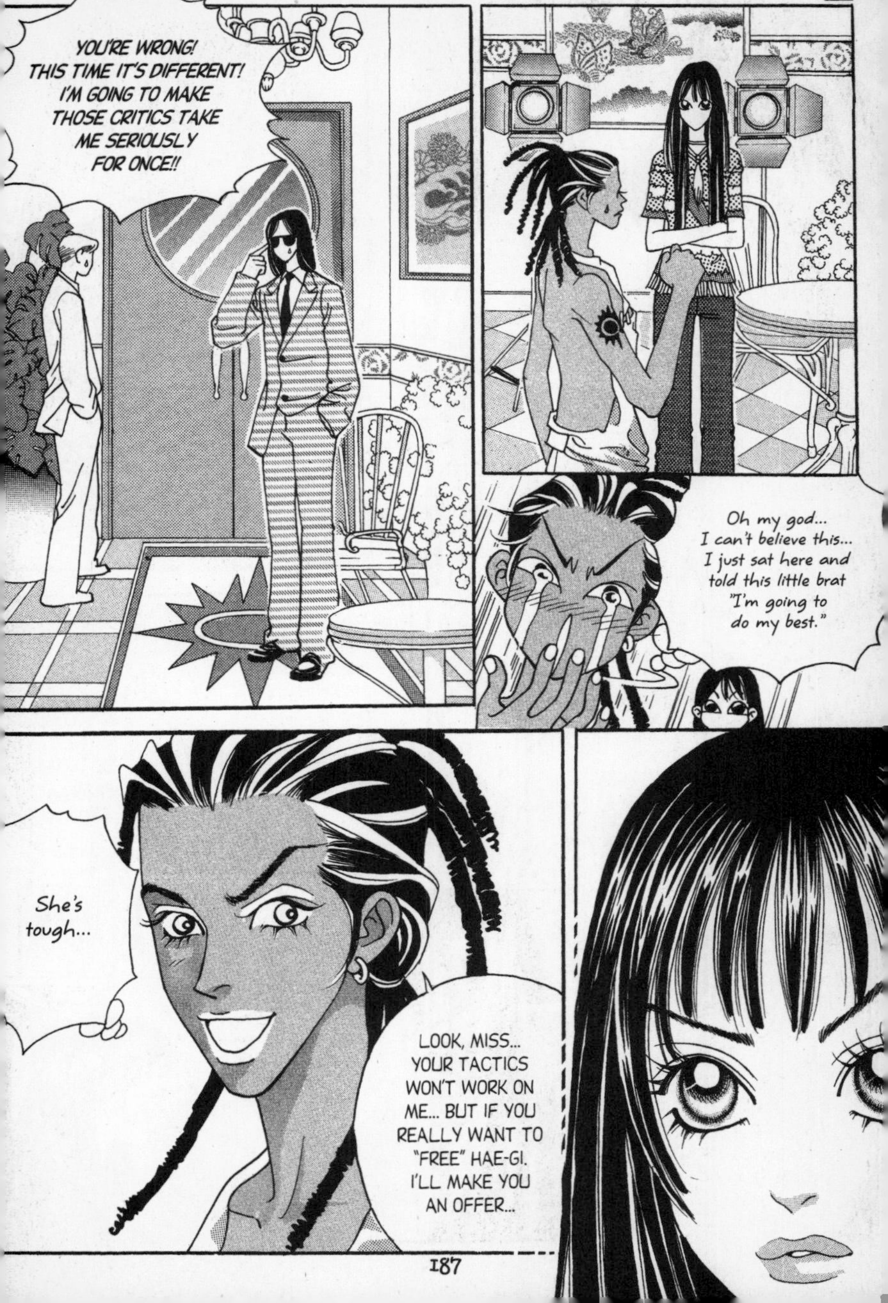
YOU'RE WRONG! THIS TIME IT'S DIFFERENT! I'M GOING TO MAKE THOSE CRITICS TAKE ME SERIOUSLY FOR ONCE!!
Oh my god... I can't believe this... I just sat here and told this little brat "I'm going to do my best."
She's tough...
LOOK, MISS... YOUR TACTICS WON'T WORK ON ME... BUT IF YOU REALLY WANT TO "FREE" HAE-GI. I'LL MAKE YOU AN OFFER...

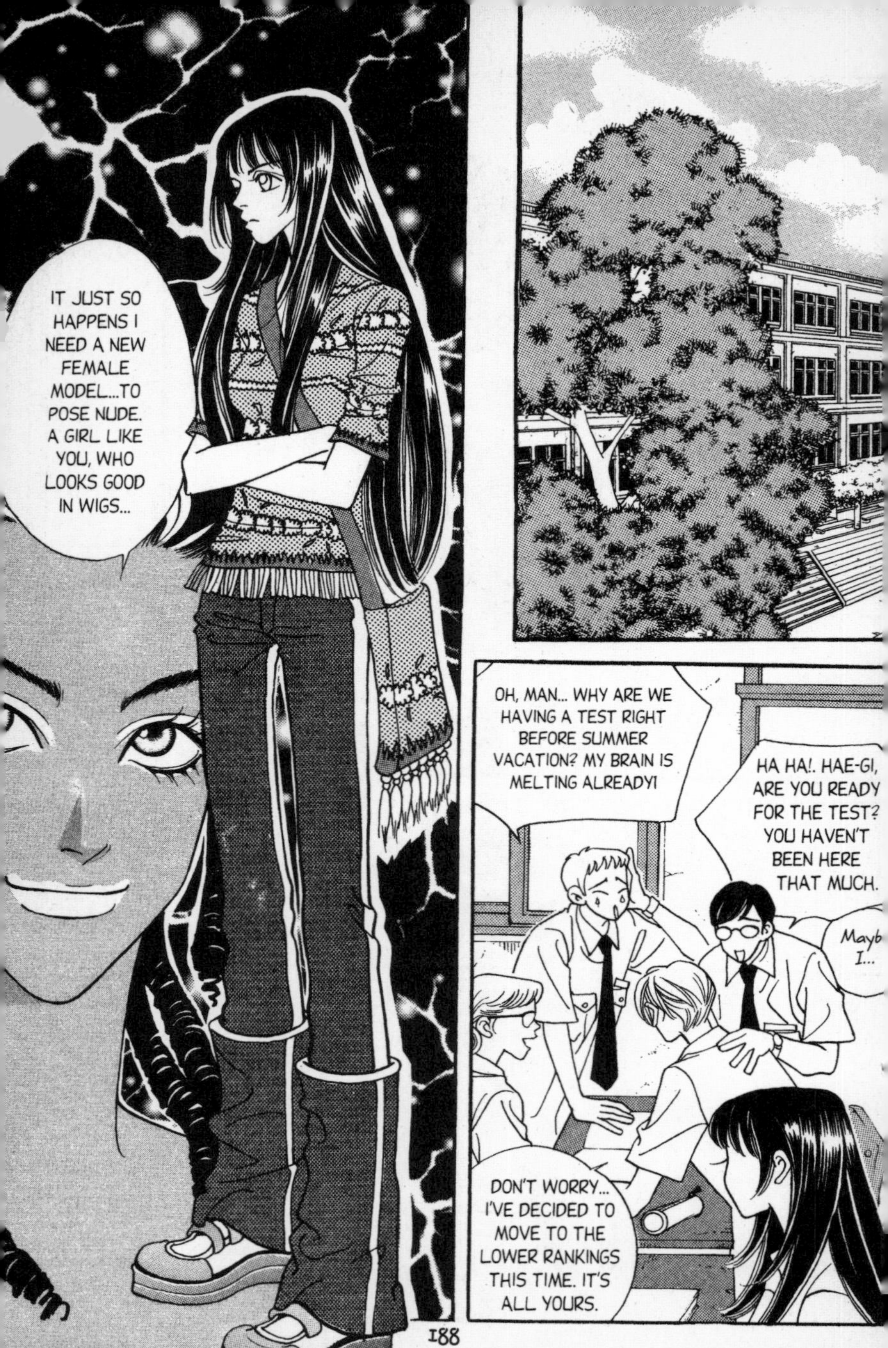
IT JUST SO HAPPENS I NEED A NEW FEMALE MODEL...TO POSE NUDE. A GIRL LIKE YOU, WHO LOOKS GOOD IN WIGS...
OH, MAN... WHY ARE WE HAVING A TEST RIGHT BEFORE SUMMER VACATION? MY BRAIN IS MELTING ALREADY!
HA HA!. HAE-GI, ARE YOU READY FOR THE TEST? YOU HAVEN'T BEEN HERE THAT MUCH.
Mayb
I...
DON'T WORRY... I'VE DECIDED TO MOVE TO THE LOWER RANKINGS THIS TIME. IT'S ALL YOURS.

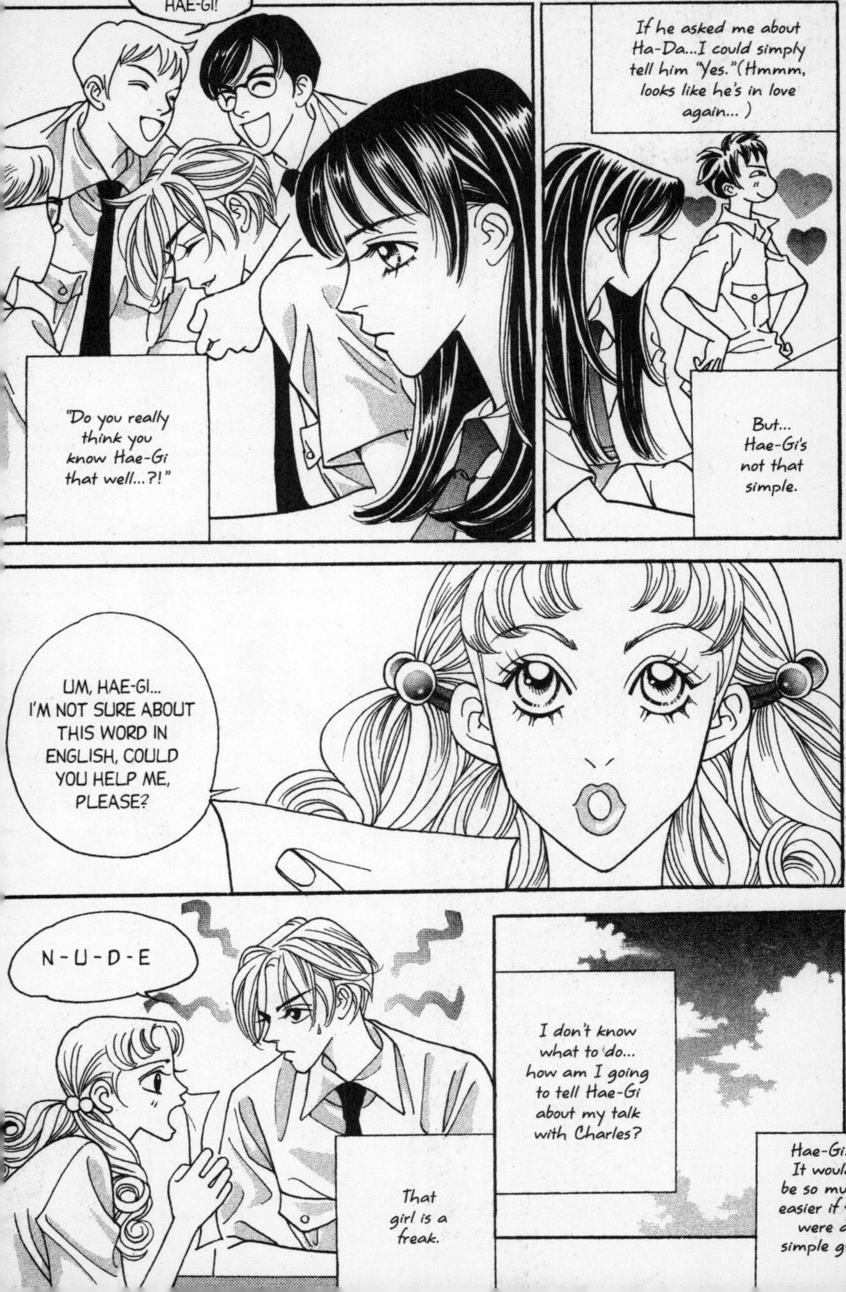
THANKS, HAE-GI!
"Do you really think you know Hae-Gi that well...?!"
If he asked me about Ha-Da...I could simply tell him "Yes." (Hmmm, looks like he's in love again... )
But... Hae-Gi's not that simple.
UM, HAE-GI... I'M NOT SURE ABOUT THIS WORD IN ENGLISH, COULD YOU HELP ME, PLEASE?
N-U-D-E
That girl is a freak.
I don't know what to do... how am I going to tell Hae-Gi about my talk with Charles?
Hae-Gi... It would be so much easier if you were a simple guy.

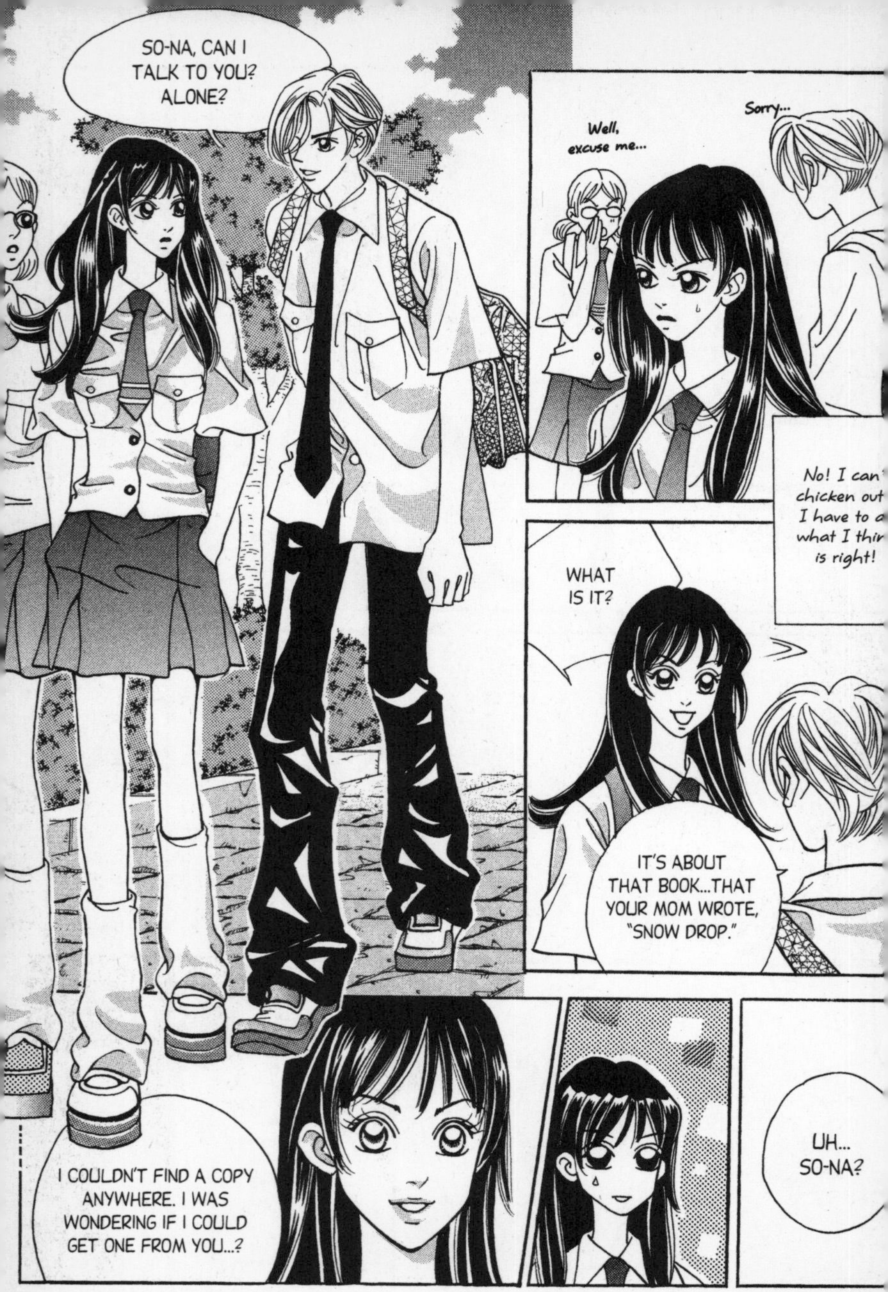

SO-NA, CAN I TALK TO YOU? ALONE?
Well, excuse me...
Sorry...
No! I can chicken out I have to a what I thir is right!
WHAT IS IT?
IT'S ABOUT THAT BOOK...THAT YOUR MOM WROTE, "SNOW DROP."
I COULDN'T FIND A COPY ANYWHERE. I WAS WONDERING IF I COULD GET ONE FROM YOU...?
UH... SO-NA?

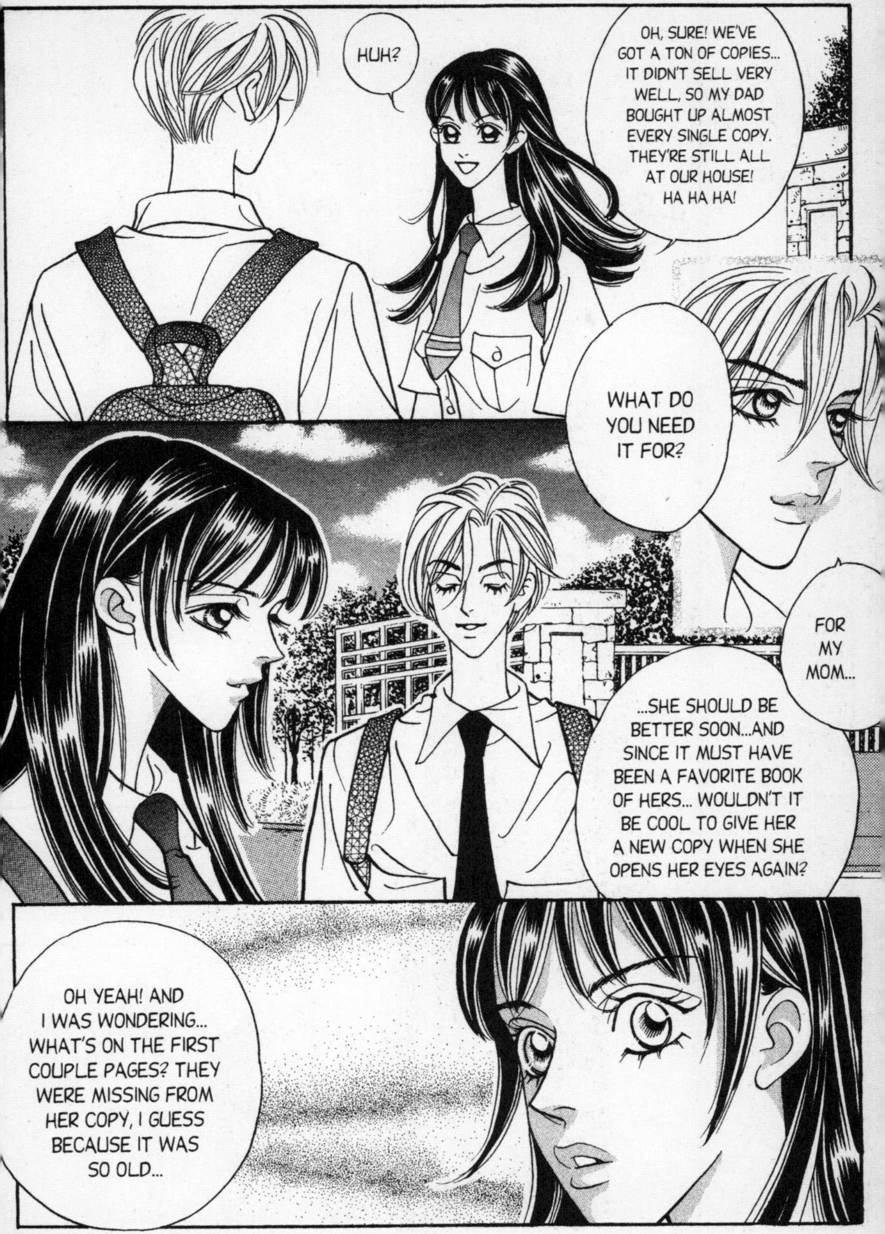
HUH?
OH, SURE! WE'VE GOT A TON OF COPIES... IT DIDN'T SELL VERY WELL, SO MY DAD BOUGHT UP ALMOST EVERY SINGLE COPY. THEY'RE STILL ALL AT OUR HOUSE! HA HA HA!
WHAT DO YOU NEED IT FOR?
FOR MY MOM...
...SHE SHOULD BE BETTER SOON...AND SINCE IT MUST HAVE BEEN A FAVORITE BOOK OF HERS... WOULDN'T IT BE COOL TO GIVE HER A NEW COPY WHEN SHE OPENS HER EYES AGAIN?
OH YEAH! AND I WAS WONDERING... WHAT'S ON THE FIRST COUPLE PAGES? THEY WERE MISSING FROM HER COPY, I GUESS BECAUSE IT WAS SO OLD...

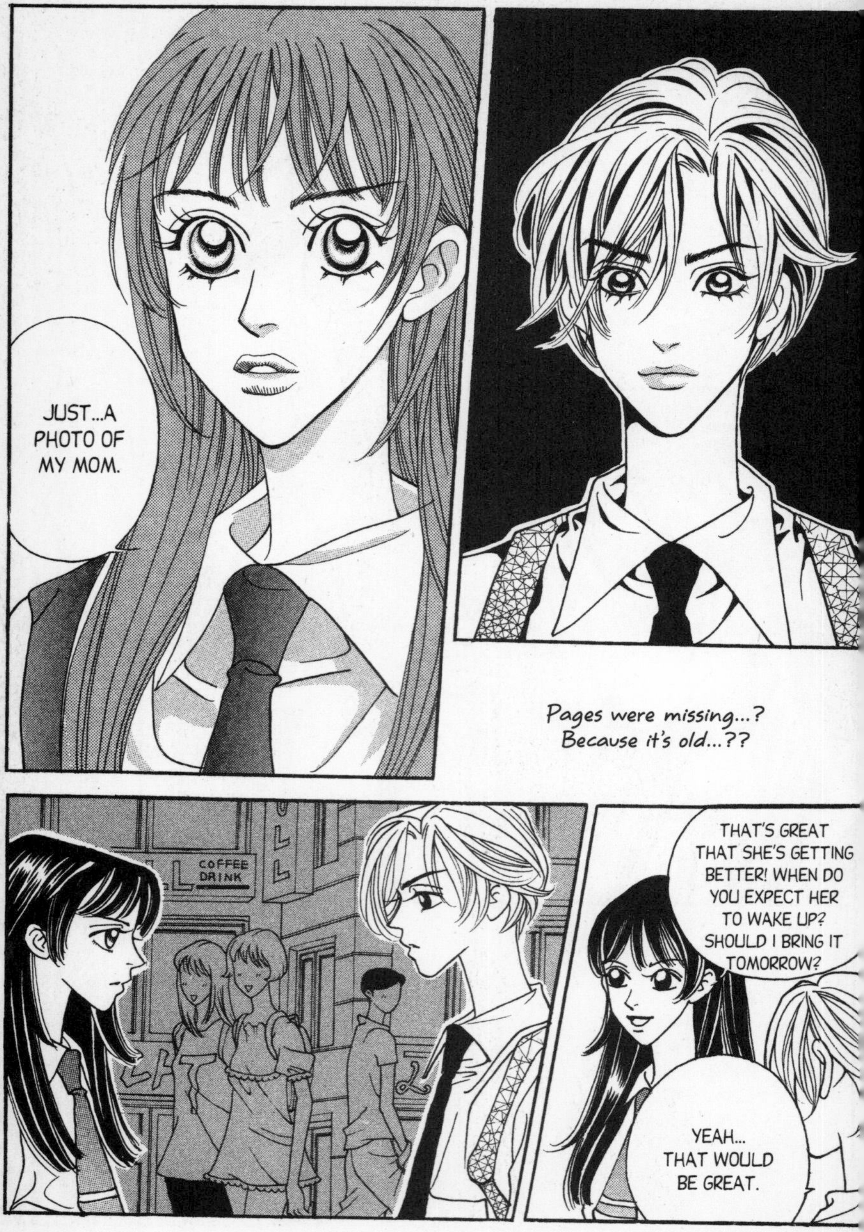
JUST...A PHOTO OF MY MOM.
Pages were missing...? Because it's old...??
COFFEE DRINK
THAT'S GREAT THAT SHE'S GETTING BETTER! WHEN DO YOU EXPECT HER TO WAKE UP? SHOULD I BRING IT TOMORROW?
YEAH... THAT WOULD BE GREAT.

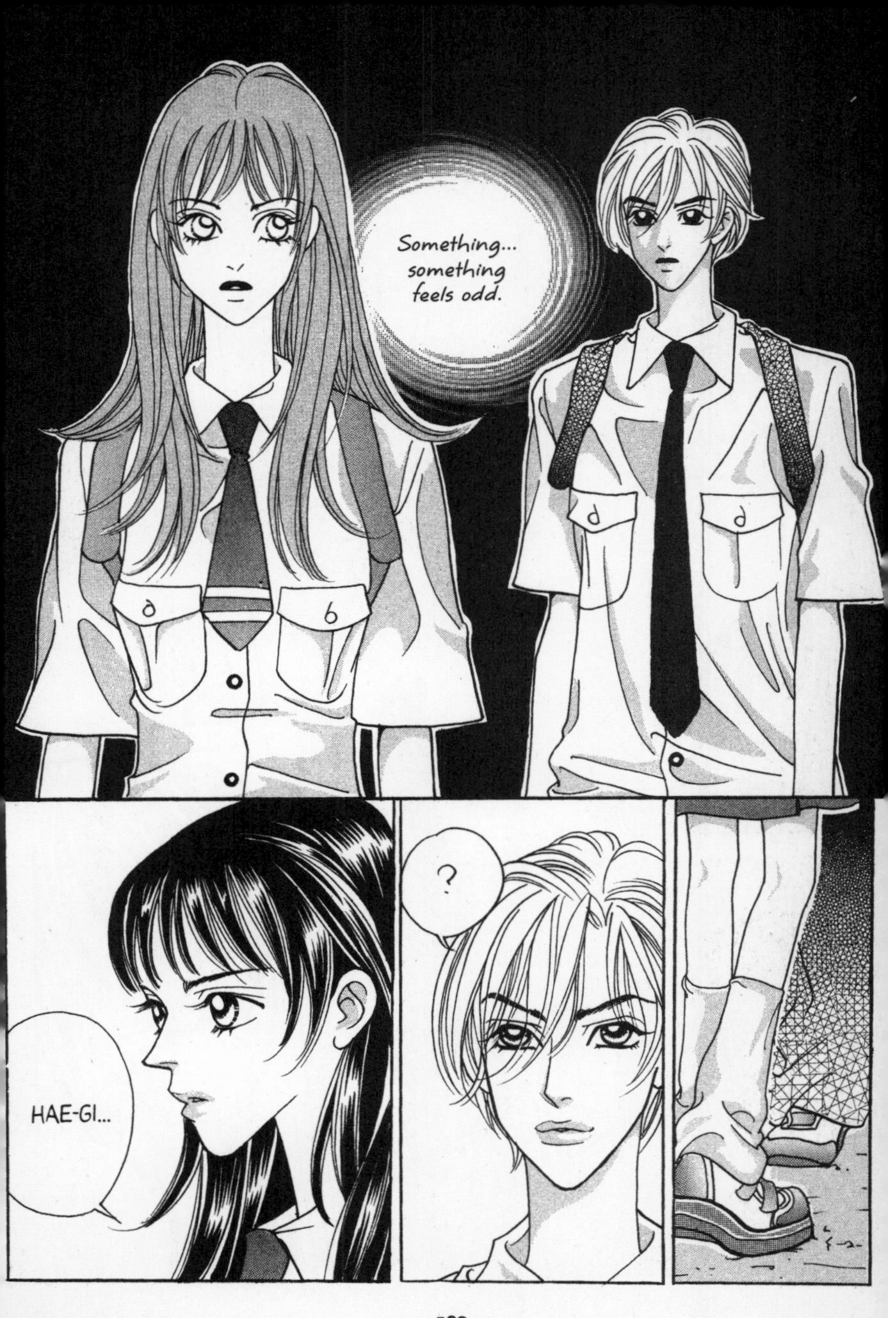

Something... something feels odd.
HAE-GI...
?

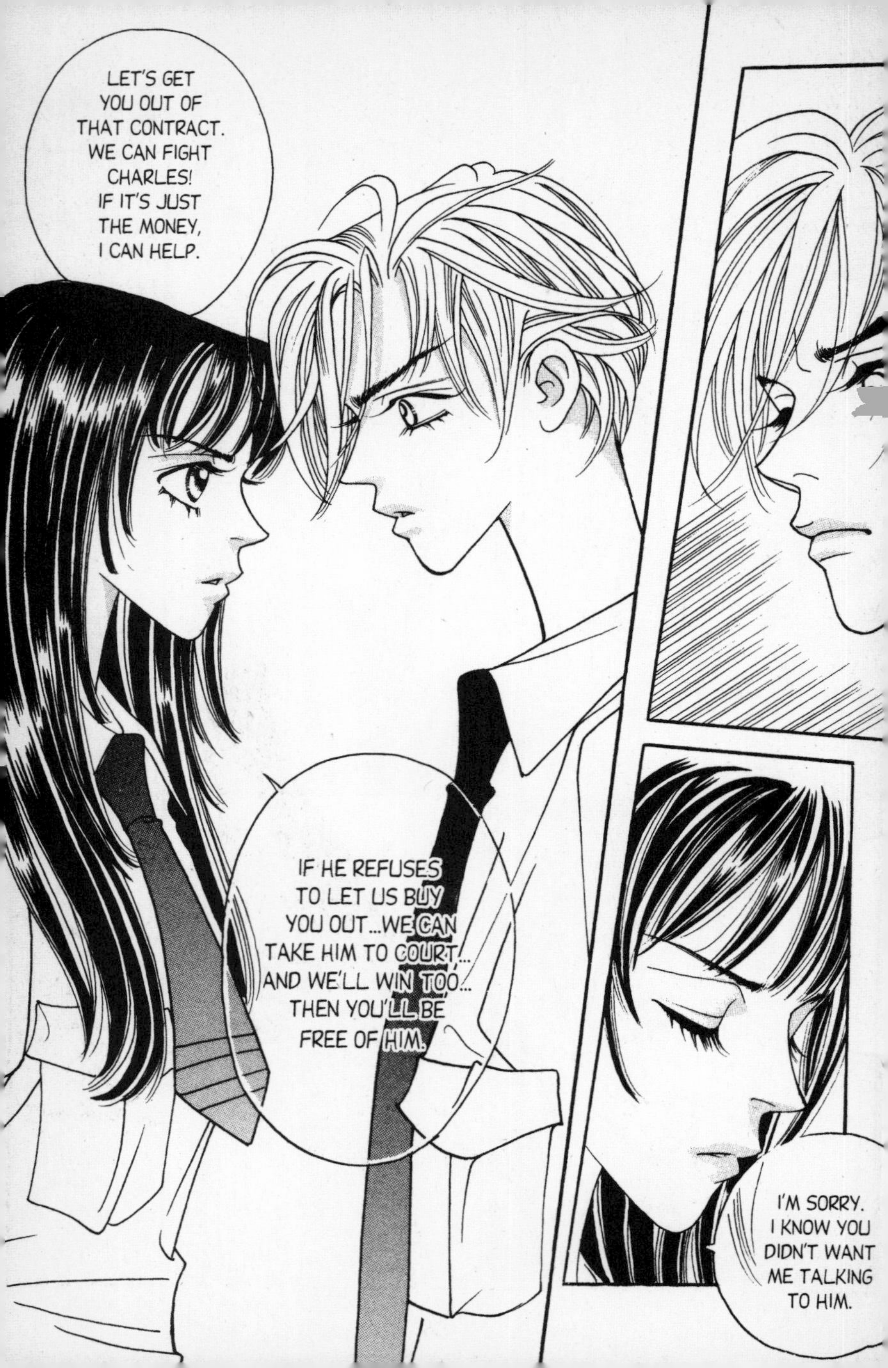
LET'S GET YOU OUT OF THAT CONTRACT. WE CAN FIGHT CHARLES! IF IT'S JUST THE MONEY, I CAN HELP.
IF HE REFUSES TO LET US BUY YOU OUT...WE CAN TAKE HIM TO COURT... AND WE'LL WIN TOO... THEN YOU'LL BE FREE OF HIM.
I'M SORRY. I KNOW YOU DIDN'T WANT ME TALKING TO HIM.

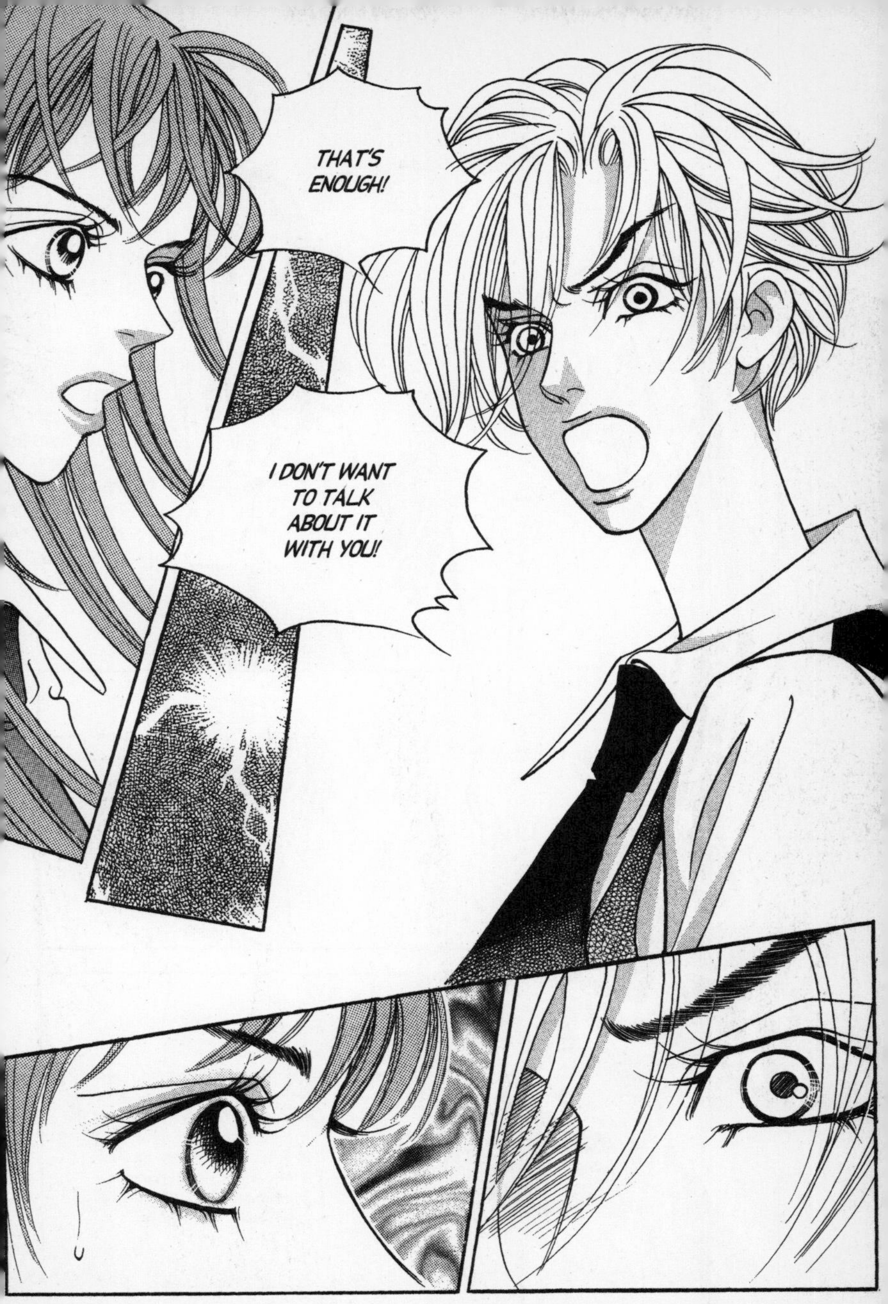
THAT'S ENOUGH!
I DON'T WANT TO TALK ABOUT IT WITH YOU!

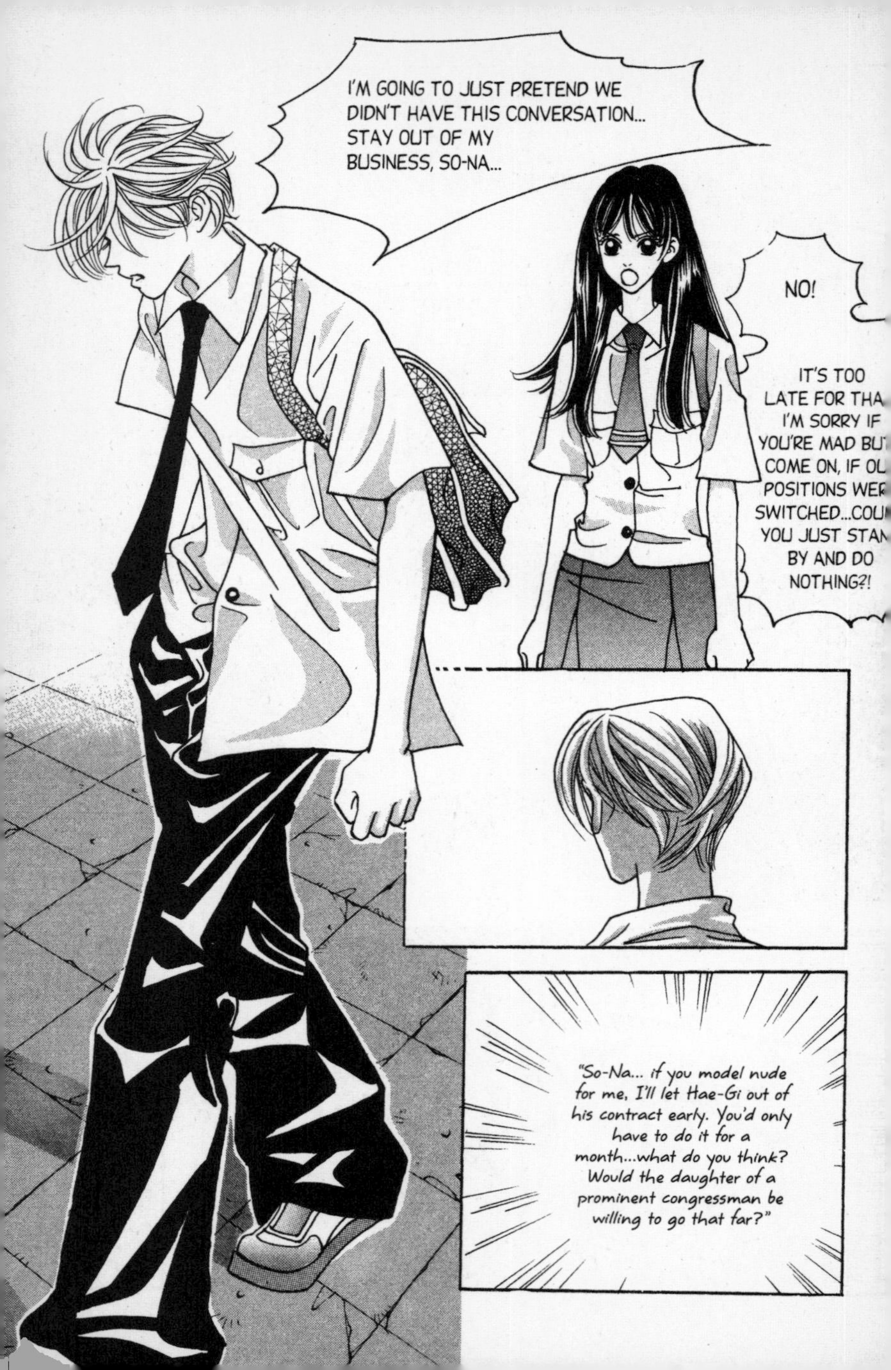
I'M GOING TO JUST PRETEND WE DIDN'T HAVE THIS CONVERSATION... STAY OUT OF MY BUSINESS, SO-NA...
NO!
IT'S TOO LATE FOR THA I'M SORRY IF YOU'RE MAD BU COME ON, IF O POSITIONS WER SWITCHED...COU YOU JUST STA BY AND DO NOTHING?!
"So-Na... if you model nude for me, I'll let Hae-Gi out of his contract early. You'd only have to do it for a month...what do you think? Would the daughter of a prominent congressman be willing to go that far?"

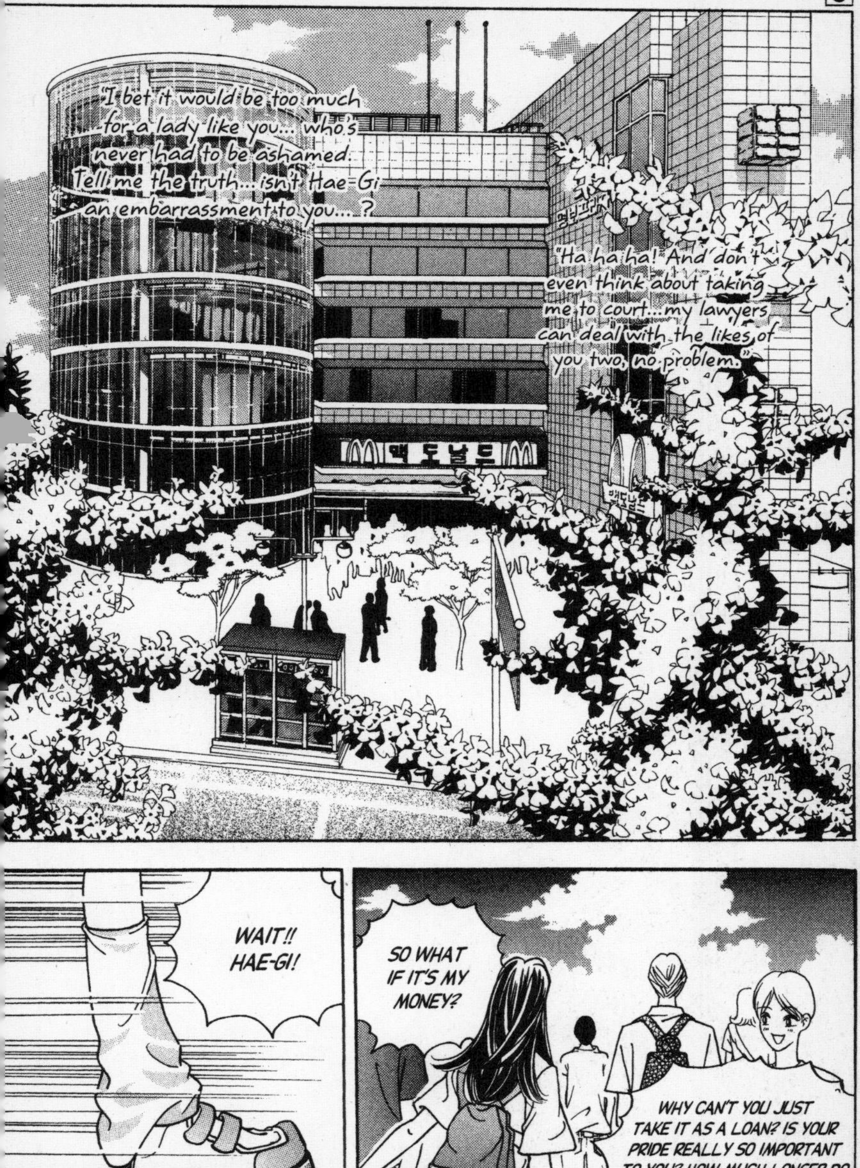
"I bet it would be too much for a lady like you... who's never had to be ashamed. Tell me the truth... isn't Hae-Gi an embarrassment to you...?
"Ha ha ha! And don't even think about taking me to court...my lawyers can deal with the likes of you two, no problem."
맥도날드
WAIT!! HAE-GI!
SO WHAT IF IT'S MY MONEY?
WHY CAN'T YOU JUST TAKE IT AS A LOAN? IS YOUR PRIDE REALLY SO IMPORTANT TO YOU? HOW MUCH LONGER DO YOU THINK YOU CAN HANDLE BEING CHARLES' LITTLE TOY?

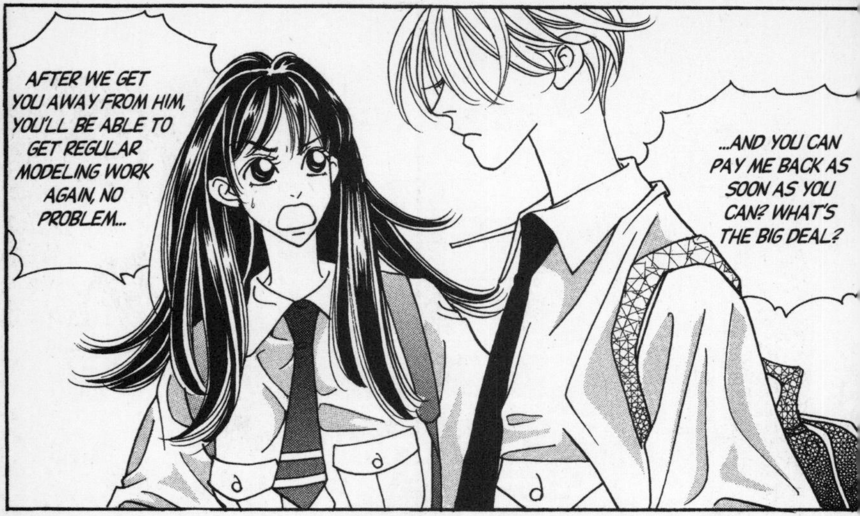
AFTER WE GET YOU AWAY FROM HIM, YOU'LL BE ABLE TO GET REGULAR MODELING WORK AGAIN, NO PROBLEM...
...AND YOU CAN PAY ME BACK AS SOON AS YOU CAN? WHAT'S THE BIG DEAL?
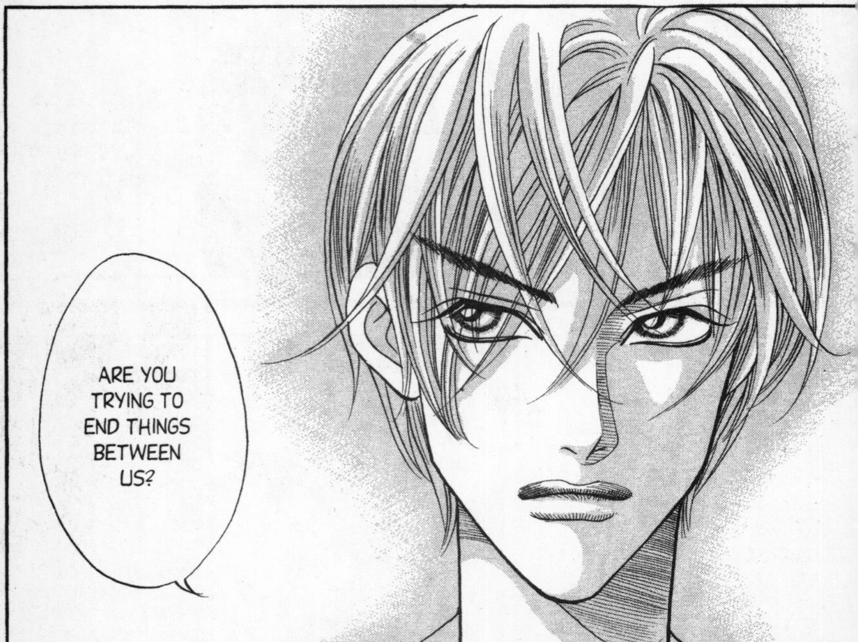
ARE YOU TRYING TO END THINGS BETWEEN US?

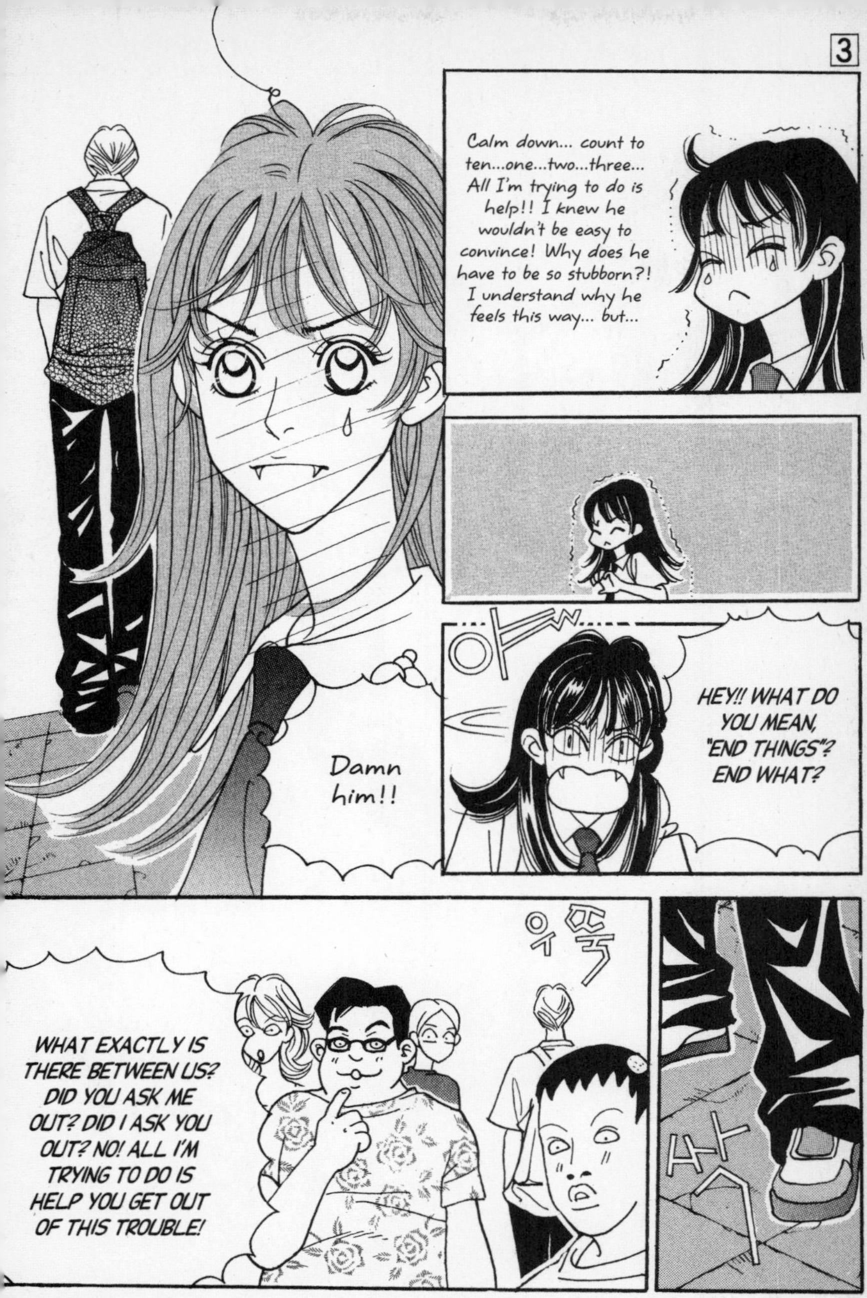
3
Damn him!!
Calm down... count to ten...one...two...three... All I'm trying to do is help!! I knew he wouldn't be easy to convince! Why does he have to be so stubborn?! I understand why he feels this way... but...
HEY!! WHAT DO YOU MEAN, "END THINGS"? END WHAT?
WHAT EXACTLY IS THERE BETWEEN US? DID YOU ASK ME OUT? DID I ASK YOU OUT? NO! ALL I'M TRYING TO DO IS HELP YOU GET OUT OF THIS TROUBLE!

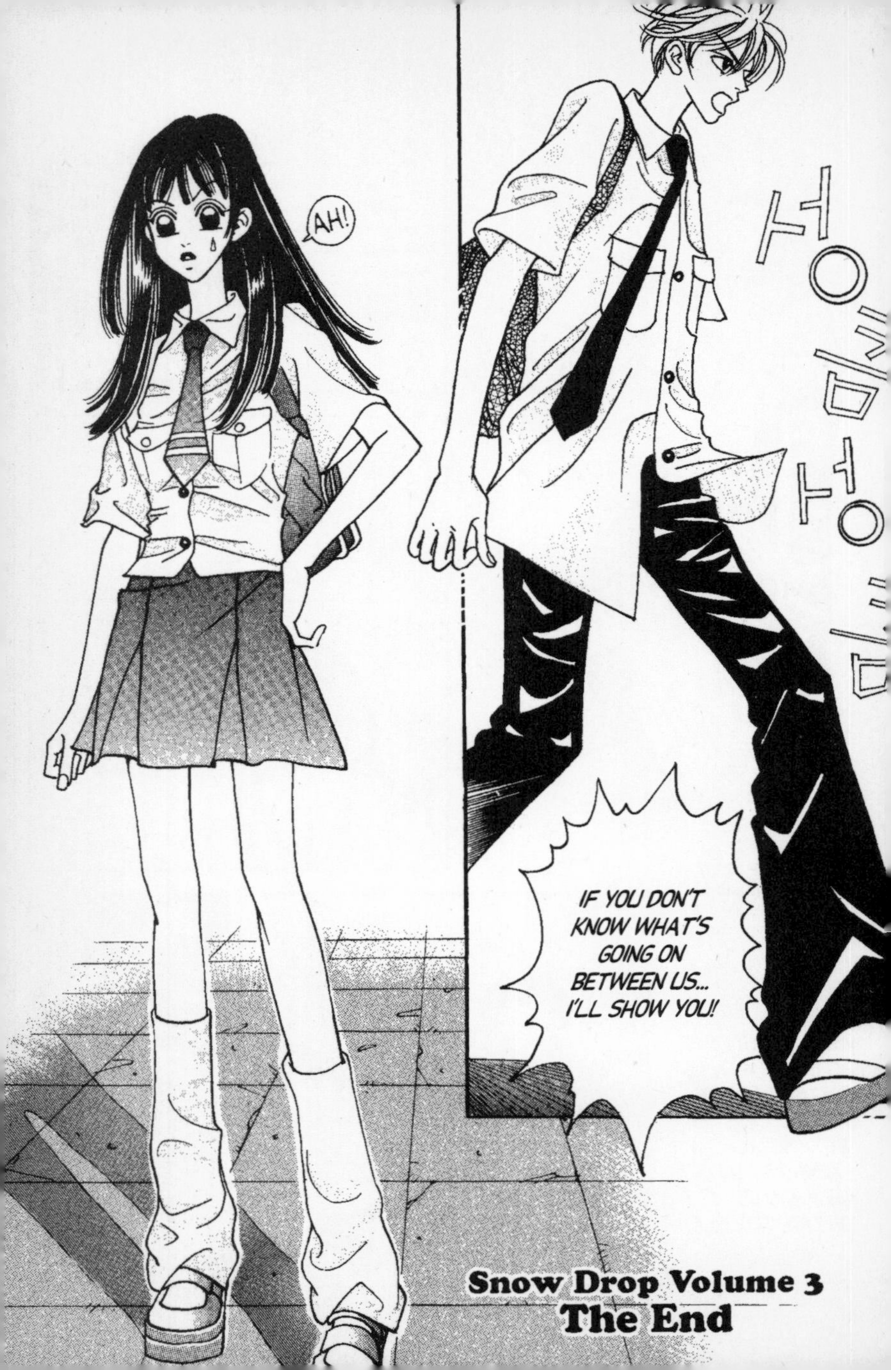
AH!
성큼성큼
IF YOU DON'T KNOW WHAT'S GOING ON BETWEEN US... I'LL SHOW YOU!
Snow Drop Volume 3
The End

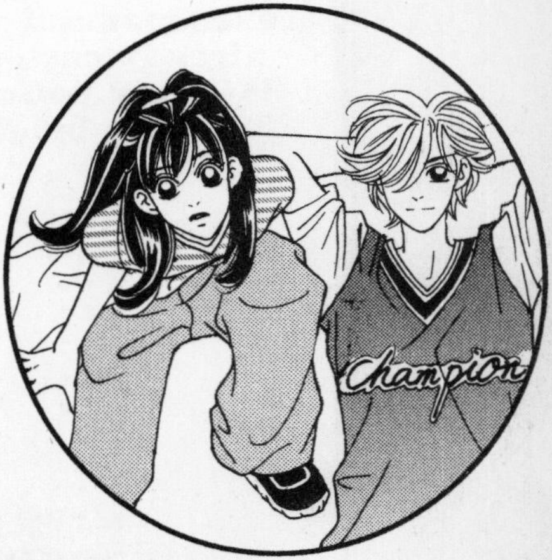
Champion

## Coming in July...

# Snow Drop

## Volume Four

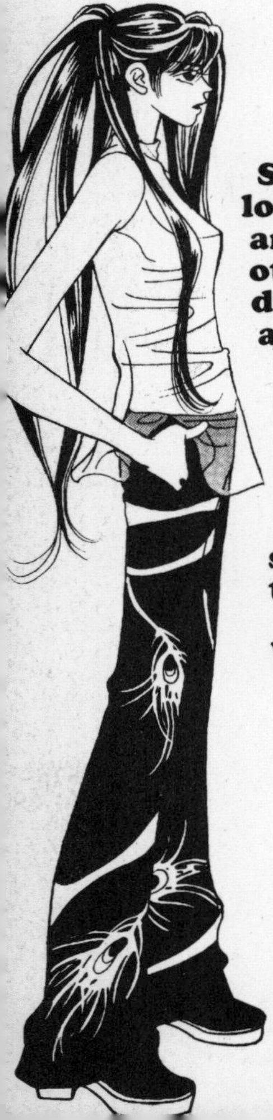

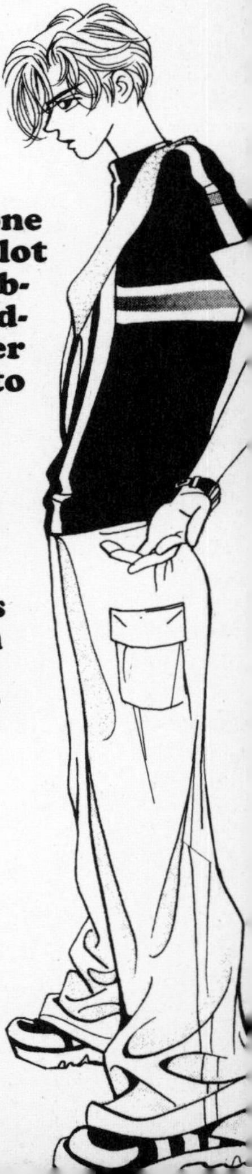

**Sun-Mi, the rich girl everyone loves to hate, continues to plot and scheme over ways to sabotage So-Na and Hae-Gi's budding romance. But when her attempts to bring Ha-Da into the conspiracy don't bear fruit, Sun-Mi decides to take a more direct—and brutal—approach. She's not the only one playing hardball though, as the shady photog, Charles puts the financial squeeze on an already cash-poor, Hae-Gi. Will our young lovers ever see a brighter day?**

**Drop in for SNOW DROP Volume 4!**

GTO™
GREAT TEACHER ONIZUKA
AS SEEN ON SHOWTIME!
DVD VIDEO
TOKYOPOP®
NO BIG EYES
NO MAGICAL POWERS
NO GIANT ROBOTS
GTO
OT OLDER TEEN AGE 16+
©Tohru Fujisawa – KODANSHA – FUJI TV – SME Visual Works – ST. PIERROT.
©2002 TOKYOPOP Inc. All Rights Reserved.
www.TOKYOPOP.com

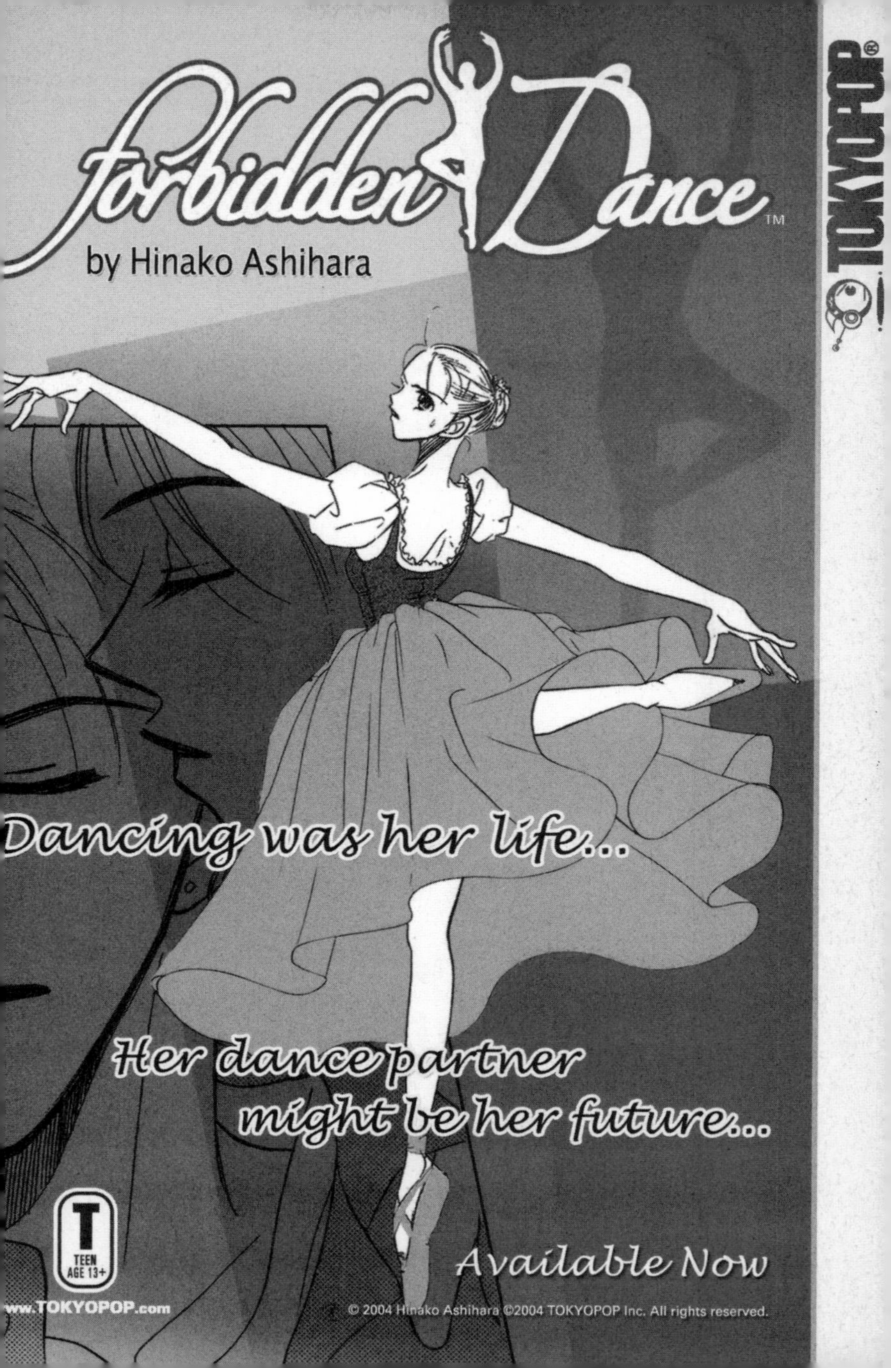
TOKYOPOP®
Forbidden Dance™
by Hinako Ashihara
Dancing was her life...
Her dance partner
might be her future...
T
TEEN
AGE 13+
Available Now
www.TOKYOPOP.com
© 2004 Hinako Ashihara ©2004 TOKYOPOP Inc. All rights reserved.

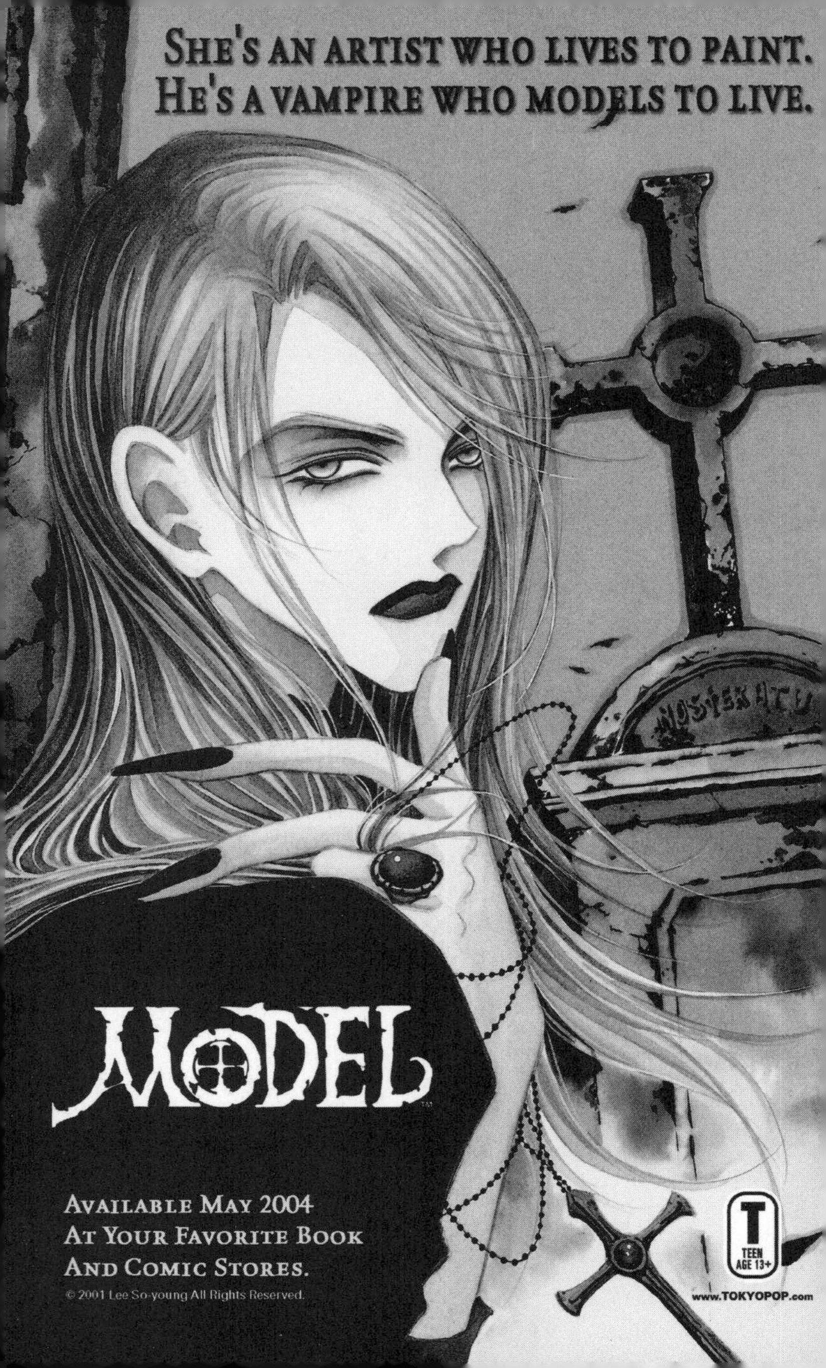

SHE'S AN ARTIST WHO LIVES TO PAINT.
HE'S A VAMPIRE WHO MODELS TO LIVE.
MODEL
AVAILABLE MAY 2004
AT YOUR FAVORITE BOOK
AND COMIC STORES.
© 2001 Lee So-young All Rights Reserved.
T
TEEN
AGE 13+
www.TOKYOPOP.com